A General History
History
Of Music

From the Earliest Times

Da Capo Press Music Reprint Series

GENERAL EDITOR
FREDERICK FREEDMAN
VASSAR COLLEGE

A General History Of Music

From the Earliest Times

By Thomas Busby

Volume I

DA CAPO PRESS • NEW YORK • 1968

A Da Capo Press Reprint Edition

This edition of Thomas Busby's
A General History of Music
is an unabridged republication
of the first edition published in London in 1819.

Library of Congress Catalog Card No. 68-21091

Da Capo Press
A Division of Plenum Publishing Corporation
227 West 17th Street
New York, N. Y. 10011

Printed in the United States of America

11/68

A

GENERAL

HISTORY OF MUSIC,

FROM

THE EARLIEST TIMES TO THE PRESENT;

COMPRISING

THE LIVES

OF

EMINENT COMPOSERS AND MUSICAL WRITERS.

THE WHOLE ACCOMPANIED WITH

NOTES AND OBSERVATIONS, CRITICAL AND ILLUSTRATIVE.

By **THOMAS BUSBY**, Mus. Doc.

AUTHOR OF A MUSICAL DICTIONARY, MUSICAL GRAMMAR, TRANSLATION OF LUCRETIUS, &c. &c.

IN TWO VOLUMES.

VOL. I.

London:

PRINTED FOR G. AND W. B. WHITTAKER, AVE-MARIA LANE; AND
SIMPKIN AND MARSHALL, STATIONERS' COURT.

1819.

PREFACE.

DESCANTING on the value, or effects, of a particular science, writers seem more subject to the anomaly of over-charging, or under-rating, its peculiar claims to cultivation and patronage, than to any other error. This remark applies with particular force to disquisitions on the properties of Music! Treated by a professed theorist, or a scientific amateur, Harmony and Melody are apt to assume moral and intellectual importance,—to affect to ameliorate the heart, and edify the mind; while, in the estimation of an author unacquainted with their principles, and insensible to their real though limited pretensions, they sink, perhaps, into empty recreation; and, represented by his coldness, as amusements barely rational, appear little worthy of the philosopher's cultivation, or of occupying the leisure hours of the reflecting portions of society.

An esteemed writer of our own country *, asserts, That Music raises noble sentiments, and fills
the mind with great conceptions ; while a clas-
sic of a neighbouring nation affirms, That harmony aims but to please the ear, and is qualified
only to entertain the idle and effeminate †.   But
assuredly, neither of these speculatists is perfectly correct.   Truth lies between the extremes
they maintain.   If Music aspires not to the
value of ethics, political economy, or natural
philosophy, neither does it yield to the beauty of
imaginative poetry, or the dignity of the nobler
species of architecture.   If mellifluous numbers
and lively description sooth the sense, and enchant
the fancy, and temples and palaces present to us
images of symmetry and grandeur, musical composition is qualified to charm our ear, awaken our
finest feelings, and elevate the soul.

Sensible to the effects of harmony, and not uninformed upon the subject of its principles, I have
easily been induced to devote several months to
the history of a science, the progress and powers of
which the learned of all ages have not disdained to
discuss and develop ; and may be allowed to confess, that the task was undertaken, not without a
degree of confidence in the qualifications derived
from the uninterrupted study of many years.

---

* Addison, Spect. N°. 405.
† Fenelon, Treat. on Eloq.

To some, probably, it will appear problematical, whether, since the public already possessed two English Histories of Music, the present undertaking was necessary : and were the case simply a question of *merit*, it might soon be decided by the admitted claims of the works to which I allude. But when it is recollected, that Dr. Burney's production occupies *four bulky quarto volumes*, and that of Sir John Hawkins *five ;* and when it shall appear, that not only all the requisite points on which those writers touch, but a variety of super-added particulars connected with the more recent state of Music in this and other countries, are included in *two volumes octavo*, the propriety of supplying the lovers and cultivators of the science, with a Musical History upon such a scale, will scarcely fail to be obvious.

Though with two authors before me respectable as those just mentioned, it was natural, if not indispensable, to make some use of the materials afforded by the ample latitude of their matter, and the general justness of their criticism, I have, I hope, been sparing in the appropriation of their ideas, scrupulous in the adoption of their language, and, duly careful not to descend to servile imitation. But while every invasion of the property of Hawkins, and of Burney, whether in their conceptions, or their expressions, is denied, it will not, perhaps, be improper, or unnecessary, to conciliate the reader's candour towards my occasional dissensions from their sentiments. The best apology, however, for differing from such precursors, will be deduced from the *meditation* which dictated, and the *independence* which emboldened, criticisms equally free and well considered.

But the present work differs not more in its critical remarks, than in its plan and conduct, from the several musical histories, English and foreign, by which it has been preceded. Designed for the entertainment of the general, as well as intelligence of the curious, reader, it is sparingly encumbered with the dry and unengaging theories of the ancient speculatists; preferring to dwell upon topics, at once more modern, and better calculated to invite, and repay, the amateur's attention, it chiefly devotes its pages to the narration of interesting events, and the investigation and eulogium due to sound science and extraordinary talents.

Nevertheless, the several casts, or species of the Grecian and Roman, Jewish and Christian Music, have been considered ; and their various principles laid down and discussed. The characters and powers of the ancient instruments, and the abilities of those who excelled as vocal or instrumental performers, have also been thought too worthy of notice to be neglected, as well as the effects ascribed to the ancient melopœia, and afterwards to such harmonic combinations as were known in the times of the earliest contrapuntists.

Of the subsequent practical musicians and theoretical writers, the principal have been honourably distinguished, their respective merits examined, and the obligations of the musical science to their industry and talents, patiently ascertained, and faithfully stated. On the more modern masters of eminence, a still closer attention has been bestowed. Their comparative pretensions have been weighed and determined, and the learning and taste of themselves, and of their times, illustrated by a variety of examples.

Though, while cheerfully subscribing to the opinion, That other countries have earned the laurels they wear, I have not slighted the wreaths acquired by England (wreaths, which, cherished as they deserve, will bloom as long as those either of Italy or Germany) yet superlative foreign merit has received the *honours due.* The encomiastic notice taken of a Tallis, an Orlando Gibbons, or a Blow, is balanced by the just praise of an Orlando Lasso, a Gluck, or a Steffani. If to the life and works of the unrivalled Purcell, a distinct and entire chapter has been devoted, the sublime genius of Handel has received equal homage : and Haydn and Mozart, Arne and Arnold, Boyce and Battishill, are the worthy occupiers of three separate chapters.

A full delineation of the latter six composers was, indeed, the more necessary, since by Sir John Hawkins they are not even named ; and when Dr. Burney wrote, their careers were not terminated. To *one* of these ornaments of my time and country, two reasons have urged my particular attention ; the magnitude of his deserts, and the slight, I may say, ungenerous, mention made of his merits by the last of our two musical historians. *Dr. Arne* was the possessor of talents of the first order ; and an English cotemporary, (his pupil too!) by weaving for him a crown, would have accumulated honours for himself*.

When I first surveyed my accumulated materials, so vast and diversified a mass, native and exotic, presented itself to my attention, that some degree of perseverance was necessary, to examine, and some judgment requisite, to discriminate—to separate, and to arrange—to approve, and to select, the minor authors most worthy of appearing in company with examples of superior merit. Every admitted master could not be a diamond of the first lustre : but in a work, from its *compass,* needfully choice in its subjects, it would be expected that each should contribute to the general lustre of the casket.

To make this selection was, at least, a task of some trouble. To preserve the judgment unperplexed—to reject and to adopt by system ; in one instance to resist the influence of an over-estimated name—to subdue, in another, the prejudice exist-

---

* Burney's three years' tuition under the composer of *Comus,* was, it seems, as insufficient to infuse into his mind the amiable liberality, as the practical taste, of his illustrious master.

ing against obsolete excellence; to decide by the desert, not the reputation, of an author;—to give connexion and order to prominent incidents, and judiciously omit whatever would rather serve to surcharge, than to adorn, a concise though not uncomprehensive history—required, perhaps, not only much patience, but some little ability. To the Italian and the English opera, a sedulous and delicate attention was required ; and modern German, and English, church composition, demanded an equally careful consideration. These have been duly regarded, as well as the general state of Music in England, from its earliest cultivation among us, to the present time.

Thus, though for general convenience, the subject matter of this undertaking has been limited to the size in which it is here presented, (and consequently offered to the public at a price much more moderate than that of the works which have been named) truth and justice will sanction my saying, that nothing material to the reader's information has been omitted ; nothing forgotten by which needful knowledge might be communicated, or tasteful curiosity gratified ; nothing overlooked, of a nature calculated to instruct, or to amuse.

Further, to promote these eligible purposes, annotations have been freely and copiously subjoined. While some of these convey collateral narrative, or suggestions elucidatory of the main text, others, it is presumed, will inform, as critical illustrations, or entertain, as curious anecdotes, or appropriate comments.

How far these several, and desirable objects, have really been attained, remains for the public judgment to determine. In palliation of the defects of his work, the author can only plead the haste in which it has necessarily been produced. Formerly announced in his *Dictionary of Music* *, and lately in his *Musical Grammar* †, the long-promised History has been too frequently inquired after, not to have rendered those now concerned in its publication, anxious for its speedy appearance; and almost the whole of the matter has been written *currente calamo*, and sent to press the moment it was committed to paper.

If in a work produced under such circumstances, the style should not be found perfectly equal; if, in some instances, the phraseology should appear prolix, and in others too succinct; if the sentiment be not always strictly just, nor the diction uniformly select, candour will concede something to the urgency of the case, and criticism divide its regret between the deficiencies of the author, and the disadvantages with which he had to contend.

Chiswick, July, 1819.

. * Published by Sir Richard Phillips.

† Printed for Walker, and G. and W. B. Whittaker.

CONTENTS.

VOL. I.

———◆———

CHAP. I.

Page.

ORIGIN, and early Progress of Music 1

CHAP. II.

The Ancient Melopœia 21

CHAP. III.

Disputed Counterpoint of the Ancients 43

CHAP. IV.

Reputed Effects of the Ancient Music 62

CHAP. V.

Egyptian and Hebrew Music 84

CHAP. VI.

Ancient Music, as connected with the Grecian Mythology .. 109

CHAP. VII.

Musicians and Poets, subsequent to Hesiod and Homer 132

CHAP. VIII.

The Grecian Games 153

CHAP. IX.

The Ancient Musical Theorists, and their Works 169

CHAP. X.

Practical View of the Ancient Music, Vocal, and Instrumental 205

CHAP. XI.

Page.

Music of the Ancient Romans 229

CHAP. XII.

Music of the early Christians to the Time of Guido, and the
Introduction of the modern Organ 246

CHAP. XIII.

State of Music from the Time of Guido to the Formation of
the Time Table 268

CHAP. XIV.

Invention of the Time Table, and the further Progress of Harmonical Composition 295

CHAP. XV.

Minstrels, Troubadours, &c. &c.—General State of Music
from the Introduction of the Time Table to the Fourteenth Century 320

CHAP. XVI.

General State of Music, from the Beginning of the Fourteenth Century to the Time of Hambois, the first Doctor
in Music.. 353

CHAP. XVII.

State of Music, from the Time of Hambois, the first Doctor
in Music, to the Invention of Printing................ 382

CHAP. XVIII.

State of Music, from the Invention of Printing to the Time
of Josquin del Prato............................. 412

CHAP. XIX.

Josquin del Prato; and the State of Music during the early
part of the Sixteenth Century 445

CHAP. XX.

State of Music from the early part of the Sixteenth Century,
to the Reign of Elizabeth......................... 481

HISTORY OF MUSIC.

CHAP. I.

ORIGIN, AND EARLY PROGRESS, OF MUSIC.

IN contemplating the origin of music, a writer finds himself upon the margin of a boundless and unknown ocean, an ocean in which he fears to launch, because he has for his guide, neither compass, chart, nor polar star. If he keep to the coast, he finds nothing new, to add to the stock of existing information, or to gratify curiosity; and if he venture into the wild waste of conjecture, he is lost. He cannot hope that fortune will throw into his way a new continent, or unvisited island: he is on a voyage of discovery in the regions of imagination, and out of the very tract of truth and reality.

Any one doubting the verity of these remarks, will soon arrive at a settled opinion, by comparing the related effects of the ancient music with the imperfect knowledge we have, not only of the Egyptian and Grecian instruments, but of the system by which those instruments were tuned, and the manner in which they were performed. Much more sensible, then, will he be of their justness, if he compare the various fables in which it has been attempted to account for the *birth* of artificial music. *One* of those fanciful narratives bestows the honour of its parentage upon the Trismegistus, or *thrice-illustrious*, EGYPTIAN MERCURY. "The Nile," says Apollodorus, " after having overflowed the whole country of Egypt, when it returned within its natural bounds, left on the shore a great number of dead animals of various kinds, and, among the rest, a tortoise, the flesh of which being dried and wasted by the sun, nothing was left within the shell but nerves and cartilages, which, braced and contracted by desiccation, were rendered sonorous. Mercury, walking along the banks of the river, chanced to strike his foot against the shell of this tortoise, was pleased with the sound it produced, and upon reflection, conceived the idea of a *lyre*, which instrument he afterwards constructed in the form of a tortoise, stringing it with the dried sinews of dead animals."

The *flute*, or *monaulos*, according to Plutarch, was the invention of APOLLO; while Athenæus (in Juba's *Theatrical History*) attributes its origin to the great Egyptian ruler and legislator, Osiris. Its first shape is said to have been that of a bull's horn; and Apuleius, speaking of its uses in the mysteries of Isis, calls it the *crooked flute*.

With respect to the forms of these instruments, whoever suggested the first rude ideas of the frame and effect of the lyre, did, most probably, borrow the approximate conceptions from the vibrations of a distended string: and it is natural to suppose, that the *flute*, in its original simplicity, was but a slight improvement upon the whistling reed of the field. Of this opinion we find the sublime poet, Lucretius, than whom no ancient philosopher ever looked into nature, and nature's secrets, with a more penetrating eye*.

---

* Dr. Burney having found all the representations of the flute which he had seen, to be crooked, and formed pretty much like natural

Et zephyri cava per calamorum sibila primum
Agresteis docuere cavas inflare cicutas,
Inde minutatim dulceis didicere querelas,
Tibia quas fundit digitis pulsata canentum,
Avia per nemora, ac sylvas saltusque reperta,
Per loca pastorum deserta, atque otia dia.—LIB. v. 1381.

And moved by gentle gales, their murm'ring sound
The tuneful reeds, soft waving, whisper'd round ;
To wake the hollow reed, hence, man acquired
The melting art, and all the soul inspired.
Then sounds he learnt to breathe, like those we hear,
When the soft pipe salutes th' enchanted ear ;
When to the nimble finger it replies,
And with the blended voice in sweetness vies ;—
That pipe that now delights the lawns and groves,
Where'er the solitary shepherd roves,
And speaks the dulcet language of the Loves.

BUSBY.

But however early the formation of the first musical instruments, we cannot reasonably doubt that their invention was preceded by the use of the natural voice. Vocal music was a gift of nature ; and a susceptibility favourable to its reception, an unacquired property of the ear. But at what period vocal music assumed any thing like a systematic regulation of tones,

---

horns, supposed that the first instruments of the flute kind were suggested by the horns of dead animals ; but such a reason ought not to have satisfied a mind so inquisitive as his. Graphic representations of *crooked flutes* bring proofs that such flutes have been in use ; but afford no argument that they were the *first kind* of flutes. The *horn* inadvertently receiving the living breath, might suggest the idea of the shawm and trumpet ; but the reed, a *flute* ready formed by the hand of nature, and inflated by the passing gale, sent forth its melody, and left nothing to man but to improve the music he heard.

or intervals, remains, and ever must remain, a problem un-
solved. One fact, nevertheless, appears tolerably certain,
that vocal music could not be reduced to any settled rule,
without the aid of instruments. A wild and rude succession
of sounds, the unguided voice might be capable of producing; but without instruments, to give order, stability, and
mechanical precision to the distances; to fix their gradations,
and, in a word, form a determined and intelligible *scale*, the
sounds themselves, however agreeable to the raw, untutored
ear, could not be understood by the mind, and, therefore,
could not be sentimentally felt.

In saying that vocal music was a natural gift, I do not
mean that it was wholly unborrowed, perfectly independent
of example. The notes of birds, as a living melody, a melody not subject to chance, but no less constantly than
agreeably saluting the sense, could not but excite human imitation. This idea forcibly struck the poet whose verses have
just been quoted.

> *At liquidas avium voces imitarier ore*
> *Ante fuit multo, quam lævia carmina cantu*
> *Concelebrare homines possent, aureisque juvare.*—LIB. v. 1377.

> Then with their liquid lays the birds began
> To teach the ear of imitative man;
> Long ere with polish'd notes he cheer'd the plains,
> Or pour'd his extacies in measur'd strains.   BUSBY.

The opinion that man received his first musical tuition
from birds, derives no little corroboration from the fact, that
most of the winged tribes are distinguished by their own
specific and exclusive specimens of song. The melody of
the blackbird is not only composed of certain of the elements
of one of our two modern scales, but of the very notes of

that scale, which, in-combination, form its fundamental harmony. They are the following:

The song of the cuckoo is well known to consist of two notes.

Cuckoo,   Cuckoo,   Cuckoo.

And Kircher, in his *Musurgia,* has given the melodies of other tribes of birds, which his ingenious industry investigated and ascertained.

A sufficient reason having been given for the conclusion, that vocal melody was borrowed from living models, and that, though its rude state preceded the use of instruments, yet the music of the voice could not be governed by any system, till the mechanical production and modulation of sound had provided the means of arranging and fixing the intervals, the inquiry that next presents itself, concerns the inventors and improvers of those ancient instruments, whose origin we are best able to trace. Of these, the pipe and the lyre were certainly the two first that were used ; and though the story of the *tortoise-*

---

* Here we have the key-note, with its third, fifth, and eighth ; that is, the complete common chord, or harmony, of **G.**

† Here we have the third and fifth of the key-note ; that is, two of the component parts of the common chord, or harmony, of **G.**

*shell** may reasonably be doubted, there is no necessity to rob Mercury of the honour he has so long enjoyed, as the original fabricator of the latter instrument. It was in the year of the world 2000 that it was produced, a distance of time that hath as effectually concealed from antiquarians the first form of the lyre, as it has disappointed their inquiry concerning the first number of its strings. Some writers assert that it had only three, and that the inventor assimilated these to as many seasons of the year, summer, winter, and spring—assigning the acute string to the first, the grave to the second, and the mean to the third. Others affirm, that his lyre had four strings; that the first and fourth were octaves to each other; that the second was a fourth from the first, the fourth the same distance from the third, and that from the second to the third was a whole tone†. Others, again, contend that the lyre of Mercury had seven strings. To gratify curiosity, and to convince the readers how necessary it is to concede much to the ancient spirit of fiction (even in historical narration,) it will be sufficient to submit to him the account left us by

---

* It is worthy of remark, that the ancient statues of Apollo, Orpheus, and others, on bass reliefs, antique marbles, medals, and gems, do not all favour the supposition, that the lyre was formed of a tortoise-shell. If a single sample of this instrument, a part of which consists of a tortoise-shell, actually exists in Rome, others are found there formed of the bones of a goat standing in parallel positions; and others, again, constructed of the horns of a bull. Isaac Vossius contends, that the condition of these remaining monuments of antiquity is scarcely such as to demonstrate the real forms of the ancient cithara, or lyre.

† That is, the two extreme terms being included (which is the uniform custom in musical reckoning) the sounds of these four strings consisted of the first, fourth, fifth, and eighth, of the octave in which they lay.

Nicomachus, a follower of Pythagoras. " The lyre," says he, " formed of the shell, was invented by Mercury; and the knowledge of it, as it was constructed by him of seven strings, was transmitted to Orpheus ; Orpheus communicated its use to Thamyris and Linus, the latter of whom instructed Hercules, from whom the mystery passed to Amphion the Theban, who, to the seven strings of the lyre, built the seven gates of Thebes."

The same author further informs us, that Orpheus was afterwards killed by the Thracian women; that they were reported to have cast his lyre into the sea, and that it was afterwards thrown up at Antissa, a city of Lesbos; that, found by certain fishers, it was by them brought to Terpander, who carried it to Egypt, exquisitely improved, and shewing it to the Egyptian priests, assumed to himself the honour of its invention.

The pipe, the most simple, and, probably, the first of musical instruments, is ascribed to a variety of inventors, as Apollo, Pan, Orpheus, Linus, and many other revered cultivators and patrons of music. By some writers, the honour of first combining into one instrument, pipes of different lengths, is awarded to Marsyas; by others, to Silenus; but Virgil seems to decide the fact, when he says—

> *Pan primos calamos cera conjungere plures*
> *Instituit.*   ECLOG. II. 32.

> Pan taught to join with wax unequal reeds ;
> Pan loves the shepherds, and their flocks he feeds.
>   DRYDEN.

By Isidore, bishop of Seville, and others after him, this in strument, (frequently represented in collections of antiquities,)

has been called a *Pandorium,* while some writers have given
it the name of *syringa,* or the syrinx*.

An instrument consisting of strings distended upon a frame,
and by their comparative tensity or laxity, rendered capable
of producing different sounds, or a pipe perforated at equal
distances, are instruments, the simple forms and powers of
which our minds might easily conceive, even without the
instruction of the remaining monuments of antiquity; and,
therefore, I have preferred to speak of them before mentioning the instruments of which we read in the Pentateuch, or
the less ancient parts of sacred history; instruments, with the
figures and constructions of which the translators were so
little acquainted, as to be reduced to the necessity of so rendering the Hebrew appellations as to approach the nearest,
not to any founded or sanctioned idea of the things named,
but to their own conceptions of those things; conceptions
borrowed from *present* things, and, consequently, not to be
relied upon, as conveying ideas corresponding with the things
of which they speak†.

Any regular construction of a musical instrument, as that
of the lyre, or the pipe, supposes a *system;* and a system
once instituted, opens the road to the production of that
appreciable succession of sounds which forms *melody.*

---

* So called, from *Syrinx,* a nymph of Arcadia.   Pan became
enamoured of her; but she fled from his embraces, and at her own request, was changed by the gods into a reed called *syrinx.*   Pan made
himself a pipe of the reeds into which his favourite nymph had been
changed.—Ovid. Met. i. 691.

† How grossly would they deceive themselves who should assimi-
late in their minds the *organ* handled by those of whom Jubal is represented to be the father, to the instrument now known among us by
that name!

Melody, however, must for a long time have been vague, evanescent, and unsettled, because it was long before *notation* was invented. It does not appear, from history, that the Egyptians, Phœnicians, Hebrews, or any ancient people, except the Greeks and Romans, had *musical characters;* and even they could boast of no better symbols of sound than the letters of their alphabet, which also served them for arithmetical numbers, and chronological dates. The art of notation, nevertheless, was understood by the Greeks while yet the holes of the flute, and the strings of the lyre, were few, and, consequently, before they thought of the simplicity of expressing the octave of any sound by the same sign. The *diatesseron*, or fourth, was the constant limitation of the scale, the extremes of which were fixed, or *soni stabiles,* though the intermediate sounds were mutable, or *soni mobiles:* and the different rules by which the intermediate strings were tuned, formed the several *genera,* or various systems of graduated tones*.

The first improvement upon the tetrachord, or fourth, appears to have been, that of engrafting upon it a conjunct tetrachord, which addition extended the series to a heptachord, or scale of seven sounds. The last string of this heptachord was added by Terpander, and this system, considered as the second state of the lyre, was distinguished by his name. It was the following :

---

* That the *diatesseron*, or fourth, was a favourite and important interval in the ancient music, is manifest from the great system of two octaves having been composed of five of these tetrachords.

System of Terpander in modern notation.

First Tetrachord*.   Second Tetrachord.

It will be observed, that each of these tetrachords consists of an interval of a semitone, followed by two whole tones. But there were three different systems of fourths: one in which the semitone was between the first and second string, as above; one in which it was between the second and third string; and one in which it was between the third and fourth string.

EXAMPLE.

Semitone.   Semitone.   Semitone.

1st & 2d string.   2d & 3d.   3d & 4th.

---

* Here are eight *notes;* but the last sound of the first of these tetrachords being the same with the first of the second tetrachord, it is obvious, that one string would be sufficient for the termination of one tetrachord, and the commencement of the other. It will also be manifest that the two tetrachords meeting in one common sound (A,) are properly called *conjunct tetrachords*, in contra-distinction to a *disjunct tetrachord*, that is, to two tetrachords, the first sound of the second of which is one degree higher than the fourth sound of the first, as in the following example :—

Disjunct Tetrachord.

First Tetrachord.

Second Tetrachord.

The sound which constituted the last of the first four, and the first

To Terpander's lyre of seven strings, were afterwards added two other tetrachords; and it continued to be gradually improved, down to the time of Philolaus: when the genius of Pythagoras not only regulated, and gave order to the octave, but investigated the ratios of the consonances, and demonstrated, that the foundations of sonorous order lay deeper than had been imagined. The occasion of his discovery is too curious and interesting to be omitted.

" Pythagoras," says Mr. Stanley, in his History of Philosophy, " being in an intense thought whether he might invent any instrumental help to the ear, solid and infallible, such as the sight, both by a compass and a rule, and by a diopte ; or the touch, by a balance, or by the invention of measures; as he passed by a smith's shop, by a happy chance, he heard the iron hammers striking on the anvil, and rendering sounds most consonant to one another, in all combinations except one. He observed in them those three concords—the diapason (octave), the diapente (fifth), and the diatesseron (fourth). But the composition of the diatesseron and the diapente he found to be discordant. Apprehending that this new intelligence proceeded immediately from God, he enthusiastically hastened into the shop, and by various trials, finding the difference of the sounds to be according to the weight of the hammers, and not according to the force of those who struck, nor according to the fashion of the hammers, nor according to the turning of the iron which was in beating out; having exactly taken the weight of the hammers, he went straitway home, and to one beam fastened to the walls, across from one corner of the

---

of the second four of the *conjunct tetrachord*, was denominated the *mese*, or middle.

room to the other, lest any difference might arise from thence, or be suspected to arise from the properties of several beams, tying four strings of the same substance, length, and twist, upon each of them he hung a several weight, fastening it at the lower end, and making the length of the strings altogether equal; then striking the strings by two at a time interchangeably, he found out the aforesaid concord, each in its own combination: for that which was stretched by the greatest weight, in respect of that which was stretched by the least weight, he found to sound a diapason. The greatest weight was of twelve pounds, the least of six; thence he determined that the diapason did consist in double proportion, which the weights themselves did shew. Next he found, that the greatest to the least but one, which was of eight pounds, sounded a diapente; whence he inferred this to consist in the proportion called sesquialtera, in which proportion the weights were to one another; but unto that which was less than itself in weight, yet greater than the rest, being of nine pounds, he found it to sound a diatesseron; and discovered that, proportionably to the weights, this concord was sesquitertia; which string of nine pounds is naturally sesquialtera to the least; for nine to six is so, viz. sesquialtera, as the least but one, which is eight, was to that which had the weight six, in proportion in sesquitertia; and twelve to eight is sesquialtera; and that which is in the middle, between diapente and diatesseron, whereby diapente exceeds diatesseron, is confirmed to be in sesquioctave proportion, or the proportion in which nine is to eight. The system of both was called diapason, that is, both of the diapente and diatesseron joined together, as double proportion is compounded of sesquialtera and sesquitertia; such as are twelve, eight, six, or on the contrary, of diatesseron and diapente, as duple proportion is compounded of sesquitertia and sesquialtera, as twelve, nine, six, being taken in that order.

" Applying both his hand and ear to the weights which he hung on, and by them confirming the proportion of relations, he ingeniously transferred the common result of the strings upon the cross beam to the ridge of an instrument which he called *Chordotonos ;* and for stretching them proportionally to the weights, he invented pegs, by the turning of which he distended or relaxed them at pleasure. Making use of this foundation as an infallible rule, he extended the experiment to many kinds of instruments, as well pipes and flutes, as those which have strings; and he found, that this conclusion made by numbers, was invariably consonant in all*."

Till the time of this great philosopher and intellectual musician, the stated gradation, or order of sounds, was that which both ancient and modern writers term the *diatonic,* as proceeding by tones; that is, speaking in reference to a settled key, a progression from the unison to its fourth, by two tones and a semitone, two *disjunct tetrachords* of which constitute our octave in the major mode, and are confessedly

---

* Other writers attribute the discovery of the consonances to *Diocles,* who, they inform us, passing by a potter's shop, chanced to strike his stick against some empty vessels which were standing there, when observing the sounds of grave and acute resulting from the strokes on vessels of different magnitudes, he investigated the proportions of music, and found them to be as above related. But the almost uniform opinion of mankind gives the invention to Pythagoras. To whomsoever it belongs, its importance is great; since it proves consonance to be founded on geometrical principles, the contemplation of which, and the making them the test of beauty and harmony, is a pleasure separate and distinct from that received merely by the external sense.

very natural, and grateful to the ear*.   Refinement, and the
love of novelty, however, by a different division of the
integral parts of each of the tetrachords, formed another
series of progression, to which, from the flexibility of its
nature, they gave the epithet *chromatic ;* and to this they
added another, still more subtle, which they termed *enharmonic.*

In the *diatonic genus*†, the melody proceeded by a semitone and two tones, as

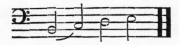

The *chromatic*‡ proceeded by two successive semitones,
and a minor third, as

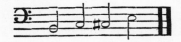

---

* TWO DISJUNCT TETRACHORDS,
OR
DIATONIC OCTAVE.

(MAJOR MODE.)

1st tetrachord.   2d tetrachord.

† Called *diatonic,* from its containing a succession of two whole
tones.

‡ This genus, holding the middle place between the diatonic and
enharmonic, has been supposed by Martianus Capella and Bayennius,
to derive its name from the word *chroma,* colour.

The *enharmonic** proceeded by two quarter tones, and a major third, as

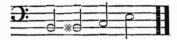

These *genera* given in rotation, will at once represent the degrees of which they consisted, and the order in which those degrees were disposed.

DIATONIC GENUS, OR SCALE.

CHROMATIC GENUS, OR SCALE.

---

* The *enharmonic* tetrachord is often called by Aristoxenus, and others, simply *harmonia*, that is, *well arranged*.

† This note, called *Proslambanomenos*, was added at the bottom of each of the scales, forming a kind of foundation for the whole series of sounds, but not included in the tetrachords: consequently, the first tetrachord of each genus commenced at the note immediately following the *proslambanomenos*. The whole series of each scale was divided into tetrachords; and the purpose of the curves here drawn under the notes, is to designate them.

The octave to the *proslambanomenos* completed the second tetrachord, formed the final of the first octave, and the initial of the second, that is, the centre of the two octaves, and therefore was called the *mese*, or middle sound of the system; as that sound, which formed the

ENHARMONIC GENUS, or SCALE.

By these diagrams, we see, that the regular *diatonic* scale was similar to our own, inasmuch as it consisted of tones and semitones: while the *chromatic* comprised semitones and minor thirds; and the *enharmonic,* quarter tones and major thirds.

Till the time of Euclid, these three were all the genera or scales in use; but we find that author speaking of a fourth or *mixed genus,* the scale of which he has left us.

FOURTH, or MIXED GENUS†.

According to this scale, six strings, instead of four, were

---

final of the first of two conjunct tetrachords, and the initial of the second, was denominated the *mese*, or middle sound of the hepta-chord. Vide note, p. 10.

* This sign of the diesis, or quarter tone, is, from necessity, arbitrarily applied. Modern musicians, not dividing the semitone into two equal portions, have no character by which to imply such division.

† This *mixed* genus in *music*, may not unaptly be compared with the *composite* order, in *architecture*. As the *composite order* is but a commixture of the Corinthian and the Ionic, so this *fourth scale* is only a compound of the Diatonic and Enharmonic.

required, to fill up the *tetrachord;* and the octave from *proslambanomenos* to *mese,* must have been supplied with twelve*.

The above three *genera,* as differing from each other in respect of their intervals, may be said to correspond with the three scales of the moderns ; that is, with the diatonic major scale, the diatonic minor scale, and the Scotch scale, in which the fourth and seventh are omitted. But not only was the music of the ancients, like our own, founded upon different scales ; it had under the name of *modes,* all our different keys. Yet in one remarkable particular, this branch of their system differed from ours ; it was confined to the *minor*†. They had their *grave,* their *middle,* and their *acute* modes ; but the comparative gravity and cheerfulness of each, related merely to its locality in the GREAT COMPASS, which comprised three octaves and a tone ; that is, from our A above G gamut, in the bass, to B in alt, in the treble.

The following table, exhibiting the different modes, with

---

* Aristides Quintilianus, (p. III.) speaking of the different *genera,* says, that the *diatonic genus* is manly and severe, the *chromatic* sweet and pathetic, and the *enharmonic* animating and mild. With whatever justice these *properties* might once have been attributed to the Grecian scales, they will not be recognised by modern ears. When the same author, in another place, observes that the *diatonic* is the most natural of all the genera, we can comprehend and feel the truth of his remark ; and the fact, that even the uninstructed are capable of singing it, confirms the assertion.

† This limitation of the mode, to the *minor,* speaking generally, must have imparted a melancholy cast to their melodies : yet, strange as it may appear, no provision is made in any of the treatises that have come down to us, for that ordinal disposition of the tones and semitones which constitute a major key.

their appropriate flats and sharps, together with their ancient denominations, and their divisions into *grave*, *mean*, and *acute*, will give the reader a clear idea of their relative characters, as well as of their affinity to the modern bearings and distinctions of keys.

GRAVE MODES.

Key of A Minor; ——— of B flat Minor; ——— of B ♮ Minor;

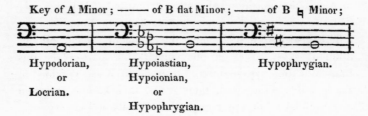

Hypodorian,   Hypoiastian,   Hypophrygian.
or   Hypoionian,
Locrian.   or
      Hypophrygian.

Of C Minor; ——— of C ♯ Minor:

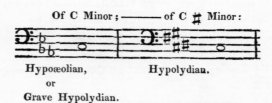

Hypoæolian,   Hypolydian.
or
Grave Hypolydian.

MIDDLE MODES.

Key of D Minor; ——— of E flat Minor; ——— of E ♮ Minor;

Dorian.   Ionian,   Phrygian.
or
Iastian.

Of F Minor; ——— of F ♯ Minor:

Æolian.   Lydian.

ACUTE MODES.

Key of G Minor; ———— of G ♯ Minor; ———— of A Minor;

Hyperdorian,	Hyperiastian,	Hyperphrygian,
or	or	or
Mixolydian.	Hyperionian.	Hypermixolydian

Of B flat Minor; ————of B ♮ Minor*.

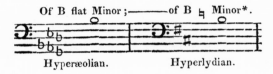

Hyperæolian.   Hyperlydian.

Since these modes correspond in their variations from each other, with the manner, and the extent of the differences in our modern keys, we are left to wonder at the very striking and transporting effects that ancient authors have attributed to a mere change from one mode to another,—to a transition from scale to scale,—to an elevation or depression of the same range and description of intervals†.

Of all the several modes of the Greeks, the *Phrygian* and the *Lydian* appear to have been the most opposed to

---

* The two last of these fifteen modes are only octaves, or repli-cates, of the second and third; for which reason Aristoxenus very properly rejected them.

† In modern music, *a change of key* without a change of time, is not sufficient either to sink or to animate, the spirits in any great degree; to a change of pitch in the scale (for melodial modulation is no more), a variation of measure must add its auxiliary influence; and even then, the result will not be comparable to what is related of the effects of a sudden transition from the *soft* Lydian, or *grave* Dorian, to the *furious* Phrygian.

each other.   Apuleius tells us, that the *Lydian* was appropriated to the expression of sorrow and complaint; and the *Phrygian* to religious ceremonies; that is, to the passionate and vehement ebullitions of phrenetical adoration. Thus Lucretius, in his description of the public honours paid to Cybele, *magna deûm mater*, the great common mother of gods, men, and brutes,

> *Et Phrygio stimulat numero cava Tibia menteis.*
>
> B. ii. 620.

And Phrygian airs the raptur'd soul inspire,
Rouze the strong passions, and to phrenzy fire.

BUSBY.

And Dryden, in celebrating the powers of *Timotheus*, was mindful of the melting magic of the *Lydian* mode,

> Softly sweet, in Lydian Measures,
> Soon he sooth'd the soul to pleasures.

ALEXANDER'S FEAST.

Dryden, by the whole cast and allusions of this fine poem, was evidently of opinion (and it would be difficult not to think with him) that the surprising effects of the ancient music are chiefly ascribable to *changes of measure*. But to whatever extent these changes might be carried, both in the poetry and its instrumental accompaniments, the lyrical numbers of their melodial delivery, we still have to give the ancient *Melopœia* credit for arts of expression and modulation not explained in the treatises that have come down to us, before we can yield our unqualified belief to what the gravity of history relates, not to mention the lively flourishes of poetry.

CHAP. II.

THE ANCIENT MELOPŒIA.

OF the system of the erudite and philosophical Pytha-goras*, who so sedulously and successfully gleaned the garden of Egyptian science, and to whose instructions Cicero imputes whatever knowledge the old Romans might possess, I shall take no further notice, than to add, that its truth has been disputed by the noble Florentine, Vincentio Galileo, and disproved by his illustrious son, Galileo Galilei; refer-ring the reader for a knowledge of the laws of appreciable sounds, to Malcolm, Holden, and other of our patient inves-tigators of that branch of acoustics.

It has been said, that the Greeks employed, for musical signs, the letters of their alphabet. The method of applying those letters is explained by Boetius. Speaking in his fourth book upon music (chap. 3) of the early manner of notation, he says, " The ancient musicians, to avoid the necessity of always writing them at length, invented certain characters to express the names of the chords in their several

---

* This philosopher was the founder of the *Italic sect*, that flourished in Italy about the time of the expulsion of the Tarquins. He was also the author of the custom of singing (accompanied by the flute) the praises of famous men, at great entertainments, a practice which is said to have been introduced by that sect.

genera and modes; this short method was the more eagerly embraced, that in case a musician should be inclined to adopt music to any poem, he might, by means of these characters, in the same manner as the words of the poem were designated by letters, express the music, and transmit it to posterity." The author then proceeds to exhibit his examples, some of which consist of certain letters imperfectly formed, some of letters standing rightly, and some of letters reversed, while others again are supine, others erect, some simple, and some compound.

The difference, therefore, between the ancient and modern method of notation, is as striking, as the advantage of the latter is obvious. By the adoption of staves, we obtain an analogy between the *situations* of our notes and the gravity and acuteness they represent. The ancient notation, defective in this most essential particular, induced the necessity of re-particularizing their signs, by the words *acumen* and *gravitas*, which perpetually occur. It may be true, that there is no positive likeness or connexion between *local elevation* or profundity, and what we call a *high* or a *low sound;* but the respective assimilations are very natural, seem to be sanctioned by the fact, that the deeper sounds of the voice are produced from the lower parts of the larynx, and the more acute by the higher*, and by, as it were, ren-

---

* Mr. Chilmead, the publisher of the Oxford edition of Aratus, and of Eratosthenes de Astris, has annexed to the work three hymns, or odes, of a Greek poet, named Dionysius, with the ancient musical characters, which he has rendered by *breves* only; but Kircher, in his *Musurgia*, has inserted a fragment of Pindar, with the musical notes, which he has explained by the different signs of a breve, semi-breve, crotchet, and quaver. Meibomius also has given, from an ancient manuscript, a *Te Deum* with the Greek characters, and in

dering sound *visible*, enable us to learn them with our eyes.
This, however, is not the only advantage of the notation now
in use, over that of the ancients. They had no characters
to designate the precise length or duration of their sounds ;
a defect that was very inadequately supplied by the *measure*
and the *feet* of the verse to which the melody was accommodated. It is very true, that some among the learned who
have undertaken a translation of a few remaining fragments
of ancient music, into modern notes, have in particular instances, ventured to render the characters in the original by
acknowledged signs of various durations ; but it is only fair
to insinuate that their choice was determined rather by the
cadence of the verse, than by any rhythmical designation or
implied temporal precision, observable in any of their characteristic archetypes*.

So far, however, was the notation of the ancients (with all
its defects) adequate to the purposes to which *they* applied
the powers of music, that it not only furnished the means of
distinguishing the several *genera* and the *modes*, but of
expressing all the d.fferent branches, offices, and operations

---

modern notes, consisting of the *breve*, the *semibreve*, and the *minim :*
but upon what authority those several modes of translation were
founded, it would not be easy to discover.

It would, perhaps, be wrong to discuss this note without observing
that the *Te Deum*, commonly styled the Song of St. Ambrose, is generally conjectured to have been composed jointly by him and St. Augustine, early in the fourth century ; though Archbishop Usher ascribes it to Nicetius, and supposes it not to have been composed till
about the year 500, which was long after the time of Ambrose and
Augustine.

* It is a circumstance of surprise, that this fact escaped the sagacity of the ancient Greeks ; a fact, the knowledge of which would
have determined them at once to consider slower vibrations as the
low, or grave, and the quicker as the high, or acute.

of the *Melopœia;* in which may be included *Mutation,* resembling our *modulation; Melos,* consisting of several *musical sounds* of a *certain pitch of voice; Melodia,* or the *singing of poetry* to such sounds; *Rhythm,* or the adjustment of sounds to equable measures or times; and *Prosody,* or that adaptation of the length of the sounds to the syllables, which makes music of the poetry, as the melodious variations of the verse cause poetry to be music.

Melopœia had its particular rules, several of which are come down to us, and are still clear and intelligible. A principal law was, that an air, or melody, should be composed in some particular *genus,* and be chiefly, if not wholly, confined to the sounds of some one *mode.* The successions, or order of sounds, in each air, as we learn from Euclid, was, in general, limited to four kinds. Their description will throw some light upon the nature of ancient melody.

One *licence,* rather than a *rule,* was, that sounds may move either ascending or descending, regularly; that is, in consecutive degrees ;—as thus :

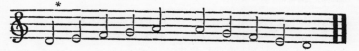

Secondly, they might proceed by leaps, or intervals, greater than that of a tone ;—thus :

---

* A manner of succession, called *agoge.*
† Called *ploche,* or *interwoven.*

Thirdly, the same sound might be repeated several times;
—as thus:

The *mutation* of the *melopœia* corresponded with that
variation, or excursion of the voice, which in the language of
poetry rather than that of music, is called *modulation*†. Instead of being a transition from one mode, or key, to another,
it was limited to a diversified arrangement of sounds in the
same mode; as, in modern music, thus:

Mutation, however, was occasionally permitted to trans-
gress the prescribed bounds; passing from one *genus* to
another; from the chromatic, for instance, to the diatonic, or

---

* Called *petreia*, or *iteration*.

† That *modulation*, with the ancients, was no more than the
change of sounds in singing, or, as we should call it, *melody*, is clear
from a passage in Bacchius, senior, who, in his "Introduction to the
Art of Music, by Question and Answer," asks, "How many kinds
of *modulation* there are?" the answer is, "Four." And these, he

enharmonic, and the contrary. Also *mutation* took place, sometimes, in the *mode ;* as from the *Dorian* to the *Lydian*, or *Phrygian*, &c. and lastly, there was a mutation of style; as from grave to gay, or from a languid to an impetuous strain. But this last kind of *mutation* was never allowed to be too sudden, or irrelative, lest the pleasure arising from reminiscence should be lessened or destroyed*. These rules, it must be confessed, afford us but general notions of the ancient *modulation ;* and to render them clear and determinate would require the illustration of examples, and the aid of those *minutiæ* which private and personal tuition easily conveys, but which we do not find in any one of the seven treatises collected by the care and industry of Meibomius.

An important, because an intellectual and animating part of the *melopœia*, was the *rhythm*, or *measure.*

So strict was the ancient union between poetry and music, that a violation of the *rhythm*, or *time*, was an unpardonable offence†. *Rhythm*, either in vocal or instru-

---

afterwards tells us, are " *rising, falling*, repeating the same sound to different words, and remaining upon, or holding out, a musical tone."

* It is a remark of Aristoxenus, that the understanding music depends upon sensation and memory. " We must not only," says he, " feel sounds at the instant they strike the external sense, but remember those with which it has already been struck, in order to be able to compose them together ; for otherwise it will be impossible to follow a melody or modulation with pleasure to the ear, or to form a judgment of its degree of excellence in the mind."

† Plato refused the title of musician to every one who was not perfectly versed in *rhythm :* Pythagoras used to call *rhythm*, in music, *male*, and *melos, female;* and Doni has compared *rhythm* to *design* in painting, and *melos* to *colouring.* And certain it is, that an ordinary melody, in which the *time* is strongly marked, and the

mental music, is indispensable : but, if possible, less to be
spared in the vocal. Consequently, with the Greeks, almost
the whole of whose music was but a musical recital of
poetry, *rhythm* was the first object of attention. Their
verses, all composed of long and short syllables, depended,
for their just and emphatic delivery, wholly upon this branch
of the *melopœia*, which includes both accent and quantity.
The ancient rule was, to give the short syllable half the time
of the long : by consequence, the sound which was applied
to the long syllables was equal in duration to two such
sounds as were sung to the short syllables. It must be remembered that the verses thus sung consisted of a certain
number of feet, formed by these long and short syllables
differently combined : and that the *rhythm* of the melody
was regulated by these feet; as, whatever was their length,
they were always divided into two parts, equal or unequal,
the first of which was called *arsis, elevation,* and the second
thesis, depression. In like manner, the *rhythm* of the
melody corresponded with these feet, was divided into two
parts, equal or unequal, corresponding with our *ascending*
and *descending* parts of a bar, expressed by raising and sink-
ing the hand or foot*.

---

accents well placed, is more effective than one that fails in those
qualities, even though more refined and uncommon, and aided by all
the richness of harmony, and variety of modulation.

* To regulate the *time* was generally the office of the music
director, or *coryphæus*, who was placed in the middle of the orchestra,
among the musicians, and in an exalted and conspicuous situation,
that he might be the more easily seen by the whole band. To
render their *beating* the more audible, their feet were generally furnished with wooden or iron sandals. The time was sometimes beaten
by the open right hand upon the hollow of the left, and then the director was called the *manu-ductor*. The ancient measures, or times,

This was the *rhythm* of the ancient *vocal* music. We will now consider that of the *instrumental*. In this, since the notes were constantly written over the syllables of the verses that were to be sung, while the quantity of each syllable was perfectly understood by musicians, and the duration of each sound regulated by the syllables, it did not seem necessary that the *time* should be marked by any particular sign or character. However, for the ease and convenience of the performer, a canon, or rule, was given of the *rhythm* at the beginning of a lyric poem. This canon consisted of nothing but the numbers 1 and 2, that is, the *alpha* and *beta* of the Greek alphabet, disposed according to the order of the breves and longs which composed and divided each verse according to the numbers of the feet. The *alpha*, or unit, marked a *breve*, because it contained only one portion of time; and the *beta*, or binary, marked a *long*, being equal to two portions*. *Rhythm*, in Latin, was called *numerous;* and this term, in process of time, was extended to the melody itself, subjected to certain numbers of rhythms, as appears from this line of Virgil :

Numeros memini, si verba tenerem.

If I knew the words, I could remember the tune.

---

were of four kinds; two equal parts, two parts the first of which was double of the second, five equal parts, and seven equal parts. The first of these (answering to our *common* time) they called *equal;* the second (corresponding with our *triple* time) they named *double ;* the second was denominated *sesquialter*, that is, *two to three ;* and the fourth was called *epitritus*, that is, *three to four*.

* Some of these poetical, or rhythmical canons, are still to be found in the Manual of Hephæstion, the grammarian, who flourished in the time of the Emperor Verus, in the second century.

It is fortunate for the curious respecting the ancient *rhythm*, that, having been regulated entirely by metrical feet, it is as well known to us as the prosody and construction of the verse; so that we have only to apply to the long and short syllables any two notes, one of which is twice the length of the other, in order to proceed as exactly as if we heard, in what manner any particular kind of *metre* was set with respect to *time* and *cadence*,—to be perfectly acquainted with that *rhythm*, which is represented as every thing in the ancient music.

From what has been said, it is evident that the Greeks and Romans had but two degrees of long and short notes*. The time of these may, indeed, have been accelerated or retarded, but still the same proportion must have been preserved; and all the variations could only have been so many different combinations of these two kinds of notes. By this fact we can account for the facility with which even the common people of Greece could discover any mistakes in the length and shortness of the syllables, both with respect to the poetry and the music; a point of history in which all writers agree. Hence it appears, that besides the intervals peculiar to the melody, *Rhythm*, or time, must have contributed to characterize the modes, though it has no kind of connexion with our flat and sharp keys; and this presents to our minds something distinct from our modern modes, taken as keys, and our music in general†. To speak truly,

---

* And even the old lozenge and square characters still used in the *Canto Fermo* of the Romish church, under the denomination of Gregorian notes, are but of two kinds.

† Tartini observes, that *we* make the prosody subservient to the music, not the music to the prosody; and adds, "that as by the laws prescribed to the ancient musicians, *they* were obliged to rigor-

we regard neither the theory nor the practice of the ancient
rhythm, beyond the mere observance of the expression of
the final cadence of verses, or the agreement and similarity
of sound in the last syllables of couplets and triplets, comprehending what are denominated *rhyme.* And, in fact,
when we examine the proportion subsisting between the
different parts of a' melody, constituting *time, measure,* and
movement, we find it to consist but of two kinds, differently
modified; that of *common time,* and *triple time,* with their
compounds.

The invention and adoption of musical characters, must,
for some time, have occasioned infinite labour and perplexity
to the practical musician. The study of the new relations
was almost a new science, and begat, as it were, a necessity
for his re-acquiring his profession. Not only were these
characters new in their figures, but gifted with different
value and velocity, according to other characters prefixed to a
musical composition, and likewise frequently occurring in the
course of a piece, to announce a change of measure: as
from common time to triple, from quick to slow, and *vice
versa.* Other characters were called *moods,* but they were
so extremely embarrassing and ill understood, till the invention of bars, by which musical notes were divided into equal
portions, that scarcely two musicians agreed in their defini-
tion*. But to this invention of musical signs for *time,* and

---

ously preserve in their music the quantity of syllables, it was impossible to prolong a vowel, in singing, beyond the time which belonged
to a syllable : *we,* on the contrary, often prolong the vowels through
several bars, though in reading, they are often short."

* Since technical terms, chiefly borrowed from the Italian language, have been adopted, these moods, by which the kind of movement, with respect to quick and slow, as well as the proportion of the

to the consequent introduction of *bars,* we have certainly been much indebted for a rapid advance in the composition and performance of instrumental music. Not only has it attained a degree of energy unknown, till aided by adscititious advantages, but its expression is now accentuated; and it possesses a cadence and feet of its own more marked and more sensible than those of poetry, by which its motions were guided, and to which they were subservient*.

Quitting the comparatively confined and sterile tracts of *recitative* and *chanting* (for the Greek music was certainly little more) *we* indulge in the enlarged and gratifying regions of the *florid song.* Our airs, limited in their freedom, only by the accent and cadence of the words they adorn and illustrate, offer an augmented scope for the fancy, and a more favourable display to taste and genius†. To this is to be added the fact, that our *instrumental music* has almost attained the sentiment and expression of language; that it actually *does speak* to the heart and to the passions, and is

---

notes, used to be known, serve for no other purpose than to mark the number and kind of notes in each bar.

* This great improvement upon the ancient *rhythmopœia* was first introduced in the fourteenth century, by John de Muris, a doctor of the Sorbonne, and a native of England, though the generality of writers suppose him to have been a Norman. It was he who invented characters significative of the different durations of sounds, and supplied a system of metrical music.

† It must not, however, be dissembled, that modern melody is not always sufficiently compliable with the demands of poetry; that, too frequently, the finest sentiments and most polished verses are injured by the composer's inattention to *prosody.* But Salinas tells us, from St. Augustine, that poets and musicians have ever been at strife concerning long and short syllables, accents, and quantity, since their respective arts have ceased to be united in one and the same person.

capable of moving and exciting our interest and our feelings.

To return, however, to the more immediate consideration of the ancient *melopœia*: —It was long very earnestly wished that a collection of some of the most beautiful melodies of antiquity might be found among the manuscripts that have escaped the ravages of time, as a means to accurately determine the nature of the ancient music to which such marvellous effects have been attributed. A few of these were, at length, discovered; but for the honor of the Greeks, it becomes us to conclude, that if we have found the *form*, we are still strangers to the *spirit* of their musical composition; that it is the *body*, not the *soul*, of their melody, we have obtained; and that with respect to the principle from which emanated its resistless influence, of which ancient writers boast, we remain as uninformed as ever.

At the end of a Greek edition of the astronomical poems of Aratus, called *Phœnomena*, and their *Scholia*, published at Oxford, in 1672, the anonymous editor, among several other pieces, has enriched the volume with three hymns, which he supposed to have been written by a Greek poet, called Dionysius, of which, the first is addressed to the Muse Calliope, the second to Apollo, and the third to Nemesis; and, fortunately, these hymns are accompanied with the notes of ancient music, to which they were originally sung*.

---

* This precious manuscript was found in Ireland, among the papers of the famous Archbishop Usher. The ancient musical characters being reduced to those in present use (by the Reverend Mr. Chilmead, of Christ Church, Oxford, into whose hands they passed from the library of Mr. Bernard, fellow of St. John's College) it appeared that the music was composed in the Lydian mode, and diatonic genus.

Dr. Burney, after explaining the manner in which these curious fragments were discovered, and tracing them from Vicenzo Galilei, father of the great Galileo, to the Rev. Mr. Mead, of Christ-church, Oxford, tell us, that "after being sifted, collated, and corrected by the most able critics in the Greek language, as well as the most skilful musicians of the last and present centuries, he presents them to his readers, not only as they appear in the original manuscript, (that is, with the Greek musical characters over the words) but in the equivalent and modern notes." The veil of obscurity thus removed, they come before the eye in all their native destitution of beauty, and excite quite as much wonder, that such music should ever have been admired and eulogized, as the accounts which ascribe the astonishing effects of the ancient melodies, created, before these compositions made their appearance among us*.

These airs (if airs they can be justly termed) comprise no other sounds than those of the Lydian mode, yet very frequently change the *key* and the *time,* speaking according to the modern sense of those words, which shews in what different acceptations the ancients used the terms *mode* and *rhythm,* from those in which we employ the technical expressions *time* and *key.* By *mode* they understood no more than a certain degree of elevation, or acuteness, in their

---

* Through all the simplicity of these melodies, which, as Dr. Burney correctly observes, somewhat resemble the *Canto Fermo* of the Romish Church, the musician appears to have aimed at the just expression of the words. By the *appogiaturas,* something more seems to be meant than meets the eye. Evidently the music does not fully unfold itself. To affirm that it does, would be to say that it is very bad ; for it is so little susceptible of harmony, that it would be difficult to give a tolerable bass to either of the compositions, especially to the first.

general system, in which the sounds always followed in the same order; whereas in our music, keys are distinguished from each other, not only by their situation in the scale with respect to high and low, but by their different arrangement in regard of mutable intervals, such as thirds and sixths, which constitute major and minor, or sharp and flat keys, besides the different modifications that these keys receive from *temperament*, which, in instruments where tones are fixed, are characterized and diversified by a greater or less degree of perfection in the intervals and concords, though all the intervals of major and minor keys are nominally, and essentially the same.

Dr. Burney, as if sensible that his readers in general would deem themselves little obliged to him for presenting them with these unintelligible specimens of the ancient *melopœia*, the entire exposition of which seems to deter modern patience and defy modern sagacity, says, with diffidence and ingenuousness, " I know not whether justice has been done to these melodies; all I can say is, that no pains have been spared to place them in the clearest and most favourable point of view : and yet, with all the advantages of modern notes and modern measure, if I had been told that they came from the Cherokees, or the Hottentots, I should not have been surprised at their excellence*." The truth is, that after all the light that the most patient and ingenious inquiry can throw upon these pieces, they are too rude, irregular, and inelegant to seem worthy of so ingenious, so polished, and sentimental

---

* The Doctor tried these series of sounds in every key, and in every measure that the feet of the verses would allow; and as it has been the opinion of some, that the Greek scale and music should be read Hebrew-wise, he even inverted the order of the notes, but without being able to reduce them to the least grace or elegance.

a people as the ancient Greeks. The most charitable sup-
osition, therefore, that can be admitted concerning them, is,
that the Greek language being in itself accentuated and sonorous, wanted the less assistance from musical refinements;
and that music being with them the slave of poetry, and
wholly governed by its *feet*, derived all its merit and effects
from the excellence of the verse, and sweetness of the voice
by which it was sung, or rather, recited.

Another ancient composition (found by M. Burette in
the collection of Father Montfaucon, a literary and scientific
antiquarian, known to be in possession of copies of all the
most valuable manuscripts in the principal libraries of Europe) exhibits claims to a somewhat better account than the
pieces we have already described. The words consist of the
first eight verses of the first Pythic of Pindar; and they are
accompanied with the ancient Greek musical notes, which
are the same as Alypius attributes to the Lydian mode*.
The first four of these verses have a melody set to them for
one or several voices; the four last constitute a different melody, at the beginning of which were (in Greek) the following
words—*Chorus sung to the sound of the Cithara;* and over
the words of each verse are written, the characters peculiar
to instrumental music; which shews that the second melody
was not only executed by voices, but accompanied by one or
more citharas, playing in unisons, or octaves, to the voice.
The melody set to these eight verses is extremely simple,
and composed of only six different sounds; a cogent proof of
the antiquity of the music, since the lyre of seven strings had
more notes than were sufficient for its execution.

---

* But for the musical characters over the notes, which belong to
the Lydian mode, this melody might, with more propriety, be said to
be in the Phrygian mode.

The whole composition (reduced to modern notes by M. Burette, in the *Memoires de l'Academie des Inscriptions*, tome 5) consists of thirty-eight bars, some of which are in triple, and others in common time; but without any regular, or orderly interchange of measure.   The series of the sounds are, however, so connected and natural, that by reducing them to a stated measure, or time, whether triple or common, and subscribing a bass, which it is very capable of receiving, it will have the appearance and effect of a religious hymn of the last century.

The following examples (the one of Burette's rendering, and the other a later and equalized transcript) will both gratify the reader's curiosity respecting the ancient construction of melody, and serve as indices to the affinity between the old and the modern school.

ANCIENT GREEK MUSIC,

TO THE

FIRST EIGHT VERSES OF THE FIRST PYTHIC OF PINDAR,

REDUCED TO MODERN NOTATION,

BY

M. BURETTE.

κον Μοι - σαν - κτεα - νον, Τας α -

κου - ει μεν βασις αγλαι -

ας αρ - χα.

Χορος εἰς Κυθαραν.

Πει - θον - ται δ'α - οι - δοι σαμα -

σιν, 'Α - γησιχο - ρων ο - πο ταν των

φροι - μι - ων 'Αμ - βο - λας τευ -

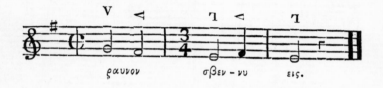

THE SAME,

IN MODERN NOTATION, AND EQUABLE TIME,

WITH A FIGURED BASS.

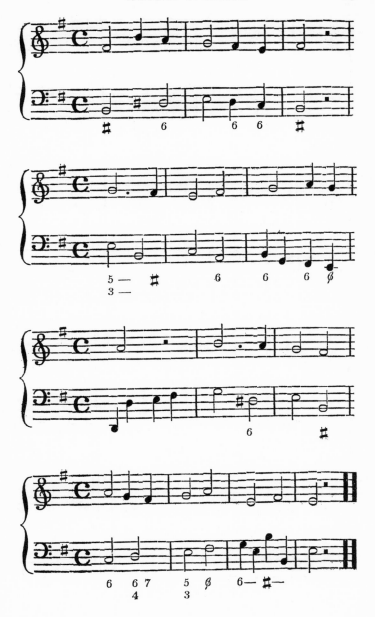

TRANSLATION.

Hail, golden lyre! whose heav'n-invented string
  To Phœbus, and the black-hair'd nine belongs;
Who in sweet chorus round the tuneful king,
  Mix with thy sounding chords their sacred songs.

The dance, gay queen of pleasure, thee attends ;
  Thy jocund strains her list'ning feet inspire:
And each melodious tongue its voice suspends,
  'Till thou, great leader of the heav'nly quire,
With wanton art preluding giv'st the sign—
  Swells the full concert then with harmony divine.

                                West's Pindar, vol. i. *p.* 84.

It will be impossible for the reader to peruse these bold and animated verses, and not be sensible of the utter insufficiency of the above music, to express their fire and force. Bearable as it might be, associated with the words of a parochial charity hymn, or of a common love ditty, in such company as that of the muse of Pindar, it is beyond toleration. Taking this, then, as a sample of the *melopœia* of the ancients, (and they have left us nothing better by which to guide our judgment, supposing this to be authentic) we are compelled to conclude, either that their music possessed some powerful adjunct, some extrinsic auxiliary, at the knowledge of which we have not been able to arrive, or that it was far from possessing that extraordinary influence over the mind and the passions, ascribed to it by the fiction of poetry, and the zeal and enthusiasm of historians.

CHAP. III.

DISPUTED COUNTERPOINT OF THE ANCIENTS.

HAVING exhibited the exposition of the elements of ancient melody, we will now enter upon the consideration of the arguments in favour of, and against, the opinion, that the art of *Counterpoint*, or composition in *parts*, was known to those early cultivators of Music, the *Greek Harmonicians*.

It has been rather unfortunate for those whose curiosity would be satisfied upon this point, that, for the most part, it has been discussed by writers not qualified by an acquaintance with the science upon which the question is founded. Some of these authors have failed to distinguish between simultaneous concordance, and the connexion of successive impressions, as they have confounded the accident of *tone* with the permanency of gravity and acuteness, and the term *key*, as implying an independent sound, and as the representative of the foundation of a scale to each degree of which it bears a certain relation, and the intervals of which it prescribes and governs. If those of the learned, who have written *ex-professo*, have not been able to come to an agreement upon a topic that has excited their most earnest and sedulous inquiry, much less would those ignorant of the principles of music find it possible to solve the problem. Therefore,

taking no notice of such unqualified disquisitors, we will
weigh the arguments, and collate the opinions of those
whose theoretical intelligence, entitle their *dicta* to our consideration, if not to our implicit confidence.

The most distinguished advocates for ancient *Counterpoint,*
are, Gaffurio, Zarlino, Gio. Battista Doni, Isaac Vossius,
Zaccharia Tevo, the Abbé Fraguier, and Stillingfleet, author
of *The Principles and Power of Harmony.* Those against
it are, Glareanus, Salinas, Bottrigari, Artusi, Cerone, Kepler,
Mersennus, Kircher, Claude Perrault, Wallis, Bontempi,
Burette, the Fathers Bougeant and Cerceau, Padre Martini,
M. Marpurg, and M. Rousseau.

Gaffurio, in his *Practica Musicæ utriusque Cantus,* has
affected to quote Bacchius, senior, as his authority for the
ancients having practised simultaneous harmony; a writer
in whom not a single word is to be found on the subject.
Bacchius only treats of the laws of *melody,* no inquiries
into the nature of which can throw the least light upon those
of *harmony,* or corroborate, or weaken, the probability that
harmony was known to the ancients. Zarlino asserts, (in his
Supplimenti Musicali) that it could not well be possible
that the ancients should have made use of instruments of
many strings, without playing in consonance; and lays much
stress upon the opportunity afforded them by the *hydraulicon,* or water-organ, to cultivate the science of concording
combination. This is necessitating harmonical knowledge
from plural audibility; as if to hear a combination of sounds,
were to be endued with the faculty of understanding their relation in respect of consonance. Dr. Burney pertinently observes, that, for a long time, the lyre had but very few strings;
and that it was several ages before their number exceeded
eight. But I should argue that, however numerous the
strings, the science of simultaneous concord would not

necessarily grow out of such a provision*. And as to the
hydraulicon, the idea of which was probably suggested by
the *Syrinx*, or *Fistula Panis*, even admitting, agreeably to
the opinion of Barlotinus and Blanchinus, that it was ultimately furnished with keys, it must have been a long time
before that instrument was rendered capable of being played
in *parts ;* and still longer, ere that science existed by which
alone its sounds could be systematically combined†. Doni,
a Florentine nobleman, who flourished in the last century
but one, defends ancient counterpoint with as much perti-
nacity of opinion as dissonance of argument. He is unwilling that the Greeks and Romans should be robbed of the
honour of its invention and practice ; and yet calls it *ne-
mico della musica.* His reasoning is sometimes specious ;
as when he refers to the difference between the vocal and
the instrumental notes of the ancients, and avails himself of
a striking passage in Plutarch, noticing, that though they
used but few strings, yet these were *tuned in consonance,*
and *disposed with art.* But far, indeed, is it from following,
that because the vocal *parts* and instrumental accompaniments of the ancients did not consist of the same sounds,
the two *parts* together constituted what we mean by *Harmonical Construction.* The one *part* might be an octave or
fifteenth above the other‡ : and the mere possibility of the

---

* The doctor himself adduces a case in point, when he observes,
" that, for a long time, the Irish harp had a greater number of strings
than the ancient lyre, without suggesting to the performers the idea
of *counterpoint*, or of performing in *parts*."

† If the hydraulic organs, still to be found in Italy, are to be considered as remnants of the ancient instruments so named, they will
excite no very exalted idea of their powers.

‡ That this was really the case, plainly appears, from a passage in
Aristotle, (Prob. 39. sect. 19.) in which he says, " *Antiphony is con-*

circumstance, would alone be sufficient to invalidate any conclusion in favour of the reality of ancient counterpoint, deduced from an admitted difference between the vocal and instrumental sounds of the Greek music.   And from the consonant tuning of the strings of the lyre, no argument can fairly be drawn; since the art of harmonical evolution is by no means a necessary consequence of a tuning that was regulated purely by a regard to interval, or melodial relation. Few men, perhaps, ever considered this subject with greater attention than Doni; but the difficulties he encountered were insuperable.

Of all the champions for ancient harmony, none delivered his sentiments in more elegant and classical Latin, than Vossius.   Had his reasoning been as pure as his style, he would not in his celebrated work *(De Poem. Cantu et Virib. Rhythmi)* have attempted to support the poetical fables, or mythological allegories, relative to the power of the ancient music*.   He seems to rank among mortal sins, the doubt, that the Greeks invented and practised *counterpoint ;* and is highly indignant, that the moderns should presume to imagine that they were not masters of the art of

---

sonance in the octave :" and also in another (Prob. 34), where he inquires, " *Why the double fifth and double fourth cannot be used in concert as well as the double octave ?*"   A query that explains the nature of that part of the Grecian music which Doni and others dignify with the name of *harmony.*

* He tells his readers, that "to build cities, surround them with walls, to assemble or dismiss the people, to celebrate the praises of gods and men, to govern fleets and armies, to accompany all the functions and ceremonies of peace and war, and to temper the human passions, were the original offices of music :" and he gravely concludes by observing, " that ancient Greece may be said to have been wholly governed by the lyre."

constructing simultaneous harmony. Yet, in one part of his work, relaxing a little from his rigid maintenance of the dignity of the ancient *consonance of parts*, he says, in favour of rhythm, " so long as music flourished in this form (the *rhythmical*) so long flourished that power which was so adapted to excite and calm the passions*." The next favourer of ancient counterpoint, assumes no higher import-ance than that of a *collector* and *compiler* of the opinions of others. After citing passages from the most respectable writers of antiquity, corroborated by remarks from the most eminent moderns, in support of the supposition of a Greek system of harmony, he draws from them the conclusion, " that *from* the minute and accurate description of concords by ancient authors, it is natural to suppose they were no strangers to the use of them." He gives it as his opinion, that harmony, properly so called, was known before the time of Plato and Aristotle; but that it was lost, together with other arts and sciences, during the barbarism of the middle ages†. The learned academician, Fraquier, was incapable of believing, that antiquity, so enlightened, and so ingenious in the cultivation of the fine arts, could have been ignorant of the *union* of sounds; and thinking that he had happily discovered, in a passage of Plato, an indubitable proof that the ancients possessed the art of *counterpoint*, he,

---

* According to this, a drum, a cymbal, or the violent stroke of the Curetes and Salii, on their shields, as more emphatically marking the time, would have produced effects even more marvellous than those to which he so implicitly yields his credence.

† About the year 1430, according to Vincentio Galilei, who also believed in the verity of an ancient consonance, the restored art was greatly improved, its limits extended, and its rules established on principles that still remain in force.

in 1716, drew up his opinion in the form of a memoir, and presented it to the Academy of Inscriptions and *Belles Lettres.* The passage alluded to is in the seventh book of laws ; and runs thus : " As to the difference and variety in the accompaniment of the lyre, in which the strings produce one air, while the melody composed by the poet produces another, whence results the assemblage of dense and rare, of quick and slow, acute and grave, as well as of concord and discord; besides, the knowing how to adjust the rhythm, or measure, to all the sounds of the lyre; these are not studies fit for youth, to whom three years only are allowed for learning what may merely be of use to them. Such contrarieties of different difficulties in the study and practice of music, are too embarrassing, and may render young minds less fit for sciences, which they ought to learn with facility." This passage of Plato, (as M. Burette, Fraquier's brother academician, will be found to shew) brings no proof or even indication, of the existence of *ancient consonance.* Not the least formidable champion of the ancients on this subject, was our countryman, the learned and tasteful Stillingfleet, who, in his *Principles and Power of Harmony,* forming a commentary upon a musical Treatise by Tartini, acquits himself as a scholar, a gentleman, and a musician. After deliberately considering the very passage of Plato cited above, he deduces from it the evidence, that the ancient Greeks were acquainted with *music in parts,* but did not generally make use of it. Tartini*, in his *Trattato di Musica,* ad-

---

* Tartini was not, strictly speaking, a man of letters ; but he was gifted with native discernment, had well informed himself upon the subject of dispute, and was capable of that patient research necessary to arrive at a just conclusion, on any topic involved in the obscurity of distant ages.

vances the following strong proposition: " that if simultaneous harmony was known to the Greeks, they could not,
and ought not, to use it, in order to arrive at the end proposed; but ought to employ a single voice in their songs."
Stillingfleet, instead of answering this assertion, peaceably
allows Tartini to doubt of the ancient union of sounds,
during the examination of his book; but in the appendix,
takes up the matter seriously. " Dr. Wallis," says he,
" tells us, that the ancients had not *consorts* of two, three,
four, or more *parts*, or voices. Meibomius declares much
the same thing; and this is, one may almost say, the universal
opinion. Some, however, of the writers on music, have
produced passages out of the ancients, which seem to imply
the contrary, but which are not regarded as conclusive by
others: such as that out of Seneca, (Epistle 84), ' Non
vides quam multorum vocibus,' &c. where, perhaps, nothing
more than octaves are implied. Another passage, cited by
Isaac Vossius, De Poemat. Cant. &c. out of the piece *de
Mundo*, attributed to Aristotle, seems to be more to the
purpose, μυσικηοξεις, &c. that is, music, mixing togethei
acute and grave, long and short sounds, forms one harmony
out of different voices. Wallis also has produced a passage
out of Ptolemy, which he thinks may infer *music in parts*.
(Ptol. Harm. p. 317.) But the strongest which I have met
with, in relation to this long disputed point, is in Plato."
Stillingfleet then gives his own translation of the very passage,
with a version of which Traguier had already presented his
readers; professes to have been as faithful as possible to the
sense of his original, and draws from it the conclusion, that
the ancients *were* acquainted with *music in parts*, but did not
generally make use of it.

In opposition to these speculatists, Glareanus and Salinas
positively deny that the Greeks practised, or had even any
conception of harmonical combination. From the *Dodeca-*

chordon of the first, and the *Treatise on Music* by the second, we collect their opinion to be, that the great musicians of antiquity, when they accompanied themselves on the lyre, played only in unison with the voice; and that nothing appears in any works that have come down to us, which can be urged in proof, that *music in consonance* was known to the ancients. The musically-learned cavalier, Hercules Bottrigari, in his *Theory of Fundamental Harmony,* (a manuscript left in the hands of Padre Martini, about the latter end of the sixteenth century,) says, " as neither ancient musicians nor ecclesiastics, had characters of different value to express time, or make sounds very long, or very short, they had consequently no other measure of time in singing, as far as I have been able to discover, among the Hebrews, Greeks, or first ecclesiastics, than that of an articulately quick, or slow pronunciation; nor were they acquainted with that diversity of different *parts* in consonance, which in modern music constitutes as many different airs as there are parts set to the principal melody." Artusi, another musical writer of the same century, refuses the ancients all knowledge of counterpoint. " In the first ages of the world," says he, " during the infancy of music, there was no such thing as singing in parts, since counterpoint is a modern invention." And Cerone, author of an excellent musical treatise in Spanish, speaks to the same purpose. The celebrated Kepler was so far from allowing to the ancients any knowledge of harmony as now practised, that he has given it as his opinion, that if they ever had any accompaniment to their melodies by way of bass, it must have been perfectly monotonous; such a bass, for instance, as is produced by the drone of a bagpipe. " As to the Greeks, and people still more ancient," says Father Mersennus, " we are ignorant whether they sung in *different parts*, or accompanied a single voice with more than *one part*. They might, indeed, vary the sounds of the lyre, or strike several strings together, as at present; but as all the ancient books are silent with respect to counterpoint, it is natural to suppose that antiquity was unacquainted with the art." Marsilius Ficinus, author of a commentary written in the fifteenth century, upon the *Timœus* of Plato, asserts that the Platonists could not have understood music so well as the moderns, since they were insensible to the pleasure arising from *thirds* and their replicates, which they regarded as *discords*. It is the opinion of Kircher, that although the ancients might use some of the concords in counterpoint, yet there were others, such as the thirds and sixths, so grateful to our ears, that were absolutely rejected; and that, of the intermixture and relief of *discords,* they had not the remotest conception*.

---

* The weight and authority of Kircher will excuse my presenting the reader with his opinion, at length. " It has for some time," says he, " been a question among musicians, whether or not the ancients made use of several *parts* in their harmony; in order to determine which, we are to consider their *polyodia*, as three-fold,—natural, artificial, and unisonous. I call that natural which is not regulated by any certain rules or precepts, but is performed by an extemporary and arbitrary symphony of many voices, intermixing acute and grave sounds; such as we observe even at this time, happens amongst a company of sailors or reapers, and such people, who no sooner hear any certain melody begun by any one of them, than some other immediately invents a bass or tenor, and thus produces an extemporary harmony, not confined by any certain laws, and which is very ·rude and imperfect; and it is almost always in unison, or in the octave, and contains nothing of harmony, and therefore is of no worth. That the Greeks had such a kind of music, none can doubt. But the question is not concerning this kind of Polyodia, but whether they had compositions for several voices, framed according to the rules of art. I have taken great pains to be satisfied in this matter; and as in none of the Greek and Latin writers I have met with, any mention is made of

With this subject, the consideration of which has employed the attention, and excited the researches, of so many ingenious antiquarians, literati, and musicians, no one, perhaps, was more intimately conversant than Claude Perrault, the celebrated architect*, whose *Dissertation upon the Music of the Ancients*, published in 1680, exhibits strong arguments against the probability of the practice of counterpoint by the ancient Greeks and Romans. In his notes to his translation of Vitruvius, given to the world seven years before this, he had taken an opportunity of observing, that neither in Aristoxenus, nor any of the Greek authors, a single sentence was to be found, indicating that the ancients had the least idea of the use of music in *parts*. Boileau, in his translation of a certain passage in Longinus, renders the word *paraphoni*, by the expression *different parts*, being of opinion, that the ancients had counterpoint : " For I cannot easily think," says he, " with those who deny the union of sounds to that music of which such wonders are related ; since, without *parts*, there could be no *harmony*†." He after-

---

this kind of music, it seems to me, that either they were ignorant of it, or that they did not make use of it, as imagining, perhaps, that it interrupted the melody, and took away from the energy of the words."

* Of this ingenious scholar and artist, M. de Voltaire delivers his opinion, by affirming, that he was not only a most accurate naturalist, profoundly skilled in mechanics, and an excellent architect ; but that he was endowed with great knowledge and skill in many of the arts, a familiarity with which he acquired without the aid of masters.

† The French poet, evidently, was not aware, that by the term *harmony*, the ancients always understood what we mean by the word *melody*. That their *harmony* really was no more than a mere succession of sounds, Longinus himself gives proof positive, when, in his *Treatise on the Sublime*, (cap. 33) he applies the expression *har-*

wards, however, modestly says, " I submit this matter, nevertheless, to the learned in music; for I have not sufficient
knowledge in the art, to determine the point." Angelini
Bontempi (an excellent practical musician, and profound
theorist, as well as a respectable scholar) after the most
sedulous examination of all the ancient genera, systems and
proportions, aided by a careful perusal of the Greek authors,
on the subject of music, declares his conviction of the certainty, that the ancient *harmony* consisted of only a *single
part*. Dr. Wallis is a powerful advocate for the same opinion. Qualified by a more thorough knowledge of ancient
music than any modern, except Meibomius, to judge and

---

mony to the human voice in the single number. Boileau, however,
only made a mistake common to the writers of other countries. By
many of our own authors, the words *harmony* and *melody* are received
as synonymous.

I had intended to present my readers with my own explanation of
the terms *harmony* and *melody*, both as they were used by the
ancients, and as they are employed by the moderns: but our excellent
and erudite poet, the late Mr. Mason, has performed the task so
accurately and ably, that I cannot do better than avail myself, as Dr.
Burney has done, of his full, perspicuous, and distinctive definitions.
" The *harmony* of the ancients was a succession of simple sounds,
according to their scale, with respect to their acuteness or gravity.
Their *melody* was a succession of these harmonical sounds, according
to the laws of rhythm or metre, or, in other words, according to time,
measure, and cadence. The *harmony* of the moderns is a succession
of combined sounds, or chords, according to the laws of counterpoint.
Their *melody* is what the ancients understood by *harmony;* that is,
a simple succession of unaccompanied, or unharmonized sounds.
According to these definitions," adds Mr. Mason, (and, assuredly,
his definitions are correct) " it appears, that *harmony*, as *we* call it,
was unknown to the ancients ; that they used that term as we use the
term *melody*, when we speak of it as distinguished from modulated
air ; and that their term *melody* was applied to what we call *air*, or
song."

decide upon the question before us, he has, in his Appendix
to the *Harmonics of Ptolemy*, and in the *Philosophical
Translations*, treated the ancient music almost with contempt.   In the latter, he expressly says, " I do not find
amongst the ancients any footsteps of what we call *several
parts* or *voices* (as bass, treble, tenor, &c. sung in *consort*)
answering each other, to complete the music."   M. Burette,
in a Dissertation upon the *Symphony* of the Ancients, published 1723, in the *Memoires des Inscriptions*, advances
against the supposition of a Greek consonance of *parts*, a
variety of arguments which have never been controverted.
Yet, either by design, or inadvertence, he admits of the
ancient usage of *thirds :* in allusion to which, Voltaire said,
" *Le sceptique Bayle n'est pas assez sceptique.*"   Burette,
examining the structure of the ancient lyre, and the number
of its strings, shews how far it was capable of the harmony
of double stops : then making the result of this inquiry the
basis for the determination, whether the ancients availed
themselves of all the powers of the instrument in this particular, he finds himself obliged to conclude, that no ground
could possibly be derived from it to sanction the opinion of
an ancient consonance of *parts*.   Padre Martini is too respectable an opponent of ancient counterpoint not to add
great weight to the above testimonies on his own side of the
question.   After inspecting all the repositories, all the arch-
ives of Italy, he relinquishes his primitive opinion in favour
of the ancient Greeks, and avows himself to be satisfied, that
since they limited their concordant intervals to the octave,
fourth, and fifth, with their replicates, it indubitably robs
them of the merit of having invented and practised what we
call counterpoint; and, certainly, this decision receives additional force from the testimony of several writers of the middle
ages, cited in his book, who call music in parts, the *new music*,
the *new art*, the *new invention*.   Mersennus was not only

decidedly of opinion that the ancient Greeks had no counter-point, but directly denies that it is any reproach to them, to have been ignorant of it*. Rousseau, in his *Musical Dictionary*, coincides with those sentiments. His article, *Counterpoint*, concludes thus : " It has long been disputed whether the ancients knew counterpoint ; but it clearly appears from the remains of their music and writings, especially the rules of practice in the third book of Aristoxenus, that *they never had the least idea of it*." And in his discussion on the word *harmony*, he says, " when we reflect, that of all the people on the globe, none are without music and melody, yet only the Europeans have harmony and chords, and find their mixture agreeable; when we reflect how many ages the world has endured, without any of the nations who have cultivated the polite arts, knowing this *harmony ;* that no animal, no bird, or being in nature, produces any other sound than unison, or other music than mere melody ; that neither the oriental languages, so sonorous and musical, nor the ears of the Greeks, endowed with so

---

* " It is difficult," says this father, "to prevail upon modern composers to allow that simple melody is more agreeable than when it is accompanied by different *parts*, because they are in fear of diminishing the public esteem for the learning and contrivance of their own compositions ; which, indeed, would be the case, if a method could be devised of finding the most beautiful melodies possible, and of executing them with the utmost perfection. For it seems as if the art of composing in *parts, which has been practised only for these last hundred and fifty, or two hundred years,* had been invented merely to supply the defects of air, and to cover the ignorance of modern musicians in this part of *melopœia*, as practised by the Greeks, who have preserved some vestiges of it in the Levant, according to the testimony of travellers, who have heard the Persians and modern Greeks." And this author carries his predilection for simplicity so far as to say, that " as the beauties of a *trio* cannot be so easily discovered and compre-

much delicacy and sensibility, and cultivated with so much art, ever led that enthusiastic and voluptuous people to the discovery of our *harmony;* that their music, without it, had such prodigious effects, and ours, such feeble ones, with it; in short, when we think," continues he, " of its being reserved for a northern people, whose coarse and obtuse organs are more touched with the *force* and *noise* of voices, than with the sweetness of accents, and melody of inflexions, to make this great discovery, and to build all the principles and rules of the art upon it; when," says he, " we reflect upon all this, it is hard to avoid suspecting, that all our harmony, of which we are so vain, is only a Gothic and barbarous invention, which we should never have thought of, if we had been more sensible to the real beauties of the art, and to music that is truly natural and affecting." This latter opinion of Rousseau, bold and extraordinary as it may seem, is surpassed by the assertions of Vincenzi, Galilei, and Mersennus, who imagined that the contrary effects of grave and acute sounds in different progressions, must mutually weaken and destroy each other*.

---

hended as those of a *duo,* (the mind and the ear having too many things to attend to at the same time;) when lovers of music are more delighted with *trios* than *duos,* it must proceed from their being more fond of *crowds* and confusion, than of *unity* and *clearness:* and he compares them to those who love to fish in troubled waters, or who like fighting pell-mell with the multitude, better than in duel, where a want of courage and conduct is more easily discovered."

* We read, that when the celebrated composer, Claude le Jeun, first presented his pieces of five, six, and seven *parts,* to the masters of Italy and Flanders, they regarded them with contempt; and his compositions would never have been performed by them, if he had not written something in two parts; in which, however, he at first succeeded so ill, that he confessed himself to have been ignorant of the true principles of music.

To these testimonies, if we add the facts, that Plato speaks of *harmony* as *a current order of sounds, as to acute and grave ;* that the word *harmony* is defined by Hesychius and Suidas, *a well-ordered succession ;* that Aristotle (Prob. 33) says, *Antiphony* is *consonance in the octave ;* that Theocritus (Idyll. 18) describes the bride-maids of Helen in the act of dancing and singing together, *one and the same melody* * *;* that Aristoxenus and others, speaking of the enharmonic genus, are in the habit of calling it *harmonia,* meaning that its *successive* sounds are *well arranged ;* and further, if we consider, that the Greeks gave the appellation of *harmony* to every thing that possessed proportion, or was reduced to any systematic arrangement, we shall find ample reason for concluding, that the term when used by them in a musical sense, implied *melody,* and no more; that with the ancients, *musical harmony,* like *dramatic harmony,* (as that of the unity of character) was a symmetrical order of impressions, arising from a consistent course of actions or operations; so that it was as proper to speak of the *harmony* of a verse, as of the *harmony* of an air; of the *harmony* of music, as of the *harmony* of conduct, or moral principles.

If, however, any reader be sceptic enough to harbour the least doubt of the ancients being ignorant of simultaneous consonance, the following argument will, perhaps, determine his opinion.

If the Greeks *performed* music in *parts,* they *composed* it in *parts :* and if they composed it in *parts,* not only were they masters of the art of fabricating chords, but of so modulating their order, so differing and variegating the successive

---

* Αειδον δ'αρα πασαι ες εν μελος εγκροτεοισαι.

   Chanting *one simple melody,* advance

   The beauteous bride-maids, in a well-tim'd dance.

BUSBY.

harmonies, as at once to produce a congruity in each combination, and a connexion and consistency in the changes: in
a word, their skill, not confined to the formation of the
chords, was capable of preparing and resolving them, according to the rules prescribed by the very natures of harmonic
structure and harmonic evolution.   An art so extended,
would infer a code of rules, no less bulky than profound, and
which, as lying in a province of music more abstruse and
more important than the regulations of melody, would first
have engaged the study and attention of the theoretical and
philosophical musicians : yet, in the most elaborate treatises
that the most learned of the ancient writers on the subject of
music have left us, we do not find a single law relating to
composition in *simultaneous parts.*   In their introductory
chapters, they profess to have treated of, and to have ex-
pounded every thing connected with the science ; they me-
thodically separate the heads of their works ; present us,
under their eight proper titles, the arcana of *sounds, intervals, systems, genera, tones, mutations, melody,* and *rhythm,*
but say not a word of *united parts ; parts* to be sung or
played *together;* not a syllable upon the subject of *counterpoint.*   The obvious truth is, that they *did* explain all
they could ; for they explained all that concerned the music
with which they were acquainted—all that concerned *melody.*

To some modern writers, it has appeared strange, that so
meditative, enlightened, and refined a people as the Greeks,
who penetrated deeply into the general secrets of science,
should have failed to discover the art of combining musical
parts.   But would it not have been equally extraordinary,
had they made themselves masters of the most occult branch
of so captivating a science as that of music, written long and
elaborate treatises upon its principles and powers, and
wholly omitted to speak of what most demanded their at-

tention*? Again: If the Greeks *performed* music in *parts,* they *wrote* it in *parts:* what then has become of their *compositions in parts?* Why have they not descended to us, together with their *treatises?* Of the latter description of their works we have many; what have we of the former?

Another point, and of no light consideration in this long-agitated question, is, that of their three *genera,* or scales, as delivered and explained to us by their most competent theorists, two were by no means calculated for the structure of consonant combination, or evolution. The two contiguous semitones and succeeding hemiditone, or minor third of the *chromatic* genus, were even more hostile to the conduct than to the formation of harmony. No *relation* could have been obtained between one union and another; each chord would have constituted an isolated body of sounds; and all harmonical connexion or bearing, all lead-

---

* The general opinion of Mersennus, as collected from his *Harmonie Universelle,* has been adduced in a former note; nevertheless, his very words on this point, will neither be out of place here, nor superfluous, as appended to, and confirmative of, an argument which occurred to me long since.

Quant aux Grecs, et aux plus anciens, nous ne sçavons pas s'ils chantoient, a plusieurs voix, et bien qu'ils ne joinissent qu'une voix a leurs instrumens, ils pouvoient neanmoins faire trois ou plusieurs parties sur la lyre, comme l'on fait encore aujourd'hui, et une autre avec la voix. Joint que les livres que les Grecs nous ont laissés de leur musique, ne tesmoignent pas qu'ils ayent si bien connu et pratiqué la musique, particulierement celle qui est a plusieurs parties, comme l'on fait maintenant, et consequemment il n'est pas raisonable de les prendre pour nos juges en cette matiere.

MERSENNUS. *Harmonie Universelle. Livre* iv. *p.* 204.

And Kircher, it will be remembered, speaks to the same effect. See the note given in page 5 of this volume.

ing of the ear from harmony to harmony, as, in simple melody, it is conducted from note to note, would have been beyond the achievement of the most comprehensive genius, most patient exertion, and most subtle management.   Much further, then, from practicable, would have proved the task of eliciting *concording parts* from the elements of the *enharmonic* genus, from its two adjacent *quarter tones* and *major third*.   Should it be objected to this latter reasoning, that as having no application to the *diatonic genus*, it brings no conclusive argument against the ancient counterpoint, it will remain to be observed, that since the Greek writers have taken so much notice of the characteristic and efficient distinctions between the several modes, as the *Lydian* and the *Phrygian*, they would never have omitted to inform us of the extraordinary superiority of the elements of the *diatonic* over those of the *chromatic* and the *enharmonic* genus, as affording the means of concording construction and modulation.   We should have heard of that genus as the *master genus ;* as the exclusive foundation of the sublimity of amassed intonations, and as symbolical of the music of the spheres*.

All things, therefore, duly regarded, we are compelled to conclude, that the ancient Greeks possessed no music similar to our compositions in *parts ;* that the grand pile of *sound upon sound,* an under *part* supporting a complicated superstructure of coinciding materials, all moving in consentaneous

---

* It is not unworthy of remark, that the ecclesiastical modes and *canto fermo* of the Romish church, are generally admitted to be remains of the ancient Greek music ; and that as these have ever been written in manuscript missals *without parts*, and always been chanted in *unison* and *octaves*, it is a strong presumptive proof, as Dr. Burney most justly observes, against the ancients having had counterpoint.

junction, and in principle, ultimately bearing upon a fundamental bass, or bed, like the waters of a stately river, flowing with a majesty commensurate with their bulk and weight,
—this august contrivance transcended the bounds of their contemplation, and, by its magnitude and complexity, was necessarily reserved for the discovery of a later period than that of
classical Greece.

CHAP. IV.

REPUTED EFFECTS OF THE ANCIENT MUSIC.

WE are now entering the enchanted regions of imagination; regions which, in regard of musical power, poetry has fertilized with all that she could conceive, and eloquence adorned with all that she could express. The reader, whose expectation looks for prodigies, will not be disappointed; nor will his fancy be ungratified, who delights in decorated hyperbole. The *Golden Legend* is not more enriched with the narrative of *saintly* miracles, than the remains of the Grecian and Roman historians and philosophers with *harmonical* wonders, borrowed from the fanciful Muses, and commended by the copious and ornate style of mythological enthusiasm, secular interest, and tasteful diligence. Gods and goddesses have succumbed to the domination of sonorous appeals, and the spheres have been put in motion but to yield their mundane music; female chastity has been preserved, men have been humanized, their manners softened, and their civilization promoted, by " the concord of sweet sounds;" and while the passions have been excited and repressed by their influence, bodily disease has felt their charmful power, and fled!

It is remarkable, that though a particular art or science is ascribed to one muse, and a different accomplishment to another, mythology represents the whole Nine as *singers*. *This* is a historian, *that* an astronomer, *that*, again, the inspirer of tragedy, and *that* the mistress of comic dialogue; but each is a *musician.*

> " Hear the Muses in a ring,
> Round about Jove's altar sing."
> *Milton's Il Penseroso.*

And Apollo is not only the sacred source and regulator of harmony, the heavenly *Coryphœus,* but the tutelary deity of earthly musicians, and the pleased auditor of their perform-ances.

> " With hymns divine the joyous banquet ends,
> The poems lengthen'd till the sun descends:
> The Greeks restor'd, the grateful notes prolong;
> *Apollo listens, and approves the song.*"
> *Pope's Homer's Iliad,* B. I.

The grave historian, Polybius, speaking of the cruelty and injustice of the Ætolians towards the Cynætheans, their neighbours, has the following passage, declaratory of his opinion of the influence of music over the morals and man-ners of nations.

" With regard to the inhabitants of Cynætha, whose mis-fortunes we have just now mentioned, it is certain, that no people ever were esteemed so justly to deserve that cruel treatment to which they were exposed. And since the Arcadians, in general, have been always celebrated for their virtue, throughout Greece; and have obtained the highest fame, as well from their humane and hospitable disposition, as from their piety towards the gods, and their veneration of all things sacred; it may, perhaps, be useful to inquire, from whence it could arise, that the people of this single city, though confessed to be Arcadians, should, on the con-

trary, be noted, for the savage roughness of their lives and
manners, and distinguished by their wickedness and cruelty
above all the Greeks. *In my judgment*, this difference has
happened from no other cause, than that the Cynætheans,
threw away that institution, which their ancestors had established with the greatest wisdom, and with a nice regard
to the natural genius, and peculiar disposition of the people
of the country; I mean, the discipline and exercise of music:
of that genuine and perfect music, which is useful indeed in
every state, but absolutely necessary to the people of Arcadia.
For we ought by no means to adopt the sentiment that is
thrown out by Ephorus in the preface to his history, and
which, indeed, is very unworthy of that writer, ' That music
' was invented to deceive and delude mankind.' Nor can it
be supposed, that the Lacedæmonians, and the ancient
Cretans, were not influenced by some good reason, when,
in the place of trumpets, they introduced the sound of
flutes, and harmony of verse, to animate their soldiers in the
time of battle : or that the first Arcadians acted without
strong necessity, who, though their lives and manners, in all
other points, were rigid and austere, incorporated this art
into the very essence of their government; and obliged, not
their children only, but the young men likewise, till they had
gained the age of thirty years, to persist in its constant study
and practice. For all men know, that Arcadia is almost
the only country in which the children, even from their
most tender age, are taught to sing in measure their
songs and hymns, composed in honor of their gods and
heroes : and that afterwards, when they have learned the
music of Timotheus and Philocenus, they assemble once in
every year in the public theatres, at the feast of Bacchus;
and there dance, with emulation, to the sound of flutes, and
celebrate, according to their proper age, (the children, those
that are called the *puerile*, and the young men, the *manly*

games. And even in their private feasts and meetings, they
are never known to employ any hired bands of music for
their entertainment; but each man is obliged himself to sing
in turn. For though they may, without shame or censure,
disown all knowledge of every other science, they dare not,
on the one hand, dissemble or deny that they are skilled in
music, since the laws require, that every one should be instructed in it; nor can they, on the other hand, refuse to
give some proofs of their skill when asked, because such
refusal would be esteemed dishonourable. They are also
taught to perform, in order, all the military steps and motions,
to the sound of instruments : and this is likewise practised
every year in the theatres, at the public charge, and in sight
of all the citizens." *Hampton's Translation.*

Polybius then proceeds to show, that the ancients introduced these customs purely to soften that natural austerity
of the Arcadians, attributed to their cold and heavy atmo-
sphere: and insists, that their neglect by the Cynætheans,
was the cause of those fierce and savage manners, on account
of which they were despised and hated by all the other cities
of Arcadia.

Homer places a musician over Clytemnestra, during the
absence of Agamemnon, as a guard upon her chastity ; and,
till he was sent away, her seducer, Ægisthus, had no power
over her affections :

> At first, with worthy shame, and decent pride,
> The royal dame his lawless suit denied :
> For virtue's image yet possess'd her mind,
> Taught by a master of the tuneful kind.
> > *Pope' Homer's Iliad,* B. III.

By Plutarch, we are told, that Terpander appeased a
violent sedition among the Lacedæmonians, by the aid of
music. *Dialogue on Music.*

The same author records of Antigenides, what others have said of Timotheus,—That in performing to Alexander a bold and animated air, he so roused the warrior's fury, that he started from his seat and seized his arms*.

Pythagoras (according to Boetius) seeing a young man so inflamed with jealousy, music, and wine, as to be resolved to set fire to his mistress's dwelling, restored the lover to his reason, by causing the *Tibicina,* or female flute-player, to change from the Phrygian mode to a grave and soothing style.

Thucydides, as quoted by Aulus Gellius, supports the idea of the restraining power of music, by what he relates of the Lacedemonians, who going to battle, were attended by a *Tibicen,* playing soft and assuasive melodies, to temper their martial fire, lest a rash temerity should overcome their discretion, and endanger their success. He also gives in favour of its exciting force, an evidence not less positive, in the case of the same people, who, when their discomfiture was near at hand, became so re-animated by the music of the celebrated Tyrtæus, upon his quitting the Lydian mode for the Phrygian, that they rushed forward with irresistible courage, and gained over the Messenians a decisive victory. And Diogenes Laertius, Pausanias, and Polyænus, relate that Solon, the renowned law-giver, by singing an elegy of his own composing, excited the Athenians to a revival of the war against the Megarians, the renewal of which had been forbidden to be proposed, on pain of death. Xenophon

---

* Dryden, in his *Alexander's Feast*, has not shown more judgment in alluding to this story, than felicity in its treatment.

" Sooth'd with the sound, the king grew vain,

Fought all his battles o'er again,

And thrice he routed all his foes, and thrice he slew the slain."

speaks of a Thracian prince, who by the sound of flutes and trumpets made of raw hides, was roused to such a degree of martial ardour, that he danced with as much impetuosity and quickness, as if he had tried to avoid a dart: and, according to Athenæus, the trumpeter, Herodorus, of Megara, possessed the power of so highly inspiriting the troops of Demetrius, by sounding two trumpets at a time, during the siege of Argos, as to enable them to move a machine towards the ramparts, the ponderosity of which, had, for several days, baffled all their endeavours to stir it*.

Yielding to the principle of impartiality, I give the believers of these antiquated tales, the advantage of the following *modern* narratives, which, in order to sanction and defend any liberality of faith, only require to be *substantiated*.

When Ericus, King of Denmark, surnamed *the Good,* who reigned about 1130, returned into his kingdom, and held the yearly assembly, he was greatly pleased with the industry both of his soldiers and artificers. Among others of his attendants, was one who asserted, that by the power of his art, he was able to excite in men whatsoever affections he thought proper; to make the sad cheerful, the cheerful sad, the angry placid, and such as were pleased, discontented; and even to drive them into a raging madness: and the more he insisted on his abilities, the greater was the king's desire to try them.

The artist, at length, began to repent of his having thus

---

* That the sound of trumpets, should put the animal spirits in motion, and their activity augment the body's strength, ought not, perhaps, to excite astonishment: but the case here stated seems to border on the extravagant. May not the whole miraculous part of this exploit be construed into *a signal given by the musician to the soldiers,* for exerting themselves in concert?

magnified his talent, foreseeing the danger of his making such
experiments on a king; and he was afraid, that if he failed in
the performance of what he had undertaken, he should be
esteemed a liar : he therefore entreated all who had any influence over the king, to endeavour to divert him from his
intention to make proof of his art; but all without effect;
for the more desirous he was to evade the trial of his skill,
the more the king insisted on it. When the musician perceived that he could not be excused, he begged that all
weapons capable of doing mischief might be removed; and
took care that some persons should be placed out of the
hearing of the Cithara, who might be called in to his assistance, and who, if necessity required it, should snatch the instrument from his hands, and break it on his head.

Every thing being thus prepared, the Citharist began to
make proof of his art on the king, who sat with some few
about him in an open hall. First, by a grave mode, he threw
a certain melancholy into the minds of his auditors; but
changing it into one more cheerful, he converted their sadness into mirth, that almost incited his hearers to dancing;
then varying his modulation, on the sudden he inspired the
king with fury and indignation, which he continued to work
up in him till it was easy to see he was approaching to
frenzy. The sign was then given for those who were in
waiting to enter; they first broke the Cithara according to
their directions, and then seized on the king; but such was
his strength, that he killed some of them with his fist; being
afterwards overwhelmed with several beds, his fury became
pacified, and, recovering his reason, he was grievously afflicted that he had turned his wrath against his friends.—
(Saxo Grammaticus, in Hist. Danicæ, edit. Basil, lib. 12, p.
113.) The same author adds, that the king broke open the
doors of a chamber, and, snatching up a sword, ran four men
through the body ; and that when he returned to his senses,

he made a pilgrimage to Jerusalem as an expiation of his crime. Olaus Magnus (in Hist. Gent. Sept. lib. 15, cap. 28.) and Krantzius (in Chron. Regn. Daniæ, Sueciæ, et Norvegiæ) who relate the same story, say that he died in the island of Cyprus.

By Hieronymus Magius (Var. Lect. seu Miscell. Venet. 1564) we are told, that when Cardinal Hippolyto de Medicis was a legate in the army at Pannonia, the troops being about to engage, upon the alarm being sounded by the trumpets and drums, he was so inflamed with a martial ardour, that, girding on his sword, he mounted his horse, and could not be restrained from charging the enemy at the head of those whose duty it was to make the onset. And in Bayle (art. *Goudimel*, in not. Vol. III. p. 205) we find it related, that at the celebration of the marriage of the Duke of Joyeuse, a gentleman was so transported with the music of Claude le Jeune, performed at that solemnity, that he seized his sword, and swore that, unless prevented, he must fight with some one present; but that a sudden change in the music calmed him *.

These effects of musical sounds, much as they appear to partake of the marvellous, shrink into insignificance, when compared with what are still to be adduced. The *medicinal* virtues of ancient melody rival both its moral and mental operations. Fever, lunacy, epilepsy, pestilence, chronic disorders, and the bite of the viper, have yielded to its influ-

---

* We see by these relations, that to grant the effects imputed by history to the *ancient music*, is to admit the same powers in the *modern*, since history lends its grave authority to the wonderful results of both. A reflecting reader cannot, indeed, peruse such extravagant stories, and think it more miraculous that they should find believers, than that they should be true.

ence.   But what are even these results of the application of *song* and the *lyre*, compared with their power to build walls, attract dolphins, and humanize the savage inhabitants of the woods *?

That music, in either a highly polite, or extremely ignorant age, is capable of great effects, cannot be denied. A people utterly unacquainted with its principles, whose feelings are not blunted by its familiarity, will listen to it as something supernatural; while a learned auditory will be gratified with the elegance, melted with the beauties, and elevated with the grandeur, begotten by genius upon science, and conferring honour upon the intellect that produced, and the taste that enjoys them. That the stronger emotions of the soul may be gradually allayed by the soothing softness, subdued force, liquid tones, and gliding gentleness, of slow and tender music, the mind's languor be wrought to cheerfulness and hilarity by the operations of its brisk and sprightly strains, the animal spirits put into a new and vigorous activity by its rapid movements and violent transitions, and the warmer and bolder passions become awakened and inflamed by its strong percussions, massy combinations, dignified dispositions, and rich varieties, almost every susceptible heart and cultivated mind, has experienced. The province of music is the province of passion ; even when it directly appeals to the intellect, it is indebted to the feelings. It is

---

* That—

> *Music hath charms to soothe the savage breast,*
> *To soften rocks, and bend the knotted oak,*—

was an idea of Rowe's, not the less poetical for being at variance with reason. Perhaps the beauty of the thought becomes heightened, when we reflect, that neither the bosom, nor the ear, even of *man*, is always susceptible of musical impression.

a corporeal motion communicating with, and operating upon our corporeal nature, and most delights the soul when it thrills the nerve. Music furnishes no sensible object, but readily becomes connected with whatever being or circumstance presents itself to its influence. With regard to passion, it may, perhaps, be assimilated to abstract reasoning, with respect to the understanding. As the one awakens the mind, the other excites the heart, to a determinate disposition; but neither of them *applies* the stimulated feeling. To hear the music of a song without understanding the words, is seeing an historical picture without knowing its story: but the story known, and the words understood, the musical composition claims in its motion and its transitions, an advantage over the picture. The considerate connoisseur tells the artist, that his figures breathe; but an agitated audience assures the composer, that his music both lives, and communicates its animation *.

With respect to the accounts from Polybius and Homer, were they to be understood literally, they would rather prove the natural and quick sensibility of the Greeks, than the

---

* According to Ælian, (l. 2. 44.) Theon, at the exhibition of one of his own pictures, representing a soldier ready to fall on the enemy, prepared the spectators by employing a *Tibicen* to sound the charge. At the moment when their excited enthusiasm had reached its highest possible elevation, the painter uncovered his piece, and received their warmest admiration. Theon, in resorting to this ingenious manœuvre, manifested the resources of his mind, but betrayed the impotence of his art. Sensible that the still colours on his canvas could not move the soul to rage, he with music inflamed his spectators, whose kindled imaginations, he knew, would transfer their own emotions to the figures of his picture. The general passion previously excited, found an object for its application in the incident represented by the artist, and demonstrated its Promethean power.

superior excellence of their music, in the early periods of its progress. The Grecian lyre, it is pretty generally understood, was, at first, only furnished with three or four strings, and for many ages had not more than seven or eight, by which to regulate and govern the voice: yet the music of those dark and fabulous times is honoured with the miraculous effects which have been described. But it will be but candid to inquire, whether, in ages so remote, it was necessary that the science of music, and the art of its performance, should have attained any great perfection, in order to be capable of operating so powerfully upon the human mind and frame *.

In the case of the sedition of Sparta being appeased by Terpander, the question, whether it was achieved more by the lyre, or the language, the music or the poetry of the *enchanter*, naturally suggests itself. As a *bard*, in the poetical sense of the word, he greatly excelled : and from what we experimentally know of the power of verse, sung or recited to musical accompaniment, it seems difficult not to conclude, that the animated and florid expression of his sentiments operated upon his Spartan auditory, and found in the modulations of his voice and the suited tones of his instrument, auxiliaries, and no more than auxiliaries †. With respect to the adventure of Solon, the prepared disposition

---

* The Scalds or Bards of the Scandinavians, availing themselves of the weakness of reason and the force of superstition in their auditors, boasted a power of disturbing the repose of the dead, and even of dragging them out of their gloomy abodes, by means of certain songs which they knew how to compose. *Note in Cottle's* EDDA.

† Of this, still more will the reader be persuaded, when he considers the small compass of Terpander's lyre, and the consequent confinement of the range of his melody.

of the minds and feelings of the Athenian youth, enhanced by the martial persuasion of his elegiac muse, was so favourable to the operation of his musical powers, that we can scarcely be surprised, they should have contributed to the influence for which he exerted himself. That brisk music, exercised upon persons heated by wine, should increase the motion of their animal spirits, will not much surprise any one, any more than it will excite their wonder, that soft and gentle strains should gradually moderate their impetuosity, and induce tranquillity, and even sleep *.

At the tales of epilepsies cured, and maniacs restored, and the virus of the viper subdued, by the power of musical incantation, the reader will smile: yet Cœlius Aurelianus gravely informs us how the enchantment is effected : viz. *by causing a vibration in the fibres* of the disordered part: and Galen as seriously speaks of the efficacy of the flute, when played on the seat of the disease. Indeed, many of the ancients consider music to be a recipe for every kind of malady : and Dr. Burney sagaciously observes on the probability, that the Latin word *præcinere,* to charm away pain, *incantare,* to enchant, and the English word *incantation,* came from the imputed medicinal influence of song. On this particular branch of musical superstition, Burette has been explicit and candid. We find him, in his Dissertations

---

* The effects of the flutes of Pythagoras and Damon, like those of the lyre of Empedocles, are not to be regarded with that wonder with which they have generally been viewed. In even the reputed powers of the latter, what do we find beyond the fact of a furious young man restored to reason and self-command by the persuasions of good counsel conveyed to him in lyric verse, aided by musical accompaniment? And why should we be surprised that the flute of Timotheus, or of Antigenedes, should rouse the martial feelings of a mind incessantly devoted to war, like that of Alexander?

on the subject, allowing the possibility that music, by reiterated strokes and vibrations given to the nerves, fibres, and
animal spirits, may be useful in curing diseases, but at the
same time, not making any concessions in favour of the
power of ancient music over that of the modern. On the
contrary, he says, that *a very coarse and vulgar music is as
likely to operate on such occasions as the most refined and
perfect**. Accounting for the remedial result, by the oscil-
lations and vibratory action produced in the nerves, and not
by the elegance, beauty, or strongly-conceived passages of
the music, he conceives that even the pains of the sciatica
may be relieved by the performance of the most indifferent
composition; that is, that the successive sounds may be capable of giving motion to the humours, and removing the
obstructions which occasion the disorder. And, certainly,
not only Burette, but many modern philosophers, physicians,
and anatomists, have believed, that musical sounds are endued with the power of affecting not only the mind, but the
nervous system, to a degree that will effect a temporary relief of certain disorders. " It is," says M. de Mairan, (in
the Memoirs of the Academy of Sciences, 1737) " from
the mechanical and involuntary connexion between the organ
of hearing, and the consonances excited in the outward air,
joined to the rapid communication of the vibrations of this
organ to the whole nervous system, that we owe the cure of

---

* The savages of America pretend to perform cures by the noise
and jargon of their musical instruments; and every body has heard
of the story of the bite of the *Tarantula*, and of the particular tune to
the performance of which the power of the virus yields. It is curious,
that Dr. Mead, Baglier, and all the learned of their time, should have
had faith in an assertion, the fallacy of which philosophical inquiry
has since so satisfactorily proved.

spasmodic disorders, and of fevers attended with a delirium and convulsions, of which our Memoirs furnish numerous examples." From Dr. Bianchini's work, consisting of a collection of all the passages preserved in ancient authors, relative to the medicinal application of music by Asclepiades, it appears that music was used as a remedy by the Egyptians, Hebrews, Greeks and Romans, not only in acute, but chronical disorders. Though most of these instances of the power of melody over diseases are, perhaps, exaggerated, or altogether imaginary, some of them may really have happened; since great effects have sometimes arisen from trivial causes. It is by no means difficult to conceive, that as the poetry of the ancients stimulated the mind, the sounds of the music gave motion to the nerves; that the fervid conceptions in the one, and the emphatic intonations of the other, were sometimes capable of influencing both intellect and sensation, and that transient changes in the mental or corporeal economy, might result. This, it is natural to imagine, would be more likely to take place, as the music was more simple and intelligible to the plain untutored ear.

That *some* extraordinary effects have been produced by the combination of poetry and music, it would be too much to deny. So much fable, fable though it be, was not built upon a vacuum. Some basis was necessary to support the superstructure, light as it is; and this is the only question to be asked—How has it happened, that, occasionally, effects thus arose from the operation of musical sounds, which, in our days, those sounds cannot command? Why,

" When Music, heav'nly Maid! was young,
    While yet in early Greece she sung,
    Had she more strength, diviner rage,
    Than all which charms this laggard age?"

The reason for this appears to be, that in after times,

music became too refined; that art superseding nature, directed modulated sound more to the mental than the passionate faculty; that instead of remaining the rude, but robust and efficient child of fancy and simplicity, she became the adopted and delicate offspring of complex science and sophisticated taste. By degrees, every thing that was natural, was deserted, and every thing that was artificial adopted. Harmony, and a multiplicity of *parts*, destroyed the *unity*, and thereby divided the *force* of the effect. The ear became cultivated, but sensation enfeebled. All things have their price; and the price of a more polished and complicated music was, the loss of those irresistible and transporting excitations, of which we read in the accounts of the ancient melopœia. What I have said in one of my commentaries on a passage in the fifth book of Lucretius, expresses my sentiments (I may say my *conviction*) so fully on this topic, that I request to be indulged in its insertion in this place.

" Since, as a science operating by the emotions it arbitrarily excites, music may be felt without our acquaintance with its principles, we may conclude that sounds were gratifying to the ear, even before they were modulated into appreciable intervals, or supposed to have any harmonic relation. *Poetry* speaks to the mind through the medium of some sentiment, founded on principles previously comprehended; and *Painting*, by the representation of objects familiar to the sense: but *Music*, as a power operating by the variety of the successive vibrations imparted to the nerve, works on the mind and moves the soul, agreeably to the relation between the excited tremulations and this or that passion of our nature. Music, therefore, to arrive at some of its most powerful effects, had not to wait for that scientific form which it gradually assumed. Not only was the uninstructed sense better qualified to be impressed, and the mind, in its most simple state, more subject to the vibratory communication, but the mechanical force of the sounds was neither evaded nor weakened by any systematic regulation or re-modelling of the ear; and the soul, unoccupied by the consideration of the complicated structure of what it heard, received at once, pure and unmixed, the sonorous appeal. But when Science formed her diagram of harmony, her *preparations* and *resolutions of discords,* and her *dilated* and *contracted intervals,* the general ear began unconsciously to receive an education, which in part diverted the mind from the natural impulse it had at first involuntarily obeyed ; and though the feelings now awakened were more elegant and refined, thepassions were less powerfully roused.

" If we are surprised at the extraordinary effects said to have been produced by the Grecian music, especially by that of their seven modes called the *Phrygian,* it is because we forget, that with the growth of our science, our ears are, as it were, newly modelled. By the refinement of our melody, and complex construction and evolutions of our harmony, we have obtained a sweetness, elegance, dignity, and grandeur, of which the ancient Greeks had no conception ; but have lost the means of making, and the fitness for receiving, those powerful and transporting impressions which their music was calculated to impart, and the comparatively natural susceptibility of their ear, to feel. How far the rule may hold in the other arts, we need not here inquire; but, certainly, with respect to *music,* the most simple is the most sensible state of the mind; the state in which it is most alive to warm and passionate impressions.

" In vain, were it in our power, would it now be to revive the softness of the Lydian mode, and the fury of the Phrygian; to strive to melt the soul to pity, or exasperate it to rage, by the power of music; much less possible were it to excite its raptures by any efforts of our present profound and complicated theory. To admit that the ancients were acquainted

with counterpoint, would not be to sanction the extraordinary
relations respecting the effects of their music.   The voluminous, pealing masses of plain harmony, and the puissant
majesty of the high-wrought fugue, may impress the soul with
greatness, and elevate the solemnity of public devotion; but
will not kindle the ecstacy of love, or the paroxysm of anger.
For the dissolving, exhilarating, and inflaming strains, said to
have been enjoyed by the Greeks, we substitute the noble
and the sublime; for their simple softness, a laboured refinement; and indulge in an elegance of expression and grandeur of combination, suitable to our more delicate sentiment,
our tranquil dignity, and profundity of science *."

Since in a former page, I have endeavoured to demonstrate, that Greek music was indebted to " its combination
with poetry, for such of the related effects as really may
have occurred," it will be but just to show, that the ancient
poetry was under equal obligations to the charms of music;
that it was imperfect and inefficient without its aid.   The
strongest possible proof of the necessity of the aid of music
in poetical recital, is, undoubtedly, to be drawn from its constant employment in the drama.   Could the ancients have
dispensed with it in any province of the metric art, that province would have been in *representative* poetry.   Not only
the dignity of the epic muse, and the description of the
pastoral, the rage of the ode, and the pathos of the elegy,

---

* A more decisive evidence than the following fact cannot be given
or required, that either we are entirely ignorant respecting what constituted the *charm* of the Greek music, or have spoiled our ears by
science and excessive refinement. Meibomius (the learned Meibomius, who had devoted his life to the study of the ancient melopœia,
and the discovery of its principles and powers) being prevailed on at
the court of Stockholm to sing *Greek strophes*, set his whole audience
in a roar of laughter.

required to be recommended and enforced by musical intonation, but even the *drama*, dignified by plot, embellished
by the grace of action, and elevated by the influence of
character, incident, and situation, derived an accession of
strength from that melodial auxiliary, with which the poet
never ventured to dispense; that aid by which he added
passion to interest, and arrived at the acmé of his power
over the souls of his audience.

Even *then*, that species of poetry which enjoyed every
other support, was dependent on music. And, again, not
only was music necessary to the drama *generally*, but most
necessary to its *higher order*. Aristotle calls it *the greatest
embellishment that Tragedy can receive*. And from innumerable passages in the ancient writers, we learn, that all the
dramas of the Greeks and Romans, were not only sung, but
accompanied by musical instruments. While metric dialogue delighted the ear, and story in representation fixed
and interested the mind, music heightened the passion, and
completed the triumph. Of the advantage of theatrical
music the ancients were, indeed, so sensible, that they never
omitted to avail themselves of its advantage. Dramatic recitation was constantly called by the Greeks, *melos*, melody ;
and by the Latins, *modulatio*, *modus*, *canticum ;* terms which
signify *singing**.

---

* The theatres of Greece and Italy were so spacious, that a *musical declamation* must have been necessary to a performer's being distinctly heard. In such immense areas, common speech would scarcely
have been audible : and it is well known, that the necessity for aug-
menting the force of the voice first suggested the idea of the *metallic
masks*, used by the actor, as speaking trumpets ; and to that of the
Echeia, or harmonic vases, said by Vitruvius, to have been provided
for the augmentation of the sound. But it is difficult to imagine how,
even with these, or any other aids, a performer would be heard and

The management of the voice was the actor's peculiar
care. Nothing was omitted that could render it more sonorous ; even in the heat of action, it was governed by the
tones of instruments, that regulated the intervals by which
it was to move. The *melos*, however, which was used in
the declamation of the actors, was not employed in the
chorus. As in the rehearsal of the epic, there were two different kinds of rhapsodists ; those who *recited*, and those
who *sung ;* so in the performance of the drama, there were
those who *chanted*, and those who *melodized ;* those who de-
claimed in *recitative*, and those who vociferated in *song*.
The first served to render speech more articulate, and the
second, to give a more imposing grandeur to the assemblage
of the dancers whose exhibitions formed the interlude, or
inter-act, first introduced by Æschylus. Hence, with the
ancients, the word *chorus*, equally meant a group of singers,
or a company of dancers*.

The ancient declamation being but a species of recitative,
though it possessed a poetical rhythm, it could not, in its
measures, be *strictly musical ;* it was incapable of partaking
of that uniform division of time indispensable to tune, or
air. Voltaire, speaking of the *musical character* of the ancient drama, asserts in unqualified terms, that the *melopœia*
of the ancients was a declamation directly similar to that of

---

understood, in a theatre capable of containing forty thousand persons,
as that of Pompey, or twice that number, as that of Icaurus. (Vide
Pliny, l. 36. 15.)

* *Dancing*, in the old drama of the Greeks, sometimes meant no
more than moving and acting gracefully. According to Lucian, a
single dancer, or *mime*, was able to express all the incidents and sentiments of a whole tragedy, or epic poem, by dumb signs, aided by
music. And, for a long time, singing and dancing were regularly
united, and professed by the same person.

the modern Italian opera : and feels as well assured, that our operatical chorus equally resembles the chorus of the Greek tragedy.* It seems, that not only modern musicians, but modern poets, flatter themselves, with having discovered, to exactness, what the ancient dramatic music must have been ; that the former, from their intimacy with musical principles, and the latter, from their knowledge of poetical construction, confidently assume to judge, and to determine. But, after all, plain good sense, and an assiduous examination of the testimonies left us, are the best guides : for instance, we learn more from a few passages in *Cicero* concerning *Roscius,* than from the most ingenious conjectures of the learned, whether in science or letters. The Roman orator tells us (*de Orat.*) that Roscius had always said, when age should diminish his force, he would not abandon the stage, but would proportion his performance to his powers, and make music conform to the weakness of his voice ; which, indeed, really happened ; for the same author informs us (*de Leg.*) that in his old age, that actor sung in a lower pitch of voice, and made the tibicines play slower†. This circumstance of

---

* " *This* I know," says this celebrated author and critic, " that *our* musical tragedies, (operas) so bewitching by the charms of their melodies, and magnificence of their decorations, have a *defect* which the Greeks always avoided ; a defect which has transformed the most beautiful, and, in other respects, the most regular tragedies that ever were written, into monsters : for can any thing be more absurd, than to terminate every scene by one of those *detached airs,* which interrupt the business, and destroy the interest of the drama, in order to afford an opportunity to an effeminate throat, to shine in trills and divisions, at the expence of poetry and good sense. (Dissert. sur la Tragedie Ancienne et Moderne.)

† Our English Roscius was wiser. He quitted the boards while his mental powers, corporeal activity, and the public admiration, were yet in their zenith.

the tibicines being made to *play slower,* would alone be sufficient to prove, that the accompanying music was not measured melody, or air, since such an alteration of the time, in *song,* would have amounted to a change of the sentimental effect, and have ruined the interest it was intended to support.

In the Greek tragedy, Plutarch informs us, the accompaniment of the recitation was performed by the *cithara,* and other stringed instruments, after the manner in which Archilochus had embellished his iambics; a position supported by Athenæus, who (lib. 1. cap. 17. p. 20) speaks of Sophocles *playing the cithara himself,* in his tragedy of Thamyris. But the Roman comedy was accompanied with *equal* and *unequal flutes,* as we learn from all the most ancient manuscripts of Terence. *

It appears, then, that neither tragedy nor comedy, did, or could, dispense with *music :* that the dialogue and the chorus of the one, and the diverbia of the other, were uniformly under the necessity of being *accompanied ;* that is, that poetry, even when surrounded and adorned by all its other aids, required, for its command over the passions, the stimulant of appreciable intonation ; that the lights and shades of elocution, without the varieties and beauties of modulated sound, were impotent; that neither Melpomene could afflict, nor Thalia exhilarate, unless aided by the voice of Polyhymnia.

The *dramatic music* of the ancients is a subject of that extent and importance, that had the prescribed plan of this work permitted, it would have excused my devoting a chap-

---

* Dr. Burney, before he had been in Italy, thought that these *equal* flutes were unisons, and the *unequal,* octaves to each other ; but the numerous representations of them, which he afterwards saw there, rather shook than confirmed this opinion.

ter to its separate discussion. The remarks that have been offered, will, however, afford the reader a tolerably perspicuous idea of its nature and extent; and while they serve to illustrate the position, that poetry and music are not only mutually, but equally, indebted to each other, will convince the unprejudiced, that not only was it impossible that music alone should have worked those wonders, of which we read, but that, without poetry, to excite sentiment, and supply an object upon which to fix that sentiment, melodious sounds can only awaken general and vague sensations, which however gratifying to our animal nature, will not reach the rational soul; and that, consequently, the ancient music, merely as music, could not produce those effects attributed to it by many of the ancient writers.

CHAP. V

EGYPTIAN AND HEBREW MUSIC.

AFTER all that has been said of Mercury, Apollo, and the Muses, as the inventors of MUSIC, *from whose ingenuity it originally sprung*, still remains a problem. But if the praise due to its first cultivation, is to be awarded to some one country, that which first distinguished itself by its superior excellence in other arts and sciences, seems to have the higher claim to the honour. Where Geometry was invented, and Architecture exhibited in its most grand and magnificent aspect, it is perfectly natural to suppose that music first arrived at some degree of refinement; that there it first attained the power to gratify tasteful ears, and sentimental minds. Indeed, to endeavour to trace the harmonic science to a higher source than that of ancient Egypt, the state of whose music we are now about to examine, would be a fruitless task.

The assertion of Diodorus Siculus, that the Egyptians prohibited the cultivation of music, is contradicted by Plato, who studied and taught in that country thirteen years.

" *Athen.* The plan which we have been laying down for the education of youth, was known long ago to the Egyptians, viz. : that nothing but beautiful forms, and fine music, should be permitted to enter into the assemblies of young people. Having settled what those forms and that music should be, they exhibited them in their temples ; nor was it allowable for painters, or other imitative artists, to innovate, or invent, any forms different from what were established ; nor is it now lawful, either in painting, statuary, or any of the branches of music, to make any alteration. Upon examining, therefore, you will find, that the pictures and statues made ten thousand years ago, are, in no one particular, better or worse than what they are now.

" *Clin.*   What you say is wonderful.

" *Athen.*   Yes : it is in the true spirit of legislation and policy.   Other things practised among that people may, perhaps, be blameable ; but what they ordained about *music* is right ; and it deserves consideration, that they were able to make laws about things of this kind, firmly establishing such melody as was fitted to rectify the perverseness of nature. This must have been the work of the Deity, or of some divine man ; as, in fact, they say in Egypt, that the music which has been so long preserved, was composed by Isis, as was likewise the poetry." (*Plat.* p. 789.)

And Herodotus, after telling us, that the Egyptians were the first who introduced festivals, ceremonies, and mediatory transactions with the gods, says, that at the annual festivities at Bubastis, where they assembled to worship Diana, men and women embarked in great numbers ; and that during the voyage, some of the women beat upon a tabor, while part of the men played on the pipe ; the rest, of both sexes, singing, and clapping their hands together at the same time. At every city that lies in their passage, they haul in the vessel, and some of the women continue their music.   From this *Father of History* we also learn, that in the processions of Osiris, or Bacchus, the Egyptian women carried the images, *singing* the praises of the god, preceded by a *flute ;* and that among other memorable customs, the Egyp-

tians sung the song of Linus*, like that which was chanted
by the Phœnicians, Cyprians, and other nations, who varied
the name according to the different languages they spoke.
And Strabo (B. 1.) says, that the children of the Egyptians
were taught letters, the songs appointed by law, and a certain species of music established by government, exclusive
of all others.   To these testimonies we may add, that most
of the musical instruments of the ancient Greeks were of
Egyptian invention†.

These evidences of the high estimation and general use
of music, in Egypt, corroborated by the proofs still remaining at Rome, and at Thebes, render its high antiquity
indubitable.

With the story of Mercury, and the shell of the tortoise
left on the shore by the Nile, the reader has already been
made acquainted.   But it is generally imagined, that there
were two Mercuries in Egypt, both persons of eminent abilities, but who lived at very distant periods.   To these are ascribed the invention of the Dichord, or lyre of two strings,
and the Trichord, or lyre of three strings; while the *Monaulos* is said, by Athenæus, to have been originally constructed by Osiris, first an Egyptian king, and then the proto-
type of almost every other god of antiquity.

---

* Linus, according to the same author, was by the Egyptians called
Maneros, and thought to have been the only son of the first of their
kings.   Dying in the flower of his age, he was lamented in this
mournful song.

† As the triangular lyre, the monaulos, or single flute; the cymbal,
or kettle-drum; and the sistrum, an instrument of sacrifice, which
was so multiplied by the priests in religious ceremonies, and in such
great favour with the Egyptians in general, that Egypt was often
called *the country of Sistrums.*

Dr. Pococke, in his *Description of the East*, speaking of the remains of the magnificent tomb of Ismandes, or Osymanduos, observes that the walls of its chambers are still adorned with sculpture, and *with instruments of music*. What kind of instruments these were, the Doctor does not explain; but by the following friendly communication from Mr. Bruce, the celebrated searcher of the source of the Nile, to Dr. Burney, who had requested information respecting them, we are enabled to form a tolerably accurate idea of their forms and effects, as well as of the state of music in Abyssinia.

" Dear Sir,

" I have employed the first leisure that bad weather has enabled me to steal from the curiosity and kindness of my friends, to make you two distinct drawings of the musical instruments, you desired of me. I sit down now to give you some particulars relative to them, and to other instruments of less consequence, which I found in my voyage in Abyssinia to the fountains of the Nile.

" I need not tell you, that I shall think myself overpaid, if this, or any thing else in my power, can be of service to you, or towards the history of a science, which I have always cultivated, with more application than genius; and to which I may say, however, that I owe some of the happiest moments of my life.

" I have kept both the lyre and harp of such a size as not to exceed a quarto page: but I hope you will find, that all the parts appear distinctly. I did not choose to embarrass the harp with the figure which is playing upon it, because this would necessarily conceal great part of the instrument; and your business is with the instrument, not with the figure.

" There are six musical instruments known in Abyssinia;

the *flute,* the *trumpet,* the *kettle-drum,* the *tambourine,* the *systrum* and the *lyre.*

" The four first are used in war, and are by much the most common; the fifth is dedicated to the service of the church; and the sixth is peculiarly an attendant on festivity and rejoicings.

" There are two principal languages in Abyssinia, the *Æthiopic,* which is the literal, or dead language; and the *Amharic,* or language of *Amhara,* spoken by the court.

" The flute in the Æthiopic, is called *Kwetz,* a word difficult to be written or sounded in English: in the Amharic it is called Agădă; it is about the shape and size of the German flute, but played upon long-ways, with a mouth-piece, resembling that of the clarinet; its tone is not loud, but accompanied with a kind of jar, like a broken hautbois; not owing to any accidental defect, but to construction or design, as it would not be esteemed without it*.

The kettle-drum is called, in both languages, *Nagareet,* because all proclamations are made by the sound of this drum, (these are called Năgăr) if made by governors, they have the force of laws in their provinces; but if made by the king, they are for all Abyssinia. The kettle-drum is a mark of sovereign power. Whenever the king promotes a subject to be a governor, or his lieutenant-general in a province, he gives him a kettle-drum and standard, as his inves-

---

* I think with Dr. Burney, that the *jar* Mr. Bruce mentions as *conformable to the construction and design of this instrument,* must have arisen either from the vibration of the reed, or some unfixed part of the instrument left loose for the purpose of that particular effect. It is from the tremulation of their reeds, that the hautbois and bassoons derive the murmuring thickness of their tones.

titure. The king has forty-five of these drums always beating before him when he marches. They are in shape and size like ours, only they are braced very disadvantageously; for the skin is strained over the outer rim, or lip of the drum, and brought a third down its outside, which deadens it exceedingly, and deprives it of that clear metallic sound which ours has. Each man has but a single drum upon the left side of his mule, and beats it with a crooked stick about three feet long. Upon the whole, its sound is not disagreeable, and I have heard it at an incredible distance.

"The third instrument is the small drum, called Kăbăro, in Æthiopic and Amharic; though in some parts of Amhara, it is also called Hătămo. It is about half the diameter, and twice the length, of our common drum; it is just the *tambourine* of Provence, only rounded to a point at the lower end. This is beaten always with the hand, and carried sometimes on foot, sometimes on horseback, when an inferior officer (not having a *Nagareet*) marches.

"The trumpet is called Mĕlĕket, and *Kenet* in Amharic, but *Keren* in Æthiopic (or horn); which shews of what materials it was anciently formed. It is now made of a cane that has less than half an inch aperture, and about five feet four inches in length. To this long stalk is fixed at the end, a round piece of the neck of a gourd, which has just the form of the round end of our trumpet, and is on the outside ornamented with small white shells; it is all covered over with parchment, and is a very neat instrument. This trumpet sounds only one note, E, in a loud, hoarse, and terrible tone*. It is played slow when on a march, or before an

---

* This is the description of the New Zealand trumpet, which is extremely sonorous; but when blown by the natives, merely monotonous. It is, however, said to be really capable of all the variety of tones produced by the European trumpet.

enemy appears in sight ; but afterwards, it is repeated very quick, and with great violence, and has the effect upon the Abyssinian soldiers, of transporting them absolutely to fury and madness, and of making them so regardless of life, as to throw themselves into the middle of the enemy, which they do with great gallantry.   I have often, in time of peace, tried what effect this charge would have upon them, and found that none who heard it, could continue seated, but that all rose up, and continued the whole time in motion.

" The fifth instrument is the *sistrum :* it is used in the quick measure, or in allegros, in singing psalms of thanksgiving.   Each priest has a sistrum, which he shakes in a very threatening manner at his neighbour, dancing, leaping, and turning round, with such an indecent violence, that he resembles rather a priest of paganism, whence this instrument was derived, than a Christian.

" The sixth and last instrument is the *lyre,* which is never played *solo,* but always in accompanying the voice, with which it plays constantly in unison ; nor did I ever hear *music in parts,* in any nation, savage or polished, out of Europe.   This was the last refinement music received, after it was in possession of complete instruments, and it received it probably in Italy *.

" The lyre has sometimes five, sometimes six, but most frequently seven strings, made of the strings of raw sheep or goat skins, but extremely fine, and twisted ; they rot soon, are very subject to break in dry weather, and have scarce

---

* Mr. Bruce, though no musician, speaks on this subject, with the intelligence of an informed and sound professor.   Nothing can be farther from the verge of probability, than that the arcana of counterpoint should have revealed themselves to the early ages of the world, or to uncivilized nations.

any sound in wet. From the idea, however, of this instrument being to accompany and sustain a voice, one would think that it was better mounted formerly.

" The Abyssinians have a tradition, that the sistrum, lyre and tambourine, were brought from Egypt into Æthiopia, by Thot, in the very first ages of the world. The flute, kettle-drum, and trumpet, they say, were brought from Palestine, with *Menelek*, the son of their queen of Saba, by Solomon, who was their first Jewish king.

" The lyre in Amharic, is called Bēg, (the sheep); in Ethiopic it is called mĕsīnkō; the verb *sinko* signifies to strike strings with the fingers : no *plectrum* is ever used in Abyssinia; so that *mesinko* being literally interpreted, will signify *the stringed instrument played upon with the fingers.* This would seem as if anciently there was no other stringed instrument in Abyssinia, nor is there any other still.

" Indeed, the guittar is sometimes seen in the hands of the Mahometans, but they have brought it with them from Arabia, where they go every year for trade or devotion. This instrument having a neck, is from that circumstance, surely modern. Necks were probably inserted after strings of different lengths and sizes had been so multiplied upon the harp and lyre, that more could not be added without confusion. This improvement of producing several notes upon one string, by shortening it with the momentary pressure of the fingers, was then introduced, and left little more to do, besides the invention of the bow, towards bringing stringed instruments to their utmost perfection.

" The sides which constitute the frame of the lyre, were anciently composed of the horns of an animal of the goat kind, called Agazān, about the size of a small cow, and common in the provinces of Tigre. I have seen several of these instruments very elegantly made of such horns, which nature seems to have shaped on purpose. Some of the

horns of an African species of this animal, may be seen in
M. Buffon's History of the King of France's Cabinet.
They are bent, and less regular than the Abyssinian; but
after fire-arms became common in the province of Tigrē,
and the woods were cut down, this animal being more scarce,
the lyre was made of a light red wood : however, it is always
cut into a spiral twisted form, in imitation of the ancient
materials of which the lyre was composed. The kingdom
of Tigrē, which is the largest and most populous province
of Abyssinia, and was, during many ages, the seat of the
court, was the first which received letters, and civil and re-
religious government; it extended once to the Red Sea.
Various reasons and revolutions have obliged the inhabitants
to resign their sea-coast to different barbarous nations,
Pagan and Mahometan ; while they were in possession of it,
they say that the Red Sea furnished them with tortoise-shells,
of which they made the bellies of their lyres, as the Egyptians did formerly, according to Apollodorus and Lucian ;
but having now lost that resource, they have adopted in its
place, a particular species of gourd, or pumpkin, very hard
and thin in the bark, still imitating with the knife the squares,
compartments, and figure of the shell of the tortoise*.

" The lyre is generally from three feet to three feet six
inches high; that is, from a line drawn through the points of
the horns, to the lower part of the base of the sounding-

---

* Upon Mount Parthenius there was an excellent breed of tortoises,
for the purpose of making the *bellies of lyres ;* but the inhabitants
supposing these animals sacred to Pan, would neither use them, nor
suffer strangers to take them away. (Pausanias, *In Arcad.* ad Cal-
cem.) Dr. Burney justly observes, that this proves it to have been at
one time the common practice in Greece, as well as in Abyssinia and
Egypt, to apply the shell of the tortoise to the lyre.

board. It is exceedingly light, and easy of carriage, as an instrument should naturally be, in so rugged and mountainous a country.

" When we consider the parts which compose this lyre, we cannot deny it the earliest antiquity. Man in his first state, was a hunter, and a fisher, and the oldest instrument was that which partakes of that state *. The lyre, composed of two principal pieces, owes the one to the horns of an animal, the other to the shell of a fish.

" It is probable that the lyre continued with the Ethiopians in this rude state, as long as they confined themselves to their rainy, steep and rugged mountains; and afterwards, when many descended from the Nile in Egypt, its portability would recommend it to the extreme heats and weariness of their way. Upon their arrival in Egypt, they took up their habitation in caves, in the sides of mountains, which are inhabited to this day. Even in these circumstances, an instrument larger than the lyre, must have been inconvenient, and liable to accidents, in those caverns; but when the people increased in their numbers and courage, they ventured down into the plain, and built Thebes. Being now at their ease, and in a fine climate, all nature smiled around them, music and other arts, were cultivated and refined, and the imperfect lyre was extended into an instrument of double its former compass and volume. The size of the harp could be now no longer an objection; the Nile carried the inhabitants every where easily, and without effort : and we may naturally suppose, in the fine evenings of that country, that the Nile was the favourite scene upon which this instrument was practised; at least, the sphinx and lotus upon its head, seem to hint that it was some way connected with the overflowings of the river.

---

* Mr. Bruce overlooks the *reed;* a musical instrument formed by Nature ! *Vide Note.*

" Behind the ruins of the Egyptian Thebes, and a very
little to the N. W. of it, are a great number of mountains,
hollowed into monstrous caverns ; the sepulchres, according
to tradition, of the first kings of Thebes. The most considerable of these mountains thus hollowed, contains a large
sarcophagus ; there are two pannels, one on each side; on
that of the right is the figure of the *Scarabœus Thebaicus*,
supposed to have been the hieroglyphic of immortality; on
the left is the crocodile, fixed upon the apis with his teeth,
and plunging him into the waves : these are both moulded
into basso relievo, in the stucco itself. This is a sufficient
indication of the grotto, to any one who may wish to examine it again.   At the end of the passage on the left hand,
is the picture of a man playing upon the harp, painted in
fresco, and quite entire.

" He is clad in a habit made like a shirt, such as the
women still wear in Abyssinia, and the men in Nubia. This
seems to be white linen, or muslin, with narrow stripes of
red.   It reaches down to his ancles ; his feet are without
sandals, and bare; his neck and arms are also bare ; his
loose, wide sleeves are gathered above his elbows ; his head
is close shaved ; he seems a corpulent man, of about fifty
years of age, in colour rather of the darkest, for an Egyptian.

" To guess by the detail of the figure, the painter should
have had about the same degree of merit with a good sign-
painter in Europe ; yet he has represented the action of the
musician in a manner never to be mistaken.   His left hand
seems employed in the upper part of the instrument, among
the notes in *alto,* as if in an *Arpeggio ;* while stooping forwards, he seems with his right hand to be beginning with
the lowest string, and promising to ascend with the most
rapid execution ; this action, so obviously rendered by an
indifferent artist, shews that it was a common one in his
time, or in other words, that great hands were then frequent,

and consequently, that music was well understood, and diligently followed.

" If we allow the performer's stature to be about five feet ten inches, then we may compute the harp, in its extreme length, to be something less than six feet and a half. It seems to support itself in equilibrio on its foot, or base, and needs only the player's guidance, to keep it steady. It has thirteen strings; the length of these, and the force and liberty with which they are treated, shew that they are made in a very different manner from those of the lyre.

" This instrument is of a much more elegant form than the triangular Grecian harp. It wants the fore-piece of the frame, opposite to the longest string, which certainly must have improved its tone, but must likewise have rendered the instrument itself weaker, and more liable to accidents, if carriage had not been so convenient in Egypt. The back part is the sounding-board, composed of four thin pieces of wood, joined together in form of a cone, that is, growing wider towards the bottom ; so that, as the length of the string increases, the square of the corresponding space in the sounding-board, in which the tone is to undulate, always increases in proportion.

" Besides that, the principles upon which the harp is constructed, are rational and ingenious ; the ornamental parts are likewise executed in the very best manner; the bottom and sides of the frame seem to be veneered, or inlaid, probably with ivory, tortoise-shell, and mother-of-pearl, the ordinary produce of the neighbouring seas and deserts. It would be, even now, impossible to finish an instrument with more taste and elegance.

" Besides the elegance of its outward form, we must observe, likewise, how near it approached to a perfect instrument; for it wanted only two strings of having two complete octaves in compass. Whether these were intentionally omitted or not, we cannot now determine, as we have no idea of the music or taste of that time; but if the harp be painted in the proportions in which it was made, it might be demonstrated, that it could scarce bear more than the thirteen strings with which it was furnished. Indeed, the cross bar would break with the tension of the four longest, if they were made of the size and consistence, and tuned to the pitch that ours are at present.

" I look upon this instrument, then, as the Theban harp, before and at the time of Sesostris, who adorned Thebes, and probably caused it to be painted there, as well as the other figures in the sepulchre of his father, as a monument of the superiority which Egypt had in music at that time, over all the barbarous nations that he had seen or conquered.

" Astronomy, and, we may imagine, the other arts, made a rapid progress at this period in Upper Egypt, and continued to do so for fifty years after, between which time, and the Persian conquest, some catastrophe must have happened that reduced them to their lowest ebb, which historians have mistaken for their original.

" We know about the time of Sesostris, if, as Sir Isaac Newton supposes, this prince and Sevac were the same, that in Palestine, the harp had only ten strings; but as David, while he played upon it, both danced and sung before the ark, it is plain that the instrument upon which he played, could have been but of small volume, and, we may suppose, little exceeded the weight of our guittar ; though the origin of this harp was probably Egyptian, and from the days of Moses, had been reduced in its size, that it might be more portable in the many peregrinations of the Israelites.

" The harp, that approaches nearest to this in antiquity, is represented upon a basso-relievo at Ptolemais, in the Cyrenaicum, a city built by Ptolemy Philadelphus; and it is there twice represented.

" It has fifteen strings, or two complete octaves ; but the adding these two notes has occasioned likewise the addition of a fore-piece, to sustain the cross-bar above, so that its form is triangular; the extremity of the base is rounded into a ram's head, which seems to allude to its Theban original ; and I should imagine that this instrument is likewise Egyptian, as no harp with such a number of strings has ever been seen, that I know of, in Grecian sculpture.

" As the application of pedals has enabled us to disengage the modern harp from its multiplicity of strings, and brought it nearer to Theban simplicity, I hope our artists, and Merlin* in particular, will endeavour to introduce into its form, a little of the Theban elegance. It is the favourite of the fair sex, and nothing should be spared to make it beautiful ; for it should be a principal object of mankind to attach them by every means to music, as it is the only amuse-

---

* Mr. Bruce here alludes to a most ingenious German mechanic, who during many years gratified the curious and tasteful, by the public exhibition of his inventions in Princes-street, Hanover-square. With a judgment unbiassed by his civility in pressing upon my acceptance for myself and friends, a card of general admission to his Museum, I decidedly subscribe to the opinion of his warmest admirers, and add to theirs my testimony to his mathematical, mechanical, and *musical* knowledge.

Mr. Merlin's mind was adequate to the embracing the whole compass of mechanical science and execution ; at least, in the articles connected with elegant and domestic amusement. One of his ingenious novelties was *a pair of skaites* contrived to run on small metallic wheels. Supplied with a pair of these, he in the character of a Dutchman, mixed in the group of one of the celebrated Mrs. Corneily's masquerades at Carlisle House, Soho Square ; when not having provided the means of retarding his velocity, or commanding its direction, he impelled himself against a mirror of more than five hundred pounds value, dashed it to atoms, and wounded himself most severely.

ment that may be enjoyed to excess, and the heart still remain virtuous and uncorrupted.

" I shall say nothing of the capabilities of this harp, nor
what may be proved from it relative to the state of music,
at a time when men were able to make such an instrument;
I shall with patience expect this detail from you, better qualified than any one I know in Europe, for this disquisition;
it is a curious one, and merits your utmost reflection and
attention.

" It overturns all the accounts of the earliest state of ancient music and instruments in Egypt, and is altogether in
its form, ornaments, and compass, an incontestable proof,
stronger than a thousand Greek quotations, that geometry,
drawing, mechanics, and music, were at the greatest perfection when this harp was made; and that what we think in
Egypt was the invention of arts, was only the beginning of
the era of their restoration.

" I am, &c.

" JAMES BRUCE*."

That many arts, after having arrived at perfection, have
shared the same fate as the kingdoms in which they have
been cultivated, can scarcely be doubted. The instrument
represented upon a basso-relievo at Ptolemais, and so satisfactorily described by Mr. Bruce, seems to have been originally invented in Ethiopia, and not in Greece; for we do
not learn from history, that any of the inhabitants of the

---

* I have presented the reader with the whole of this long letter,
because it not only conveys much curious and valuable information
on a subject directly connected with that of the state of the ancient
Egyptian and Hebrew music; but contains many collateral observations highly worthy of attention.

Grecian states penetrated into that country. Even Alexander the Great never undertook an expedition against the Ethiopians.

One of the most elegant and curious of ancient musical instruments, is the *Theban lyre*. It is, perhaps, speaking generally, of no great importance, to know what kind of instruments were used, either in Upper or Lower Egypt, in times so remote ; but the *Theban lyre* has too many claims to our notice to be passed by in silence. Since it possessed thirteen strings, three ideas respecting their several degrees, and the extent of their scale, will naturally present themselves. One will be, that their intervals were semitonic; in which case, the sounds would correspond with those of the modern octave. The other, that their adjustment resembled the Grecian principle of tuning. For instance; if the longest string represented *Proslambenomenos*, the remaining twelve strings would more than supply all the tones, semitones, and quarter-tones of the *Diatonic, Chromatic,* and *Enharmonic* genera of the ancients, within the compass of an octave. The third probable conjecture is, that the strings furnished the four tetrachords, *Hypaton, Meson, Synemmenon,* and *Diezeugmenon,* with *Proslambenomenos* for their foundation; as here given :—

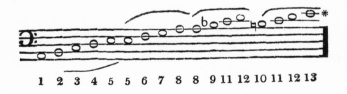

1   2   3   4   5   5   6   7   8   8   9 11 12 10 11 12 13

_____

* Here are *seventeen* notes : but, for the purpose of representing the *signs* of the four tetrachords, independent of each other, and

We can hardly withhold our surprise, that with such a model before them as an instrument of this compass and powers, the lovers of music and musical practice, should have descended, or retrograded, to the adoption of a lyre of fewer strings. It is a proof of the alternate losses and acquisitions of science. Ptolemy Soter, Ptolemy Philadelphus, and Ptolemy Euergetes, were such sumptuous and voluptuous princes, that it is impossible to doubt of the high cultivation of music at Alexandria, during their reigns*. It is remarkable, that the title of Auletes (*flute-player*) was given to the father of Cleopatra, and the last of the Ptolemies. He instituted musical contests at his palaces, and in the robe, the buskins, and the crown, and the bandage and veil of a Tibicen, disputed the prize with the first musicians of his time. But however exalted the personages who cultivated music, and to whatever degree of excellence it was brought by the taste and ingenuity of the Egyptians in remote antiquity, by the time their country became a Roman province, they had not only lost all appetite for its enjoyment, but, according to Diodorus Siculus and Plutarch, actually prohibited its practice†. That country to which Pythagoras had

---

thereby rendering their distinction the more obvious, the fifth, eighth, eleventh and twelfth notes, (E, A, C, D) are given twice; so that, in fact, the seventeen express only the sounds of thirteen strings.

* Athenæus (lib. 5.) affirms, that in the Bacchic festival given by Philadelphus, more than six hundred musicians were employed in the chorus; and that among these, there were three hundred performers on the cithara. And from the same writer (lib. 4.) we learn, that " there never was a people better skilled in music than those of Alexandria."

† Be it however, observed, *en passant*, that when Diodorus and Plutarch visited the Egyptians, they were in a state of slavery; and though not, like the Jews, in a strange land, yet, like them, " they had hung their harps on the willows."

travelled, and where the Samian sage had collected the material portion of his musical as well as other scientific knowledge, had lost with their independence, every elegant propensity and virtuous ambition, and, with the pencil, the chissel, the line, and the rule, the flute and lyre were resigned, and the cheerful sounds of the flageolet, and the horn, the syrinx, the trumpet, and the systrum, were heard no more.

On the subject of the music of the Hebrews, it will not be possible to speak with all the clearness and perspicuity that would be desirable. Enveloped in almost impenetrable obscurity, it defies elucidation, and discourages research. Among the inventions attributed by the Jewish lawgiver to the most remote race of men, the construction and performance of musical instruments, take a very early station. Though the Scriptures do not mention the practice of music, till more than six hundred years after the flood, (excepting that Jubal, the sixth descendant from Cain, is called " The father of all such as handle the harp and organ") no one can reasonably doubt, that long before the Deluge, it was in very considerable, if not high cultivation. Guided by the Hebrew chronology, we may say, that more than seventeen hundred years before Christ, music must have been in familiar use, because we find it spoken of as understood and practised about that time. And at a period nearly as low as thirteen hundred years before Christ, we have the lyrical effusions of Moses, upon the escape of the people of Israel across the Red Sea; in which Miriam the prophetess is represented as using a timbrel, followed by women *with timbrels and dances**.

---

* " Then sang Moses and the children of Israel this song unto the Lord, and spake, saying, I will sing unto the Lord, for he hath tri-

Without noticing every link of the chain of musical events furnished by Holy Writ, the circumstance of David having been called in to administer relief to Saul afflicted with an evil spirit, by the palliative powers of his harp; (1 Sam. xvi.) his being met when returning from his victory over Goliath by the women of all the cities of Israel, " *singing* and *dancing* with *tabrets,* with joy, and with *instruments* of *music ;*" (1 Sam. xviii.*) the damsels playing with *timbrels* in the procession before the ark (Psalm lxviii. 25) the sons and daughters of Haman being the musical pupils of their father †; David appointing four thousand of the Levites to praise the Lord with *instruments ;* (1 Chron. xxiii. 5.) the information in the twenty-fifth chapter of the same book, that two hundred and fourscore and eight persons were *in-structed* and *cunning* in *song ;* and again, the intelligence in the thirty-third chapter, that the *singers,* chief of the fathers of the Levites, who remained in the chambers, were *free ;* all these facts are so many evidences to prove, that music was held in high estimation by the Hebrews, and very gene-

---

umphed gloriously : the horse and his rider hath he thrown into the sea."—Exod. xv. 1.

" And Miriam the prophetess, the sister of Aaron, took a timbrel in her hand ; and all the women went out after her with timbrels and with dances."

* And in the following verse, we read—" And the women answered one another as they played, and said," where the word *answered* clearly indicates a musical dialogue; an additional proof that some-thing like a dramatical management of music then existed.

† " God gave to Haman fourteen sons and three daughters. And all these were under the hands of their father for *song,* in the house of the Lord, with cymbals, psalteries, and harps." (1 Chron. xxv.) And Deborah, Judith, and Anne, the mother of Samuel, are all regarded by the Jews as poetesses and prophetesses ; that is, *singers* and *musicians.*

rally cultivated among them, especially in solemn and religious ceremonies.

To these striking particulars ought to be added the *cure
of Saul.* An examination of this incident would involve
the question, whether the evil spirit fled before the miraculous power of God, or yielded to the musical skill of David.
Kircher, however, not afraid of making the inquiry, has, in
his Musurgia (tom. 2, p. 214, et seq.) ventured to expatiate
at length upon that extraordinary event, not hesitating to
state it in detail, nor to accompany his account with reasoning too curious to be properly omitted in a chapter dedicated
to the review of the music of the ancient Egyptians and
Hebrews.

" That we may be the better able to resolve this question,"
says Kircher, " How did David free Saul from the evil spirit?
I shall first quote the words of the Holy Scripture, as found in
the first book of Samuel, chap. xvi. ver. 23. ' *And it came to
pass, when the evil spirit from God was upon Saul, that
David took a harp, and played with his hand : so Saul was re-
freshed, and was well, and the evil spirit departed from him.'*
The passage in the holy text informs us very clearly, that the
evil spirit, whatever it was, was driven away by music ; but
how that came to pass is differently explained. The Rabbins, speaking on this passage, say, that when David cured
Saul, he played on a cithara of ten strings ; they say also,
that David knew that star, by which it was necessary the
music should be regulated, in order to effect the cure : thus
Rabbi Abenezra. But Picus of Mirandola says, that music
sets the spirits in motion, and thereby produces the like
effects on the mind, as a medicine does on the body ; from
whence it may be seen, that the comment of Abenezra, is
vain and trifling, and that David regarded not the aspect of
the stars ; but trusting to the power of his instrument, struck
it with his hand as his fancy suggested.

" And we, rejecting such astrological fictions, assert, that David freed Saul, not with herbs, potions, or other medicaments, as some maintain, but by the sole force and efficacy of music. In order to demonstrate which, let it be observed, that those applications which unlock the pores, remove obstructions, dispel vapours, and cheer the heart, are best calculated to cure madness, and allay the fury of the mind; now music produces these effects; for as it consists in sounds, generated by the motion of the air, it follows that it will attenuate the spirits, which by that motion are rendered warmer, and more quick in their action, and so dissipate at length the melancholy humour. On the contrary, where it is necessary to relax the spirits, and prevent the wounding or affecting the membranes of the brain; in that case, it is proper to use slow progressions of sound, that those spirits and biting vapours, which ascend thither from the stomach, spleen and hypochondria may be quietly dismissed. Therefore, the music of David might appease Saul, in either of these two ways of attenuation or dismission : by the one, he might have expelled the melancholy from the cells of the brain, or he might, by the other, have dissolved it, and sent it off in thin vapours, by insensible perspiration. In either case, when the melancholy had left him, he could not be mad until the return of it, he being terrestrial, and as it were, destitute of action, unless moved thereto by the vital spirits, which had led him here and there; but they had left him, when for the sake of the harmony they had flown to the ears, abandoning, as I may say, their rule over him. And though, upon the cessation of the harmony, they might return, yet, the patient having been elevated, and rendered cheerful, the melancholy might have acquired a more favourable habit. From all which, it is manifest, that this effect proceeded not from any casual sound of the cithara, but from the great art and excellent skill of David in playing on it; for, as he had a consummate and penetrating judgment, and was always in the presence of Saul, as being his armour-bearer, he must have been perfectly acquainted with the inclination and bent of his mind, and to what passions it was most subject: hence, without doubt, he being enabled, not so much by his own skill, as impelled by a divine instinct, knew so dexterously, and with sounds suited to the humour and distemper of the king, to touch the cithara, or indeed, any other instrument; for, as hath been mentioned, he was skilled in the use of no fewer than thirty-six, of different kinds.

" It might be, that at the instant we are speaking of, David recited some certain rhythmi, proper for his purpose, and which Saul might delight to hear; or, that by the power of metrical dancing, joined to the melody of the instrument, he wrought this effect: for Saul was apt to be affected in this manner, by the music and dancing of his armour-bearer; as he was a youth of a very beautiful aspect, these roused up the spirits, and the words, which were rhythmically joined to the harmony, tickling the hearing, lifted up the mind, as from a dark prison, into the high region of light, whereby the gloomy spirits which oppressed the heart were dissipated, and room was left for it to dilate itself, which dilatation was naturally followed by tranquillity and gladness*."

---

* Kircher was a man of considerable learning, and upon most points that come under his consideration, speaks with much sobriety and judgment: but in the passage just cited, candour must own, he is fantastic and extravagant. I will not say with Sir John Hawkins, that it is hardly possible *to compress more nonsense into an equal number of words* than is contained in this quotation; but I will readily allow, that its reasoning is unsubstantial, and proves the author less fortunate in forming just conclusions, than fertile in suggesting wild and visionary systems of argument.

Since the application of music is purely corporeal, the animal spirits, are of course, subject to its operation. But whether David worked upon the disorder of Saul by means of the agitations communicated to the air by his cithara, (I mean the agitations of the air simply as such) or by virtue of a power arising from the constitution of melody,—of that ordered succession of vibrations which the soul feels and enjoys, as something congenial with its own spirituality, and as independent of the quantity and quality of tone, can never be decided.

Of the musical instruments of the Hebrews, which Rabbi Hannase, the author of a work called *Schilti Haggiborim*, says were thirty-six in number, nothing certain can be known. The psalms speak of the *lute*, the *harp*, and the *cymbal;* the *psaltery*, the *organ*, and the *flute ;* the *cithara*, the *cornet*, and the *sacbut ;* the *dulcimer*, the *sistrum*, the *bells*, and the *trumpet **. At least, all these different names are given to them in the various translations. But neither the ancient rabbins nor modern Jews are agreed with re-

---

* The trumpet appears to have been considered as the most sacred of all the Hebrew instruments. During the life of Moses, none but the priests blew the trumpets, whether in peace or war. And indeed, in Joshua's administration, we find the office of blowing the trumpets was still confined to the priesthood. To this may be added, the avowal of the Hebrews, that they owed many of their victories to the inspiring effect of their trumpets. In the twenty-third chapter of the first book of Chronicles (twelfth verse) we read—"And behold, God himself is with us, for our captain, and his priests with sounding *trumpets*, to cry alarm against you. And when Judah looked back, behold, the battle was before and behind, and they cried unto the Lord, and the priests sounded with the trumpets." The trumpet having been ordered to be sounded, after the flight from Egypt, seems to argue, that it had been brought by the Hebrews from that country ; and that, consequently, it was of Egyptian invention.

spect to the instruments mentioned in the Old Testament.
It would, therefore, be as vain to assign to them the forms
and characters indicated by their modern appellations, as to
enter upon the wide field of unguided conjecture.

If this research would be idle and futile, to endeavour to
discover the Jewish *theory* would be more so. If finding
no guides in the correspondence of the names of their instruments with those of some of our own, we are at a loss to
determine what their *instruments* were; we have still less
evidence to guide us to the discovery of their *system*.

Kircher thinks that the *psaltery* of David has never been
justly described. And many have been of opinion, that the
word implied certain *genera* of harmony, or modulations of
the voice. According to Josephus, the *psaltery* had twelve
sounds, and was performed on with the fingers. Hilarius,
Didymus, Basilius, and Euthymius, upon what authority we
know not, call it the *straitest* of all musical instruments:
and Augustine, unsanctioned by any authentic documents,
assumes, that it was borne by the hand of the player, and
that a part of its construction consisted of a shell, or con-
cave piece of wood, that caused the strings to resound.
Hieronimus tells us, that the *psaltery* had ten strings, and
in its form resembled a square shield: while Hilarius pronounces this instrument to have been the same as the *Nablium;* an idea that Kircher himself, on the ground that
the Nablium, like the Psalterium, was struck by both hands,
has adopted, and endeavoured to support, by citing the following passage from Ovid:

> *Disce etiam duplici genialia Naulia palmâ*
> *Verrere: conveniunt dulcibus illa modis.*
>
> Art. Amat. lib. 3. l. 327.

> Learn with *both hands* to sweep the *Naulian* lyre,
> And pour enchantment from th' according wire.
>
> Busby.

But from so vague a description, no inquisitive mind can draw any satisfactory conclusion. And, surely, to substitute the harp of David, for the musical scale or theory of the Hebrews, is scarcely less irrational than to confound the Jewish musician, Idithus, with the ancient Orpheus.

A much later writer than any here quoted, Giambatista Martini, of Bologna, has in his *Storia Musica,* gone into the most elaborate research upon the ancient Hebrew music. But a work, the information of which is drawn from few other sources than those of the Talmud and the lucubrations of the Rabbins, can only present us with surmised systems : and every candid inquirer will confess, that to pursue this investigation, is to follow a subject enveloped in a mist so dense, as to evade conjecture, baffle patience, and defy even indefatigability.

CHAP. VI.

ANCIENT MUSIC, AS CONNECTED WITH THE GRECIAN MYTHOLOGY.

WE are now entering upon the visionary but elegant scheme of the Grecian religion and deification. Of all the various regions of fancy, none, perhaps, are so delightful, so animating, and so sublime, even in error, as those which hope and fear, people with beings capable of disposing of us at their pleasure; beings awfully potent, and whose hands dispense every evil and every good. If men ascribe to these beings their misfortunes and inconveniences, they view in them also the sources of their happiness and their gratifications, and for the existence of the arts, the springs of their most refined enjoyments, look up to their inventive and creative attributes.

As of all the numerous Pagan divinities there was not one to whose protection the polite arts were so directly indebted as to the god Apollo, so there was no art to which that deity was so especially addicted, and to which he was equally propitious, as Music. Identifying *Apollo* with the Sun, mankind, from the harmonious motions of his attending planets, inferred his immediate power and presidency over " the concord of sweet sounds *."

---

* Plato, following Pythagoras, makes Apollo and his attendant Muses the soul of the planets. The Emperor Julian, viewing the su-

The power to captivate the ear, and, through the ear, to excite the affections and the passions, was the most distinguishing
of the numerous attributes of this god; hence he is never

---

perstition more rationally, says, " It is not without cause, that mankind
have been impressed with a religious veneration for the sun and
stars. As they must, at all times, have observed that no change ever
happened in celestial things ; that they were subjected neither to augmentation nor diminution ; and that their motions and laws were
always equal, and proportioned to their situations in the heavens.
From this admirable order, therefore, men have reasonably concluded
that the sun itself was either a God, or the residence of some divinity." (Ap. I. Cyril. cont. Julian.)

From this order, they have also derived the idea of the *Music of
the Spheres*, a music far surpassing the susceptibility of human sense,
and even transcending the reach of mortal conception. The account
collected by Stanley upon this subject from Nicomachus, Manobius,
Pliny, and Porphyry, is too curious not to be worthy of being laid
before the reader.

" The names of sounds in all probability were derived from the
seven stars, which move circularly in the heavens, and compass the
earth. The circumagitation of these bodies must of necessity cause a
sound ; for air being struck from the intervention of the blow, sends
forth a noise. Nature herself constraining that the violent collision
of two bodies should end in sound.

" Now, all bodies which are carried round with noise, one yielding
to, and gently receding from the other, must necessarily cause sounds
different from each other, in the swiftness of voice, and magnitude of
place, which (according to the reason of their proper sounds, or their
swiftness, or the orbs of repressions, in which the impetuous trans-
portation of each is performed) are either more fluctuating, or, on
the contrary, more reluctant. But these three differences of magnitude, celerity and local distance, are manifestly existent in the planets,
which are constantly, with sound, circumagitated through the æthereal
diffusion ; whence every one is called *aster*, or star, as void of *stastis*,
or station. Moreover, the sound which is made by striking the air,

represented without his lyre in his hand,—that lyre, whose
transporting sounds conquered the pipe of *Pan*, and the
flute of *Marsyas*. *Apollo*, however, it is to be remembered,
was not the original fabricator of the lyre, but received it
from the inventor, *Mercury*. He, nevertheless, gave the
first example of performing upon it with method ; and, by
combining with it the sounds of his voice, made it the constant companion of poetry. Homer, in his hymn to *Mercury*, informs us, that the lyre was presented by that god to

---

induceth into the ear something sweet and musical, or harsh and discordant: for if a certain observation of numbers moderate the blow,
it effects a harmony consonant to itself; but if it be temerarious, not
governed by measures, there proceeds a troubled, unpleasant noise,
which offends the ear.   Now in heaven, nothing is produced casually,
nothing is temerarious ; but all things there proceed according to divine
rules and settled proportions : whence irrefragably is it inferred, that the
sounds which proceed from the conversion of the *Celestial Spheres*,
are musical.   For sound necessarily proceeds from motion, and the
proportion which is in all divine things, causeth the harmony of this
sound.   This Pythagoras, first of all the Greeks, conceived in his
mind ; and understood that the spheres sounded something concordant, because of the necessity of proportion, which never forsakes celestial beings."

This notion of the *Music of the Spheres* has been variously received by different authors in different instances.   Cicero, Boetius,
and Macrobius, are in its favour, while Valesius and others treat it as
an idle conceit.   Our own Milton in a small tract called *De Sphæra-
rum concentu*, defended the doctrine : and it has been attempted to be
maintained, upon the strength of various passages in the Holy Scriptures, which Hume, however, judiciously observes, are merely the
language of metaphor, and only to be understood, as annunciative of
the wonderful proportions observed by the heavenly bodies in their
various forms, dimensions, distances, and motions.

Apollo, as a peace-offering and indemnification for the oxen
which he had stolen from him.

> To Phœbus, Maia's son presents the lyre,
> A gift intended to appease his ire ;
> The God receives it gladly, and essays
> The novel instrument a thousand ways.
> With dext'rous skill the plectrum wields, and sings
> With voice accordant to the trembling strings,
> Such strains as gods and men approv'd, from whence
> The close alliance sprang of sound and sense.

If in the first ages, Poetry and Music were in constant
coalescence, so was Philosophy and Poetry. All the precepts
of wisdom were delivered in verse. Homer and Hesiod
were the first Grecian philosophers ; and hence the great
credit given by their cotemporaries, and those who followed
them, to the maxims of reason and ethics, which soon began to prevail in their country. Every prophecy, and every
speculative dogma, was *sung.* Measured language and
beautiful figures, heightened and adorned by the charms of
musical sound, formed an enchantment that could not be
resisted ; and not unfrequently, the understanding was subdued by the pleasure afforded to the external sense. From
Oenomous, the loss of whose works, a few fragments ex-
cepted, is much to be lamented, we indirectly learn, that
even the hades of *Apollo* were musically delivered. This
author, treating the God rather cavalierly, on the subject of
his predictions, says to him, " What dost thou do at Delphos, wretchedly employed as thou art in *singing* idle, use-
less prophecies?"

Since, then, *Apollo prophesied* in *music,* gave in *melody*
the stern decrees of Fate, we are obliged to conclude, that
all his less imposing *dicta* were *sung ;* that, in fact, his current speech was *music ;* and that, as the orb of which he is
the living emblem, dispenses light and warmth to the cir-

cumvolving planets, so his inspiring breath instilled the gift
of harmony into the souls of inferior deities; especially of
the *Muses*; since, of all the pagan divinities, none are so
immediately allied to the *God of Song* as those harmonious
immortals; none are known whose powers claim so direct
an affinity with the attributes by which that deity is most
distinguished, as the influence of those celebrated female
musicians; those soul-enchanting and indispensable patron-
esses of genius and of art.   Some ancient writers have asserted, that originally, the *Muses* were only *three* in number; but following the poetical fabulists, Homer and Hesiod, most mythologists have admitted *nine*.   They say, that
the citizens of Sicyon having directed three distinguished
sculptors to make each of them statues of the three original
Muses, they were all so perfectly executed, that they knew
not which to prefer, therefore erected them all; and that
the above authors did no more than furnish their appellations.
In Hesiod's *Theogony*, we find them mentioned; as also in
an epigram of Callimachus, which not only enumerates the
nine names in so many lines, but describes their several
powers and offices.

> *Calliope* the deeds of heroes sung;
> The choral lyre by *Clio* first was strung;
> *Euterpe* the full tragic chorus found;
> *Melpomene* taught lutes their soothing sound;
> *Terpsichore* the flute's soft pow'r display'd;
> By *Erato* the pious hymn was made;
> *Polymnia* to the dance her care applied;
> *Urania* wise, the starry course descried;
> And gay *Thalia's* glass was life's and manners' guide.

Other authors, however, assign to these sacred choirists,
provinces not exactly agreeing with the above: and among the
pictures found in the ruins of Herculaneum, are portraits of
Apollo and the Muses, in which the god is seated on a

throne, with a cithara of eleven strings in his left hand, in the character of Musagetes, or conductor of the Muses. *Clio* is represented as the inventress of history; the picture of *Euterpe* is obliterated; (but the poets generally consider the flute as her proper symbol) *Thalia* is made the authoress of comedy, as *Melpomene* is of tragedy. *Terpsichore* presides over the lyre, and *Erato* appropriates the psaltery, or long lyre of nine strings. *Polymnia* is exhibited as a fabulist; *Urania* as the patroness of astronomy, and *Calliope* as the inspiring projectress of poetry.

Though authors do not concur in regard of the particular or principal powers and employments of the *Muses*, they all, ancient and modern, agree that every one of them excels in *song*. Homer, in his Hymn to Apollo, tells us that—

By turns the Nine delight to sing;

And in the *English* Homer's *Il Penseroso*, we read

" Hear the Muses in a ring,
Round about Jove's altar sing."

The *Muses* had their terrestrial secondaries. While *they* were delighting the ears of the gods, the *Sirens* were the charmers of mortal auditors. The number of these celebrated songstresses, inhabitants of the coast of Sicily, was three : their names were *Parthenope, Lygea,* and *Leucosia.* They have been represented under more than one form. By some ancient artists, they are exhibited as half-women and half-fish; by others as half-women and half-birds. Persuaded by Juno, they emulated the confidence and temerity of Pan, Marsyas, and Silenus, by vying with heavenly skill. They challenged the Muses, and, vanquished, saw their golden feathers plucked from their wings, and formed into crowns for the embellishment of the heads of their sacred adversaries.

So seductive were the strains of the Syrens, that the powers of Orpheus were scarcely sufficient to save the Argonauts, by diverting their attention: and Ulysses experienced the greatest difficulty in avoiding their snares. *Circe,* apprizing the hero of his danger, says to him earnestly, before he leaves her,—

> Next where the Syrens dwell, you plough the seas,
> Their song is death, and makes destruction please.
>
> Fly swift the dang'rous coast ! let ev'ry ear
> Be stopp'd against the song ! 'tis death to hear !   Od. l. 12.

The whole story of the Syrens seems little else than an allegory, illustrative of the dangerous seduction of thoughtless and enervating pleasure, as opposed to the meditative and strenuous pursuit of knowledge and wisdom. But as affording another proof of the ravishing power of the ancient melody, it possesses interest ; and in a general History of Music, could not have been omitted without leaving a blank *.

---

* There are other particulars connected with this fable, which Mr. Pope, when writing his notes on the twelfth book of the *Odyssey,* deemed worthy of being collected.

"The critics have greatly laboured to explain what was the foundation of this fiction of the *syrens.* We are told by some, that the syrens were queens of certain small islands, named Sirenusæ, that lie near Capreæ in Italy, and chiefly inhabited ; the promontory of Minerva, upon the top of which that goddess had a temple, as some affirm, was built by Ulysses. Here there was a renowned academy in the reign of the *Sirens,* famous for eloquence and the liberal sciences, which gave occasion to the invention of this fable of the

With the stories of the contests of Pan and Marsyas
with Apollo, I shall suppose the reader to be already acquainted. The punishment of Midas * for his decision in
favour of the god of the woods, by having his ears changed
to those of an ass, and the severer resentment suffered by
Marsyas † for presuming to dispute the prize with so pre-

---

sweetness of the voice, and attracting songs of the *Sirens*. But why,
then, are they fabled to be destroyers, and painted in such dreadful
colours? We are told, that at last the students abused their knowledge, to the colouring of wrong, the corruption of manners, and the
subversion of government : that is, in the language of poetry, they
were feigned to be transformed into monsters, and with their music to
have enticed passengers to their ruin, who there consumed their pa-
trimonies, and poisoned their virtues with riot and effeminacy."

* Midas, Pausanias informs us (in Atticus) was the son of Gordius
and Cybele, and reigned in the greater Phrygia. He was as wealthy
as usurious ; and, according to the poets, converted into gold whatever he touched.

† According to Apuleius, Apollo and Marsyas had tried their strength
at invective and sarcasm, previous to the musical contest; and Marsyas was so indiscreet as to irritate the god, by opposing his own en-
tangled hair, his frightful and shaggy beard, to the flowing locks, and
the dainty effeminacy of his rival ; for which he was kissed by all the
Muses. (Floridor, p. 341.) It is to be presumed, that this musician
set too much value upon the approbation of these harmonious goddesses, to find such a salute a very pleasant prelude to his being *flead
alive ;* a fact which, however, it is to be observed, many authors consider as purely allegorical. The great ingenuity of the musician,
Diodorus Siculus informs us, was evinced " by his invention of a
single and of a double flute ; the power of which, by means of holes,
like that of Minerva, expressed all the sounds of the several pipes, of
which the syrinx was composed." We learn, from the same author,
that Apollo, repenting of his cruelty to Marsyas, broke the strings of
his lyre ; and, by consequence, stopped for a time, all further improvement upon that instrument, whether in its construction, or its
practice. The satyr, Silenus, also contended with Apollo ; but though
with no better success, escaped the punishment of his temerity.

eminent an antagonist, seem to prove the high value set upon the accomplishment of music, and therefore are worthy of notice in this place; but *Olympus* is a name too much and too deservedly revered by the most eminent of the Greek writers, for his history not to claim our immediate attention. I cannot do better than give it in the very words of Dr. Burney.

" There were two great musicians in antiquity of the name of *Olympus*, both of them celebrated performers on the flute. One flourished before the Trojan war, and the other was cotemporary with Midas, who died six hundred and ninety-seven years before Christ. The first was a scholar of Marsyas, and a Mysian ; the second, according to Suidas, was a Phrygian, and the author of several poems, which were by some attributed to the first *Olympus*. But the most important addition which the disciple of Marsyas made to the musical knowledge of his time, was the invention of the *Enharmonic Genus*. Plato and Aristotle, as well as Plutarch, celebrate his musical and poetical talents ; and tell us, that some of his airs were still subsisting in their time *. Plato says the music of *Olympus* was, in a particular manner, adapted to affect and animate its hearers; Aristotle affirms, that it swelled the soul with enthusiasm; and Plutarch declares, that it surpassed, in simplicity and effect, every other music then known. According to this biographer, he was author of the Curule song, which caused Alexander to seize his arms, when it was performed to him by Antigeni-

---

* The airs of *Olympus* used in the temple worship during the time of Plutarch, were not more ancient than the *Chants, or Canto Fermo,* to some of the hymns of the Romish church : and the melodies now sung to many of the hymns and psalms of the Lutherans and Calvinists, are such as were applied to them at the time of the Reformation.

des. To great musical abilities he joined those of poetry; and according to Suidas, and Jul. Pollux, he composed elegies, and other plaintive songs, which were sung to the sound of the flute ; and the melodies of these poems were so much celebrated in antiquity, for their pathetic and plaintive cast, that Aristophanes, in the beginning of his comedy called *The Knights,* where he introduces the two generals, Demosthenes and Nicias, travestied into valets, and complaining of their master, makes them say, " Let us weep and wail, like two flutes, breathing some air of *Olympus.*"

Besides the *Curule,* or chariot air, just mentioned, Plutarch ascribes to him several *nomes,* or airs, that are frequently mentioned by ancient writers; among which is the *spondean,* or celebrated libation melody.

Among the first musicians after Apollo, handed down to us by what may be called fabulous record, is Philammon of Delphos *. He sung to the accompaniment of his lyre. According to Tatian, he was not only a practical artist, but a scientific student in music, and flourished as a speculatist before the time of Homer: and the scholiast of Apollonius Rhodius, speaking after Pherecydes, affirms, that it was this musical poet, and not Orpheus, who accompanied the Argonauts in their expedition †. Little, however, of certainty can be expected, in regard of the music and musicians of a period so early : and after all that industry can collect, and learning and ingenuity suggest, we are, in a great measure, left to the reasonableness of our own conjectures. The exploits of Amphion, Chiron, Linus, Orpheus, and Mu-

---

* He invented the dances performed in the temple of Apollo. Those who cultivated the fine arts were called the *sons of that god;* and Philammon was one of them.

† If we could confide in this assertion, it would ascertain the time in which he lived, to be the era immediately preceding the Trojan war.

sæus, are gravely marshalled before us, only to move our wonder, and excite a curiosity that can never be gratified.

Of Bœotian Thebes, said to be built by Cadmus, Pausanias has left us a list of sixteen kings, among whom we find *Amphion*. He is the first Theban musician upon record. Homer tells us, that to secure the crown which he had usurped, he enclosed the city; but says nothing of the miraculous powers of his lyre ; nothing of his having built the wall by virtue of its sound *. Pliny supposed him to have been the inventor of music, and of the cithara ; and both Pliny and Pausanias say, that Amphion acquired his musical knowledge in Lydia ; and that merely because he brought the art into Greece, he was complimented as the author of the Lydian mode.

The age immediately after Deucalion's deluge, commonly called the *golden era*, produced *Chiron*†, styled by Plutarch, the *Wise Centaur*. He was not only a musician, but a distinguished astronomer and general scholar. He is said to have been a native of Thessaly, and to have inhabited a grotto, or cave, at the fount of Mount Pelion, which his renown and learning rendered the most famous and frequented school throughout Greece. We are told, that one of his most favourite scholars was the Grecian Bacchus, who learned of him the revels, orgies, Bacchanalia, and other ceremonious worship ‡. The grandfather of Achilles, he was also his tutor : and Apollodorus tells us, that music

---

* " For my part," says Pausanias, " I believe that Amphion only acquired his musical reputation from his alliance with the family of Tantalus, whose daughter, Niobe, he had married."

† According to Sir Isaac Newton's reckoning.

‡ Pausanias speaks of a place at Athens consecrated to *Bacchus* the *singer;* " thus named," says he, " for the same reason that Apollo is called the chief and conductor of the Muses." Of the three Grecian *Orgia*, one was dedicated to *Cybele*, one to *Ceres*, and one to *Bacchus*.

formed a principal accomplishment in his education*. Chiron, after a long life of honour and celebrity, died of an accidental wound in the knee, given by a poisoned arrow, shot by his scholar, Hercules.

With respect to the priority of Linus and Orpheus, authors are far from being agreed; but the majority are in favour of the superior antiquity of the former. The learned antiquarian, Archbishop Usher, says that Linus flourished 1280 years before Christ; and Eusebius includes him among the poets who wrote before the time of Moses. From Diodorus Siculus, speaking from Dionysius of Mitylene, we learn that Linus was the first among the Greeks who invented verse and music, as Cadmus first taught that people the use of letters. The same author gives him credit for having added the string *Lichanos* to the Mercurian lyre, and also for the invention of rhythm and melody, in which Suidas coincides, and regards him as the most ancient of lyric poets. Hercules was one of his pupils. Being both dull and obstinate, he provoked his master to strike him; when, enraged at the blow, the rebellious scholar seized the lyre, and, with its frame, beat out his tutor's brains. Pausanias asserts, that the Thebans profess to have buried him in their city; and say, that Philip, the son of Amyntas, excited by a dream, removed his bones into Macedon; whence, instigated by a second dream, he sent them back to Thebes †.

---

* One of the best remains of antique painting now subsisting, is a picture dug out of Herculaneum, in which Chiron is represented teaching the young Achilles to play on the lyre. That ancient authors all agree in thinking the knowledge of music one of the necessary acquisitions of kings and heroes, is certain. *Nec fides didicit, nec natare*, was in antiquity, a reproach to every man above the rank of a plebeian.

† Plutarch, speaking after Heraclides of Pontus, speaks of certain dirges written by Linus; but they are not mentioned by any other an-

Homer, in his description of the shield of Achilles, has not omitted the tribute due to this illustrious poet and musician:

> To these a youth awakes the warbling strings,
> Whose tender lay the fate of *Linus* sings ;
> In measured dance, behind him move the train,
> Tune soft the voice, and answer to the strain *.

Of the great merit of another ancient and venerable name among the Greek poets and musicians, Apollonius Rhodius speaks in the strongest terms. *Orpheus,* he says, enjoyed an established and exalted reputation as early as the time of the Argonautic expedition, in which he was himself an adventurer; and by the music of his lyre, not only incited the Argonauts to labour at the oar with extraordinary ardour, but even silenced the Syrens by the superiority of his strains. Of the abilities, and acquirements, of this renowned bard, Dr. Cudworth speaks in a very full and ample manner. After combating the supposed opinion of Aristotle, that no such man as Orpheus ever existed, (an idea erroneously derived by some modern writers from a passage in Cicero) the Doctor proceeds to tell us, that Orpheus was the son of Oeager, by birth a Thracian, the father, or chief founder of the mythological and allegorical theology amongst the Greeks, and of all their most sacred and religious rites and mysteries; who is commonly supposed to have lived before the Trojan war; that is, in the time of the Israelitish judges,

---

cient author. Many songs of that kind, however, were conferred in honour of his memory.

* The ancient Greeks annually lamented the death of this their first poet: and, as Pausanias relates, before the yearly sacrifice to the Muses on Mount Helicon, the obsequies of Linus were performed, and he had a shrine and statue erected to him in that place.

or at least to have been senior both to Hesiod and Homer,
and to have died a violent death; some saying that he was
killed by a thunderbolt; though most writers affirm, that he
was torn to pieces by Thracian women *. For which reason, in the vision of Herus Pamphylius, in Plato, Orpheus's
soul passing into another body, is said to have chosen that of
a swan, a reputed musical animal, on account of the great
hatred he had conceived for all women, from the death
which they had inflicted on him. And the historic truth of
Orpheus, was acknowledged not only by Plato, but also by
Isocrates, (who lived before Aristotle) in his oration in
praise of Busiris; and confirmed by the grave historian
Diodorus Siculus, who says, that Orpheus diligently applied
himself to literature; and that when he had learned the
mythological part of theology, he travelled into Egypt,
where he soon became the greatest proficient among the
Greeks in the mysteries of religion, theology, and poetry †."
(*Intellectual System.*)

Orpheus is universally allowed to have excelled in poetry
and music; especially on the lyre; so that his successors
were content to be his imitators: whereas, says Plutarch, *he*
adopted *no* model; for before his time, no music was known,
except a few airs for the flute ‡. Every one is acquainted

---

* From some of the ancient writers we learn, that the bard's lyre
happening to fall into the Hebrus during his struggle with his female
murderers, it was carried by the waters to Lesbos, where it was taken
up, and deposited in the temple of Apollo.

† Sir Isaac Newton has traced the family of Orpheus for several
generations. " Sisac," says this great man, " passing over the Hel-
lespont, conquered Thrace, killed Lycurgus, king of that country,
and gave his kingdom, and one of his singing-women, to Oeagrus,
the son of Tharops, and father of Orpheus; hence Orpheus is said
to have had the muse Calliope for his mother."

‡ Orpheus was pretty generally regarded as a magician, as well as a

with the incident of Orpheus's success in drawing his wife
from the infernal regions, purely by the power of his lyre,
and ultimately losing her again, from looking back upon her
before she had reached the upper air. Virgil relates the
transaction beautifully; and Dryden has not disgraced his
description.

> All dangers past, at length the lovely bride
> In safety goes, with her melodious guide;
> Longing the common light again to share,
> And draw the vital breath of upper air;
> He first, and close behind him follow'd she,
> For such was Proserpine's severe decree.
> When strong desires the impatient youth invade,
> By little caution, and much love betray'd:
> A fault which easy pardon may receive,
> Were lovers judges, or could hell forgive,
> For near the confines of etherial light,
> And longing for the glimmering of a sight,
> Th' unwary lover cast a look behind,
> Forgetful of the law, nor master of his mind.
> Straight all his hopes exhal'd in empty smoke;
> And his long toils were forfeit for a look.   *Georg.* 4.

To the strings added by Amphion to the Mercurian lyre,
(consisting originally of only four, at the most) Orpheus
contributed others, thereby completing the second tetra
chord, which two tetrachords, being *conjunct,* would constitute a heptachord, or that series of seven sounds implied
by the following verses in the sixth book of the Æneid;
which may be regarded as historical.

---

master in the arts of poetry and music. Many writers speak of him
as the inventor of that species of necromancy called *evocation of the
manes,* or raising ghosts; and this is sanctioned by the hymns he has
left, which can be regarded only as so many pieces of incantation.

—— Threïcius longa cum veste sacerdos
Obloquitur numeris septem discrimina vocum :
Jamque eadem digitis, jam pectine pulsat eburno.   v. 645.

Thus translated by Dryden :

The Thracian bard surrounded by the rest
There stands conspicuous in his flowing vest :
His flying fingers, and harmonious quill,
Strike sev'n distinguish'd notes, and seven they fill.

Pausanias informs us, that the hymns of this musical pa-
triarch, though not numerous, were rapturously admired ;
and that the *Lycomides,* an Athenian family, knew them all
by heart.   And we find Pindar, in his fourth Pythic, saying,
or to speak poetically, singing, " Oh, Orpheus, father of the
lyre and of song !   Orpheus, whom the universe celebrates,
and whose sire is Apollo * !"

According to Plato and other writers, the inheritor of the
lyre of Orpheus was his own illustrious son, Musæus †.
He was born at Athens 1426 years before Christ, and was
created chief of the Eleusinian mysteries, instituted in honor
of Ceres.   This philosopher, astronomer, priest, poet, and
musician, (for he combined in his own person and faculties
all those characters in a very eminent degree) was one of the
first versifiers of the oracles.   Virgil celebrates Musæus in
the character of Hierophant, or priest of Ceres, among the
most illustrious mortals who have merited a place in Ely-
sium.

---

* Those in the very first rank of poetical and musical excellence,
and those only, were called the *sons* of this deity.

† Some, however, dispute the descent of Musæus from Orpheus ;
and say, that he was only the disciple of that great master of the lyre.

Though Plutarch does not include this scientific and distinguished scholar in his catalogue of musicians, yet, since his hymns were set to music, and sung by himself, in the mysteries, his title to a place among the *sons of Apollo,* does not require to be defended. It was the habit of Musæus to retire to a certain hill near the citadel of Athens, for the purpose of meditation: on which account, it was called *Musæum.* None of his works have reached modern times ; and even in those of Pausanias, there only remained a hymn to Ceres, which he produced for the use of the *Lycomedes.*

Among the first poets and musicians of Greece, *two* yet remain to be mentioned; *Eumolpus* and *Melampus.* These were both priests of Ceres, and the authors of hymns dedicated to her worship.

Eumolpus, as appears from the Oxford marbles, was the son of *Musæus,* and the publisher of his father's verses. He united in himself the three characters that in the early ages of the world, almost constantly went together; the *priest, poet,* and *musician ;* qualifications for which, he chiefly obtained in Egypt, to which country, like most of his accomplished compatriots, he travelled for the acquisition of knowledge. Unremitted application rendered *Eumolpus* so eminent, and enabled him to so greatly distinguish himself at Athens, as Hierophant in the Eleusinian mysteries, that (as we are told by Diodorus Siculus) the priests and singers were afterwards known by the appellation of the *Eumolpides.*

Melampus did not visit Egypt less profitably than *Eumolpus.* However extended his acquirements there in music, it should seem, that at his return, he assumed the professions of a physician and a diviner ; arts, the union of which, he had witnessed in the great scene of his studies. In both these faculties he was highly skilled ; and in his practice of the first, was so fortunate as to restore to health, the two daughters of Prœtus, king of Argos, who laboured under an atrabilious complaint; in return for which service, he received the hand of one of his royal patients*.

---

* Since Melampus was by profession a *diviner*, as well as a physician, he must have included in his character the qualities of a poet and practical musician : and poetical and musical accomplishments were held in much too high esteem, not to be supposed to have contributed to his obtaining this illustrious and munificent honour.

As *poetry* and *music* were necessary ministrants to divination, so *dancing* was the almost indispensable companion of music and poetry. The following description, or rather painting of a dance, in the eighteenth book of the *Iliad*, is too lively, and too satisfactory, to be properly omitted in this note. The Greeks had two sorts of dances, the Pyrrhic, and the merely festive dance. Both in a degree are here represented clearly.

> A figur'd dance succeeds: such once was seen
> In lofty Gnossus, for the Cretan queen,
> Form'd by Dædalean art, a comely band
> Of youths and maidens, bounding hand in hand;
> The maids in soft cymarrs of linen drest;
> The youths all graceful in the glossy vest;
> Of those, the locks with flow'ry wreaths enroll'd;
> Of these, the sides adorn'd with swords of gold,
> That glitt'ring gay, from silver belts depend.
> Now all at once they rise, now all descend,
> With well-taught feet : now shape, in oblique ways,
> Confus'dly regular the moving maze.
> Now forth at once, too swift for sight they spring,
> And undistinguish'd, blend the flying ring.   POPE.

This elegant and animated picture is not so explicit in regard of the military manner of dancing, as of that exhibitory of the joys of peace. This deficiency, however, is well supplied by the fine description given by Lucretius in his second book, of the procession of Cybele.

To fill up the interval between the Argonautic expedition and the regular celebration of the Olympic games, it will not now be unreasonable to take notice of the chief of the bards mentioned in the *Iliad* and *Odyssey;* poems in which the harmonic art is often alluded to, and always with rapture and encomium; though not, in every instance, so distinctly, as to make it evident whether the author is extolling the powers of music, or verse; or of verse and music in conjunction.

The instruments chiefly, if not exclusively, mentioned by Homer, are the *lyre,* the *flute,* and the *syrinx;* the latter two of which, as hath been already mentioned, were of Egyptian origin. He introduces the name of the trumpet; but it is pretty generally agreed, that however common the use of that inflatile might be in the time of the poet, it was

---

Lo! armed bands for pious antics fam'd,
(Phrygian Curetes by the Grecians nam'd)
Leap wildly round (while victim blood distains
Their furious forms) and shake their rattling chains.
On well-brac'd drums their hands transported beat,
To hollow cymbals move their madden'd feet;
The roaring horns increase the horrid sounds,
And threat'ning music to the skies rebounds;
While Phrygian airs the raptur'd soul inspire,
Rouse the strong passions, and to phrenzy fire.   BUSBY.

It may not be superfluous to observe, that *Cybele,* the daughter of Meon, a Phrygian king, who exposed her upon a mountain called *Cybele,* after being suckled by wild beasts, was fostered by shepherds, and by them named after the mountain on which she had been left. As she grew up, she surpassed all her companions as much in wisdom and talents, as in beauty of person; for she invented a flute, composed of many pipes, and was the first of that country who introduced the use of *dances* and *cymbals.* Hence, when celebrated as the *mother of the gods,* those were the chief instruments with which she was saluted.

unknown to the Greeks during the Trojan war *. According to Plutarch, the flute and lyre were the principal military instruments; and it was the former that the Lacedemonians used when approaching the enemy, performing upon it the melody appertaining to the song or hymn addressed to Castor. The same writer informs us, that the Cretans played their military marches on the lyre. We find, however, that at the siege of Troy, heralds gave the signal of battle with their voices. Nestor (in the Iliad, book the second) says to Agamemnon,—

> Now bid thy heralds sound the loud alarms,
> And call the squadrons sheath'd in brazen arms.

At feasts and banquets, celestial and terrestrial, the lyre was the instrument preferred :

> Thus the blest gods the genial day prolong
> In feasts ambrosial, and celestial song ;
> Apollo tun'd the *lyre*, the Muses round
> With voice alternate aid the silver sound.   IL. l. 1.

And in the Odyssey, Homer thus describes the reception of Telemachus at the palace of Menelaus in Sparta :

> While this gay friendly troop the king surround,
> With festival and mirth the roofs resound :
> A bard amid the joyous circle sings
> High airs, attemper'd to the *vocal strings* †.   OD. l. 4.

---

* Archbishop Potter says in his *Archæologia Græca*, that before the invention of trumpets, the first signals of battle were lighted torches ; and that to them succeeded shell-fishes, which were sounded like trumpets.

† The general panegyric Homer puts in the mouth of Ulysses, upon the pleasures produced by poetry and music, is worthy of notice.

Both Achilles and Paris are represented to us as proficients on the lyre. When Agamemnon's ambassadors arrived at the tent of the Grecian hero,

> Amus'd at ease, the god-like man they found,
> Pleas'd with the solemn harp's harmonious sound.

And when the Trojan lover declines the combat with Menelaus, Hector speaks reproachfully of—

> His graceful form, instilling soft desire,
> His curling tresses, and his sylvan lyre.   Il. l. 3.

Among the bards, rhapsodists, or musical seers, immortalized by the father of poetry, *Tiresias* is the most ancient; and no prophet in the Grecian annals was more celebrated. Circe, directing Ulysses to consult him in the shades, says—

> There seek the Theban bard depriv'd of sight,
> Within irradiate with prophetic light.   Od. l. 2.

In the Catalogue of Ships, *Thamyris* is introduced as having contended with the Muses:

> Too daring bard! whose unsuccessful pride
> Th' immortal Muses in their art defied:
> Th' avenging Muses of the light of day
> Depriv'd his eyes, and snatch'd his voice away * ;

> How sweet the products of a peaceful reign;
> The heav'n-taught poet and enchanting strain!   Od. l. 9.

And Maximus Tyrius, alluding to the festive scene described in the succeeding lines, liberally observes, that the poet, by representing a social company in the midst of their entertainments, delighted with song and music, intended to recommend a more noble pleasure than that of eating and drinking.

* We learn from Pausanias, that the celebrated painter *Polygnus,*

No more his heav'nly voice was heard to sing,
His hand no more awak'd the silver string.   IL. l. 2.

Of *Demodocus* Homer speaks with the generous rapture
of one bard admiring the exalted genius of another. The
king of the Phœacians being about to entertain Ulysses, he
makes that monarch say—

Let none to strangers, honours due disclaim ;
Be there *Demodocus*, the bard of fame,
Taught by the gods to please when high he sings
The vocal lay, responsive to the strings *.   OD. l. 8.

Nor is he less liberal in his praises of *Phemius,* said by
Eustathius to have been the brother of *Demodocus.*

To Phemius was consign'd the chorded lyre,
Whose hand reluctant touch'd the warbling wire :

---

in his picture of the descent of Ulysses into hell, represented *Thamyris* with his eyes put out. According to the same author, this unfortunate bard was not only the subject of painting and poetry, but of
sculpture ; since among the statues which decorated Mount Helicon,
he saw one of *Thamyris*, blind, and with a broken lyre in his hand.
Diodorus Siculus says he learnt music of Linus. Pliny informs us,
that he was the first who performed on an instrument without the
voice. Plato compares him with Orpheus : and Clemens Alexandrinus calls him the inventor of the Dorian mode.

* Homer, who by some has been thought to represent himself in
the person of Demodocus, allows him the gift of inspiration ; and intimates that he sung and played extempore, when he says,

The bard advancing, *meditates* the lay.   OD. l. 8.

The instrument on which he excelled was the phorminx. It ought
not to be omitted, that (as we read in Plutarch's *De Musica*) he wrote
the *Fall of Troy* in verse, and also a poem called the *Nuptials of
Venus.*

Phemius whose voice divine could sweetest sing
High strains, responsive to the vocal string.   Od. l. 1.

And in other passages of the same book, conveying to us ideas of the kind of songs usually performed at royal banquets, and showing to what an extent the *immediate inspiration* of poets was accredited, further and still higher praise is bestowed upon this minstrel. " *Phemius, the sweet, the heav'n-instructed bard*," who " *High on a radiant throne, sublime in state*," is requested to sing " *What ancient bards in* HALL and BOWER, *have told*," and " *To tune what graces* EVERY FEAST, *the* LYRE."

From Homer, then, alone, we might collect, that anciently, poetry and music were in constant union, and universally honoured * ; that the great masters of those arts were esteemed and caressed by kings, princes, and heroes ; that no banquet or public solemnity was complete without the tributary skill of the poet and musician ; and that the general companion and supporter of the voice, was the *lyre*.

---

* A stronger proof cannot be adduced of the importance given to music in Homer's time, and the ages anterior to his own, than that of his feeling it necessary to give it a place in four of the twelve compartments of his *Shield of Achilles*.

CHAP. VII.

MUSICIANS AND POETS, SUBSEQUENT TO HESIOD AND HOMER.

THE almost total blank in literature, from the time of Homer to that of Sappho, from that of Sappho to the age of Anacreon, and between the birth of Anacreon and the appearance of Pindar, renders it impossible to be regularly progressive in this stage of our history. As we proceed, large fertilized spots will exhibit themselves amid a barren waste ; and we must be content, that if the intermediate spaces are nearly destitute both of flowers and grain, we can transport ourselves from one scene of pleasure and plenty to another, and are not necessitated, like other travellers, to encounter the fatigue of traversing the intervening deserts. When, however, I call these spaces intervening *deserts*, the appellation is not to be understood rigidly. The distance between one genius of the very first order, and another of the same rank, is not wholly unoccupied with specimens of merit sufficiently illustrious, perhaps, to be entitled to, and to repay, our attention.

Among these, the first presented to our notice, is Thaletas of Crete. This *Poet-musician,* by some writers confounded with *Thales,* lived about three hundred years after the Trojan war. He was so distinguished in philosophy and politics, that Lycurgus, when establishing his new form of government, was glad to avail himself of his advice. From Plato and Plutarch we learn, that his manner of *singing* was highly captivating ; and that his odes were so many exhortations to obedience and concord. Athenæus tells us, that the Spartans long continued to sing his melodies; and it appears that he was the first who composed the *Hyporchemes* * for the armed, or military dance.

Thaletas was succeeded by *Eumelus.* Of *his* productions not much is now known. Pausanias and other authors, however, speak of his talents, and quote his works, not only as the productions of a musician and poet, but as an historian. He flourished between seven and eight hundred years before Christ. It has been very truly observed, that if he wrote the history of Corinth, his own country, as several writers have declared, it must have been composed in verse ; because, in his time, prose-writing was unknown in Greece. *Eumelus's* history, therefore, it is most probable, formed a kind of *historical ballad;* a production not very unlike our own old poetical legends, which were originally sung to the flute, or lyre. His name is so obscure, that, except for the purpose of preserving something like a chain of characters, however distant the links, I should scarcely have suffered him to detain me from the notice of a name so much better known, and of so much more interest.

Archilochus, the inventor of *Dramatic Melody*, was born at Paros ; and according to modern chronology, flourished about one century later than *Eumelus ;* though Herodotus says he was cotemporary with Candaules and Gyges, kings

---

* The composition called *Hyporchemes*, consisted of a kind of poetry intended to be sung to the sound of flutes and citharas, during a military dance.

of Lydia; but Plutarch gives him the credit of having done more for the advancement of poetry and music than any other bard of antiquity. *Archilochus* discovered an early attachment to poetry and music; yet these arts had not charms sufficient to detain him from the army. The very first engagement, however, in which he was engaged, proved that nature had not designed him for a soldier. In a word, it was his misfortune to *lose* his buckler, which, to repeat a pleasantry of his own, he felt it was much easier for a man to renew, than to restore his existence. This disgrace so affected Lycambes, the father of his mistress, that he refused him his daughter, to whom he had long been betrothed.

Archilochus, among many other mental qualifications, possessed the powers of a satirist; the exercise of which, it appears, created him many enemies. But his lyrical and musical talents are what chiefly concern our present inquiry. He was largely gifted with invention. He discovered, Plutarch tells us, the *Rhythmopœia* of trimeter iambics, the sudden transition from one kind of rhythm to another, and the manner of accompanying those irregular measures upon the lyre *; which latter invention, as a peculiarity in lyric poetry, constitutes him the author of that species of versification. Also to his ingenuity is ascribed the origin of *Epodes* †.

---

* It is worthy of remark, that since, according to the nature of the ancient recitation, the measure of the verse rigorously governed the melody to which it was set, this operation was nothing less than musical composition perpetually diversified.

† In the most general acceptation of the word, an *Epode* is a composition consisting of a number of lyric verses of different construction, comprised in a single stanza. But in a less common sense, it implied a small lyric poem, composed in *Trimeter Iambics*, of six feet, and *Dimeters* of four feet, alternately. In process of time, the signification of the word *Epode* was extended to every poem which had a short verse placed at the end of several that were longer.

From an epigram in the *Anthologia*, as also from the epistles of Cicero, it appears, that the name of *Archilochus* vied, in the regard it challenged, with that of Homer himself. And Aristophanes, the most scrupulous critic of his time, said, the longest poem of *Archilochus* was to him always the most acceptable.

Of *Tyrtœus*, an Athenian general and musician, all antiquity speaks as the admired composer of military songs and airs; and also as an excellent musical performer. A memorable victory obtained by the Lacedemonians in their second war with the Messenians, about 685 years before Christ, was attributed to the animating sound of a new flute *, invented, and played upon, by *Tyrtœus*. So powerful, indeed, were his compositions, that, according to Lycurgus the orator, the Spartans made a law, that previous to their going upon any military expedition, they should all be summoned to the king's tent, to hear the songs of *Tyrtœus*. A celebrated song and dance performed at festivals by *three choirs*, was also of his production. In the performance of this composition, the first choir consisted of *old men*, the second of *young men*, and the third of *boys*. The disposition of this choral dialogue was as follows :

---

* From this, and many similar instances, in proof of the effects of the flute in animating the soldiers, besides the fact, that in warlike expeditions, it was the instrument more generally used than any other, it is evident, that its construction and character must have been very different from that of the modern flute, as well as from that simple form and soft mellowness of tone of the original pipe or reed. Probably, it was of the cornute kind; an idea sanctioned by the following verses in the description of the music used in the procession of *Cybele*. (Vide Lucretius, l. 2.)

The roaring horns increase the horrid sounds,
And threat'ning music to the sky rebounds. Busby.

Old Men.—In youth, our souls with martial ardour glow'd.
Young Men.—We present glory seek: Point out the road.
Boys.—Though now with children we can only class,
Our future deeds, we hope, will your's surpass.

On the extraordinary talents of *Terpander,* most of the ancient writers expatiate ; though scarcely any two of them agree concerning the time and place of his birth.   According to the Oxford marbles, he was the son of Derdeneus of Lesbos, and flourished about 670 years before Christ. From the same source we learn, that *he taught the nomes, or airs, of the lyre and flute, which he performed himself upon this last instrument, in concert with other players upon the flute.*   In confirmation of the general opinion, that he added three strings to the lyre, which, till his time, had only four, both Euclid and Strabo quote two verses, which they ascribe to *Terpander* himself* :

The *Tetrachord's* restraint we now despise,
The *sev'n-string'd Lyre* a nobler strain supplies.

To the genius of *Terpander,* the Greeks, it is said, owed the introduction of *notation,* for ascertaining and pre-

---

If to this we add the circumstance, that Lysander, the Spartan general, beat down the walls of Athens, and burned the Athenian ships *to the sound of flutes,* we shall want no further proof, that the tones and power of the ancient *tibia* were sufficiently boisterous to come under the description of those of the *clarion.*

* If, however, the hymn to Mercury, which is attributed to Homer, and in which the *seven-stringed lyre* is mentioned, be genuine, it deprives *Terpander* of this glory.   But it is only being just to him, to observe, that the learned have great doubts respecting its authenticity ; and that the *Marbles* tell us the Lacedemonians were offended by his innovations.

serving melody; which, till his time, was traditionary and fleeting *.

Plutarch enumerates among the other compositions of this distinguished poet and musician, his excellent *poems,* or hymns, for the cithara, in heroic verse, which, in after times, were used by the rhapsodists, as prologues to the poems of Homer. But it does not appear that his name derived more lustre from any talent than from his accomplishments as a *citharist,* and as a performer on the *flute* †. His skill on these instruments obtained him the first prize in the musical contests at the *Carnean* games; and four prizes at the *Py-thic* games ‡.

Mimnermus was a musician and lyric poet of Smyrna; and flourished at the beginning of the sixth century before the Christian era. He first attracted notice, and obtained admiration, by his excellent performance (on the flute) of a *nome* called *Cradias,* usually played at Athens during the march, or procession, of the victims of expiation. According to Athenæus, he was the inventor of the *pentameter verse :* and his genius shone so conspicuously in his elegies, (which Horace preferred to those of Callimachus) as to place him in the highest of the bardic ranks. These, and his

---

* It is, nevertheless, to be observed, that the honour of inventing the first *musical characters,* has, by Alipius and Gaudentius, been awarded to Pythagoras.

† The flute, Aristotle informs us, after its first invention, was used by mean people, and deemed an ignoble instrument, unworthy of a free man, till after the invasion and defeat of the Persians; when ease, affluence, and luxury, soon so augmented its estimation, that it was a disgrace to a person of birth not to be master of its performance.

‡ For a full account of the four principal *Grecian games,* viz. the *Olympic,* the *Pythic,* the *Nemean,* and the *Isthmean,* see the following chapter.

poem upon the battle between the people of Smyrna and the Lydians, under Gyges, together with his *Nanno* *, an exquisite elegiac composition extolled and quoted by Strabo, induced Propertius to declare, that, in his opinion, his verses were more valuable than all the writings of Homer. And Horace, struck with the beauty of some lines of this poet-musician, written in his earlier years, and preserved by Stobœus, bears testimony to his talents in describing the passion of love. Their sense is as follows :

> Say, what is life, and all its pride,
> If Love's pure pleasure be denied ?
> O, snatch me hence, ye Fates, whene'er
> His tender joys I cease to share.
> Now let us cull each fragrant flow'r,
> While youth's bright season grants the pow'r ;
> For frozen age will soon destroy
> The force to give or take a joy ;
> And then, a prey to pain and care,
> Avoided by the young and fair ;
> The sun's blest beams will loathsome grow,
> And only shine on scenes of woe.

After *Mimnermus*, we find no lyric poet whose works have survived, till we descend to the time of *Stesichorus*, who, Athenæus informs us, was born at Himera in Sicily, and who, according to the most authentic chronologers, died near the end of the fifth century before Christ. His original name was *Tisias ;* but, as some say, he acquired that of *Stesichorus*, from the changes he made in the manner of performing the dithyrambic chorus, which was *sung* and *danced*

---

* *Nanno*, according to Athenæus, was a young and beautiful girl, an excellent performer on the flute, and with whom, in his old age, Mimnermus was deeply enamoured.

round the altar of Bacchus; while others, among whom is Suidas, affirm that he was so called, because he was the first who accompanied a chorus with *citharodia*, or *singing to the lyre*.

Quintilian, who speaks of the poems of *Stesichorus* as extant in his time, gives them a high character. Of these, however, only a few fragments are remaining. His genius led him to the projecting several musical improvements, among which, Plutarch mentions the changes he made in the *Harmation*, or chariot air, composed by Olympus *.

Of *Simonides*, who flourished much about the same time as *Stesichorus*, it will be necessary to speak somewhat more at large. Though there were several poets and musicians of that name, the eldest, born 538 years anterior to Christ, was the most illustrious. He was a native of Ceos, and had the honour of being the preceptor of Pindar. Among his numerous poetical productions, are many songs of victory and triumph at the public games, at which he himself gained the prize in elegiac poetry, when Æschylus was his competitor; and another when he was fourscore years of age †.

The tender, sweet, and plaintive character of his verse, procured him the appellation of *Melicertes;* and of the *tearful eye* of his muse every one spoke. Both Plato and Cicero give him the character, not only of an excellent

---

* The *Harmatian* air was so denominated, as Hesychius informs us, on account of its imitating the rapid motion of a chariot wheel; or because its fire and spirit was calculated to animate the horses that drew the chariot in battle.

† From Suidas we learn, that he added four letters to the Greek alphabet; and Pliny gives him credit as the contributor of an eighth string to the lyre; claims which, however, it is difficult to allow him.

poet and musician, but speak in admiration of his wisdom
and virtue : and Dr. Johnson (*Adventurer*, No. 89) says
" Simonides was celebrated by the ancients for the sweetness, correctness, and purity of his style, and his irresistible
skill in moving the passions."

This distinguished genius lived to his ninetieth year.
Such an extraordinary longevity afforded him the opportunity
of personally knowing many of the first characters in antiquity. Xenophon in his Dialogue upon Tyranny, makes
him one of the interlocutors with Hiero, king of Syracuse *.

Not the least curious part of the history of Simonides,
is, that being frequently applied to by the victors at the
games, to write odes in their praise, he would never gratify
their vanity till he had secured the sum for which he stipulated. He had two coffers, he told his employers ; one
for the deposit of honours, verbal thanks, and promises,
and the other to receive his pecuniary rewards. He added,
that as he charged the latter coffer, he found it filled ; but
that however liberally the first was supplied, it still remained
empty †.

Being asked by Hiero's queen, whether it was most desirable to be learned or rich, he answered that it was far
better to be rich ; for the learned were always dependent on
the rich, and waiting at their doors; but he never saw rich
men waiting at the doors of the learned. Carrying the
principle of economy to the excess of selling part of the
provision with which his table was furnished by Hiero,

---

* The reader will not fail to recollect the story of Hiero's demanding to know of *Simonides* the nature of God : and that after much
meditation he gave that despot the answer he should have returned at
first :—that the nature of God was inscrutable.

† Simonides is said to have been the first who sold his muse to
the best bidder.

some one on the part of the king reprobated his meanness; upon which he said, he so acted for two reasons ; to display to the world the magnificence of his patron, and to show his own frugality. One maxim of his, (never out of his recollection) was, that it is better to leave money to your enemies, after death, than to be troublesome to your friends, while living *.

We are now approaching the most exalted lyric genius of Greece : but impatience to contemplate his refulgence must not prevent our taking a glance at a great though inferior luminary. *Simonides* left behind him a nephew (born at Cos) who rivalled his uncle's talents. *Bacchilydes*, like his relation and tutor, sung the victories of Hiero at the public

---

* Dionysius has preserved the following fragment of this poet. The occasion is as interesting as the ideas are natural and beautiful. Danaë being, by her merciless father, enclosed in a chest, and thrown into the sea with her child, when night comes on, and a storm arises, which threatens to overset the chest, weeping, and embracing the young Perseus, she exclaims :

> Sweet child! what anguish does thy mother know,
> Ere cruel grief has taught thy tears to flow!
> Amidst the roaring wind's tremendous sound,
> Which threats destruction as it howls around,
> In balmy sleep thou liest, as at the breast,
> Without one bitter thought to break thy rest.
> While in pale, glimm'ring interrupted light,
> The moon but shows the horrors of the night.
> Didst thou but know, sweet innocent! our woes,
> Not opiate's pow'r thy eyelids now could close.
> Sleep on, sweet babe! ye waves in silence roll,
> And lull, oh lull to rest my tortur'd soul.

There is a second great poet and musician of the name of Simonides, recorded on the *Marbles*, supposed to have been the grandson of the present ; and who, in 478 B. C. gained the prize in the games at Athens.

games. He was also the author of numerous *Love Verses*, *Prosodies*, *Dithyrambics*, *Hymens*, *Pæans*, *Hyporchemes*, and *Parthenia*, or songs to be sung by a chorus of virgins at festivals. Unfortunately, though his claims to our notice are great, the particulars now known of him are limited to these. This historical defect, however, permits us to pass with less delay to the history of *Pindar*.

PINDAR, whose genius, every hero, prince, and potentate, was prone to court, whose *muse of fire* was retained and pensioned at Delphos, was a native of Thebes, in Bœotia, and born about 520 years before the Christian era. From his father, a flute-player by profession, he received his first musical instructions. His second teacher was *Myrtis*, a lady distinguished by her talents for lyric poetry. *Myrtis* had also a female pupil of the name of *Corinna*, who, more advanced in her studies than Pindar, contributed to facilitate his progress. Shewing his fair fellow pupil the exordium of a poem, in which he had crowded an immense variety of historical subjects, she, smiling, told him, he should *sow with the hand*, and not empty his whole sack at once. He was not, however, long in outstripping the knowledge of his tutoresses, whom he quitted for the instruction of Simonides, then in extreme old age.

The institution of public trials of poetical and musical merit was now so general through Greece, that the fame of a young student and practitioner could be promoted only by his entering the lists ; and it so happened that both Myrtis and Corinna publicly disputed the prize with him at Thebes. Over the former he obtained a victory ; but was vanquished by Corinna no less than five different times *.

---

* Pausanias attributes these victories of Corinna to the partiality of the judges, more sensible to the charms of beauty than to the powers of music and poetry. A very natural conjecture.

The hypercritics and satirists, taking advantage of the impression made on the public mind by these his defeats, traduced, abused, and turned into ridicule, his poetical and musical abilities. But this treatment he was wise enough to turn to his own account, by making it the spur to his future industry. His first measure was to quit Thebes: after which he arduously and incessantly exerted himself to remove other faults besides those of which ill-nature and sarcasm had made him sensible, and soon became the wonder and delight of Greece.

His performances then frequently graced and dignified the four great festivals of the Olympian, Pythian, Nemean and Isthmean games. Those candidates for fame, who were ambitious of having their achievements celebrated by Pindar, applied to him for an ode, which was always sung in the *Prytaneum*, or town hall of Olympia, before it was performed at the *triumphal entry* *.

The character of a poet, Pausanias says, was positively consecrated in the person of *Pindar*, by the god of verse himself, whose oracle commanded the inhabitants of Delphos to set apart for that bard one half of the first-fruit offerings, brought by the religious to his shrine, and to allow him a conspicuous place in his temple †.

According to Fabricius, *Pindar* lived to the age of ninety;

---

* Gratian advises the man who would arrive at the most consummate greatness, to perform extraordinary actions, and then secure a good poet. But this latter provision could not always be made: and those conquerors who were not so fortunate as to have poets and musicians for their friends, or so rich as to be able to purchase odes for their own particular victories, were content to have the old *Hymn to Hercules* of Archilochus performed by a band of musicians; or if they could not afford that expense, to get it sung by their friends.

† In consequence of this divine favour, an iron chair was provided for *Pindar*, and placed in the temple. This chair, sitting in which

but the chronology of Dr. Blair makes it appear that he died 437 years before Christ, at the age of eighty-six. The Thebans erected a monument to him in the Hippodrome: and his renown continued so great, that his posterity derived from it considerable honours and privileges. It is an incident as striking in the page of history, as honourable to the character of Alexander, that when that warrior attacked the city of Thebes, he gave express orders to his soldiers to spare the house and family of *Pindar*. One, and one only circumstance, is to be compared with this mark of honour: When the Lacedemonians ravaged Bœotia, and burned the capital, these words were written upon the door of the bard: *Forbear to burn this house ;* it was *the dwelling of Pindar.*

Concerning the celebrated musician and poet, *Pylades* of Megalopolis, no more is known than the few particulars, or rather single incident, transmitted to us by Plutarch and Pausanias. He lived in the time of Philopœmen, general of the Achæan league. This hero, soon after he had gained the battle of Mantinea, happened to visit the theatre during the Nemean games, while the musicians were disputing the musical prize. At the moment he entered, *Pylades*, accompanied by the lyre, was singing the beginning of a song composed by Timotheus, called *the Persians.* The words were—

> Behold the hero from whose glorious deeds
> Our greatest blessing, *liberty*, proceeds!

This extraordinary coincidence struck the whole assembly with pleasure and surprise. Roused to instant enthusiasm by the exact application of the verse to the general's

---

the bard sung his hymns in honour of the god, was remaining in the time of Pausanias.

late victory, the energy with which it was uttered, and the excellence of the singer's voice, the auditors cast their eyes upon Philopœmen, burst into violent applauses, and felt confident of entirely recovering the dignity they had lost by former defeats.

We will now take a view of the great poet-musician, the fire, vigour, and accidental appropriateness of whose verses formed the basis of this remarkable incident in the life of a general, who, proposing Epaminondas for his model, was not unsuccessful in imitating the prudence and the simplicity, the courage, skill, and disinterestedness, of that celebrated Theban.

Timotheus, son of Thersander, or Philopolis, and one of the most shining ornaments of antiquity, was born at Miletus, an Ionian city of Caria, 346 years before Christ. His excellence lay in lyric and dithyrambic poetry, and the performance of the cithara. He is said to have added four strings to the seven, of which the lyre then consisted *. The first time he performed in the assembly of the people

---

* This is the account given by Pausanias: but Suidas says, the Grecian lyre had already nine strings, and that Timotheus only added two : but the famous *Senatus Consultum* settles the question.

The greatest progressive improvement of this instrument, as generally stated, is that from the time of Amphion to that of Terpander, a period of 856 years. It had only four strings; when the latter, by adding to it three new ones, extended its scale to a *heptachord*. One hundred and fifty years after this period, Pythagoras added an eighth string, completing the octave.

To the strings that were afterwards added to these (by which the scale was extended to two octaves) there are various claimants, which, perhaps, only proves, that music was cultivated at the same time, in different countries; and that the inhabitants of each country invented and improved their own instruments, some of which were confounded with those of other parts of Greece, which they resembled.

he experienced such violent marks of disapprobation, that had not his cotemporary, Euripides, been sensible of his extraordinary abilities, and encouraged him to pursue a profession in which he afterwards so highly succeeded, he would have abandoned it for ever.

It seems extremely likely, that the great offence given to his countrymen, by his innovation upon the then state of the lyre, was in a great measure the cause of his unfavourable reception at his first public appearance *. How decided the opposition was to his extension of the scale, is evident, from the following curious decree of antiquity (or Spartan *Act of Parliament*) preserved by Boethius : —

" *Whereas* TIMOTHEUS *the Milesian, coming to our city, has dishonoured our ancient music, and despising the lyre of seven strings, has, by the introduction of a greater variety of notes, corrupted the ears of our youth ; and by the number of his strings, and the novelty of his melody, has given to our music an effeminate and artificial dress, instead of the plain and orderly one in which it has hitherto appeared ; rendering melody infamous, by composing in the chromatic, instead of the enharmonic ;*

" *The Kings and the Ephori, have, therefore, resolved to pass censure upon* TIMOTHEUS *for these things : and, farther, to oblige him to cut all the superfluous strings of his eleven, leaving only the* SEVEN TONES ; *and to banish him from our city ; that men may be warned for the future, not to introduce into Sparta any unbecoming customs.*"——

Timotheus, however, was afterwards pardoned†; and rose

---

* Severe as we find this edict, Timotheus was not the first who used eleven strings. Melanippidas had long before performed on a lyre with *twelve* strings.

† In the relation of this affair, as given by Athenæus, we find it

to such exalted celebrity, that he received from the Ephesians the immense sum of a thousand pieces of gold, as his reward for composing and setting to music a poem in honour of Diana.

According to the account left of this extraordinary genius, by Suidas, his poetical and musical compositions were very numerous, and of various kinds. They are said to have consisted of nineteen *nomes*, or canticles, in hexameters; thirty-six *proems*, or preludes; eighteen *dithyrambics;* twenty-one *hymns;* the *poem* in honour of Diana; one *panegyric;* four tragedies (the *Persians, Phinidas, Laertes,* and *Niobe*), and the rhapsody on the *Birth of Bacchus;* to which are to be added, eighteen books of *nomes*, or airs, composed expressly for the cithara, and set to eight thousand verses, and a thousand *prooimia*, or preludes, for the *nomes* of the flute, as mentioned by Stephen of Byzantium.

The same author informs us, that *Timotheus* died in Macedonia, at the advanced age of ninety-seven[*].

Among the distinguished musicians of ancient Greece, few held a higher station than ANTIGENIDES. We learn from Suidas, that he was a native of Thebes, in Bœotia, and the son of Satyrus, a celebrated flute-player. He studied under Philoxenus, to whom he became flute-player in ordinary, constantly accompanying him in the musical airs which that celebrated poet-musician set to his own verses.

---

added, that when the public officer was on the point of executing the sentence by cutting off the new strings, Timotheus, perceiving a little statue in the same place, with a lyre in its hand of *eleven* chords, and directing to it the attention of the judges, was acquitted.

[*] According to the *Marbles* (certainly much better authority) he was only ninety when he died.

Stephen Byzantium fixes his death in the fourth year of the 105th Olympiad, two years before the birth of Alexander the Great; whence

By attention and practice, aided by the instruction of so excellent a master, he brought the art of flute-playing to
greater perfection than it had ever reached before; and when
he quitted Philoxenus, obtained pupils of the first class, and
was caressed by the greatest princes. Pericles, having undertaken the education of his nephew Alcibiades, preferred
Antigenides for his flute-master.

According to Athenæus, it was *Antigenides* who performed upon the flute at the nuptials of Iphicrates, when
that Athenian general espoused the daughter of Cotys, King
of Thrace : and it is to him that Plutarch attributes the
power that, by the performance of the *Harmatian* air at a
banquet, transported Alexander to such a degree, that he
seized his arms, and was on the point of attacking his
guests *.

However high the reputation of this musician, he was too
sensible of the precariousness of public favour, to place in
it any great confidence, or to suffer himself to be elated by
the applause of the multitude. Endeavouring to inspire
his pupil Ismenias with the same sentiment, and to teach
him to despise the judgment of the populace, one day he
consoled him on the coldness of his auditors, by saying,
Mihi cane et Musis : Sing to me and the Muses.

Antigenides had so great a command of the flute, that he
could express with it minute intervals and inflexions of
sound : and, according to Apuleius, play in all the modes.
But such a variety of execution necessitated many novelties
in the construction of the instrument : among these, one

---

it would appear that this Timotheus was not the famous performer
on the flute, so much esteemed by that prince, and over whose passions his musical powers are said to have had such an entire command.

* The same story has been told of Timotheus.

was, an increase in the number of its holes, which, probably, not only extended the compass, but rendered the tones more flexible and various *. His innovations were not confined to the instrument itself: he appeared in public with delicate Milesian slippers, and a robe of saffron colour, called *Crocoton*.

A *bon mot* of the general Epaminondas (himself a skilful musician) relative to *Antigenides*, is recorded by Plutarch. The Theban leader, upon being informed, as if to alarm him, that the Athenians had sent troops into the Peloponnessus, equipped with entire new arms, asked " Whether *Antigenides* was disturbed when he saw new flutes in the hands of Tellis † ?"

If *Dorion* is entitled to a place among these poetical and musical luminaries, it is, perhaps, more on account of his wit than his professional superiority. He, however, distinguished himself, by introducing a number of changes in the music of his time; and was at the head of a sect of performers, opponents to another sect, of which Antigenides was the chief. Though both his poetry and his music are lost, many of his pleasantries are preserved.

Being at Milo in Egypt, and unable to procure a lodging, he inquired of a priest, who was sacrificing in a chapel, to

---

* Theophrastus, in his History of Plants, has recorded how, and at what season, Antigenides cut the reeds for his flute, in order to obtain such as should be capable of expressing all the delicacy and refinements in which he prided himself.

† A Greek lyric poet and musician, the father of *Brasidas*, the famous Lacedemonian general, to whose memory a superb monument was raised ; and in whose honour public festivals were held at Lacedemon, called Brasideia. *Tellis*, by the jut of Epaminondas's *jeu d'esprit*, did not, as a flute-player, rival the talents of his son as a general.

what divinity it was dedicated, who answered, *To Jupiter, and to Neptune.* "How should I be able," says *Dorion,* "to get a lodging in a place where the gods are obliged to lie double?"

Supping with Nicocreon in the Island of Cyprus, and admiring a rich cup of gold that was placed on the sideboard,—"The goldsmith will make you just such another," says the prince, "whenever you please." "He'll obey your orders much better than mine, Sir," answered *Dorion;* "so let me have that, and do you bespeak another."

Upon hearing the description of a tempest, in the *Nauplius* of Timotheus, *Dorion* said, he had seen a better in a boiling caldron.

Being robbed of a gouty shoe at a banquet, "The only harm I wish the thief," says he, "is, that my shoe may fit him."

Dorion's wit and talents made him a welcome guest wherever he went. Philip of Macedon often invited him to his parties of pleasure, which he never failed to animate and delight.

The number of illustrious poet-musicians in antiquity is too great to admit the inclusion of every one. The present list is, perhaps, already too long; but it is impossible to refuse the claims of a *lady* to our notice; a lady whose merits rank so high as those of *Lamia.*

This celebrated female was as much admired for her abilities as a flute-player, as for her wit and beauty. If an exquisite engraving of her head upon an amethyst, with the veil and bandage of her profession, which was in the possession of the late King of France, proves her to have been uncommonly handsome, the honours her *talents* received, sufficiently testify their power over the hearts and minds of her hearers.

Lamia was the daughter of Cleanora, mistress to Demetrius Poliorcetes, at whose court she became the object of universal admiration. But her personal charms and abilities were not long limited to so narrow a sphere as that of a single court, city, or country. From Athens, the place of her birth, she travelled into Egypt, whither she was attracted by the fame of its flute-players. Her person and performance soon engaged the attention of Ptolemy Soter, with whom she abided till she became the captive of Demetrius, who contending with Ptolemy for the Island of Cyprus, conquered him in a sea engagement, and took prisoners his wives and domestics.

The prince whose captive *Lamia* became, conceived for her the most violent passion. At her request, he conferred such extraordinary benefits upon the Athenians, that they rendered him divine honours; and in gratitude for the influence she had exercised in their favour, dedicated to her a temple, under the name of *Venus Lamia* *.

These are the chief and most celebrated poet-musicians of Greece, subsequent to the times of Hesiod and Homer; excepting such as *Anacreon, Æschylus, Sophocles, Euripides,* and *Theocritus;* who, though they all flourished before the separation of Music and Poetry, are not only too well known, for their characters and lives to require to be related here, but have so long been familiar to us simply as poets and dramatists, that a *musical* account of them would seem foreign from their established fame and recognised merits †.

---

* A great number of Grecian *Tibicinæ*, or female flute-players, are mentioned by Athenæus; and yet, by the account which Parmenio gives to Alexander of the female musicians in the service of Darius, the use of the flute among ladies, appears to have been much more general in Persia than in Greece.

† And it is scarcely necessary to observe, that of names obscure as

From the time of Alexander the Great, down to which we have traced the principal professors of the poetical and musical arts, but few masters of eminence are upon record. Of these notice will hereafter be taken.

We are now about to take a view of those national institutions, which not only opened a field for the display of Grecian genius, Grecian taste, and Grecian emulation; but which, from their memorable character and important objects, have been made so many grand bases for chronological calculation, and historical certainty.

Anthes, Polyodes, Zenodemus, Zenocritus, Telesilla, Rhianus, Ibycus, and other lyrics, no memorials remain sufficiently interesting to entitle them to any detailed notice.

CHAP. VIII.

THE GRECIAN GAMES.

Of the GRECIAN GAMES, or PUBLIC SPORTS, consisting of trials of skill, in arts and bodily exercises, and instituted in honour of distinguished personages, or auspicious events, there were a great variety; but of these, the chief were, the *Olympic Games*, founded, according to some, by Hercules; the *Pythian Games*, first established, as Pausanias informs us, by Jason, or Diomedes, King of Etolia, and re-established by Iphitus; the *Nemœan Games*, instituted by Adrastus, and subsequently augmented by Hercules; the *Isthmean Games*, founded in commemoration of Melicertes; and the *Panathenœan Games*, appointed in honour of Minerva.

The OLYMPIC GAMES, which commenced in the year of the world 2886, were held at the beginning of every fifth year, on the banks of the Alpheus, near Olympia, a city of Elis, in honour of Olympian Jupiter, and comprised personal combats, chariot-races, and musical contests.

It is remarkable, that Homer does not once mention these games; which, as dedicated to Jupiter, and forming by their regular returns, those measures or divisions of chronology most generally adopted, were superior in consequence to all the others*. It is true, that at first, the *Olympic Games*

---

* Of the superiority of these *games* over the others, no evidence can be stronger than that deducible from the speech of Socrates to the

were observed only occasionally, at very distant and irregular periods; but in the year 776 before Christ, their celebration was fixed for every fiftieth month, or the second
month after the expiration of four years, and were made to
serve as epochas.   In the first of these, the Olympiad from
which chronologers reckon, Corœbus, the Elan, was the victor.

Whether these games, which had their name from the
god in whose honour they were ordained, or from the city
of Olympia, near which they were held, were originally instituted for religious or civil purposes; they, in process of
time, became so important to all Greece, that every state
and city felt a deep and constant interest in their celebration.
From Mr. West's *Dissertation on the Olympic Games*, the
source which supplied Dr. Burney with the greater part of
his description of the manner of their exercise, we learn
that they were both religious and political.   Respect and
veneration for the gods, but particularly for Jupiter, the ingenious translator of Pindar observes, were impressed by
the noble and magnificent temple and statues erected to him
at *Olympia*, as well as by religious rites and ceremonies.
By the *horse-race*, the breed and management of that useful
animal was promoted; in the *foot-race*, manly speed and
activity.   Add to this, that a noble thirst of excellence and
victory was excited by the various other feats of manhood

---

judges, after his condemnation; because it is praise only by inference,
and not an intended eulogy.   Required to pass sentence on himself,
and to name the death he preferred, he said, " For my attempts to
teach the Athenian youth justice and moderation, and to render the
rest of my countrymen more happy, let me be maintained at the public expense the remaining years of my life in the Prytaneum; an
honour, O Athenians! which I deserve *more than the victors at the
Olympic games*.   THEY *make their countrymen more happy in appearance, but* I *made you so in reality.*"

and dexterity performed on these occasions, and the higher
and more useful feelings awakened and called into play.
But though Mr. West tells us, that " these assemblies were
frequented by persons of the greatest eminence in all the
arts of peace, such as historians, orators, philosophers, poets
and painters; who perceiving that the most compendious way
to fame was through Olympia, were then induced to exhibit their best performances, at the time of the celebration of
the *Olympic Games ;*" he has wholly omitted to mention
poetical and *musical contests*, though both had frequent admission there. The PENTATHLON, or five bodily exercises,
of leaping, running, throwing the quoit or dart, boxing, and
wrestling, were all, it appears, accompanied with the flute.
Pythocritus, of Sicyon, as we learn from Pausanias, played
six times on the flute, during the exercise of the *Pentathlon*,
at Olympia; and in testimony of his skill, a pillar and statue
were erected to him. The same author informs us, that the
horse-race was accompanied by the trumpet, and the *chariot-race* by the flute *.

The ninety-first Olympiad, it is worthy of remark, was
honoured with the dramatic exertions of Xenophon and
Euripides, who disputed the prize in that species of poetry.
The lyrical parts of the compositions were, of course, set to
music, and accompanied by instruments, as when performed
on the stage.

The *flute* was a universal favourite with the Greeks; but

---

* Near Olympia there was a *Gymnasium* called *Lolichmium*, which
was open at all times to those who were desirous of trying their
powers in poetical and musical exercises : and though sometimes
music was performed independently of poetry, poetry was never recited without music.

the *trumpet*, nevertheless, was an instrument, to the practice of which they much attended. In the ninety-sixth Olympiad, a prize was instituted at the *Olympic Games*, for the best performer on the *trumpet** ; and the first of these honours gained there, was adjudged to Timœus of Elis. In the same year, another was obtained by Crates, the countryman of Timœus, on the *cornet*, or *horn*. Archias of Hybla in Sicily, was victor on the *trumpet* at three several Olympiads : and the famous trumpeter, Herodorus of Megara, carried off the prize ten several times, (some say fifteen,) and was, Athenæus informs us, victor in the *whole circle of sacred games*, having, by turns, been crowned at the Olympian, Pythian, Nemean, and Isthmean †. According to some authors, Herodorus was as remarkable for his gigantic figure, as for the strength of his lungs; which were, so powerful, that his performance could not be heard with safety, unless at a great distance. The exertions used by the ancients in blowing the flute and the trumpet, were so great, that for the preservation of their cheeks, they were obliged to use a *capistrum*, or muzzle, which, however, was not always adequate to the purpose. According to Lucian, Harmonides, a juvenile scholar of Timotheus, at his first

---

* The trumpet, not known, or not in use, at the time of the Trojan war, was one of the instruments of later invention and slower improvement, than some others ; and is supposed, for a long time, to have been in so very imperfect state, as to have served, at first, only as a rough and noisy signal of battle.

† These trumpeters appear, speaking generally, to have been heralds and public criers, who at the *games*, gave the signal for engaging, and announced the successes. They also proclaimed peace and war, and were employed to sound signals of sacrifice and silence, at religious ceremonies.

public performance, began his flute solo with so violent a blast, that he breathed into the instrument his *last breath* *: and from an epigram of Archias, the Hyblæan, we learn, that that trumpeter dedicated a statue to Apollo, in gratitude for that deity's preservation of his cheeks and blood-vessels, while, with his utmost force, he proclaimed the *Olympic Games*.

A prominent and important feature of these *games*, was the musical recitations of the *Rhapsodists*. Their exercises chiefly consisted of *pasticios*, or collections of favourite passages of poetry and music from different masters, and of various styles, which they repeated to the accompaniment of the cithara †. The Emperor Nero's ambition to rival every other rhapsodist of his time, impelled him to enlist himself among the performers at these games; at which he was content to submit himself to all the discipline and rigour of the Olympic laws, as also to the self-humiliating practice of *supplicating* the favourable decision of the *Nomodictai*, or umpires. This is mentioned, not so much as an instance of the prostitution of imperial dignity, as to demonstrate, that poetico-musical exercises, formed a considerable portion of the Olympic exhibitions. Indeed, we have every reason to conclude, that at these numerous and splendid assemblies, poetry and music formed the principal sources of gratification; and that, as the *media* for embellishing and applauding other provinces of the arts, as well as the various corporeal

---

* By this, it would appear, that the power or fulness of the tone constituted one of the principal excellencies in instrumental performance; at least, in those of the inflatile kind.

† Not unfrequently, however, they rehearsed entire poems. It is on record, that Cleomenes sung, by memory, a very long one, composed by Empedocles, and called *The Expiations*.

feats there exhibited, these intellectual and elegant accomplishments must have been, both as accompaniments and *codas*, indispensable adjuncts. Honour, the chief incitement to the candidates in all the *sacred games*, demanded the applausive voices of bards and musicians ; and found its best supports in their rhapsodical descriptions and celebrations *. It is to the eager and universal demand for these, that we owe the noble odes of Pindar ; and to the same demand, but for the ravages of time, we should have been indebted for the possession of many valuable specimens of Greek eulogistic poetry. The hymns composed by Simonides and Bacchylides, in honour of Hiero, would not have been less gratifying to modern taste, than satisfactory to the curious ; nor would a single sample of the numerous productions of the other great poets and musicians of antiquity have proved wanting in their own interest, or unattended by our veneration.

The fate and condition of the ancient poetical and musical panegyrists, corresponded with the services they rendered the Olympic victors by their odes, which were performed in processions and temples with religious zeal and solemnity. They were held in the highest esteem, and distinguished by the public regard, and the honours universally conferred upon their names. Indeed, the successful candidates of every description were so exalted in the public estimation, and so amply protected, that it may be said, they had nothing to apprehend from the vicissitudes of fortune † ;

---

* Though the victors in the *Pentathlon* were entitled to a reward of about 500 drachmæ, or sixteen pounds, it does not appear, that in the horse or chariot-race, any other prize was bestowed on the conqueror than an *olive crown.*

† Solon found the rewards of the victors of the Olympic and Isthmean games so great, that he deemed it necessary to reduce them.

and while all their wants were gratuitously supplied, statuaries were ambitious of the honour of representing them in brass and marble *.

According to St. Chrysostom, the *Olympic Games* continued to be celebrated with splendour till the end of the fourth century.

The PYTHIAN GAMES were instituted in commemoration, and in honour, of Apollo's destruction of the serpent Python. They were celebrated in a place called *Pythium,* situated in Macedonia, and also at Delphi †. Though more ancient than the *Olympic Ludi,* they never equalled them in fame. They commenced in the third year of the forty-eighth Olympiad, from which time, the Greeks reckoned sometimes by *Olympiads* and sometimes by *Pythiades*. At their origin, they were held every eight years, but afterwards became quadrennial, which served for an epocha for the inhabitants of Delphi ‡. At first they were devoted to

---

* The sacred grove of Olympia, Pausanias informs us, contained above five hundred statues of gods and heroes of the first class, without including those that had been placed there in honour of less important personages.

† About the year 642 of their city, the Romans adopted these games, under the appellation of APOLLINARES LUDI.

‡ Swift always persisted in writing *Delphos,* instead of *Delphi;* and the word Delphi was a subject of violent dispute between Boyle and Bentley. Boyle, on the ground of *common usage,* defended Delphos. Bentley rejected it as a barbarism, and as being merely the *accusative* of the word Delphi. The story the latter tells in ridicule of Boyle's veneration for custom, right or wrong, is amusing. " A Popish priest," says he, " for more than thirty years, had in his breviary, read *mumpsimus,* instead of *sumpsimus;* and when a learned man apprized him of his blunder, he replied, ' Aye, well, well; I have always read it so; and shall not now change my old *mumpsimus* for your new *sumpsimus.*' "

poetical and musical contests, but were soon extended to the other exercises of the *Pancratium* performed in the Olympic Games. Pausanias, speaking of the original exercises in these *games*, says that the prize, which first consisted of a wreath of beech leaves, and afterwards of a crown of laurel, was adjudged to him who had composed and sung the best hymn in honour of Apollo. The first victor at the *Pythian Games* was Chrysomethis of Crete, the son of Carmanor, who purified Apollo after he had killed the Python. The second and third prizes were obtained by Philammon, the son of Chrysomethis, and Thamyris, the son of Philammon. Sometimes, the crown was bestowed upon the merits of execution only, as in the case of Eleutherus, who won it purely by the power and sweetness of his voice.

That the *Pythian Games* were conducted with the greatest order and solemnity, is obvious from the circumstance, that the *Pythii*, whose especial office it was to consult the oracle at Delphi, and who, on account of their high and sacred character, were, like the kings, maintained at the public expense, always attended them in state, sitting in the most distinguished place. It is also pretty clear that they differed from the Olympiads little more than in name. They were attended by all the genius, learning, and skill, of that part of Greece in which they were celebrated, and witnessed by the most exalted and revered characters *.

---

* Among the distinguished victories gained at Delphi, and mentioned by Pausanias, are that of Pylades upon the cithara, about the 94th Pythiad ; and that of the *Pythic Laurel* obtained, according to Suetonius and Dio Cassius, by Nero, sixty-six years afterwards, and carried by that emperor to Rome. To these may be added, the two *Pythic* conquests recorded in the Oxford Marbles, and many others, which C. Ant. Septimius Publius, the Citharœdist, won, during the reign of Septimius Severus, about the end of the second century.

Plutarch informs us, that to the musical premiums given at Delphi, one for tragedy was added, in later times; and that, by degrees, a great variety of contests was admitted; among which were trials in the graphic art ; that is, exhibitions of paintings. This institution, second only to that of Olympia, continued, according to the testimony of many ancient authors, several centuries after the establishment of the Christian religion.

The NEMÆAN GAMES, first instituted by Adrastus (as already observed) were afterwards re-established and augmented, in honour of the conquest obtained by Hercules over the Nemæan lion *. They were celebrated in, or near to, the town of Nemæa, in Argolis, every third, or according to some writers, every fifth year. At these festivals, the Argives, the Corinthians, and the inhabitants of Cleonœ, generally presided, by turns. Like the Olympic and the Pythian games, they were gymnical and equestrian, as well as poetical and musical, and served as an era to the Argives and the surrounding country.

The Nemæan games were of such high antiquity, that the time of their origin is not correctly known. From the subjects of the Nemæan odes of Pindar, it is clear that their exercises corresponded with those of Olympia and Pythium. Did any doubt exist upon the subject of this institution, including in its amusements poetical and musical trials, the passage from Plutarch respecting Philopœmon and Pylades, noticed in the last chapter, would be sufficient to remove it. But the fact is, that Timotheus, and many of the most renowned of the ancient poet-musicians, exhibited their abilities at Nemæa, and that these games were conducted with

---

* This animal, born of the hundred-headed Typhon, infested the neighbourhood of Nemæa, and kept the inhabitants in perpetual alarm.

great pomp and solemnity. They were always opened with
sacrificing to Nemæan Jove, appointing that deity a priest,
and proclaiming rewards for those who should prove victors.
Till the war with the Medes, these rewards consisted of olive
crowns ; when a blow the Argives received in that struggle,
caused them to change the olive crown, for one composed
of *smallage*, a funeral plant *.

The ISTHMIAN GAMES received their names from the
Isthmus of Corinth, where they were first observed. They
were instituted as early as 1326 years before Christ; and for
many years, continued uninterrupted. Not long after their
discontinuance (the cause of which is not understood) Theseus, in honour of Neptune, whom he proclaimed to be his
father, reinstated them. But though their renewal was nominally in honour of that deity, they were really celebrated
in commemoration of Melicertes, who was changed into a
sea-god, when his mother Ino had thrown herself into the
ocean with him in her arms. According to some writers,

---

* Some attribute the first institution of these games to the following circumstances :—The seven chiefs, they say, sent to Thebes,
under the conduct of Polynices, being on their journey extremely
oppressed with thirst, met with Hypsipyle of Lemnos, who had in
her arms Opheltes, son of Lycurgus, priest of Jupiter, and Eurydice.
They requesting her to show them some water, she laid the child
down on the grass, and conducted them to a well. In her absence, a
venomous serpent killed the child; upon which the nurse, from an
excess of grief, grew desperate. The chiefs, at their return with her,
killed the serpent, buried the young Opheltes, and, to divert Hypsipyle, appointed the Nemæan Games. Those who thus account for the
origin of this institution, add, that it was always usual for an orator
to pronounce a funeral oration, in memory of the death of Opheltes;
and that those who distributed the prizes were always dressed in
mourning.

they were repeated every third year; but others say they were quinquennial; and others again assert, that they were observed every third, and every fifth year; the first order being ordained in honour of Neptune, and the second in commemoration of the son of Ino. However this may have been, the *Isthmian Games* were held so sacred and inviolable, that the greatest public calamity was not allowed to interrupt their regular observance. Combats of every kind, especially those consisting of poetical and musical rivalry, were exhibited on the Isthmus, and the victors were rewarded with garlands of pine leaves ; in lieu of which, however, in process of time, a crown of dry parsley was substituted *.

Dr. Burney has very properly detailed a narrative in Livy of an interesting event, which occurred during the celebration of these games, after the defeat of Philip of Macedon, who had been in possession of the principal part of Greece. The account is as follows :—

" The time," says Livy, " for observing the *Isthmian Games* had now arrived. There was always a great concourse of people at them, from the natural curiosity of the Greeks, who delighted in witnessing all kinds of combats and bodily exercises, as well as from the conveniences of the situation, between two seas, for the inhabitants of the different provinces to assemble. But being, at this time, anxious to know their own fate, and that of their country, all Greece flocked thither, the greater part silently foreboding the worst, and some not scrupling openly to express their fears. At length the Romans took their places at the games, and a herald, with a trumpet, in the usual manner,

---

* Plutarch and Strabo say, that after a time, the wreath of pine-leaves was resumed, and that to this was added a reward of one hundred silver drachmæ.

advanced into the middle of the Arena, as if to pronounce the common form of words ; but when silence was ordered, he proclaimed, *that the Roman senate and people, and T. Quintius Flaminius, their general, after vanquishing Philip and his Macedonians, declared the Corinthians, Phocœans, all the Locrians, the island Eubœa, the Magnesians, Thessalonians, Perrhœbi, Achœans, and Phthiotes, all which states had been possessed by Philip, were free, independent, and subject only to their own laws.* The joy of the whole assembly, on hearing this proclamation, was too great to be expressed. The spectators could scarcely credit what they heard ; they regarded each other with astonishment, as if they had waked out of a dream. Each diffident of his own ears, with what particularly concerned himself and his own country, inquired of his neighbour what had been said. The herald was even called back, so strong a desire had they all, not only to hear, but to see again the messenger of their liberty; and they had the satisfaction to hear him repeat the decree. When the news was fully confirmed, they expressed their joy in such loud and reiterated shouts of applause, that it was evident, liberty was dearer to them than all the other advantages of life *."

So long as paganism continued to be the established religion of Greece, the *Isthmian Games,* by which the years were reckoned, as among the Romans from the consular government, were celebrated with great magnificence and splendor ; and even when Corinth was sacked and burnt by Mummius, they were not omitted †.

---

* Plutarch, (*v. T. Flamin.*) says the shouts of the people on this occasion, were so loud, that some crows which happened to be flying over their heads. *fell dead* into the Stadium.

† These games were of such celebrity, and the concourse at them

The PANATHENÆAN GAMES, so denominated, because established in honour of Minerva, the patroness of *Athens*, were first appointed by Orpheus, and called *Athenæa:* but Theseus afterwards renewed, or re-modelled them, when they were celebrated by *all* the tribes of Athens, and received the appellation by which they have been since distinguished.

In the first year of their institution, these festivals were observed only during one day; but subsequently, the time was prolonged, and the celebration was conducted with great pomp and solemnity. Horse-races and foot-races, with torches, dances by boys in armour, and gymnical trials, followed by musical contentions on the harp and flute, (first ordained by Pericles*) constituted the exhibitions in which the first musical victor was the lyrist Phrynis of Mitylene †.

---

was so great, that only the prime persons of the most distinguished cities could have places at them. The Athenians had only as much space allotted them, as the sail of a ship, which they sent yearly to Delos, could cover.

* Pericles, once a disciple of the musician Damon, and an excellent musical performer himself, and than whom antiquity cannot boast a more accomplished character, was equally a judge and encourager of all the arts. Plutarch, in the life of this illustrious man, tells us, "that the Muses bore a principal share in all the public spectacles with which he entertained the people. Not only did he regulate and augment the poetical and musical conflicts at the *Panathenæan Games*, but built the Odeum, or music-room, in which poets and musicians daily exercised themselves in their art, and rehearsed new compositions, before they were performed in the theatre. And it is worthy of notice, that it was Pericles who invited to Athens the renowned *Antigenides*.

† In the songs, they celebrated the generous undertaking of Harmodius and Aristogiton, who opposed the Pisistratidæ, and of Thrasybulus, who delivered Athens from its thirty tyrants.

Homer's poems were sung; aud the poets contended in four plays, called from their number, *Tetralogia.* Conquest was rewarded with a vessel of oil, and a crown made of the olives which grew in the groves of Academus, and were sacred to Minerva. The rites and ceremonies were of the most sumptuous and magnificent description. In the procession, Minerva's sacred *Peplus*, or white garment, without sleeves, and woven by a select number of virgins, was borne along by them, attended by two young girls under eleven years of age, attired in white, ornamented with gold : and no person was permitted to appear in dyed hal iliments.

At the period of celebrating the *Panathenæan Games*, it was usual to proclaim a general amnesty in favour of prisoners, and to present golden crowns to such as had deserved well of their country. Of these festivals there were two kinds ; the greater, exhibited every five years, and the lesser, observed every three years. The greater festivals were more splendid and pompous than the lesser. In the greater, it was that the grand procession of the *Peplus* was observed, the ceremonies of which were too important and imposing not to demand particular notice in this account of the chief Grecian games.

In the *ceramicus* *, without the city, an engine was erected in the form of a ship, upon which Minerva's garment, embroidered with gold, and having upon it the representation of the achievements of the goddess, was suspended as a sail; and the whole, put in motion by subterraneous machines, was conveyed to the temple of Ceres Eleusinia, and thence to the citadel, where the *Peplus* was placed upon Minerva's statue, which was laid upon a bed woven, or

---

* A bay of Caria, now called *Keramo*, which received its original name from *Ceramus*, a town in its vicinity.

strewed, with flowers. Persons of all ages, of every sex and every quality, attended the procession, which was preceded by old men and women, carrying olive branches in their hands, and followed by men of full age, bearing shields and spears, and attended by a certain number of foreigners. After these, came the women, accompanied by the wives of the foreigners. Then succeeded young men crowned with millet, and singing hymns to the goddess ; and after them select virgins of the noblest families, carrying baskets filled with articles necessary for the celebration, and attended by the daughters of the foreigners, who bore in their hands umbrellas and little seats ; and boys in uniforms brought up the rear *.

To the particulars which have been mentioned in this account of the five principal *public games,* or festivals of ancient Greece, it is proper to add some notice of the *orations,* the delivery of which formed a part of the solemn portion of the ceremonies of them all. These included each kind, or province of the art; the demonstrative, deliberative, and judicial, including every subdivision of each ; of which subdivisions, however, the principal were the *panegyrical,* or laudatory, the originator of which is not known; and the *epicedial,* or funeral, first introduced by Solon. To render the *panegyrics* the more solemn and imposing, the speakers commenced with the eulogy of the deity, or monarch, or hero, in whose honour the *games* were celebrated ; then they descended to the praise of the people of the country where the festival was held ; then to the presiding magistrates, and then to the victors in the various contests. They were preceded, or followed, and sometimes both, by hymns, or other

---

* It was the custom in this and every quinquennial festival, to pray for the prosperity of the Platæans, whose services had been so conspicuous at the battle of Marathon.

vocal performances, analogous to the orator's subject, and thus were so connected with the musical part of the exhibitions as to render some remarks upon them not only relevant, but necessary, in a chapter, the object of which has been to elucidate, *generally*, the character, extent, and tendency, of the principal GRECIAN GAMES, and *especially* whatever in them bears any relation to the subject of this History.

CHAP. IX.

THE ANCIENT MUSICAL THEORISTS, AND THEIR WORKS.

No national ordinations more important to the progress of the ancient music, could, perhaps, have occurred, than those which formed the subject of the preceding chapter. The *Grecian Games,* by exciting universal emulation, and rewarding real merit, went directly to the two grand means for promoting improvement, both in theory and execution. Genius and science, taste and skill, were produced to the light; excellencies were displayed and applauded, and defects exposed and disapproved. Yet then, as now (and, no doubt, as ever) licences were occasionally permitted which not only deviated from general taste and propriety, but disturbed both the measure and sense of the verse. The strings of the lyre, and the holes of the flute, increased in number, tempted even Lasus, Timotheus, and Phrynis, to admit irregularities in their verse, for the purpose of exercising their augmented powers of performance. Aristotle, disgusted at these innovations, declares his disapprobation in the strongest terms. " I hate," says the philosopher, " the difficulties and tricks practised at the public festivals, where the musician, instead of recollecting what is the object of his talent, endeavours only to flatter the corrupt taste of the multitude."

Plato, Aristoxenus, and Plutarch, all theorists, make

similar complaints : and Athenæus gives a passage from the second of these writers, which represents him saying, " I and a few others, recollecting what music once was, and considering what it now is, imitate the people of Possidonium, who annually celebrate a festival after the Greek manner, in order to keep up the memory of what they once were ; and before they depart, with tears, deplore the barbarous state to which they are brought by the Tuscans and Romans." That the ancient Greek musicians, like the musicians of every other age and country, might, by their increased power of execution, be sometimes seduced into extravagances, is extremely probable; and that a misplaced vanity might bring such extravagances before the public, and that they might find too much indulgence from the public taste, we will not dispute ; but if these eccentricities offended, by quitting the prescribed tract, they often led to the discovery of a new soil, brought to view unknown beauties, and spread and diversified the scene of science. The enemy to innovation is a foe to improvement. Without innovation, the strings of the lyre could never have been multiplied, and the world must have been contented with a monochord : without innovation, the holes of the flute would be still confined to their first number ; nay, it must have remained without any perforations at all : and again, without innovation, science itself must have stood still, or rather, never have had birth ; or being born, could not have been cherished, strengthened, maturated, brought from infancy to youth, from youth to manhood, and set fairly on its journey towards perfection ; and then our species had been unbenefited by the mental powers of such singularly-gifted men as Pythagoras, Lasus, Aristoxenus, Euclid, Didymus, and Ptolemy ; *theorists* whose learning and labours we are about to consider.

PYTHAGORAS.

Pythagoras, born at Samos, the son of a person of distinction, capable of giving him a superior education, blended with his other numerous studies, those of poetry and music. Not content with the knowledge to be acquired in his own country, he travelled into Egypt * and Chaldea, whence, after collecting whatever was to be learnt from the priests and their symbolic writings, upon the subjects of science and general policy, he returned, to adorn and instruct his native island, where he was publicly saluted with the name of *sophist*, or wise man; but he preferred to be called a *philosopher*, or lover of wisdom †. After visiting the republics of Elis and Sparta, he retired to Magna Græcia, where he fixed his habitation in the town of Crotona. It was here that he founded the sect afterwards denominated *the Italian*. His knowledge and skill in music, medicine, mathematics, and na-

---

* " At the Olympic Games," said Pythagoras, " some are attracted by the desire of obtaining crowns and honours, while curiosity draws others, and a wish to contemplate whatever deserves notice in that celebrated assembly: thus, on the more extensive theatre of the world, while many struggle for renown, and numbers pant for the advantages of fortune, a few, and, indeed, a few only, who are neither desirous of money, nor ambitious of fame, are sufficiently gratified, to be spectators of the wonder, the hurry, and the magnificence of the scene."

† The numbers this *Theorist* assigned to the several sonorous proportions, have been given in a former chapter. But how much of his system was founded on experiment, and sanctioned by demonstration, cannot now be ascertained. The great obstruction that Pythagoras had to encounter in this profound research, was in the difficulty of determining and comparing the respective bearings of vibrations, the least velocities of which are too quick to be counted, or even distinguished.

tural philosophy drew round him a great number of pupils, and friends and admirers, even amidst the voluptuousness that prevailed among the inhabitants of that place, whose manners his lessons of morality and wisdom quickly reformed. His venerable aspect, harmonious voice, persuasive eloquence, and extensive knowledge, combined with the reputation acquired by his travels, and the prizes he had obtained at the Olympic games, secured the esteem and admiration of all, especially of his pupils, among whom his authority was such, that in any dispute among themselves, the weight of any assertion depended upon whether *the master said so ;* an expression which became proverbial, in *jurare in verba magistri.*

Pythagoras considered *numbers* as the principles of every thing ; and perceived in them, the regularity, correspondence, beauty, and harmony, given to the universe, by its Creator. The importance he attributed to numbers, formed the ground of his inquiry respecting musical proportion, and led him to the discovery of the numbers expressive of the relations of the sounds produced by the blacksmith's hammers : a discovery to which music originally owed the honourable appellation of science. Perceiving that sound, considered in respect of the vibrations from which it resulted, was reducible to appreciable quantities, he made it the subject of arithmetical calculation ; and by the aid of numerical characters, rendered the ratios of those quantities *visible.*

This discovery did not only give birth to various *inaudible* species of music, under the denomination of *Divine, Mundane,* and *Elementary,* but led to the considering of musical ratios as the types of order and proportion in all things. *Harmony* was pronounced to include in itself the essence of virtue, friendship, good government, celestial motion, the human soul, and God himself *. Accordingly, Aristides Quintilianus assures us, that music comprehends arithmetic, geometry, physics, and metaphysics ; and teaches every principle appertaining to the nature of the soul, and the construction of the universe: and in confirmation of this doctrine, quotes from a writer of the name of Panacmus, a " *divine saying*," comprehending a most curious account of the *end* and *business* of music, and informing us, that its province is not only to arrange congruous sounds, but to unite and harmonize every thing in nature.

Nothing is more certain, than that Pythagoras regarded Music as something celestial and divine; and that he considered it as conducive to health, and the composure of the mind. For these salutary effects, it appears, vocal music was preferred to instrumental, and that of the lyre to the melody of the flute †. From the Egyptians he borrowed the custom, and uniformly adopted it, of having his pupils lulled to sleep every night, and waked every morning, by the soothing appeal of sweet sounds.

From the school of Pythagoras sprang many illustrious *Musical Theorists,* most of whom left treatises behind them that long continued to be studied as the great guides to

---

* Fortunately, both Philosophy and Music have since been contented with an earthly abode. The one is limited to principles that mortals can understand, and the other to sounds that human ears can receive.

† The reason given for these preferences is, that the music of the lyre was more decent and sedate than that of the flute ; and that the lyre allowed the performer to add to the quantity of its sounds, the sense and sweetness of verse, the influence of poetry, and the beauty of articulation.

science and truth.   But the genius of this sage, not circumscribed to speculation, suggested practical improvements.
Among these, was the addition of an eighth string to the
lyre, the scale of which, till his time, was that of Terpander,
comprising only a *heptachord*, or series of seven sounds *.
To a *musical*, rather than a *general* biography of the Samian
philosopher, the other numerous particulars concerning him
transmitted to us by Diogenes, Porphyry, Iamblicus, and
other ancient authors, have been deemed superfluous.   According to most chronologers, Pythagoras died 497 years
before Christ, at the age of seventy-one.

LASUS.

Lasus, who, according to Suidas, was a native of Her-
mione, a city of Peloponnesus, in the kingdom of Argos,
flourished in the fifty-eighth Olympiad; that is, 548 years
before the Christian era.   Of all the *Musical Theorists*,
he is the most ancient.   His industry, however, was not
confined to speculation; the *practice* of music had a large
share of his attention, and also, of course, poetical exercises.
In these he excelled all his cotemporaries: and had the
honour of being the first who introduced dithyrambic composition, and circular dances in the public games; the merit
of which inventions was rewarded with a premium †.   Poetry
and mathematics were the predominant objects of his medita-

---

* Many ancient writers are of opinion, that previous to the addition
of this eighth string, the scale of the lyre contained two *conjoint tetrachords*, E, F, G, A; A, B flat, C, D; and that Pythagoras, by super-
adding a sound, and varying the pitch of the fifth, (B flat) constructed
a new system, as follows : E, F, G, A; B (natural) C, D, E, forming
two *disjunct tetrachords*.

† Plutarch says he was the first who changed any thing in the
ancient music.

tions; in all which faculties he not only shone himself, but endeavoured to promote their cultivation in others; and for this purpose, established periodical conferences, or what we should now term *convcrzationi* *.

Of the circular choruses, or dances, some, denying him the honour of the authorship, will only allow him the merit of their improvement, insisting that *Arion* was the inventor; and this, indeed, is as much as the scholiast Aristophanes, pretends to demonstrate †.

Though *Lasus* lived to a good old age, the events of his life now known, unfortunately, are but few. Among those which time has not buried in oblivion, we meet with one incident, which does as much honour to his moral principles as to his sagacity. He detected and exposed a *holy fraud.* Herodotus, in his *Polymnia*, or seventh book, informs us, that the poet Onomacritus (to whom some ascribe the compositions generally attributed to Orpheus) pretending to find oracular predictions in the verses of Musæus, for *the curious in futurity*, Lasus discovered that the supposed diviner was in the habit of surreptitiously foisting into the text of Musæus, such presages as pleased his fancy, or suited his interest. Instigated by one of these motives, the impostor inserted in the verses, the prediction, *that all the islands in the neighbourhood of Lemnos would be swallowed up.* This abuse of the credulous, Lasus developed, and Hypparchus, with whose confidence Onomacritus had long been honoured, banished him from Athens.

---

* In meetings established by *one of the Seven Sages of Greece*, not only music and poetry, but general philosophy, and every science, no doubt, would be among the subjects of discussion.

† Of these dances, which were performed round the altar, both the poetry and the music were dithyrambic.

Though only a few fragments of Lasus have reached our times, his productions, both in poetry and music, appear to have been numerous. Athenæus speaks of a hymn written by Lasus, in which the *sigma,* or letter S is wholly omitted; and also of an ode, entitled *The Centaurs,* from which the same consonant has been carefully excluded. This aversion to a letter, which, in verse, never can occur too rarely, proves at least the extraordinary delicacy of an ear which could not be gratified in this particular, but at the expense of much labour and patience.

The musical discoveries of Lasus were valuable at the time they were made, and deserve to be mentioned. I record them in the words of Dr. Burney.

" First," says the Doctor, " Aristoxenus, in speaking of the nature of sound, attributes to Lasus, in common with certain Epigonians, a heterodox opinion, that *sound had a latitude.* Meibomius is perplexed by the passage, but is inclined to think it means only, that in sustaining a note, the voice varied a little upward and downward, and did not *strictly* keep to one *mathematical line* of tone. This explication, however, is not satisfactory; for the expression naturally leads to the idea of a *temperant;* and seems to say, that the intonation of the scale admitted of some variety; in other words, that the exact ratio of intervals might be departed from without offending the ear *. And what is said of Lasus by Plutarch, in his Dialogue on Music, ren-

---

* A passage of Galen, quoted by Dr. Smith in his Harmonics, sanctions this idea. " It is probable," says the philosopher, " that in the lyre, the *accurate* tuning is one, and individual; but the *practical* tuning admits of latitude." Though the ancient *Theorists* do not speak of *temperament*, this remark of Galen goes far to show, that they had such a resource for accommodating the intervals of their several scales.

ders this idea still more probable. He is there mentioned as a great innovator, who imitated the *compass* and *variety* of wind instruments; as well as Epigonius, who was the inventor of the instrument of forty strings. Among the corruptions complained of in the *new* Music, the frequent and licentious transitions from one mode and genus to another, were not the least. If, therefore, the object of this multiplication of strings may be supposed to have been the convenience of having an instrument ready tuned for all the modes, like our piano-forte, it seems probable that both Lasus and Epigonius might have been *temperers*, and have accommodated their *doctrine* to their *practice*.

Secondly, Theon of Smyrna testifies, that Lasus, as well as the Pythagorean Hippasus of Metapontus, made use of two vases of the same size and tone, in order to calculate the exact ratio or proportion of concords. For, by having one of the vases empty, and filling the other half full of water, he made them octaves to each other : and filling one a fourth part full, and the other a third, he produced by the percussion of the two vessels, the concords of fourth and fifth; from which process resulted the proportions of these three concords contained in the numbers 1, 2, 3, 4 *.

Thirdly, Lasus, according to Plutarch, introduced a dithyrambic licence, or irregularity, into musical measure, or rhythm; and upon his lyre, imitated the compass and variety of the flute.

---

* The fallacy of this theory modern experiment has evinced. Most glasses, by being half filled with water, become lowered one whole tone; and when quite filled, are found to drop about a major sixth. The musical instrument suggested to Mr. Delaval, by the tones produced from drinking-glasses, by Mr. Puckeridge of Ireland, and the improvement upon that instrument by Dr. Franklin, have shown, that the tones do not vary in the proportions stated by Lasus.

We are not to wonder, if, in an age when music was in its infancy, false calculations sometimes supplied the place of true discovery; but should rather, in candour, admit even the ingenuity of failure, and applaud every aim at scientific advancement: again, if, in times when mechanical improvements were tardy, and innovation, if not a crime, a subject of censure, invention suggested an extended system of sounds, new powers of execution, or a more varied and emphatic expression, we are but just, in admitting the claims of this *Musical Theorist* to our honourable notice. His productions, we find, were numerous, and of a quality to excite the admiration of his countrymen. He cultivated the mathematics; the poetical Muse was indulgent to his ambition: and musicians, both theoretical and practical, were indebted to his labour and his ingenuity.

ARISTOXENUS.

Aristoxenus, born at Tarentum, in Italy, about A. M. 3610, one of the disciples of Aristotle, and deeply versed in music, philosophy, and history, was the son of a musician. He first studied under his father; but subsequently, and successively, became the pupil of Lamprius, Erythræus, Xenophilus, and lastly, of the philosopher of Stagira, whom he expected to succeed in his school, but had the mortification to see its presidency left to Theophrastus, which excited his disgust, and prejudiced him against his illustrious master. He wrote on the above branches of learning four hundred and fifty-three volumes, among which were treatises on various parts of music; as the rhythmic, the metric, the organic, and the elements of harmonics; of all which, however, the only remains are his THREE BOOKS on the latter of these subjects *.

---

* Yet the writings of Aristoxenus on other subjects, are frequently quoted by ancient authors.

In the *first* of these, the *Theorist* gives the explanation of the genera, and of their colours, or species; and some general definitions of terms, particularly those of *sound*, *interval*, and *system*. His *second* contains an assertion, which, however unintelligible at this day, is to be found in the writings of all the ancient philosophers; viz. that music has a tendency to improve or corrupt the morals *.

Aristoxenus did not think, with Pythagoras, that the understanding is the ultimate judge of intervals; and that no system can justly be called harmonical, unless there be in it a mathematical coincidence. On the contrary, he expressly asserts in his second book, that " by the external sense, we judge of the magnitude of an interval, and by the understanding, consider, and decide upon, its several powers." And, again, he says, " the nature of melody is best discovered by the perception of sense, and is retained by the memory; and there is no other way of arriving at the knowledge of music :" and further, he observes, " that as it is not necessary for him who writes an iambic, to attend to the arithmetical proportions of the feet of which it is composed, so it is not necessary for him who composes a Phrygian cantus, to attend to the ratio of the sounds proper thereto." This position is obviously accurate. The musical composer takes his stand between the mere practitioner, and the philosophical theorist; and, as in order to his composing well, it is not indispensable that he should be a performer, neither is there any necessity for his being acquainted with the laws of generated sound. In fact, sounds are not music, scientifi-

---

* Plutarch is strenuous in the support of this opinion; and Aristophanes, in his CLOUDS, puts into the mouth of *Justice*, a speech to the same effect. Add to this, that it is well known what effects the Spartans attributed to Music, since they made it an essential in the education of their youth.

cally speaking, but only the elements of music; and with respect to the composer, are precisely as colours to the painter; materials, with the effects of which, by their artificial order and disposition, he is immediately concerned; but whose origin and occult constitution, need not employ his meditation *.

Proceeding on this ground of reasoning, Aristoxenus, in direct opposition to the Pythagoreans, persisted in relying on the ear, as the ultimate judge of the measure, both of the consonants and dissonants; and estimated both, not by ratios, but intervals. His opponents were equally pertinacious in affirming, that the same consonants and dissonants were to be judged of, not by intervals, but ratios; and the principles upon which the two parties defended their opinions, became subjects of violent contention. The consequence of this discrepancy, so far as it related to music, was, that for a long while, musicians, according as they adopted the one or the other of these doctrines, were denominated Pythagoreans, or Aristoxenians.

Against the position of Pythagoras there certainly lay a strong objection, inasmuch as, by wholly consulting the reason, and not the ear, it accommodated harmonical proportions to incongruous intervals. And if Aristoxenus carried his principle to the extent of entirely rejecting reason, which they asserted he did, his dictum was erroneous; since by referring to the sense alone, he rendered the very fundamental laws of the harmonical science incapable of demonstration †.

---

* This *Musical Theorist* was not always equally correct and perspicuous. Cicero and others have so often pronounced his works unintelligible, that we are almost obliged to conclude, he did not constantly comprehend himself.

† Ptolemy, who undertook the task of reviewing this controversy,

The power of Aristoxenus to hold a contest with the principles and reasoning of Pythagoras was highly honourable to his abilities and learning : and it would, perhaps, be as great an injustice to the first as to the latter, not to acknowledge, that their physical tenets concerning the production of sound, and the causes of gravity and acuteness, have been confirmed by modern philosophy : and their metaphysical speculations on the foundation and nature of consonance, approved and adopted by modern writers of no inconsiderable reputation.

The titles of several of the lost works of this *Musical Theorist*, quoted by Athenæus and others, have been collected by Meursius, in his notes upon this author ; and by Tonsus and Menage. Those which concern Music are the following :

1. Of Performers on the Flute, and concerning Flutes and other Musical Instruments.
2. Of the Manner of boring or piercing Flutes.
3. Of Music in general *.
4. Of the Tragic Dance.

EUCLID.

This great geometrician and *Musical Theorist*, flourished about 277 years before Christ. He distinguished himself by his writings on the sciences of music and mathematics. His fifteen books of problems and theorems, with demonstrations, in which he digests and regulates all the pure fundamental principles taught by Thales, Pythagoras, Eudoxus, and other illustrious philosophers, are well known to the

---

very accurately discriminates the several offices of reason and sense ; that is, the sense of hearing.

* This, a different work from his Harmonics, was devoted to the *rhythmical, metrical, organical, poetical,* and *hypocritical* parts of *Music,* combined with a *History of Music and Musicians.*

learned. Besides these, he produced an *Introduction to Harmonics*, followed by his *Section of the Canon*, a tract comprising clear definitions of the several parts of Greek music *.

In this little but valuable treatise, Euclid displays all the closeness, clearness, and method of the mathematician. The sense is compressed, but satisfactory; the words are few, but every word conveys information. No work upon the ancient music has come down, at once so dense and lucid, so limited in language, and pregnant with intelligence. If his object was (and such it appears to have been) to reduce to a scientific and elementary abridgment, the more diffused speculations of Aristoxenus, and, in a degree, to make the work his own, that object he has accomplished. But he has effected more than this, in as far as he has been to Aristoxenus, what D'Alembert was to Rameau, not only an abridger, but a corrector.

Till, in his *Section of the Canon*, Euclid gave his demonstration concerning the magnitude of the octave, it was not known that that interval consisted of somewhat less than six whole tones : nor, till he made the discovery, was it conceived that a fourth is less than two tones and a half, and a fifth not equal to three and a half †.

Euclid established a school at Alexandria, which became so famous, that from his age to the time of the Saracen

---

* This work, professing to treat of *Sounds, Intervals, Genera, Systems, Keys, Mutations,* and *Melopœia,* as the seven parts of which Music consists, would alone be sufficient to show, that the Greek music was limited to *melody.*

† But though this proves the necessity of a temperament upon instruments whose tones are fixed, he gives no rule for one : and this has been urged by some modern writers, in support of the opinion, that such instruments were not generally used by the ancients.

conquest, no mathematician was found, who had not studied there.

He enjoyed the intimacy and esteem of Plato, who, on being asked concerning the building an altar at Athens, referred his inquirers to *The mathematician at Alexandria.*

DIDYMUS.

This musician, the immediate precursor of Ptolemy, is entitled to a place in a History of Music, were it only on account of his being the first who introduced into the scale the *minor tone,* and, by consequence, the practical major third, which harmonized the whole system, and pointed out the road to counter-point.

Didymus was a cotemporary with the emperor Nero, and studied at Alexandria. He wrote upon grammar and medicine, as well as upon music : and though his works are all lost, his fame has lived, and a dispute between him and Ptolemy, produced so much notice in that writer, of his harmonical doctrines, that the essence of them may be said to have been preserved. Ptolemy confesses that Didymus was well versed in the *canon* and *harmonic divisions;* therefore, judging even from the testimony of an antagonist, he must have been an able *Musical Theorist;* and is, perhaps, besides being the rival of Ptolemy in his own province of study, better entitled than Guido, to the glory of being the original founder of modern *harmony,* or *music in parts* *.

Doni says, that the best species of diapason, and that which is the most replete with harmony, was that invented by Didymus. Ptolemy, however, objects to it as not ac-

---

* Guido, by his *Mycrologus,* seems, both in theory and practice, to have scrupulously abided by this division of the scale into *major tones and limmas.*

cording with the judgment of the ear. This being a question of the *sense* rather than of science, it is the office of the sense, rather than of science, to determine it. But what shall we hope from so capricious an arbiter? Modern ears are best pleased with *Ptolemy's* arrangement: in the seventeenth century, the diapason of Didymus was preferred.

PTOLEMY.

Ptolemy (or Claudius Ptolemeus) according to Suidas, and the evidence in his own *Magnæ Syntaxis*, flourished in the reign of the Emperor Marcus Aurelius Antoninus; that is, about the middle of the second century of the Christian era. He was born at Pelusium, anciently the principal key of Egypt. Learned in music, as well as astronomy, he constituted new scales *, corrected those of former times, and wrote a number of treatises on the harmonic science, one of which, in three books, is copious and profound. In the first chapter of the first book of this work, yielding as, indeed, he too often does, to the suggestions of a luxuriant and uncontrolled imagination, he assigns the criterion of harmony, which he makes to be sense and reason: the former of these, he tells us, discovers what is nearly allied to truth, and sanctions that which is accurate; as the latter ascertains the accurate, and approves whatever is allied to truth. In the third chapter, treating of the causes of acuteness and gravity, he compares the windpipe to a flute; and remarks, as a subject of wonder, that power or

---

* He suggested no fewer than three new forms of the diatonic scale. Five others were invented by Archytas of Tarentum, Aristoxenus, Eratosthenes, and Didymus; most of which, however, according to our present ideas of harmony and temperament, seem but to differ in deformity.

faculty which enables a singer readily and instantaneously to hit those degrees of dilatation and contraction necessary to the production of sounds in any given proportion of grave or acute. In the sixth chapter, we find him condemning the Pythagoreans, and in the ninth, the Aristoxenians, in their adjustments of the consonances: the former, as not sufficiently attending to the ear, the latter, as submitting all to the determination of the external sense. For the correction of the different methods employed by these two sects, he contrived an instrument of the most simple construction, and, in truth, nothing more than a monochord, which he called the *harmonic canon*, and which has preserved that appellation in the writings of succeeding authors.

How the *monochord* of Pythagoras was constructed, is not known; but whatever were its form and divisions, Ptolemy charges the followers of that philosopher with not knowing how to reason about the consonances *. At the same time, he condemns the division of Aristoxenus, as well as that of Archytas of Tarentum, whose definition of the genera by the interjacent intervals, rather than by the ratios of the sounds themselves, he heavily censures.

Ptolemy, gifted with a facility in calculation, seems to have delighted in speculations upon the *scale*. Having tried many systems, it is, perhaps, no subject of wonder, that he should have hit upon one that should become permanent; nor does it follow, as some have hastily concluded, that because it suits our present practice, *counterpoint* was among its objects, or that Ptolemy had arrived at the conception of that advanced state of composition.

It is but just to say, that this distinguished astronomer

---

* The scale of the Pythagoreans, as the Abbé Roussier has shewn, consisted of a series of perfect fifths.

and musician, was the most learned, close, and philosophical writer among the younger Greeks. On the subject of the sonorous science, he appears to have had the merit of being unshackled by authority ; and not to have been deficient in a just and manly sense of the superiority of his own know-ledge and discernment *. Candour, however, must confess, that too confident a reliance on his own powers sometimes led Ptolemy into eccentricities : and that as often as he set his foot within the beloved circle of imagination, the philosopher was transformed by its magic into a visionary. Then it was, that, deserting accurate reasoning and demonstration, he was the sport of his own dreams ; saw music in the human soul, and the celestial motions ; discovered the principle of con-cupiscence in the eighth, fifth, and fourth of the octave, and found that some of the human virtues were *diatonic*, some *chromatic*, and others *enharmonic*.

GERASENUS.

This philosopher and musician, the author of an Intro-duction to Harmony, lived in the last century before Christ, and was born in Gerasa, in Arabia, from which city he de-rived his name. *Nichomachus Gerasenus* was a follower of Pythagoras ; and it is by the above work that we know how his master discovered the consonances Professing, in his book, to be a Pythagorean, he considers the human voice as emit-ting sounds which are commensurable by intervals, as when

---

* The ruling law with the ancients seems to have been that of keeping unmoved the *soni stabiles* of the *tetrachords;* that is, the sounds forming the extremities of their fourths : but in the disposi-tion of the two intermediate sounds, they often yielded to the sugges-tions of unguided caprice. Hence all the various colours, or shades, of the three genera.

we are said to sing; or incommensurable, as when we converse by the medium of speech. In this latter use of the voice, he says, we are not restricted by any rule ; but that in the former, we are bound to an observance of those intervals in which harmony consists.

Deluded by the prevailing extravagances of the imagination, Gerasenus supposed the sounds and their names to be taken from the seven planets in the heavens which surround this earth; for it is said, observes he, that all bodies which are carried round with any considerable degree of velocity, must necessarily cause a sound, weaker or stronger, more grave, or more acute, according to their several magnitudes and celerities, or the repression of the orb wherein they act. The system he builds on this fantastic idea is curious. The motion of Saturn, the most distant from us, says he, produces the gravest sound ; and that of the moon, the lowest of the orbs, the acutest sound. He then proceeds to expound the analogy between the motions of the other planets and the intermediate chords *.

This treatise, written at the request of some learned female cotemporary, to whom the work is expressly dedicated, contains all the musical knowledge of the time in which it was written, and proves the author to have been a profound theorist; though, both by its internal evidence, as well as by his own confession, it is but the part of a work he intended to write. What other works Gerasenus produced, and when and where he died, is not known.

---

* The ancients were not unanimously of opinion that the graver sounds were produced by the bodies of greatest magnitude. Cicero, in particular, is by Glareanus (in his Dodecachordon) said to have maintained, that the lesser bodies produce the gravest sounds, and the greater the more acute.

PLUTARCH.

Plutarch, a native of Chæronea, and descended of a respectable family, was not only a philosopher, mathematician, and historian, but one of the most distinguished of the ancient theoretical musicians. After travelling to Egypt and Greece in quest of knowledge, he returned to Rome, where he opened a school, and where he continued to dwell, till the death of his imperial patron, Trajan, who was so sensible of his great abilities, as to honour him with the office of consul. Soon after this event, he returned to Chæronea, where he closely applied himself to study, and wrote the greater part of his works; among which we find his *Symposiacs*, a discourse containing more of the history of ancient music and musicians, than is to be met with any where else. It is written in dialogue, and is truly curious. The speakers are *Onesicrates, Soterichus,* and *Lysias;* the latter of whom, at the request of Onesicrates, gives a relation of the origin and progress of the harmonic science, down to the time at which he writes, which would alone almost furnish a substitute for its regular history. Not to insert this composition, would be to omit the most satisfactory elucidation of which the several accounts of the Grecian music are capable.

" According to the assertion of Heraclides," says the interlocutor, Lysias, " Amphion, the son of Jupiter and Antiope, was the inventor of the harp, and of lyric poesy; and in the same age, Linus the Eubean composed elegies; Anthes of Anthedon, in Bœotia, was the author of hymns, and Pierius of Pieria, of verses in honour of the Muses; Philammon the Delphian also wrote a poem, in celebration of the nativity of Latona, Diana, and Apollo; and was the original institutor of the dances performed before the temple of Delphos. Thamyris, of Thracian extraction, had the finest voice, and was the best singer of his time; for which reason he is by the poets feigned to have contended with the Muses; he wrought into a poem the war of the Titans against the gods. Demodocus the Corcyrean, wrote in verse the history of the destruction of Troy, and the nuptials of Vulcan and Venus. To him succeeded Phemius of Ithaca, who composed a poem upon the return of those who came back with Agamemnon from the siege of Troy; and besides that these poems were severally written by the person above named, they were also set to musical notes by their respective authors. The same Heraclides also writes, that Terpander was the institutor of those laws by which the metre of verses, and, consequently, the musical measure, were regulated: and according to these rules, he set musical notes, both to his own and Homer's words, and sung them at the public games, to the music of the lyre. Clonas, an epic and elegiac poet, taking Terpander for his example, constituted rules which should adjust and govern the tuning and the melody of flutes, or pipes, and similar wind instruments; and in this, he was followed by Polymnestes the Colophonian.

" Timotheus is said to have made lyric preludes to his epic poems, and to have first introduced the dithyrambic, a melody adapted to the songs in the praise of Bacchus, which songs required a violent motion of the body, and certain diversities in the measure.

" Terpander, one of the most ancient of musicians, is recorded to have been four times a victor at the Pythian games.

" Alexander the historian informs us, that Olympus brought into Greece the practice of touching the strings of the lyre with a quill; for before his time, they were vibrated by the fingers: and that Hyagnis was the first that sung to the pipe, and Marsyas, his son, the next; and that both these were prior to Olympus. He farther says, that Terpander imitated Homer in his verses, and Orpheus in his music ; but that Orpheus imitated no one. That Clonas, who was some time later than Terpander, was, as the Arcadians affirm, a native of Tegea, a city of Arcadia ; though others contend that he was born in Thebes ; and that after Terpander and Clonas, flourished Archilochus : yet some writers affirm, that Ardalus the Troezenian, taught wind music before Clonas.

" The music appropriated to the lyre under the regulations of Terpander, continued without any variation, till Phrynis, who altered both the ancient rules, and the form of the instrument to which they were adapted, had acquired considerable fame.

" Olympus, a Phrygian, and a player on the flute, invented a certain measure in honour of Apollo, which he called Polycephalus, or of many heads. This Olympus, as it is said, was descended from the first Olympus, the son of Marsyas, who, taught by his father to play on the flute, first brought into Greece the laws of harmony. Others ascribe the invention of the Polycephalus to Crates, the disciple of Olympus. The same Olympus was the author of the Harmatian mood (as Glaucus testifies in his treatise of the ancient poets) and, as some think, also of the Orthian mood. There was another mood in use among the ancients, termed *Crodias*, in which Hipponax the Mimnermian greatly delighted. Sarcados of Argos, being himself a good poet, composed the music to several odes and elegies, and became thrice a victor at the Pythian games. It is said that this Sacadas, in conjunction with Polymnestes, invented three of the moods, the Dorian, the Phrygian, and the Lydian; and that the former composed a strophe, the music of which was a commixture of all the three. The original constitution of the modes was, undoubtedly, by Terpander, at Sparta ; but it was much improved by Thales the

Gortynian, Xenedamus the Cytherean, Xenocritus the Locrian, and Polymnestes the Colophonian.

"Aristoxenus ascribes to Olympus the invention of the enharmonic genus; for before his time, there were no other than the diatonic and chromatic genera.

"As to the measures of time, they were invented at different periods, and by different persons. Terpander, amongst other improvements which he made in music, introduced those grave and decent measures which are its greatest ornament; after him, besides those of Terpander, which he did not reject, Polymnestes brought into use other measures of his own; in which he was imitated by Thales and Sacadas, both of whom, however, though of fertile inventions, kept within the bounds of decorum. Other improvements were also made by Stesichorus and Alcmas, who, nevertheless, receded not from the ancient forms; but Croxus, Timotheus, and Philoxenus, and others of the same age, affecting greater novelty, departed from the plainness and majesty of the ancient music."

Soterichus, who is represented as not only skilled in the science, but generally and eminently learned, speaks thus of the invention and progress of music;

"Music was not the invention of any mortal; but we owe it to the god Apollo. The flute was invented neither by Marsyas, nor Olympus, nor Hyagnis; but Apollo invented both that and the lyre, and, in a word, all manner of vocal and instrumental music. This is manifest from the dances and sacrifices which were solemnized in honour of Apollo. His statue, placed in the temple of Delos, holds in his right hand a bow, and at his left the Graces stand, with each a musical instrument in her hand, one bearing a lyre, another a flute, and another a shepherd's pipe; and this statue is reported to be as ancient as the time of Hercules. The youth also that carries the tempic laurel into Delphos, is attended by one playing on the flute. Venerable, therefore, is music, as being the invention of gods; but the artists of these latter times, disdaining its ancient majesty, have introduced an effeminate kind of melody, mere sound without energy. The Lydian mode, as first instituted, was very plaintive, and suited only to lamentations; wherefore, Plato, in his *Republic*, utterly rejects it. Aristoxenus, in the first book of his Harmonics, relates that Olympus sung an elegy in that mode on the death of Python; though some attribute the invention of the Lydian mode to Menalippides, and others to Torebus. Pindar asserts, that it was used at the nuptials of Niobe; Aristoxenus, that it was invented by Sappho, and that the tragedians learned it of her, and conjoined it with the Dorian: but others say, that Pythocleides the flute performer, and also Lysis the Athenian, invented this conjunction of the Dorian with the Lydian mode. As to the softer Lydian, which was of a nature contrary to the Lydian properly so called, and more resembling the Ionian, it is said to have been first introduced by Damon the Athenian. Plato deservedly rejected the effeminate modes, and made choice of the Dorian, as more suitable to warlike tempers; not that we are to suppose him ignorant of what Aristoxenus has said in his second book, that in a wary and circumspect government, advantages might be derived from the use of the other modes; for Plato attributed much to music, as having been a hearer of Draco the Athenian, and Metellus of Agrigentum; but it was the consideration of its superior dignity and majesty, that induced his preference of the Dorian mode, together with the circumstance, that the supplications and hymns to the gods, tragical lamentations, and sometimes love-verses, were also composed in it; but he contented himself with such songs as were made in honour of Mars and Minerva; or those that were usually sung at the solemn offerings called *Spondalia*. The

Lydian and Ionian modes were chiefly employed by the tragedians ; and with these also Plato was well acquainted.

" As to the instruments of the ancients, they were generally of a narrow compass ; the lyre used by Olympus, Terpander, and their followers, had but three chords ; but this is not to be imputed to their ignorance ; for those musicians who made use of more were greatly their inferiors, both in skill and practice.

" The chromatic genus was formerly used by those who performed on the lyre ; but by the tragedians never. It is certainly of greater antiquity than the enharmonic ; yet the preference shewn to the diatonic and enharmonic, far from being the resul tofscanty science, was the effect of judgment. Telephanes of Megara was so great an enemy to the syrinx, or reed-pipe, that he would never suffer it to be joined to the tibia, or flute, or to that other pipe made of wood, generally of the lote-tree ; and for that reason, he forebore to go to the Pythian games. In short, if a man is to be deemed ignorant of that of which he makes no use, there will be found a great number of ignorant persons in this age ; for we see that the admirers of the Dorian mode make no use of the Antigenidian method of composition : and other musicians refuse to imitate Timotheus, being bewitched with the trifling and idle poems of Polycides.

" If we compare antiquity with the present times, we shall find that formerly, there was a great variety in music, and that the diversities of measure were then more esteemed than now. *We* are lovers of learning ; *they* preferred measure and time ; plain it is, therefore, that it was not on account of their ignorance, but in consequence of their judgment, that the ancients refrained from broken measures ; and if Plato preferred the Dorian to the other modes, it was only because he was the better musician.

" Aristotle, a disciple of Plato, thus labours to convince

the world of the majesty and celestial character of music.
' Harmony,' saith he, ' is of a divine, noble, and angelic
nature ; being fourfold as to its efficacy, it has two *media,*
the one arithmetical, the other harmonical. As for its numbers, its dimensions, and excesses of intervals, they are best
discovered by number and equality of measure, the whole
system being contained in two tetrachords.'

" The ancient Greeks were very careful to have their
children thoroughly instructed in the principles of music,
since they deemed it of great use in forming their minds,
and exciting in them a love of decency, sobriety, and virtue :
they also found it a powerful incentive to valour, and, accordingly, made use of pipes, or flutes, when they advanced
to battle. The Lacedemonians and the Cretans did the
same ; and in our times, the trumpet, succeeding the pipe,
as more sonorous, is used for the same purpose. The Argives, indeed, at their wrestling-matches, made use of fifes
called *Schenia,* which sort of exercise was first instituted in
honour of Danaus, but afterwards consecrated to *Jupiter
Schenius,* or *the Mighty ;* and at this day, it is the custom to
employ fifes at the games called PENTATHLA, which consist
of cuffing, running, dancing, hurling the ball, and wrestling.
But among the ancients, music in the theatres was never
known ; for either they employed it wholly in the education
of their youth, or confined it within the walls of their temples ; but now our musicians study only compositions for
the stage.

" If it should be demanded, Is music ever to remain the
same, and is there no room for new inventions ? The answer is, that new inventions are allowed, so they be grave
and decent ; the ancients themselves were continually adding to, and improving their music. Even the whole Mixolydian mode was a new invention ; such also were the Orthian and Trochean songs ; and, if we may believe Pindar,

Terpander was the inventor of the Scholian song; and Archilochus of the iambic and divers other measures, which the tragedians borrowed from him, and Croxus from them. The Hypolydian mode was the invention of Polymnestes, who also was the first that taught the manner of *alternately soft and loud.* Olympus, beside that he, in a great measure, regulated the ancient Greek music, discovered and introduced the enharmonic genus, and also the Prosodiac, the Chorian, and the Bacchian measures; all which, it is manifest, were of ancient invention. But Lasus Hermionensis, applying these measures to his dithyrambic compositions, and making use of an instrument with many bells, by the addition of tones and hemitones, made an absolute innovation in the ancient music. In like manner, Menalippides the lyric poet, Philoxenus, and Timotheus, all forsook the ancient method. The latter, until the time of Terpander of Antissa, used a lyre with only seven strings; but afterwards he increased the number. The wind instruments also received a great alteration; and in general, the plainness and simplicity of the ancient music was lost in that affected variety which these and other musicians introduced.

" In ancient times, when Poetry held the precedency of the other arts, the musicians who played on wind instruments, were retained with salaries by the poets, to assist those who taught the actors, till Menalippides appeared; after which that practice ceased."

Pherecrates the comic poet, introduces *Music* in the habit of a woman, with her face torn and bruised; and also Justice, the latter of whom, demanding the reason of her appearing in that condition, is thus answered by *Music* :

" It is my part to speak, and yours to hear; therefore attend to my complaints. I have suffered much, and long been oppressed by Menalippides, who dragged me from the fountain of Parnassus, and has tormented me with twelve strings : to complete my miseries, Cinesian the Athenian, a pretender to poetry, composed such horrid strophes and mangled verses, that I, tortured with the pain of his dithyrambics, was so distorted, that you would have vowed my right side was my left. Nor did my misfortunes end here; for Phrynis, in whose brain is a whirlwind, racked me with small wires, from which he produced twelve tiresome harmonies. But him (since he soon repented of his errors) I blame not so much as I do Timotheus, and Pyrrias the Milesian, the first of whom has furrowed my face, and ploughed my cheeks ; and the second, bound me with his twelve strings, and left me helpless."

This complaint made by *Music*, is followed by some general reflections of Soterichus, respecting the influence of harmony on the passions and manners, as also on the genera, and their several characters and powers, and the cause and nature of the music of the spheres, which remarks close this dialogue, so curious and so celebrated in antiquity, and which Meibomius calls a *golden little work*.

Plutarch, perhaps, thought it but decent in a priest of Apollo to discourage theatrical music. Its deviation, therefore, into liveliness and levity, was as constant an object of his censure, as it had ever been of that of Aristotle and Aristoxenus. A modern writer observes, that the most remarkable particulars in the *Symposiacs*, is the propensity it exposes in the musicians of all ages to make innovations, and the extreme rigour with which that disposition has almost uniformly been resisted. Had he said, " *The anxiety it displays in the musicians of all ages to advance their science and its practice, and the bigotry with which that anxiety has almost uniformly been opposed, proves that nothing is safe from the interference of pride and superstition,*" he had spoken more justly and more effectively.

Plutarch, after a long life devoted to study, adorned with

honours, and crowned with reputation and happiness, died
in his native place about the 140th year of the Christian era,
leaving behind him a variety of useful, well-known, and
greatly-admired writings, among which his " Lives" was a
work so high in the favour of Theodore Gaza, that being
asked, what single production of all the profane authors he
would prefer to save from destruction, he immediately exclaimed, " Plutarch's Lives."

QUINTILIAN.

Aristides Quintilianus flourished at the latter part of the
last century but one before Christ. The treatise *De Musica*,
by this celebrated theorist, consists of three books. The
first amply discusses the doctrine of the modes ; and what
he says of theorists, is to be understood as confined to melody. Of *time*, he gives the curious definition, That it is
of two kinds ; the one simple and indivisible, resembling a
point in geometry ; the other composite, that is, duple,
triple, and quadruple ; and he speaks of the elation and position of some part of the body, as necessary to the rythmus,
probably as the measure ; which shows the correspondence
between the ancient and modern practice of beating time.
The *second* book applies music to the regulation of the external behaviour, as philosophy is employed to improve the
mind. Among a variety of observations upon the general
utility of music, we find him asserting, that by its harmony,
it polishes the manners, while its rythmus renders the personal motions more agreeable. To divine worship, adds
he, it imparts an increased solemnity, public festivals derive
from it super-added joy, and it is capable of rendering the
most difficult and laborious undertaking easy and delightful.
Of the use of music in war, as practised by the ancients,
he has the following interesting passage :

" Numa has said, that by music he corrected and refined

the manners of the people, which before, were rough and
fierce: to that end he used it at feasts and sacrifices. In
the wars, where it is and will be used, need I say what a
help the Pyrrhic music is to martial discipline ? Certainly
this must be obvious to every one; as well as that the
issuing commands by words, in time of action, would introduce great confusion, and might convey intelligence to the
enemy. To that martial instrument, the trumpet, a particular cantus, or melody, is appropriated, varying according
to the occasion, as that of the attack by the centre, or
either of the wings, or a retreat, or the forming this or that
particular figure ; so that, without apprizing the foe of your
designs, you make yourself clearly and promptly understood
by your own army."

The *third* book relates some experiments made with
strings distended by weights, in given proportions for ascertaining the ratios of consonances, a practice which he sanctions by the authority of Pythagoras, who, he says, when
he departed this life, exhorted his disciples to strike the
monochord, and thereby rather inform their understandings,
than trust to their ears in the measure of intervals. The
following passage, replete with the creations of fancy, are
much too curious to be omitted :

" The tetrachords," says he, " it is agreed, are five in
number, and each has a relation to one or other of the
senses ; the *tetrachord hypaton* resembles the touch, which
is affected in new-born infants, when the cold makes them
cry. The *tetrachord meson* is like the taste, which is necessary to the preservation of life, and hath a similitude to
the touch. The *third,* called *synnemenon,* is compared to
the smell, because this sense is allied to the taste. The
fourth, termed diezeugmenon, is compared to the hearing,
because the ears are so remote from the other organs of
sense, and are disjoined from each other. The tetrachord

hyperboleon, is like the sight, being the most acute of the systems, as that sense is of our external powers of perception." His sportive imagination next [informs us, that the five tetrachords have a similar correspondence with the five primary elements; that *hypaton* answers to the earth, as the most grave; *meson* to the water, as nearest the earth; *synnemenon* to the air, which passes through the water, remaining in the profundities of the sea and the earth, and is necessary for the respiration of animals; *diezeugmenon,* to the fire, whose motion being upward, is against nature * : lastly, the tetrachord *hyperboleon,* is comparable to the æther, as supreme, and above all the other tetrachords."

These eccentric speculations are followed by analogies equally visionary, drawn between the tetrachords and the virtues : but these are specimens of the vagrancy of the imagination, when, quitting reason and science, it wanders amidst its

---

* The retrogradation of science during the interval between the time of Lucretius and that of Aristides Quintilian, cannot be more strikingly exemplified than by opposing to this idea of the Musical Theorist, the doctrine of the Epicurean philosopher.

———— *vacuum per Inane deorsum cuncta ferantur.*
Sic igitur debant Flammæ quoque posse per auras
Aëris expressæ sursum succedere ; quanquam
Pondera, quantum in se'st, deorsum deducere pugnent.

L. 2. v. 202.

Ne'er, in a void, would substance upward tend,
But, unsustain'd, precipitate descend :
E'en flames themselves would pond'rous bodies prove,
Resign their levity, and downward move.
Superior gravity they now obey,
And wing through lifting air their upward way.

BUSBY.

own labyrinths and wildernesses, and becomes its own blind
and unsanctioned guide. Quintilian, however, amid all the
exuberances of eccentric fancy, laid down many excellent
rules, both for theory and practice; and left the harmonic
art not a little indebted to his industry. At what age, or in
what year, he died, is not known.

Not detaining the reader with the history of Alypius,
Bryennius, Bacchius Senior, Gaudentius, and many others,
whose importance among the writers on music is scarcely
sufficient to claim our particular attention, we proceed to the
account of

CENSORINUS.

This celebrated musician and grammarian flourished in
Rome, about the latter end of the third century of the
Christian era. In a work entitled *De Die Natali;* and
published in 1628 by Ericius Putianus at Louvain, who
styles it *Doctrinæ Rarioris Thesaurus,* he treats of the birth
of man, of years, months and days; and respecting the harmonic science, relates things not known, even to musicians
themselves. This production, though limited to twenty-four
chapters, throws considerable light on learning in general.
Music, its principal subject, is defined to be *the science of
well modulating; and to consist in the voice, or sound.*
After observing, that sound is emitted, at one time graver, at
another time acuter; that sounds, however emitted, are called
pthongoi, and that the *difference* by which one sound is
more grave or more acute than another, is called *diastema,*
he proceeds as follows :—

" Many *diastemata* may be placed in order between the
lowest and the highest sound, some of which are greater,
as the tone, and others less, as the hemitone; or a *diastem*
may consist of two, three, or more tones. To produce con-

cordant effects, sounds are not joined together capriciously, but according to rule. Symphony is a sweet concert of sounds. The simple or primitive symphonies are three, of which the rest consist; the first, having a *diastem* of two tones and a hemitone, is called a diatesseron; the second, containing three tones and a hemitone, is called a diapente; the third is a diapason, and consists of the two former; for it is constituted either of six tones, as Aristoxenus and other musicians assert, or of five tones and two hemitones, as Pythagoras and the geometricians say, who demonstrate, that two hemitones do not complete the tone; wherefore this interval, or *diastem*, improperly called by Plato a hemitone, is truly and properly a diesis or limma."

The author, then, in proof that sounds are subjected to measures, goes into a review of the discoveries of Pythagoras; then takes a glance at a curious analogy drawn by Plato between sounds and the different stages of animal production, and makes some remarkable reflections on the properties of the number *seven,* as connected with music and the life of man :—

" It is not to be doubted," says he, " but that music has an effect on our birth; for whether it consists in the voice or sound only, as Socrates asserts, or, as Aristoxenus declares, in the voice and the motion of the body, or of both these and the emotion of the mind, as Theophrastus thinks, it has certainly somewhat in it of divine, and has a great influence on the mind. If it had not been grateful to the immortal gods, scenical games would never have been instituted to appease them ; neither would the tibiæ accompany our supplications in the holy temples. Triumphs would not have been celebrated with the tibia; the cithara, or lyre, would not have been attributed to Apollo, nor the tibia, nor the rest of that kind of instruments, to the Muses; neither would it have been permitted to those who perform on the tibia,

those by whom the deities are appeased, to exhibit public
shows or plays, and to eat in the capitol, or during the
lesser *Quinquatria* (or feast in honour of Minerva) to range
about the city, intoxicated, and disguised in what garments
they pleased. Human minds, and those that are divine,
though Epicurus exclaims against it, acknowledge their
nature by songs.

" Lastly, symphony is employed by the commanders of
ships, to encourage the sailors, and to enable them to bear
up under the labours and dangers of a voyage; and while
the legions are engaged in battle, the fear of death is dis-
pelled by the trumpet; wherefore Pythagoras, that he might
imbue his soul with its own divinity, before he went to sleep,
and after he awaked, was, as it is reported, accustomed to
sing to the cithara ; and Asclepiades the physician relieved
by symphony, the disturbed minds of phrenetics. Etophilus,
a physician also, says that the pulses of the veins are moved
by musical rhythmi; so that both the body and the mind
are subject to the power of harmony, and, doubtless, music
is not a stranger at our birth."

Censorinus next notices the doctrine of Pythagoras relating
to the mundane construction, as according with musical
ratios, and the mellifluous melody that must result from the
proportions of the planets, their motions, and their several
and various distances from each other, were the narrow passages of our ears capable of admitting them; and concludes
his discourse, by observing, that Pythagoras compared to the
stars many other things in music, and demonstrated that the
whole world is constituted in harmony. Agreeably to this, he
reminds us of the words of Dorylaus, who says, that " This
world is the instrument of God;" and of other writers, who
declare, that " There are seven wandering planets, which
have regular motions, that may fitly be resembled to a dance."

PORPHYRY.

This musician, scholar, and philosopher, was born at Tyre, about the middle of the third century. After studying at Athens, under Longinus the sophist, he retired to Rome, where he perfected himself in the Platonic doctrine, under Amolius, and Plotinus, the admired and valued friend of the Emperor Gallienus.

Porphyry, according to the best testimony, excelled his cotemporaries in the knowledge of history, mathematics, music, and philosophy. His language was as remarkable for its elegance and dignity, as for its simplicity and grace. Besides his most celebrated work against the Christian religion, the formidable arguments of which, not sufficiently refuted by those of the fathers, were thought to be better answered by the flames of the Church, he wrote a Commentary on the Harmonics of Ptolemy. St. Jerome says, Porphyry was a Jew; but Eunapius contradicts this assertion, and assures us, that his real name was *Malchus,* which in the Syrian language, signifies a king; and that Longinus, his first tutor, gave him the name of *Porphyrius,* in allusion to the purple usually worn by sovereigns. These are not all his works;—he wrote the lives of divers philosophers, of which only a single fragment, containing the life of Pythagoras, is now remaining; a treatise on abstinence from flesh, and an explication of the categories of Aristotle.

Unfortunately, his Commentary is imperfect. Of the three books forming the treatise of Ptolemy, the second contains fifteen chapters; but what we have of his commentary, proceeds no further than to the end of the seventh chapter of that book. He appears to have been a strenuous opposer of the Aristoxenians, and, like his author, adheres pretty closely to the tenets of Pythagoras.

This enlightened ornament of his age resided during the latter part of his life, in Sicily, where he died, about the end of the reign of Dioclesian, in his seventy-second year.

This exposé of the lives and works of the most distinguished of the ancient writers on music, will have afforded the reader a tolerably comprehensive idea of the state and progress of Musical Theory, during the latter periods of pagan history, and at the commencement, and through the first few centuries, of the Christian era. The following chapter will demonstrate how the theory was applied in practice.

CHAP. X.

PRACTICAL VIEW OF THE ANCIENT MUSIC, VOCAL AND INSTRUMENTAL.

THE expression of the passions, by vocal and appreciable sounds, is so natural, that we cannot but imagine its origin to have been coeval with that of the human race. The complaints of pain, and the exclamations of joy, required no other guide, or tutor, than the sentiment to be developed; and, nature, faithful to herself, spoke in tones inspired and modulated by her feelings. The observation applies even to language. Though, in *writing*, a word is ever the same, in *delivery*, it is susceptible of a thousand differing shadings, accommodated to the sense and the sensation meant to be conveyed. All those shadings, or variations, it is Music's very office to furnish. The heart gives her the clue, but the voice is her own providing; the grief, and the pleasure, the hatred, and the affection, exist without her; but without her, want their most forcible expression. Shall we then wonder, if hymns and songs preceded the use of letters, and, for a long time, even supplied the place of history? Laws were originally *sung*, and prayers were *chanted*. To religion and justice, Music supplied zeal and solemnity; to the social enjoyments of life, added an amiable embellishment, and a more exalted hilarity.

Of *Sacred Music*, the earliest specimens of which we have any account, were the Theurgic Hymns, or *Songs of Incantation*, like those ascribed to Orpheus, and which are supposed to have originated in Egypt. These were succeeded by popular or heroic hymns, that were sung in praise of some particular divinity, or at the head of an army. Of these, the former were distinguished by appellations indicative of the deities to whom they were addressed. Those sacred to Apollo and Mars were called *Pœans;* and those sung to Bacchus were denominated *Dithyrambics.* A third class of hymns, a class which we may style *philosophic,* or *allegorical,* were devoted to the celebration of the divine attributes.

The Hyperboreans who worshipped Apollo, celebrated all their mysteries with hymns. They chanted them before the altar at Delos, accompanied with flutes and harps. The Iberians of Bœotia, delighted in a kind of dirge and funereal music: hence, Philostratus tells us, that they were the only people in the world who celebrated the triumphs of death. The Dorian and Phrygian hymns were more manly and animated. Those of Lesbos and Æolia were particularly sweet and pleasing; yet not esteemed alone for their melody, but as *repositories of all knowledge,* and *compendiums of history.* Such were the hymns at Delphos, at Delos, and in most regions of Hellas *. The Doric

---

* To this, Homer alludes in the history of the Syrens, the power of whose voices he represents as almost irresistible; while their knowledge was still more wonderful and captivating. To the hero of the Odyssey, when approaching their shores, he represents them exclaiming—

" O stay! O pride of Greece, Ulysses stay,
O stop thy course, and listen to our lay!

hymns were universally sung in the Prytaneia and temples *.
They were chanted by the Purcones, or priests of the sun;
and by the female Hierophants.

Most writers are of opinion, that the first musical exercises of the voice were in addresses to the gods; that mankind no sooner obtained an increase of sustenance by the
arts of tillage, than their gratitude burst forth in songs of
pious acknowledgment of the bounty of heaven: that seeing
around him the promise of a plenteous repayment of his
labour,

> The *Ploughman* then, to sooth the toilsome day,
> Chanted in measur'd feet his sylvan lay,
> And seed-time o'er, he first in blithsome strain,
> Pip'd to his household gods the grateful strain.

This was natural: equally so was it, that as the human
mind advanced in knowledge, and society began to be polished, that poetry and vocal music should extend their influence from the field to the city, assume new grace and
strength, and, enriched with instrumental accompaniments,

> Blest is the man ordain'd our voice to hear,
> The song instructs the soul, and charms the ear.
> Approach ! thy soul shall into raptures rise,
> Approach! and learn new wisdom from the wise !
> We know whate'er the kings of mighty name
> Achiev'd at Ilion in the field of fame ;
> Whate'er beneath the sun's bright journey lies :
> O stay, and learn new wisdom from the wise."

(OD. l. 12.)   POPE.

* These were in the ancient Ammonian language; and said to
have been introduced by Pegasus, Agyieus, and Olen; the last of
whom, some declare to have been a Lycian, some an Hyperborean,
and others, an Egyptian.

form the most solemn and imposing parts of religious ceremonies. Of this use of poetry and music, the instances in
the royal Psalmist, and Homer and Virgil, are abundant.
Indeed, so prevalent was vocal music among the Hebrews,
the Greeks, and even the Romans, that *singer* was a common appellation among them for *poet* and *musician :* by
which we may learn how intimately poetical ideas and melodial vociferation were united.

Of the *Secular Music* of the Greeks, chiefly consisting
of their *Scolia,* or festive songs, the only remains we have,
are chiefly such as were sung at table *. At banquets, or
repasts, it was for a long time the custom for each of the
guests to sing one of these songs alone, holding a branch of
myrtle in his hand, which at the end of his strain he passed
to his next neighbour, in the direction in which the song was
going round. But at length, when music arrived at a
greater degree of perfection, the myrtle was laid aside, to
make way for the lyre, which then regularly formed the accompaniment to the voice : and the talent of *self-accompa-
niment* became so general, that a deficiency in that accomplishment was disgraceful ; and *Taking to the myrtle* became
a proverbial expression for ignorance, inasmuch as it confessed the songster's inability to give a better employment to
the hand.

These *Scolia,* or convivial songs, may be arranged under
three classes : *Moral, Mythological,* and *Patriotic.* Of the
words of each of these kinds of *Scolia,* Dr. Burney has
collected some striking specimens ; which will serve to elucidate this part of our history.

---

* Plutarch, however, as also Athenæus and Lucian, inform us,
that the *first samples* of these festive strains, were real Pœans, sacred
canticles, or hymns, sung by the whole company to some divinity.

MORAL SONGS.

Scolium by Timocreon, a comic poet of Rhodes, who lived in the five hundredth century before Christ, and obtained prizes at Olympia.

> Why should wealth such favour find
> 'Mong deluded human kind ;
> Wealth more fit for fiends below,
> Prompting crimes, and breeding woe ?
> Riches since the world began,
> Guilt and mis'ry brought to man.

Ascribed to Simonides.

> The first of human gifts is *health*,
> The next on *beauty's* pow'r attends ;
> The third is mod'rate, well-earn'd *wealth*,
> The fourth is youth, enjoy'd with *friends* *.

---

* Aristotle, having written the following canticle on the death of his friend Hermias, Prince of Atarnea, was accused of impiety : but it is not easy to discover why the composition should have subjected him to such a charge.

"O virtue! who in despite of the difficulties thou presentest to mortals, art the charming object of their desire and their search! Virtue ever pure and lovely ! with the Greeks, enviable is the death by which thou art purchased ; all calamity laudable, that is suffered for thy sake. From *thee* flow joy and immortality. Thy fruits are dearer to the heart than gold, than parental love, or the most tranquil slumbers. For *thee* the godlike Hercules, and the son of Leda, braved a thousand toils, and owed to thy power alone their illustrious triumphs. From the love of *thee* it was, that Ajax and Achilles descended to the mansions of Pluto ; and for *thee* loved Hermias, and quitted the realms of light; Hermias, whose deathless name the

MYTHOLOGICAL SONGS.

Scolia from Athenæus.

At the genial board I sing
Pleasures which from plenty spring :
While the wreath adorns our brows,
Ceres well deserves our vows.
Plutus, thy great name we'll join,
And thy sister Proserpine.
Ye our social joys augment,
From your bounty flows content.
Bless our city with increase,
So our praise shall never cease.

To Pan.

O Pan, delight of nymphs and swains,
Protector of Arcadia's plains,
  Who lead'st the frolic dance !
The laughing fair, who plays the prude,
But flies thy steps to be pursued,
  Her favour to enhance.

She loves thy rustic, oaken reed ;
She knows thy genius, force, and speed,
  And feigns a modest fear.
Our jocund strains shall swell for thee,
In them, as in our hearts, shall be
  Thy name for ever dear.

Muses shall crown with unfading glory ; whose merits, when they
tune their celestial lyres to hospitable Jove, and the blessings of a
sincere and durable friendship, shall be their lofty theme."

Vide Athenæus, lib. 15, and Diogenes Laertius in Aristot.

PATRIOTIC SONGS.

Fragments of *Scolia* on the patriots Harmodius and Aristogiton, whose courage gave the signal to the Athenians to recover their lost liberty.

> Cover'd with myrtle wreaths, I'll wear my sword,
>   Like brave Harmodius and his patriot friend,
> Aristogiton, who the laws restor'd,
>   The tyrant slew, and bade oppression end.

> Harmodius dear, thou art not dead,
> Thy soul is to Elysium fled ;
> Thy virtue there a place hath won,
> With Diomede, great Tydeus' son ;
> With swift Achilles too, thou'rt join'd,
> And every friend of human kind *.

Moral, religious, and patriotic as the Greeks were, yet, judging by the specimens of their *Scolia,* which have come

---

* Before the art of writing was invented, the simplest means were employed, for perpetuating the remembrance of important events. Among these, none were more generally resorted to than festivals, plays, and songs. In the latter, national calamities and successes were rehearsed, the anniversaries of defeats and losses lamented, and those of victories, births, and marriages, commemorated and celebrated. Hence the ancients, besides the above, had songs proper to the different professions: such as the *Bucoliasm,* or *song of the shepherd;* the *Lytierse,* or *song of the reapers;* the *Hymee,* or *song of the millers;* the *Eliné,* or *song of the weavers;* the *Yulé,* or *song of the wool-carders;* the *Nunnia,* or *song of the nurses;* the *Nomion,* or *song of lovers;* the *Calycé,* or *song of the ladies;* and the *Harpalycé,* or *song of young girls.* To these are to be added, the *Marriage Song,* called *Hymenea;* the song *Datis,* for merry occasions; for lamentation, the song *Jalema;* and for funerals, the song *Linos.*

down to us, the best were upon love and wine. That *Love is the inspirer of Music and Poetry*, was one of their most memorable maxims. Plutarch, who has made this adage the subject of one of his *Symposiacs*, supports its validity with the following reasoning :—

" Love, like wine, inspires vivacity, cheerfulness, and passion ; and in those dispositions, it is natural to *sing*, and to give energy and emphasis to our expressions. Besides, when any one is in love, he naturally uses a figurative and measured language, in order to enforce his sentiments, as gold is used in embellishing statues. Whenever a beloved object is mentioned, her perfections and beauties are published in *songs*, which impress them on the memory in a more lively and durable manner. If we send our mistress either letters or presents, we try to augment their value by a copy of *verses*, or a *song*. In short, there are three incitements to singing; sorrow, joy, and enthusiasm. During sorrow, our complaints are expressed in lengthened tones resembling those of music : the voice, too, of an orator, bespeaking the favour of an audience, is modulated into a kind of *song ;* as are the grief and lamentation of actors in tragedy. Joy causes violent agitations, and stimulates the vulgar to skip and dance ; while persons more decorous, and better educated, are inclined to *sing*. Enthusiasm agitates and transports to a degree of madness and fury ; witness the cries of the Bacchanals, and the agonies of the Pythia, both of which are uttered in measure and cadence. Now there can be no doubt but that the passion of love occasions exquisite pain as well as pleasure. This passion, therefore, uniting all the three propensities of *song*, must at all times have been regarded as the most proper to excite a desire of *singing*."

If of the Greek songs, those dedicated to love and wine, are the best, the best, again, of these are the lyrics of Anacreon.

Their native elegance and grace have produced more imitators of their author, than Pindar obtained by his odes; while both have been so pre-eminently excellent in their different provinces, that if all voluptuous and gay effusions borrow from the name of one poet the general appellation of *Anacreontics*, those of a daring and sublime order, are universally called *Pindarics*.

It is impossible to be engaged in this department of the history of Grecian music, and not feel the vacuum occasioned by the total loss of the ancient festive melodies. Our possession of some of these would have thrown considerable light upon the subject. We should have learnt from them whether the airs of the ancients consisted of a continued stream or succession of passages rising out of each other, and forming a consistent whole, imbued with variety of expression, yet unity of character; or whether they were merely comprised repetitions of some short phrase, or idea, without protracted construction, system, or diversified feature. If they were of the former description, their loss is great; and if of the latter kind, their preservation would at least have served to satisfy curiosity, and have enabled us to decide upon the Grecian taste, in this branch of musical composition.

Fortunately, though time has not preserved to us any models of the ancient structure of *melody*, we are not without information respecting the forms and characters of the Grecian instruments. These appear to have been of three kinds: *inflatile, stringed*, and *percussive*. The first kind chiefly consisted of the flute, horn, syrinx, trumpet, and water organ: the second comprehended the lyre and psaltery: the third the drum, cymbal, crotalum, and bells *.

---

* Of which, taken in the same order, the classical names will be, *Aulos*, or *Tibia; Cheras*, or *Cornu; Salpinx, Tuba, Buccina*, or

WIND INSTRUMENTS.

The first instrument of the inflatile or wind kind, it is much the most probable, was the *Avena*, or reed; this would naturally lead to a combination of tubes of the same simple description, and produce the syrinx, or *fistula*. This rude attainment of the command of different sounds by the assemblage of pipes of different lengths, would again, in time, suggest the idea of producing, by the aid of *foramina*, or holes, various sounds from a single tube: and hence the *tibia* or flute, originally formed, as some think, of the shank, or shin bone of an animal. The second sort of wind instruments were, it may be supposed, derived from the shells of fishes, and the horns of quadrupeds *.

Though the improvement of the Grecian flute was rapid; though, proceeding from the rude cane hollowed by nature, it arrived at that state which the practice of *artificial boring* would produce, and, at length, was formed of box-tree, laurel, brass, silver, and even gold; yet the defects which the moderns have found so much difficulty in surmounting, were, as we may collect from the complaints of Aristoxenus, irremediable evils. " Flutes," says that profound speculatist, " are continually shifting their pitch, and never remain in the same state." One expedient resorted to for the palliation of the dissonant intervals, was the use of *wax*, which

---

Lituus; Syrinx, Fistula, or *Calamus;* and *Hydraulicon: Phorminx,* or *Cithara; Chelys,* or *Testudo; Lyra,* or *Fides;* and *Psalterion,* or *Psalterium; Tympanon,* or *Tympanum; Tympanion, Parvum Tympanum,* or *Tympanulum; Cymbalon,* or *Cymbalum; Crotalon,* or *Crotalum; Codomion,* or *Campanum æs.*

* The *Monaulos,* or single pipe, as represented in ancient sculpture, strongly sanctions this idea.

material was applied to the holes or perforations of the instrument *.

The tubes of the *Fistula Panis* (pipes of Pan) consisting of reeds, or canes, cut just below the joint, were all *stopt-pipes*, like those in the stopt diapason in the organ, in which the wind is emitted where it enters †. That the flutes of the ancients were constructed of natural reeds and canes, we cannot doubt. Plutarch, in his Dialogue, mentions a *syrinx*, or small pipe, that was sometimes affixed to flutes, apparently, as we apply reeds to our hautboys and bassoons. But though from a musical problem in another treatise of Plutarch, we learn, that the conjoined *syrinx*, when *drawn up*, sharpened the flute *in all its sounds*, and, being *let down*, flattened its whole scale, we are left ignorant of the manner in which it was applied to the body of the instrument; and can only conclude, that as its use was so very different from that of our artificial reeds, the mode of its application must also have been very different from that adopted by modern practice.

But though the object of the ancients in attaching the *syrinx* to their flutes, had no correspondence with ours, in using the *reed*, still it appears, that the effect we derive from

---

* This resource must have been necessitated by the want of skill in *boring*. In a warm climate, the wax, it is obvious, continually subject to fusion, would be a very uncertain expedient. Yet, that wax was really used for this purpose, is evident, from an instrument of the bassoon kind, described by Mersennus, who tells us, that the *Tetines*, as he calls the projections, were not moveable, but fixtures; and that when those on one side were used, those on the other were stopped with wax.

† The *Fistula Panis* of the Island of New Amsterdam, in the South Seas, is made of canes cut below the joints, and consequently, of stopped pipes.

the latter appendage, was in a degree provided for by their *glottis*, *lingula*, or *tongue*, which it would seem was essential to their use of the instrument. We are, indeed, obliged to understand, that the flute could scarcely be made to speak without its aid ; since the musician Midas, of Agrigentum, exhibited a wonder, in being able to finish a performance, though his *reed*, or mouth-piece, separated or failed, while he was playing *.

Among the most remarkable particulars in the ancient wind instruments, are the *tibiæ pares*, or equal flutes, the *tibiæ impares*, or unequal flutes, *tibiæ dextræ*, or right-hand flutes, and *tibiæ sinistræ*, or left-hand flutes. Of the manner in which these were used, we know so little, that it has never been determined, whether the *pares* and *impares* were double and single, or equal and unequal flutes : nor are the learned better agreed upon the distinction between the right-handed and left-handed flutes. In the representations in the ancient sculpture, it is not unusual to see one of the unequal flutes strait and the other curved : and Hesychius the grammarian says, that the curved flute was held in the left hand, and the strait flute in the right. And from Pliny we collect, that the *longest* of the *impares* was for the left hand ; since, speaking of the reeds of which they were made, he says *the part next the ground being the widest, serves for the left-hand flutes* †.

---

* And it was a saying of Demades, the Athenian orator, who compared his countrymen to *flutes;* that they were good for nothing without their *tongues.*

† In the Farnese collection at Rome, there is, in *bas-relief,* the representation of a female bacchanal, blowing a double-flute, the tubes of which are of unequal lengths, and furnished with keys, or stopples : but most of the double-flute-players exhibited in sculpture, appear to grasp the instrument without any motion of the fingers ;

Vossius (speaking after Proclus) says, that every hole of
the ancient flutes furnished, at least, three different sounds ;
and that if the *paratrypemata,* or side holes, were opened,
even a greater number : and from Arcadius Grammaticus
we learn, that the inventors of the holes of the flute contrived a method of stopping and opening them at pleasure,
by certain horns, or pegs, which being turned in or out, and
moved up or down, multiplied the sounds. But as Dr.
Burney justly observes, this operation could not be practised
during performance, since, according to most of the representations he had seen of perforated flutes, the plugs, or
stopples, were out of the reach of the performer's hand.
" And though in our bassoon, hautboy, and german flute,"
adds the doctor, " we are able, my means of keys, to open
and close holes which the fingers cannot reach, yet as no
such expedients appear in the representations of ancient
wind instruments, it is difficult to assign any other use to
these plugs or stopples, than that of adjusting the scale to
some particular mode or genus, before performance."

Sometimes, the flute had a horn joined to the end of it,
by which it assumed the form of a lituus, or clarion. This
curved termination was the characteristic of the Phrygian
flute. Bartholinus (De Tib. vet. p. 48) exhibits two flutes
of this kind, with plugs ; one strait and the other curved,
and tells us, from Aristotle's acoustics, that *loudness* and
clearness were acquired by the addition of the horn : *Cornua
resonando instrumentorum sonos reddunt clariores.* Some
writers think, and apparently with great reason, that the *horn*
rendered the flutes to which it was applied, an octave lower.

---

and many of the flutes being without perforations, we are left to doubt
whether they were modulated by the hand, or by the mouth, like our
trumpets and horns.

By a bas-relief in the court of the *Santa Croce* palace at Rome, it appears that the Greeks were not wholly unacquainted with the *bag-pipe*, of which they had the close resemblance, in an instrument they named *askaulos*, and which the Romans denominated the *tibia utricularis*. Isaac Vossius, however, denies that the noun *utricularis* signifies a player on a bag-pipe; and insists that the instrument in question was an organ blown by bellows, as distinguished from the hydraulic or water-organ : but a passage in Dion Chrysostom proves him to be mistaken. For, speaking of Nero, the Greek writer says, that he played on the flute *with a bladder*, or leathern bag of wind, *under his arm*. This is the exact description of a modern bag-pipe * ; and viewed together with the equal flutes, unequal flutes, double flutes, and cornuted flutes, proves that this species of wind instrument had attained among the ancients, a state of considerable complication and refinement.

Of the ancient *horn* we know so little, as to be obliged to depend for our ideas of its form and tone, chiefly upon the inference drawn from its name. That it was invented by the Egyptians, and passed from them to the Greeks, we cannot doubt. It was the *shawm* of the former people, and the *cheras* of the latter. It has, at different times, been formed of the cornute protuberances of various animals; but chiefly from those of the wild goat. Its original construction, it is to be presumed, differed little from the form given it by nature, and that the scale of its sounds, as now, lay considerably beneath that of the flute. That with the

---

* The reason given for Nero's preference of the *Tibia Utricularis* is truly curious :—*that he might avoid those distortions of the countenance occasioned by the flutes blown by the breath, and which so greatly disgusted Minerva.*

Greeks, it was in very general use, the testimonies of a variety of ancient authors sufficiently prove. And that its power over the passions was great, Lucretius bears evidence in his description of the procession in honour of Cybele*.

To the character and effects of the ancient *trumpet*, we have a tolerable key. From one of its names, *Buccina*, it must, at some time, have been formed of the horn of an ox; and as this must have been its rudest, so it could not but be its earliest state. That the *trumpet*, like the horn, originated with the Egyptians, there is no room to doubt: yet the Hetrurians have had the credit of being its inventor: an idea, arising probably from the great and constant use they made of this instrument. Tatianus Assyrius says, that that people stationed trumpeters in their towers upon the sea-coast, where they watched day and night, in order that if any thing extraordinary occurred, they might by a blast from their instruments, give immediate notice. Hence, we are told, Triton was feigned to be Neptune's trumpeter. Nonnus accordingly (L. 17, p. 468) describes him, as *possessing the deep-toned trumpet of the Hetrurian main*†. This at once proves both the force and gravity of the tone of this instrument in its early state ; and since we know it was used in war, and in public rejoicings, its ancient utility and importance is rendered manifest ‡.

---

* See a former page of this volume.

† Besides this *deep-toned trumpet*, the ancients had a kind of clarion, a military instrument, the scale of which was an octave higher, and which they called a *Lituus*. It was crooked, made of metal, and extremely loud and shrill. By the Romans it was used for their cavalry, as the strait trumpet was for their foot. The *Lituus* frequently appears on ancient medals, as a symbol of war, and is terminated by the head of a boar, and sometimes, of a snake.

‡ A trumpet of a very extraordinary kind, was, about the middle

The most extraordinary of the wind instruments, or indeed, of any other kind, is the *hydraulicon*, or water-organ:
an instrument so denominated, because it was performed
upon, or at least blown, by water. From a description given
by Vitruvius, it would seem, that the water, by which the
air was impelled into the pipes, was put into motion by
pumps. The question whether it was played with the fingers,
or its tones modulated by some mechanical means, has excited considerable dispute. Claudian speaks of it in terms
which, if we overlook what alludes to its being filled by
water instead of wind, would describe a modern organ.

> *Vel qui magna levi detrudens murmura tactu*
> *Innumeras voces segetis moderator aënæ*
> *Intonet erranti digito, penitusque trabali*
> *Vecte laborantes in carmina concitet undas.*

> With flying fingers, as they lightsome bound,
> From brazen tubes he draws the pealing sound.
> Unnumber'd notes the captive ear surprize,
> And swell and thunder as his art he plies:
> The beamy bar he heaves! the waters wake!
> And liquid lapses liquid music make.   BUSBY.

Athenæus, who also gives a description of this instrument,

---

of the last century, dug out of Pompeia. It consisted of a large
tube of bronze, surrounded by seven small pipes of bone or ivory, inserted in as many of metal. These, terminating in one point, induce
the opinion, that they were all blown through one mouth-piece. The
small pipes are all of equal length and diameter, and seem to have
been unisons to each other, and octaves to the great tube. There is a
ring to fasten a chain to, by which it was slung over the shoulder of
the performer. This instrument was found in the *corps de garde* of
this subterraneous city, and seems, says Dr. Burney, from whom
this description is taken, to have been the true military *Clangor Tu-
barum.*

says it was invented in the time of the second Ptolemy Evergetes, by Ctesibius, a native of Alexandria. Ctesibius, however, cannot properly be called the inventor of the hydraulic organ, since it is but an improvement upon Plato's *Clepsydra*, or water-clock, that played upon flutes the hours of the night, at a time when they could not be seen on the index.

The most satisfactory idea that can be formed of this instrument, is furnished by a large beautiful medallion of Valentinian, in the collection of antiquities, bequeathed to the Vatican by Christina, queen of Sweden. On the reverse of this relic is represented an *hydraulic organ,* with two men, one on the right, and one on the left, who appear to pump the water which plays, and to be listening to the sound. It has only eight pipes, placed on a round pedestal; and has neither keys nor performers.

STRINGED INSTRUMENTS.

Of the stringed instruments, the first on record is the lyre. After all that is related in the story of the Nile and the tortoise-shell, the invention of this instrument is more generally attributed to Apollo than to Mercury*. The idea of producing music from a distended chord, is said to have been first suggested to this god by the twang of his sister Diana's bow.

Though the original form of the lyre is not known, of its construction in its improved state, we are not ignorant.

---

* Some writers make Apollo the inventor of one kind of lyre, and Mercury of another. Orpheus (Argon. 380) says of Chiron, that " he sometimes strikes the *cithara* of Apollo; sometimes the *shell-resounding phorminx* of Mercury.

From a statue of Orpheus in the Palazzo Medici, holding a lyre, a graphic representation of that instrument, by Hyginius, delineated from a passage in Philostratus, drawings of it obtained by Mersennus from Rome and other parts of Italy, and the lyre in the hand of Apollo in the Matthei Garden near Rome, we can form a tolerably perspicuous idea of its shape and its powers *. The sides, generally, consist of a bull's, a goat's, or a ram's horns; the bottoms or thick ends of which are inserted at the extremities of an oblong piece of wood, and at right angles to it, while their thinner ends are joined in the same manner to a cross bar at top, which is parallel with the base.

We read of the lyre, the cithara, the chelys, the psaltery, and the harp; but Father Montfaucon, after giving infinite attention to the subject, declares it to be very difficult, if at all possible, to determine in what the instruments bearing these names differed from each other. Nevertheless, Aristides Quintilian clearly distinguishes them. After discussing the characters of wind instruments, he says, " Among the stringed instruments, you will find the lyre of a character analogous to *masculine*, from the great depth or gravity, and roughness of its tones; the *Sambuca* of a *feminine* character, weak and delicate, and from its great acuteness, and the smallness of its strings, tending to dissolve and enervate.

---

* Isaac Vossius however, (de Poemat. cant. et virib. Rythm, p. 97) contends, that hardly any of these remaining monuments of antiquity are in such a state as to warrant any opinion respecting the form of the ancient lyre. He speaks indeed, of two statues of Apollo in the garden of his Britannic Majesty at London, in the year 1673 (probably the Privy Garden behind the then palace of Whitehall) each holding a lyre, and which, not being the least mutilated, he considers as true representations.

Of the intermediate instruments, the *Polypthongum* partakes most of the *feminine;* but the *cithara* differs not much from the *masculine* character of the lyre." Here we find a scale of stringed instruments, the extremes of which are supplied by the *lyre* and the *sambuca*, while the *polypthongum* and *cithara* form the intermediate portions *.

Among the various ancient lyres was the *tripodian,* an extraordinary instrument, of which Athenæus gives the following account, in his fourteenth book, chap. 15, page 637.

" Many ancient instruments are recorded, as we learn from Artemon, of which we have so little knowledge, that we can hardly be certain of their existence; such as the *tripod* of Pythagoras the Zacynthian, which, on account of its difficulty, continued in use but a short time. It resembled in form the Delphic tripod, whence it had its name. The legs were equidistant, and fixed upon a moveable base that was turned by the foot of the player; the strings were placed between the legs of the stool; the vase at the top served for the purpose of a sound-board, and the strings of the three sides of the instrument were tuned to three different modes, the *Doric, Lydian,* and *Phrygian.* The performer sat on a chair made on purpose, striking the strings with the fingers of the left hand, and using the plectrum with the right, at the same time turning the instrument with his foot, to whichever of the three modes he pleased;

---

* In an ancient painting in the Museum at Naples, there is the representation of a *trigonum,* or *triangular harp,* placed on the shoulder of a little dancing Cupid, who supports the instrument with his left hand, and plays upon it with his right. Sophocles calls the *trigonum* a Phrygian instrument; and one of his dipnosophists tells us, that a certain musician of the name of Alexander Alexandrinus, was so admirable a performer upon it, and had given such proofs of his abilities at Rome, that he put the inhabitants in a phrenzy.

so that by great practice, he was enabled to change the modes with such velocity, that those who did not see him, would imagine they heard three different performers playing in three different modes."

Concerning the shape and structure of these instruments, Quintilian is wholly silent. The ancient cithara may, perhaps, have been as different from the lyre, as a medium single harp from one that is double; and, indeed, it seems pretty clear that the Greeks had *two* principal species of stringed instruments; one like our harp, of full compass, that rested on its base; the other more portable, and slung over the shoulder, like our smaller harp or guitar, or similar to those represented in sculpture.

These *undefaced* passages of the old authors relating to the ancient instruments, are, perhaps, more satisfactory than the *decayed* sculpture in which they are represented; especially if we consider, that artists are not always very scrupulous in figuring secondary or indicative objects, which, introduced only to denote an attribute, or art, or a profession, have in general little of that nicety of attention bestowed upon them which is given to the principal subject*.

PERCUSSIVE INSTRUMENTS.

Of the percussive, or pulsatile instruments, the principal is the drum. Though according to a passage in the Bacchæ

---

* With one of the principal expedients for producing sound from stringed instruments, the *bow*, the ancients appear to have been wholly unacquainted. Consequently, they had no conception of some of their finest effects; their *diminuendi*, and *crescendi*, upon the same note, and their " linked sweetness long drawn out." Instead of a *bow*, they used the *plectrum*, or quill. Don Calmet says the *psaltery* was played on with a *bow;* but the very *form* of that instrument, as far as we have been made acquainted with it, contradicts his assertion,

of Euripides, antiquity ascribed the invention of this instrument to the Corybantes, there is no doubt of its being of
Egyptian origin. It was the *Thoph*, or sistrum of the Egyptians, and used by their priests in the religious ceremonies.
Kircher, on the authority of the Rabbi Hannase, relates that
it was in the form of a ship; and that by the Greeks, it was
called Cymbalum, from Cymba, a boat. He adds, that it
was covered with the skin of an animal, and was beaten with
a pestle, or rod of iron or brass. This sistrum of the
Egyptians, and the *Krousma* of the Greeks, appear to have
been the same instrument. Though generally of an oval or
boat-like form, it was frequently circular, but always flat,
like the *Tambour de Basque*. Its materials were various.
Sometimes it was made of iron, sometimes of brass, silver,
or gold. Its rim is said to have been furnished with little
bells; but Kircher, upon what authority is not known, cor-
rects this assertion, insisting that instead of bells suspended
round the rim, a number of iron rings were strung in a
lateral position, on a bar that extended over the circle. He
further informs us, that a handle was affixed to the instrument, for the purpose of swinging it backwards and forwards; and that from the collision of the rings with each
other, and their friction against the sides, the circle, and
the bar, a melancholy murmur arose.

This drum, or sistrum, was beaten by the Hebrew virgins
in the dances of the *Sistri*. Instances of this practice occur
in the books of Exodus and Judges; where we are told, that
Mary the sister of Moses, and the daughter of Jephtha,
sounded the sistrum. By the Greeks, as well as by the
Egyptians, it was used in all religious ceremonies*, and also

---

* "To well-braced drums they move their madden'd feet."
Descrip. of Process. of Cybele. Luc. b. 2.

in every musical performance, formed a regulator of the time. As an article of sacrifice, it was an instrument of such constant use with the Egyptians in general, and became so multiplied by the priests, that in derision, Egypt was often called the *country of the sistrums.* Of the abundant use of the sistrum and cymbal among the Jews, no proof is wanting. By David, they are incessantly named. " Praise him in the *cymbals* and dances," " Praise him upon the well-tuned *cymbals,*" " Praise him upon the *timbrel,*" are expressions that continually meet the eye in the book of Psalms. But prevalent as the cymbalum or crotalum, was with the Egyptians and Jews, it was an equal favourite with the Greeks, as its constant appearance in the Bacchanalian sacrifices and processions, represented in ancient sculpture, sufficiently testify *.

The Abbé Winckelman has disputed the high antiquity of the sistrum in Egypt, simply because he did not find it in the hands of such Egyptian statues as he had seen at Rome: but by an instrument of this kind in the hand of a very ancient statue of Isis, which Dr. Pococke brought into England from Egypt, that point of musical history is placed beyond dispute. Another strong evidence of the high antiquity of the ancient drum is, that it appears in the *Isiac Table :* and a further proof of the same exists in the fact, that Apuleius represents an old Greek invoking an Egyptian priest " by the stars in the firmament; by the infernal divinities; by the elements which compose the universe; by the silence of the night; by the sanctuary in the temple of Coptos; by the in-

---

* Upon a beautiful marble vase in the Justinian garden at Rome, on which is sculptured the orgies of Bacchus, the pomp of the procession is filled up by matrons and virgins beating the *crotalum,* or *cymbalum,* and the *tympanum.*

crease of the Nile; by the mysteries of Memphis; and by the *sistrum* of Pharos." And I might add, that a cymbal, or timbrel, was dug out of the ruins of Herculaneum, evidently of very high antiquity.

It remains to speak of another ancient instrument of percussion,—the *bell*. *Bells* were known to the earliest times of which we have any certain account. But the bells of the ancients were very small in comparison with those of modern times; since, according to Polydore Virgil, the invention of such as are hung in the towers, or steeples of Christian churches, did not occur till the latter end of the fourth, or beginning of the fifth century, when they were introduced by Paulinus, Bishop of Nola. The Jews employed bells, since they are mentioned in the Scriptures; and the mention of them by Thucydides, Diodorus Siculus, Suidas, Aristophanes, and other ancient classical writers, prove that they were used in Greece; while Plautus, Ovid, Tibullus, Statius, and a variety of Latin authors, speak of *bells* as in use among the Romans. But these bells of the ancients were all made for the hand, or were of a size to be affixed to other musical instruments, like those which were occasionally appended to the drum. Whether, when detached from other instruments, they were used on general occasions, or only in particular ceremonies, or as signals, is not known; nor have we any clue by which to guess whether they were tuned in concordance with any scale, or whether they were unisons to each other, not formed to any particular pitch, but merely used as sonorous auxiliaries to other instruments, without any regard to their agreement of tone, either with respect to themselves, or in regard of the instruments they accompanied *.

---

* The Chinese have always had a great predilection for bells. Most of their great towers, which are very numerous, have at their

This is but a scanty and unsatisfactory view of the *Practical Ancient Music, Vocal and Instrumental;* but yet perhaps, it may be said to be as full and clear as the reader could reasonably expect. Time, and the darkness that has intervened between antiquity and ourselves, have left but limited sources of information, and still fewer on which we can depend. Now, however, we are about to survey periods in which an ampler light will encourage our research, more variegated objects animate our patience, and facts less uncertain, repay our anxiety, and sanction our labour.

---

angles, small bells appended; which hanging loosely by chains, or wires, are moved by the lightest breezes, and produce a tinkling that is highly agreeable to the Chinese taste.

MOD. UNIV. HIST. Vol. 8, p. 300.

CHAP. XI.

MUSIC OF THE ANCIENT ROMANS.

THOUGH the Romans were even more obliged to the Greeks than the Greeks to the Egyptians, especially for their music, it will not follow, that the Romans had not originally a music of their own, however coarse and rude. Indeed, the reverse of this appears to have been the fact. In very high antiquity, they borrowed from the Etruscans such of their musical establishments as suited the wants of their armies and the service of their temples.

We learn from Dionysius Halicarnassensis, that the religious ceremonies of the Pelasgians, (inhabitants of Falerii and Fescennia, two ancient cities of Etruria) were of the same kind with those of the people of Argos. " Holy women," he tells us, " served in the temple, and a girl unmarried, called *Canephoros*, or basket-bearer, began the sacrifice ; besides which, there were choruses of virgins, who hymned the goddess in songs of their country." Therefore, since the Romans were in correspondence with the Etrurians before they became intimate with the Greeks, it is natural to conclude, that they borrowed from the Etrurians their religious ceremonies, and with them their music. According to the same writer, the Arcadians were the first who brought into Italy the use of the Greek letters, and *instrumental music*, performed on the lyre, and those instruments called the

Trigon, and also the *Lydian,* an instrument for which, no doubt, the Greeks were originally indebted to their Adriatic neighbours of Lydia *.

Romulus and Remus, Dionysius likewise informs us, on the authority of many old authors, receiving their education at Gabii, a town near Palatium, were instructed in Greek learning, which included *music:* and Plutarch tells us, that the Greek spoken by the Romans in the time of Romulus, was perfectly pure. Consequently, whatever knowledge of musical science, or skill in musical performance, the Romans might originally acquire from the Etrurians, all their subsequent improvement in music, both vocal and instrumental, was derived from the Greeks. Whatever were their musical powers, they soon found them employment. In their first triumphal procession, in honour of the victory of Romulus over the Cæninenses, the whole army followed the conqueror, *hymning* their gods, in songs of their country, and celebrating their general in extemporary verses †. On some solemn occasions, they added to their own priests and priestesses, those of other countries. In the worship they paid to Cybele, Phrygian musicians attended, striking their cymbals, and blowing their flutes, throughout the procession.

Rousseau, in the course of what he says on the subject of the *Scolia,* or Grecian songs, tells us, that they passed from the Greeks to the Romans, and pertinently observes, that many of the odes of Horace are Bacchanalian and love songs. " But this nation," says he, " more military than

---

* Till that time, we are told, the shepherd's pipe was the only musical instrument in use among the Romans.

† We here see the origin of the *Improvisatori,* or extemporary versifiers of Italy. A custom that to this day is common among the Italians, was, we find, practised in the fourth year of Rome.

sensual, for a long while, made but a very coarse use of music and songs; and, in these particulars, never approached the voluptuous grace and elegance of the Greeks. It seems as if, among the Romans, melody always remained in an un-refined state. Their Hymeneal odes were rather noise and clamour, than airs*; and it is hardly to be presumed that the satirical songs of the soldiers, in the triumphs of their generals, consisted of a very agreeable melody."

But though the vocal strains of the Romans were not comparable with those of the Greeks, as imitations of such good originals, they were too far from being contemptible; and from their constant and various use among the Romans, are rendered too important, not to claim formal notice in a work professing to give an account of the ancient music,— not to stimulate inquiry among the best and most authentic of their historians.

According to Dionysius, one of the branches of the religious institutions of Numa consisted of the *Salii,* twelve young men of the most graceful appearance, chosen from among the patricians, and whose office was to dance in procession, and sing hymns of praise to the god of war, beating time upon the *Ancilia,* or sacred shields. In this, they directly imitated the Greek *curetes ;* as still more evidently appears from the following brief detail by the same writer. " In their evolu-tions," says Dionysius, " they keep time to the music of a flute, sometimes moving together, sometimes by turns; and

---

* From Servius, Macrobius, and Horace, we, however, collect, that the original nuptial songs were after a time refined and polished into epithalamiums. Rousseau, in his complaint of the occasional coarseness of the ancient muse, obviously alludes to the primitive *Versus Fescennini,* so called, because first used by the people of Fes-cennia ; a species of poetry not remarkable, certainly, either for its elegance or delicacy.

in dancing, sing certain hymns, after the manner of their country." Servius Tullius, who began his reign 137 years after Numa, having formed the people into classes and centuries, ordained that two entire centuries should consist of *trumpeters, blowers of the horn,* &c. and of such as, *without any other instruments, sounded the charge.* And in the laws of the twelve tables, among those relating to religious rites, we find the master of the funeral, in the games, authorized to make use of three square mantles, to wear a purple fillet, and to be attended by *ten players on the flute.* And after ordering, that the praises of honoured men be displayed in an assembly of the people, the same law ordains, that *mournful songs,* accompanied with a flute, shall exalt those praises.

Dr. Burney gives from Livy a kind of history of the Roman drama, which, like the Grecian, as the Doctor truly remarks, was inseparable from music. The passage is so curious and so necessary, in an account of the music of the ancient Romans, that this chapter would be incomplete without its insertion.

Livy, speaking of the plague that raged during the consulate of C. Sulpicius Peticus, and C. Licinnius Stolo (364 B. C.) says, " The most remarkable occurrence during this period was, that, in order to obtain mercy of the gods, a public feast called *Lectisternium,* was celebrated for them, which was the third entertainment of this kind that had been made since the building of the city. But the magistrates finding that the violence of the pestilence was neither abated by human prudence, nor divine assistance, and having their minds filled with superstition, among other means which were tried, in order to appease the incensed deities, are said to have instituted the games called *Scenici,* which were amusements entirely new to a warlike people, who, before this time, had none but that of the Circus.

These theatrical representations, like the beginnings of most other things, were at first inconsiderable, and borrowed from foreigners: for actors were sent for from Etruria, who, without verses, or any action expressive of verses, danced, not ungracefully, after the Tuscan manner, to the flute. In process of time, the Roman youth began to imitate these dancers, intermixing raillery in unpolished verses, their gestures corresponding with the sense of the words. Thus were these plays received at Rome, and being improved and refined by frequent performances, the Roman actors acquired the name of *Histriones*, from the Tuscan word *Hister*, which signifies a stage-player. But their dialogue did not consist of unpremeditated, and coarse jests, in such rude verses as were used by the *Fescennini*, but of satires accompanied with music, set to the flute, and recited with suitable gestures. And some years after, Livius Andronicus first ventured to abandon satires, and write plays with a regular and connected plot. After satires (which had afforded the people subject of coarse mirth and laughter) were by this regulation reduced to form, and acting, by degrees, became an art, the Roman youth left it to players by profession, and began, as formerly, to act farces at the end of their regular pieces. These dramas were soon afterwards called *Exodia*, and were generally interwoven with the *Atellane* comedies. These were borrowed from the Osci, and always acted by the Roman youth, who would not allow them to be disgraced by professed actors. Hence it has been a rule for those who performed in such pieces, not to be degraded from their tribe, and they were allowed to serve in the army as if they never had appeared on the stage."

Among the Romans, then, we find, as well as with the ancient Greeks, plays were religious institutions ; we have, therefore, only to recollect the inseparability of music from every Roman ceremony of a religious nature, to see that

the drama was necessarily *musical**. Yet the Romans, it is
well known, were among the latest of great nations in cultivating the arts and sciences, scarcely any of which they acquired but through the medium of conquest. Before their
acquaintance with Greece and her refinements, they owed
all their mental improvements to Etruria, whither they sent

---

* A stronger proof cannot be adduced, of the importance the
Romans attached to music in all religious ceremonies, than the following curious passage in Livy, lib. 9, cap. 30. " I should omit a
circumstance hardly worth mentioning, if it did not seem connected
with religion. The *tibicines*, or flute-players, taking offence at being
refused by the preceding censors, the privilege of eating in the temple
of Jupiter, according to traditional custom, withdrew in a body to
Tibur, so that there were no performers left to play before the sacrifices. This created religious scruples in the minds of the senators,
and ambassadors were sent to Tibur to endeavour to persuade the
fugitives to return to Rome. The Tiburtines readily promised to use
their utmost endeavours to this end, and first summoning them before
their senate, exhorted them to return to Rome ; but finding them deaf
to reason and intreaty, they had recourse to an artifice well suited to
the dispositions of these men. For upon a certain festival, they were
all invited by different persons, under pretence of their assisting in
the celebration of a feast. As men of this profession are generally
much addicted to wine, they were supplied with it, till being intoxicated, they fell fast asleep, and in this condition were placed in carts,
and carried to Rome ; where they passed the remaining part of the
night in the Forum, without perceiving what had happened. The
next day, upon opening their eyes, they were accosted by the Roman
people, who flocked about them ; and having been prevailed upon to
stay in their native city, they were allowed the privilege of strolling
through all the streets in their robes, three days in every year, playing upon their instruments, and indulging themselves in those licentious excesses which are practised upon the same occasion to this
day. The privilege of *eating in the temple* was also restored to such
of them as should be employed in playing before the sacrifices."
This occurred 309 years B. C.

their sons for education, and whence they drew their first knowledge, not only of religion, but of poetry, painting, sculpture,
and music. Besides their obligation both to Etruria and to
Greece, for their taste and knowledge in the fine arts, the
Romans were not a little indebted to the Sicilians, whom
they conquered two hundred years before the Christian era.
From this elegant and ingenious people, who besides reckoning among the names of their men of talent and learning,
those of Æschylus, Diodorus Siculus, Empedocles, Gorgias,
Euclid, Archimedes, Epicharmus, and Theocritus, could
boast of being not only the inventors of pastoral poetry,
but of the wind-instruments with which the shepherds used
to accompany their rural songs, the Romans could not but
derive incalculable improvement in all the acquirements of
mind, and in none among these, more than in the science
and practice of music.

The reduction of Greece opened to the Romans a new
and almost boundless field for their further acquisition of
whatever was elegant and polite.   And it is no small honour
to their intellectual susceptibility, that they permitted the
conquered to exercise a kind of sovereignty over their
taste ; to furnish them with instruction, and to new model
their ideas.   Greece not only provided them with musical
science, but musical instruments.   Yet, their progress, both
in theory, and in vocal and manual execution, was slow.
The few of their authors who wrote professedly upon the
subject of music, such as St. Augustine, Martianus Capella,
Boethius, and Cassiodorus, did not appear till the decline of
the empire*; and in what they produced, were as much

---

* It does not appear, that during the reign of Augustus, Rome
possessed one celebrated sculptor, painter, or musician, or even a distinguished architect, except Vitruvius.

indebted to Greek principles, as to Greek terms for their explanation. Vitruvius in the chapter on music introduced in his Treatise upon Architecture, regrets the unavoidable obscurity of musical literature, on account of the deficiency of terms in the Latin tongue *. " The science of music, in itself abstruse," says he, " is particularly so to those who do not understand the Greek language." This at once shews how little music the Romans possessed in the time of Augustus, and whence that little was received.

Yet during the latter end of the republic, and the voluptuousness of the emperors, music was in great favour at Rome. The temple, the stage, and the place of banquet, derived from its aid a large portion of their splendour : and as the religious ceremonies, dramatic representations, and the indulgences of the bodily appetency became more frequent, so the importance of music would be augmented, and

---

* The poverty of the Roman language, as compared with the Greek, is also a subject of complaint with Lucretius, who, avowing his anxiety to enlighten the mind of his pupil Memmius, on the subject of Epicurean philosophy, affectingly says to him,—

> Alas ! the weakness of the *Roman* tongue
> Shrinks from the burthen of my copious song :
> For precepts new, *new diction* I explore,
> And lack the riches of the *Grecian* store ;
> But thy rare virtue, and the sweet delight
> Thy friendship yields, the grateful task invite ;
> By day no labour, no research I spare,
> And silent night prolongs my pleasing care.
> *For words I seek of comprehensive sway ;*
> In forceful numbers wisdom would convey ;
> Would teach how Nature's secrets thou may'st find,
> And aid the native lustre of thy mind. L. 1. v. 137.
>   BUSBY.

its quality improved *. Nevertheless, we must be cautious of allowing too much to the influence of these circumstances. The Roman shows and public spectacles, intended to amuse and flatter the common people, were necessarily calculated for the meridian of the vulgar appetite, and, in a great measure, must have rejected refinement and polish †. One embellishment, however, appears to have formed a characteristic of their public music; that of the *crescendo* and *diminuendo;* since Cicero (De Oratore l. 3. c. 102) after speaking of the use of *contrast* in oratory, poetry, and theatrical declamation, says, " even musicians, who have composed melody, are sensible of its power ; as is manifest from the care they take to lessen the sounds of instruments, in order to augment it afterwards : to diminish, to swell, to vary, and to diversify ‡. It is also certain, from various pas-

---

* Livy mentions a hymn composed by P. Licinius Tegula, in the 552d year from the building of the city, and sung by twenty seven virgins in procession through the streets of Rome, on occasion of some prodigies, which, from a supposition that the gods were angry, had greatly alarmed the citizens. The *Carmen Seculare* of Horace, and Catullus's hymn to Diana, are curious relics of vocal poetry ; and serve to shew the esteem, and the use, that appertained to the ancient Roman music.

† The noise and indecorum of the clowns and mechanics at the theatre, whose chief delight was in the glare and glitter of the decorations, and such music as was suited to their rude ears, are frequently complained of by Horace. And from Ovid we collect, that the style of the airs of the theatre was so adapted to the taste of the common people, and their construction so artless and practicable, that they were sung by the ploughmen in the fields.

‡ According to the same orator, it was, in Rome, a general habit with persons of rank, to keep a band of musicians, who were called *Servi Symphoniaci*, and *Pueri Symphoniaci;* musical men, and musical boys, attendants.

sages in Greek writers, that ancient vocal music had its
introductory symphonies, which were expressed by the figurative word *Mesaulici*, implying an entry, or passage : and
Meibomius, speaking of the term *Mesaulion*, calls it inter-
piping.

The following description of a musical entertainment
given by a lady (Apul. Metam. lib. ii.) shows that in that
author's time, music was pretty much cultivated. " She
ordered the cithara to be played, and it was done : she asked
for a concert of flutes, and their mellifluous sounds were
immediately heard : lastly, she signified her pleasure, that
voices should be joined to the instruments, and the souls of
the audience were instantly soothed with sweet sounds."
And the account given by the same writer, of a musical
performance in honour of Ceres, would not ill describe
some modern concerts. The occasion was the celebration
of a great festival dedicated to the goddess; and at which
Apuleius himself was initiated into the Eleusinian mysteries.
" A band of musicians," says he, " now filled the air with
a melodious concert of flutes and voices. They were followed by a chorus of youths, dressed in white robes, suitable to the solemnity, who alternately sung an ingenious
poem, which an excellent poet, inspired by the Muses, had
composed in order to explain the subject of this extraordinary festival. Among these, marched several players on
the flute, consecrated to the great Serapis, who performed
many airs dedicated to the worship of the god in his temple.
After this, the venerable ministers of the true religion, shook
with all their force the sistrums of brass, silver and gold,
which produced tones so clear and sonorous, that they might
have been heard at a great distance from the place of performance."

A greater impediment to the progress of music among the
Romans could not, perhaps, have existed, than that of their

barbarous custom of abandoning to their slaves the practice
of the liberal arts, and of treating with the greater degree of
severity those who were most distinguished by their talents.
The Greeks, too just and too wise for so bad a policy,
proceeded to the other extreme, and confined the exercise
of those arts (as the epithet *liberal* implies) to *free men*,
and persons of birth and rank, absolutely forbidding their
study among their slaves; as if they were beings of an inferior nature, and their minds unworthy of a human ornament. However, the use to be here made of the above
comparison between the domestic policy of the Greeks and
that of the Romans is, to ascertain by it one great cause of
the superiority of the former people over the latter in their
degree of perfection in the elegant arts.   Another cause for
this superiority has been assigned, which I cannot so readily
admit.   " What nature was to the Greeks," says the Abbé
Gedoyn (Mem. de Litt.) " the Greeks were to the Romans.
The Grecians had only nature for their example ; since no
nation with which they had any intercourse, was learned and
polished before them.   The Romans, on the contrary, had
the Greeks for models."   More correct had it been to say,
That what the *Egyptians* were to the Greeks, the Greeks
were to the Romans. *Egypt* was the great fount from which
Greece drew her knowledge, her science, and her arts. And
from no science did she make more copious draughts than
from that of music.   For this accomplishment the Romans
were indebted to Etruria and Sicily, a considerable while
before they were instructed by the Greeks, whatever were
the improvements they derived from their conquest, and of subsequent intimacy with, that refined people.   It is, therefore,
equally incorrect to say, that the Romans had no examples
but in the *Greeks*, and that the Greeks were without models,
save those presented to them by *nature :* especially as regarding music, in the science and practice of which, they

in a great degree, were instructed by the Egyptians, as the Romans afterwards were by the Etrurians and Sicilians.

The Romans, we well know, were for centuries, more renowned as a military, than a polite and learned people. At length, however, as if conscious of their own talents, they vied with the elegance of the Greeks, imitated their institutions of musical and poetical contests at their public games, and proved their possession of genius, and capability of taste *. It was not, however, till the time of Augustus, that the glory of their literature attained a splendour any way comparable with that of their military achievements. And after that period, a false taste, borrowed from the Asiatics, substituted for real and manly refinement, an effeminate luxury and vulgar dissipation, which pervaded their public games and exhibitions, and, while they afforded

---

* Nations, like individuals, have their fits, and changes of temper; and are sometimes governed by one kind of circumstance, sometimes by another; hence Music, like other arts, has been cultivated and heard, in particular ages of antiquity, and by certain countries, with a greater degree of enthusiasm than in others. That the Romans had genius, would be sufficiently evident, had we no other proof than the eagerness and zeal with which they copied the various excellencies of the Greeks, so soon as they became acquainted with their superiority. Admitting some of the extraordinary effects imputed to the Grecian melody, (and it is not easy *wholly* to resist the torrent of eloquence and panegyric with which they have been described by respectable historians and philosophers,) the Romans, on their first hearing it, must have been greatly struck. For though the Greek music did not include harmony, properly so termed, yet its melopœia, animated by a noble order of poetry, more solemn ceremonies, greater pomp of public exhibition, and a performance, or delivery, altogether more vivid and impressive than any thing to which the Romans had been accustomed, must have awakened in them a new and livelier sense of human capability in the elegant arts, and have instantly determined them to the exertion of their own powers.

pleasure to the powerful few, taught the multitude to forget the slavery to which they were gradually reduced. In the sixtieth year after Christ, Nero instituted quinquennial exercises in poetry, oratory, and music. Three years after this, he exhibited himself at the theatre of Naples, as a public singer: and in sixty-six, appeared on a stage in Greece. His next exploits were at the Olympic games, where, by corrupting his judges, he carried off the prize of music from professional musicians, with whom he did not scruple to enter the lists. By this means, he obtained eighteen hundred prizes, which he exultingly brought with him from Greece, and entered Naples, Antium, Albanum, and Rome, through a breach in the wall of each city, as an Olympic victor. One of the candidates whom he had conquered, (Diodorus, a celebrated performer on the cithara) was carried through the streets of Rome, in a car in which vanquished kings used to be brought in triumph; and with all the splendour, pomp, and solemnity, employed to signalize the conquering prowess of the Roman generals.

Though the state of the ancient Roman music, and not the life and conduct of a Roman emperor, is the avowed subject of this chapter, the particular propensities of Nero have so linked him with the history of the music of his time, that some further facts concerning the public display of his abilities as a musician, will not be less proper than amusing, to those who can smile at the self-degradation of imperial dignity.

We learn from Suetonius, that this prince so valued his voice, that for its preservation, he was in the habit of lying on his back, with a thin plate of lead upon his stomach; that he frequently submitted to the administration of emetics and cathartics; that he abstained from all kinds of fruit, and whatever food was deemed prejudicial to the vocal organs; that, from the apprehension of straining and hurting the glottis, he ceased to harangue the soldiery and the senate, and issued his orders in writing. His care and anxiety not stopping here, when he returned from Greece, he established about his person a *phonascus*, or officer, whose sole business was, to be the guardian and preserver of his voice. It was only in the presence of this his vocal governor, that he would speak; and when in his presence, only by his permission; and then, only as loud as the officer thought meet: if, perchance, the emperor, forgetting himself, or transported by some sudden emotion, did not attend to his keeper's remonstrances, he was to stop his mouth with a napkin *.

Though all this care and attention did not improve a voice naturally thin and husky, the only way to ensure his favour, was to commend the fulness and the brilliancy of its tones, to be in raptures while he sung, and dejected when he ceased. The emperor's particular vanity, universally known, was, of course, universally flattered; and secure of applauding audiences, he appeared on the stage almost every day, inviting not only the senators and knights, but the whole populace and rabble of Rome, to hear him in the theatre, which he

---

* This excess of folly only rendered the imperial son of Agrippina despicable. What detestation do we add to our contempt, when we read of his constant habit of sallying out from his palace at night to visit the lowest scenes of vice and infamy; of the pleasure he took in insulting all he met in the streets, and his practice of offering public violence to unprotected females; of his disguising himself in the habit of a woman, and being married to one of his eunuchs; of his afterwards celebrating his nuptials with one of his meanest catamites; of his cruelties to his wife Octavia Poppœa, and the celebrated writers, Seneca, Lucan, and Petronius; and his burning of Rome, and during the conflagration, exultingly singing to his lyre the destruction of Troy.

had built in his own palace. He frequently detained the audience, not only the whole day, but the whole night; for while he was disposed, at whatever intervals, to continue to *delight* them, no one dare think of departing*. Besides the great number of spies and informers employed to watch the countenances and behaviour of the auditory, there were many who openly set down the names of those who discovered the least symptoms of dissatisfaction: the vulgar were instantly punished by the soldiery for the least inattention; and persons of rank guilty of the same crime, were sure to experience the imperial vengeance. Suetonius, in his life of Vespasian, afterwards emperor, tells us, that that personage greatly provoked the anger of Nero, by escaping from the theatre during the time of performance: however, fearing the consequences of the offence, he returned, in order to make atonement; when, unfortunately, falling asleep while the emperor was singing, only the most earnest intercession of his friends, men of the highest rank, appeased the imperial wrath, and saved his life.

During this time, public games were celebrated, and dramas performed, in all the great cities of the empire; and these were continued and encouraged by the successors of Nero. Adrian, who had been educated at Athens, was much attached to, and a great favourer of, Grecian customs. So

---

* It sometimes happened that women, unable to get out, were delivered in the theatre. At other times, persons were so tired and disgusted with his performance, that they, by stealth, leaped over the walls, at the hazard of their lives, or counterfeited death, in order to get relieved by being carried out as corpses. Some, by continuing night and day in the same posture, were seized with mortal distempers; these, however, they dreaded less than the resentment of the emperor, which they would inevitably have incurred by their absence.

partial was he to the city where he had imbibed his knowledge, that (in the year 125 A. C.) he celebrated there the great festival of Bacchus: and the next year, presided in the public games. In 132 he instituted new games, and built temples in Egypt to the honour of his favourite, Antinous. One hundred and forty-two years after Christ, Antoninus, Adrian's successor, instituted new games called *Pia* and *Pialia*, in honour of Adrian, which were appointed to be exhibited at Puteoli on the second year of every Olympiad *.

The monuments of art which the ancient Romans have left us, sufficiently testify their powers as an ingenious people. The remaining works of their orators, their poets, their philosophers, and their historians, are illustrious proofs of talents that required only proper cultivation, to be adequate to the attainment of any excellence. Since, in copying the religious ceremonies, public games, and theatrical representations of the Greeks, it was almost impossible that they should have been inattentive to their musical accomplishments, or unambitious of acquisitions more calculated than any others, to strike the general mind, and rouse the feelings common to our nature, we are obliged to conclude, that many of the higher ranks of the Romans cultivated a taste for the Grecian melody. It is not because we are without specimens of their music, that we are entitled to con-

---

* The emperor Commodus, in monstrosity a worthy rival of Nero, and equally vain of the reputation of a great public performer, not contented with exhibiting his abilities as an actor, dancer, and singer, was ambitious of shining as a gladiator. A long series of warfare had hardened the hearts of his people, and inured them to blood; and this their emperor never thought himself so worthily employed, as when, for the sport of his Roman subjects, he was destroying a Roman life.

clude no good Roman music ever existed; since, by a parity of reasoning, we must reject the claims of the Greeks themselves to musical excellence. Destitute of direct evidence, we are compelled to depend upon collateral proofs. As far as such proofs can operate, they are strong. No two arts are so intimately connected as poetry and music. In Greece, the Romans found them blended both in theory and practice; and it is difficult to imagine, that they would be sensible to the beauties of one, and not feel the charms of the other: nay, so interwoven, so incorporated, did they find poetry and music, that it would have required their ingenuity to tear them asunder. If thus, receiving two arts combined by their mutual affinity, they have demonstrated an exalted genius for one of those arts, it is but reasonable to suppose that nature had qualified him for the cultivation of the other. If Homer and Menander had their Roman emulators, so would Terpander and Telephanes; and something like a refined species of music, would, at least, form one of the private amusements of elegant life.

To these arguments, however, in favour of the musical taste of the *higher orders* of the ancient Romans, I would not wish to attribute more force than they really possess. This and the preceding chapters have developed particulars which the reader will know how to collate; and upon which his own judgment will be adequate to decide.

CHAP. XII.

MUSIC OF THE EARLY CHRISTIANS TO THE TIME OF
GUIDO; AND THE INTRODUCTION OF THE MO-
DERN ORGAN.

THAT melody formed a principal feature and embellishment in the sacred rites of the Hebrews, Egyptians, Greeks,
and Romans, has been rendered evident. We shall now
take a view of its introduction into the Christian church;
and the progress of Music till it approached the dignity of a
consonance of parts, or *harmony,* properly so denominated.
Of the propensity of the early Christians to vociferize psalms
and hymns, no evidence is wanting. The twenty-fifth verse
of the sixteenth chapter of Acts, represents Paul and Silas
singing in their dungeon at midnight " praises unto God."
In the nineteenth verse of the fifth chapter of St. Paul to
the Ephesians, that apostle says to them, " Be not drunk
with wine, wherein is excess; but be filled with the Spirit;
speaking to yourselves *in psalms and hymns, and spiritual
songs, singing and making melody in your hearts to the
Lord.*" And in the fifteenth verse of the fourteenth chapter of the first book of the same Apostle to the Corinthians,
his words to that people are, " I will pray with the spirit,
and I will pray with the understanding also : *I will sing
with the spirit, and I will sing with the understanding.*"
And in the thirteenth verse of the fifth chapter of his gene-

ral epistle, St. James also distinguishes between prayer and song. " Is any among you afflicted? Let him pray. Is any merry? *Let him sing psalms.*" Tertullian, speaking of the younger Pliny's persecution of the Christians, says that he went no further than to accuse them of adding to their neglect of sacrifice, the practice of holding meetings before day-break, *to sing in honour of Christ as a God.* And Justin Martyr, who flourished in 163, in his Apology to the Emperor Antoninus Pius, recommends our " approving ourselves grateful to God, by *celebrating his praises with hymns.*" Origen, in his answer to Celsus, who had abused the Christians, treating them as barbarians, says, " We are told that though the Pagans sing hymns to Minerva and to Apollo, they imagine they worship the great God ;" but " We know the contrary, for *we sing hymns to none but the Supreme Being, and to his only Son,* in the same manner as they sing to the sun, moon, stars, and all the heavenly host *." But the following passage alone

---

* The following passage in Clemens Alexandrinus, alluding to the church and to religious music, is not only confirmatory of the use of hymns and psalmody among the primitive Christians, but is curious in itself:—

" This is the chosen mountain of the Lord, unlike Cithæron, which has furnished subjects to tragedy. It is dedicated to Truth: a mountain of great purity, overspread with chaste shades. It is inhabited by the daughters of God, the fair lambs, who celebrate together the *venerable orgies,* collecting the chosen *choir.* The singers are holy men, their song is the hymn of the Almighty King : virgins chant, angels glorify, prophets discourse, while music sweetly sounding is heard." Long before the promulgation of the Gospel, the Greeks and Romans spoke of their gods, their priests, and their religious ceremonies, in the same musical language : and it seems impossible to doubt, that the primitive Christians borrowed from the Pagans the habit of *vocal praise.*

would be sufficient to prove the use of music by the primitive Christians, even before they enjoyed the accommodation of churches, or the sanction of the law. " After supper," says Philo, speaking of the nocturnal assemblies of the Therapeutæ (who Eusebius tells us were Christians) " their sacred songs began. When all were arisen, they selected from the rest two choirs, one of men and one of women, in order to celebrate some festival; and from each of these a person of a majestic form, and well skilled in music, was chosen to lead the band. They then chanted hymns in honour of God, composed in different measures and modulations, now singing together, and now answering each other by turns."

If to this passage we add the fact communicated by Eusebius, that in the time of Constantine, the first Christian emperor, there was at the consecration of churches throughout the Roman dominions, one common consent in chanting forth the praises of God; that the performance of the service was exact, the rites of the church decent and majestic; and that there was a place appointed *for those who sung psalms;* for *youths and virgins, old men and young;* and if we consider, that all the early Greek fathers encouraged the singing of psalms and hymns, both by day and by night, we shall be obliged to conclude, that long before any regular ritual was established, musical performance constituted a part of the Christian worship. Consequently, Christian music, if I may be allowed so to distinguish the melodies used by the church, was, from the time of the apostles down to the reign of Theodosius, towards the end of the fourth century, in an almost uninterrupted course of improvement; and we shall not wonder that its progress during that time should have enabled St. Ambrose to produce his celebrated chant*.

---

* This celebrated composition was, at the time of its production,

St. Augustine, after observing, that the church of Milan, when it introduced this chant into its service, had not begun to practise " mutual consolation and exhortation, with a joint harmony of voices," informs us, that about the same time (the year 386) the persecution of the orthodox Christians was proceeding, in favour of the Arians; and that it was ordered by the empress Justina, mother to the young emperor Valentinian, that hymns and psalms should be sung after the manner of eastern nations, that the people might not languish and pine away with a tedious sorrow; and that from that time it was retained at Milan, and imitated by almost all the other congregations of the world *.

It is to be regretted, that no specimens of the melodies first used by the Christians, are remaining, to inform us of their style and character. That some of them were borrowed from those of the Hebrew worship, and others adopted from the music of the Pagan temples, is extremely probable, if not certain. It has been very generally supposed, that the manner of reciting and singing in the theatres formed the original model of the church service; an idea sanctioned by the fact, that the passion of our Saviour was dramatized by the early priests. Eusebius tells us, that the first regular Christian choir was established at Antioch in

---

established in the church at Milan. St. Augustine's declaration of the delight he received at hearing it sung there, is worth recording. "The voices," says he, " flowed in at my ears, truth was distilled into my heart; and the affection of piety overflowed in sweet tears of joy."

* Some of the fathers affirm, that the music of the Christians drew the Gentiles into the church; and that its effects were often such as to produce their conversion. It seems a question of no very easy solution, whether music has been more indebted to religion, or religion to music.

Syria, and that St. Ambrose brought his melodies from that capital to Milan, and that these melodies, and the original manner of their performance, by *Canonici* and *Psaltæ*, (canons and chanters) were continued in the western church till the time of Gregory the Great.

The *Antiphona*, or alternate singing (a chanting in the manner of dialogue) is said by Socrates the historian, to have been first suggested by St. Ignatius * : but Suidas assigns to this practice a much later origin. According to that writer, the choirs of churches were, in the time of Constantius, the son of Constantine the Great, first divided into two choirs, who sung the psalms of David alternately. However this may have been, it seems that the primitive Christians thought they never so nearly resembled the " heavenly host," as when they were singing. Milton, equally impressed with a sense of the celestial nature of harmony, has assigned to the cherubim and seraphim, the perpetual performance of Hosannahs :

> ————— Their golden harps they took,
> Harps ever tun'd, that glitt'ring by their side,
> Like quivers hung, and with preamble sweet
> Of charming symphony, they introduce
> Their sacred song, and waken raptures high ;
> No voice exempt, no voice but well could join
> Melodious part, such concord is in heav'n.
> PARAD. LOST, B. 3.

The Ambrosian chant is supposed to have been founded on the Greek tetrachords ; but this opinion is not supported

---

* Several of the fathers aver, that this mode of performance was revealed to St. Ignatius by a vision, in which he had seen choirs of angels praising the Holy Trinity in this manner ; and there are who believe it!

by any better authority, than is the idea, that it specifically differed from the Gregorian *. Gregory the Great, however, has the credit of having, two centuries and a half after the time of St. Ambrose, materially improved the ecclesiastical music, as well as collected the fragments of such melodies as had been approved by the first fathers of the church †. Many writers of the middle ages speak of a singing-school founded by Gregory at Rome; and give us to understand, that he banished from the church what is called the *Canto Figurato*, as having too much levity; and that his own chant received the appellation of *Canto Fermo*, from its superior gravity and plainness. Since the music of the church had its foundation in that of the Pagan temple, it might reasonably have been expected, that the *Canto Fermo* would have presented us a specimen of melody, more consonant with the idea we naturally form of music, which we are told so much delighted the Greeks and Romans; unless we are to conclude, that, driven by persecution into woods and caves, the primitive Christians were in a great degree cut off, alike from the polish and the levity

---

* Dr. Burney says, that when he heard the service performed at the Duomo of Milan, he could not discover any considerable difference between the Ambrosian chant performed there, and the melodies used in the other cathedrals in France or Italy, where the Gregorian chant is said to subsist. The truth is, as the Doctor properly remarks, there are no vestiges of the chant of St. Ambrose remaining, sufficient to ascertain its peculiar character.

† The anonymous author of his life says, that he composed, arranged, and constituted the *Antiphonarium*, and chants used in the morning and evening services : and ecclesiastical writers assert, that he was the first who separated the chanters from the regular clergy ; observing that singers were more to be admired on account of their voices, than their precepts or piety.

of society, and adopted a style of singing more analogous
to their serious cast of thinking, and the simplicity of their
manners.

The chants, responses, lessons, and antiphonaries, that
accompany the psalms, were adopted in the church at different times: yet, even though they were reformed and
digested by St. Gregory, they have not lost the marks of
the age in which they were received. The new Christians,
men of mean rank, and as unscientific as illiterate, were
unaccustomed to a refined and artificial music, and consequently incapable of forming the semitones, or singing notes
of different value : hence their *Canto Fermo* seldom mo-
dulates from key to key. This defect, those who are partial to the old ecclesiastical tones, affect to say, is considerably remedied by the *different species of octaves*, included
in the same system ; meaning the major and its relative
minor, or the minor and its relative major.

Rousseau well remarks, (Art. Plain Chant) that the
" Christians having introduced singing into their religious
worship, at a time when music was very much degenerated,
deprived the art of the chief force and energy which it had
still retained, by a total inattention to rhythm and metre,
and by transferring it from poetry, with which it had always
been connected, to the prose of the sacred writings, and to
a barbarous kind of verse, less fit for music than prose itself.
Then one of its two constituent parts vanished, and the
melody being uniformly dragged, without any kind of measure, in notes of nearly equal lengths, lost, by being deprived of rhythm and cadence, all the energy which it
received from them. Hence plain song degenerated into a
psalmody always monotonous, and often ridiculous ; and yet
such of these melodies as have been faithfully preserved,
notwithstanding the losses they have sustained, afford real
judges valuable specimens of ancient music, and its modes,

though without measure and rhythm, and merely in the diatonic genus, which can only be said to be preserved in all its purity in *Canto Fermo*. These modes, in the manner they have been retained in the ancient ecclesiastical chants, have still a beauty of character, and a variety of expression, which intelligent hearers, free from prejudice, will discover, though formed upon a system different from that in present use."

It is remarkable, that notwithstanding the grotesque, cramped, and imperfect scales in which the ecclesiastical chants were composed, secular music seems to have been restrained to the same dry and heavy rules, and to have been confined to a few keys in the diatonic genus, without even the licence of transpositions. The consequence, for a long while, was, the exclusion of all keys and scales not sanctioned by the church; and a melody inevitably quaint, barren, and destitute both of beauty and character. From the time of Gregory to that of Guido, the *authentic* and the *plagal** were the only distinctions of keys; nor were any semitones admitted, except those from E to F, from B to C, and, in some instances, from A to B flat. It is difficult to form an idea of the possibility of producing any effect, either on the ear or the passions, by music constructed with such scanty and inflexible materials; yet it is the opinion of the learned Padre Martini, that the compositions of the first five or six ages of the church, were little more than plain and simple chants of unisons and octaves, limited to the key of C major and its relative minor A. And in this idea he is certainly borne out by the many fragments still remaining in the Canto Fermo of the Romish missals *.

---

* With respect to *Music in parts*, since neither the Greeks nor Romans were yet acquainted with *harmony* or *counterpoint*, it would

Hitherto we have regarded the ecclesiastical music of these earlier ages of Christianity, purely as *vocal;* since, till the reign of Constantine, it does not appear that the introduction of instruments in Christian devotion was permitted. But when the new religion was fully established and freely exercised throughout the whole Roman empire, instrumental performance was called in, to grace the great festivals; and the pomp of the Hebrew and Pagan worship was imitated by the solemn addition of musical accompaniments to the psalms, hymns, and other parts of the religious ceremonies *.

Having seen that Music, both vocal and instrumental, was used in the earliest ages of the church, it is natural that the reader's curiosity should require some intelligence on the subject of its *notation*.

Boethius, who flourished about the latter end of the fifth century, tells us, that in his time, not only the notes of the scale were distinguished by Greek appellations, but an alphabetical notation was employed, in which the letters

---

be idle to expect to find it in the church. The truth is, that many ages elapsed after the establishment of Christianity, before it began to be cultivated. Dr. Burney says, there is not the slightest trace of it to be found in the manuscript *missals, rituals, graduals, psalters,* and *antiphonaria* of any of the great libraries of Europe, which he visited for the purpose of information on this point, so important to musical history.

* Still, only the harp and psaltery were admitted. Neither Jews nor Gentiles were imitated, in the use of abrets and cymbals. These instruments were peremptorily forbidden by the Fathers; who also continually uttered their anathemas against dancing in the church; a practice which nevertheless prevailed for a long while, and gave the name *choir* to that part of the church where the dances were performed; from the Greek word *choros*, a company of dancers.

assumed various positions and transformations.   His words
upon the subject are—

"The ancient musicians invented and published certain
symbols of sounds, by which the name of every string was
known; and of these there was a different series for each
genus and mode, in order to avoid the repetition of the
original and entire name of each sound in the system.   In
this summary manner, a musician who wished to write a
melody to verses, placed over the rhythmical composition of
metre certain signs: so that by this invention, not only the
words of the verses, which are formed of letters, but also the
melody itself, which is expressed by the like signs, might be
transmitted to posterity.   These will consist of two rows of
characters; the higher for the words, and the lower for the
instrument that accompanies the singer."

It appears that Boethius used Roman letters, merely as
references to the divisions of the monochord, not as musical
notes; since (in the sixteenth chapter of his fourth book) he
directs that the alphabetical characters A, B, C, D, E, F,
G, H, I, K, L, M, N, O, P, be made to represent the concords in the double octave.   But though the Roman letters
were not employed as musical characters during the time
of Boethius, such a notation was adopted previous to the
age of Gregory, who, according to all the posterior writers
on the subject of ecclesiastical chanting, reduced their
number from fifteen to seven; the triplication of which, in
three different forms, furnished a notation for three octaves;
the gravest of which he expressed by *capitals*, the mean, or
middlemost, by *minuscules*, and the higher by *double letters*,
thus * :

---

* Mabillon informs us, that before the ninth century, letters were
used for notes in Canto Fermo; and that about the middle of the

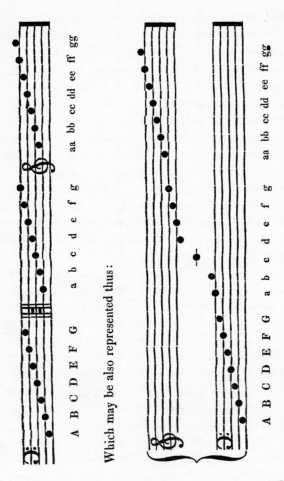

By a statute-book of Aix-la-Chapelle, and one of Charlemagne, it appears to have been ordained, that *notes*, as well

ninth century, Agobard, Archbishop of Lyons, collected into one book
all the several chants, as they were sung throughout the year at his
own church, under the title of *Antiphonarium.*

as chants and grammar should be taught in every monastery and diocese: and an ancient manuscript treatise on music, by Odo the monk, written at the beginning of the tenth century, informs us, that about that time, *lines* began to be used *.

The first notes were of a square form, and without stems. To these succeeded *points*, similar to those above † : these, again, after a time, received the addition of *stems*, sometimes detached, sometimes confluent, and sometimes distorted into hieroglyphical forms.

We learn from Zarlino, that when in the first ages of Christianity, the ancient Greek notation by letters was thrown aside, John Damascenus invented new characters, accommodated to the Greek ecclesiastical tones; and these characters, of greater powers than our own, expressed all the intervals used in melody. Such indices, must, however, have been very complex, compared even with the notation in the artless times of Canto Fermo; but how much more so would it appear to us, to whom the invention of lines and cliffs has rendered music so easily legible! It was about the time of the introduction of counterpoint, that the great advance towards this facile representation of sounds began to be made; for however florid the melody of the more modern Greeks might have been, the preference given by the heads of the western church to permanence in whatever

---

* At first, the lines were eight or nine in number; and the words of the psalm, or hymn, were placed in the spaces between them. Each space being, by a letter prefixed to it, the representative of the sound corresponding with that letter, the situation of a word in this or that space, indicated the sound to be given to that word.

† Hence the term *counterpoint;* that is, *point against point,* or *part against part.*

concerned the church, long kept music in the plain and simple state in which it was left by Gregory. But it is now time to take a view of the establishment and progress of music in England and France.

Bishop Stillingfleet, who was of opinion that St. Paul visited this island, after giving an account of the arrival here of St. Augustine, describes the English manner of performing mass, and speaks of the music employed by the early Christians of the country * ; and from the venerable Bede, and William of Malmesbury, we learn, that Austin the monk, who had been sent here from Rome, to convert the Saxons, instructed them in ecclesiastical music. Bede in his Ecclesiastical History, tells us, that when Austin and his companions had their first audience of Ethelbert, in the Isle of Thanet, they approached him in procession, *singing litanies;* and that, afterwards, when they entered the city of Canterbury, they *sung a litany,* and at the end of it, *hallelujah.* Though our British ancestors, as Bede informs us, had been instructed by St. Germanus in the rites of the Gallican church, and many years before the arrival of St. Austin, had heard him sing *hallelujah,* yet they appear to have been wholly unacquainted with the Roman ritual. For it is remarked by Bishop Stillingfleet, " that the principal difference between the Roman and Gallic ritual, which the Britons had adopted before the arrival of Austin, was in the *church music,* in which the Romans were thought to excel other western churches so far, that the goodness of their music was the chief incitement to the introduction of their offices."

From the Saxon annals we collect, that in the reign of Egbert, music, as well as the other liberal arts, began to

---

* Vide Origines Britannicæ, 1685.

flourish in England: and Bede (in his Vit. Abbot. Wire-
moth and Eccles. Hist) tells us, that in 680, John, Præcentor of St. Peter's in Rome, was commissioned by Pope
Agatho to instruct the monks of Weremouth in the art
of singing; and particularly to acquaint them with the
Roman manner of performing the festival services throughout the year. " And such was the reputation of his skill,"
says Bede, " that the masters of music from all the other
monasteries of the north, came to hear him; and prevailed
on him to open schools for teaching music in other places
of the kingdom of Northumberland."

It is a circumstance very striking, but exceedingly true,
that the French, not contented with many exalted merits in
the fine arts, have ever discovered an avidity to be thought
great musicians; not shrinking from, but rather, indeed, courting, a comparison even with the Italians. So early as the
time of Charlemagne, they had a serious dispute with the
Romans, on the subject of their own assumed superior
knowledge and taste, both in composition and performance.
The fact of that ancient quarrel is more worthy of notice,
as it was the beginning of a rivalry between the French and
Italian musicians, which, with but few intermissions, so
raged, even to the last century, as to excite the ridicule of
their own wits, as well as those of other nations. The
story, as serving to prove that the English were not the only
people obliged to the Romans, for the best style of singing
cathedral music, is not too long for admission into this
history, though the reader, perhaps, will join me in wishing
it were shorter.

" The most pious King Charles having returned to celebrate
Easter at Rome, with the Apostolic Lord, a great quarrel ensued,
during the festival, between the Roman and Gallic singers.
The French pretended to sing better, and more agreeably,
than the Italians : and the Italians, on the contrary, regard-

ing themselves as more learned in ecclesiastical music, which they had been taught by St. Gregory, accused their competitors of corrupting, disfiguring, and spoiling the true chant. The dispute being brought before our sovereign lord the King, the French, thought themselves sure of his countenance and support, and insulted the Roman singers; who, on their part, emboldened by superior knowledge, and comparing the musical abilities of their great master, St. Gregory, with the ignorance and rusticity of their rivals, treated them as fools and barbarians. As their altercation was not likely to come to a speedy issue, the most pious King Charles asked his chanters, which they thought to be the purest and best water; that which was drawn from the source, at the fountain head, or that, which, after being mixed with turbid and muddy rivulets, was found at a great distance from the original spring? They unanimously exclaimed, that all water must be more pure at its source. Upon which, our lord the king said, Mount ye then up to the pure fountain of St. Gregory, whose chant ye have manifestly corrupted. After this, our lord the king applied to Pope Adrian for singing-masters, to correct the Gallican chant; and the Pope appointed for that purpose Theodore and Benedict, two chanters of great learning and abilities, who had been instructed by St. Gregory himself; he likewise granted to him *Antiphonaria*, or choral books of that saint, which he had written himself in Roman notes. Our lord the king, at his return to France, sent one of the two singers granted to him by the pope, to Metz, and the other to Soissons; commanding all the singing-masters of his kingdom to correct their *antiphonaria*, and to conform in all respects to the Roman manner of performing the church service. Thus were the French *antiphonaria* corrected, which had before been vitiated, interpolated, and abridged, at the pleasure of every choir-man; and all the chanters of France learned from the

Romans, that chant which they now call the French chant. But as for the beats, trills, shakes, and accents of the Italians, the French were never able to execute or express them; nor, for want of sufficient flexibility in the organ of voice, were they capable of imitating, in these graces, any thing but the tremulous and guttural noise of goats. The principal school of singing was established at Metz; and in the same proportion as the Roman chant exceeded the chant of this city, the singers of Metz surpassed all those of other French schools. The Roman chanters likewise instructed those of France in the art of organizing; (or singing in thirds) and our sovereign lord Charles having, besides, brought with him into France masters in grammar and arithmetic, ordered those arts to be cultivated throughout his dominions; for, before the reign of the said lord the king, the liberal arts were neglected in France." (Vide Annal. et Hist. Francor.)

Bede (the disciple of Benedict Biscop) says, that his preceptor was the principal disseminator of the Roman chant; and that it was he who taught it to the monasteries he himself founded in the bishopric of Durham, Girwy, and Weremouth: from him we also learn, that Adrian, Stephen, (the monk of Canterbury) Friar James, and many others, were celebrated for their skill in singing *.

The latter end of the ninth century produced a *royal* musician of no common talents. Alfred was conspicuous among the lyrists of his time. Asser, Friar John, Grimbald the monk, and all his cotemporaries extol his performance,

---

* It was then the custom for the clergy to travel to Rome for improvement in music, as well as to import masters of that art from the Roman college; till the successors of Gregory established a music-school at Canterbury, when the rest of the island was furnished with masters from that seminary.

and praise his generous encouragement of the art *. This prince, whose power to impose himself upon the Danish camp as a harper, so fully proves his musical proficiency, founded in 886, (according to the annals of the church of Winchester) a professorship at Oxford for the cultivation of music as a science †.

Fuller, in his *Church History,* tells us, that St. Dunstan, who flourished in the tenth century, excelled in musical knowledge; a qualification at that time indispensable to ecclesiastical preferment. Indeed, his superiority as a harpist, was so signal as to give birth to his being suspected of the crime of musical magic; to his being actually charged with having, by the aid of the devil, constructed a harp that was capable of self-motion, and self-performance. William of Malmesbury says, that in the reign of Edgar, this prelate gave an organ to the abbey of Malmesbury; and it is upon record, that he cast two bells for Abingdon Abbey with his own hands.

Organs, as well as bells, were now in very general use. The former must, indeed, have been introduced into the church before the time of Julian the Apostate; since that Emperor (who flourished in the fourth century) is the re-

---

* During this period, music, arithmetic, geometry, and astronomy, grammar, rhetoric, and logic, (the first four constituting what was called the *quadrivium,* and the latter three the *trivium*) were the sciences which the monks pretended to cultivate: while the island was so destitute of literature during the youth of Alfred, that he was twelve years old before a tutor could be found, competent to teach him the alphabet. But in the interim, he had, by his ear, learned a variety of Saxon songs, the poetry of which awakened in him an elevation of sentiment and patriotic feeling, while their melodies improved his taste for music.

† The first who filled the chair was Friar John of St. David's.

puted author of the following Greek epigram in the *anthologia.*

Ἀλλοίην ὁράω δονακων φύσιν ηπ8 ἀπ' ἄλλης
Χαλκείης τάχα μαλλον ἀνεβλάςησαν ἀρ8ρης,
Ἀγριοι, 8δ' ἀνέμοισιν ὑφ' ἡμέτεροις δονέονται,
Ἀλλ' ὑπο ταυρείης προθορὼς σπήλυγγος ἀητης,
Νέρθεν εὔτρητον καλάμων ὑπὸ ῥίζαυ ὁδεύει.
Καί τις ἀνήρ ἀγέρωχος ἔχων θοὰ δακτυλα χειρὸς,
Ιςαται ἀμφαφόων κανόνας συμφράδμονας αὐλων·
Οἰδ' ἀπαλδη σκιρτῶτες, ἀποθλί 88σιν ἀοιδήν.

Reeds I behold, of earth the rigid spoil,
Reeds of a novel growth, and brazen soil ;
That not heav'n's wind, but blasts mechanic breathe,
From lungs that labour at their roots beneath ;
While a skill'd artist's nimble finger bounds
O'er dancing keys, and wakes celestial sounds.

BUSBY.

The *Hydraulicon*, nevertheless, appears to have been in use, as late as the beginning of the sixth century *. About that

---

* Cassiodorus, who flourished at this period, gives the following description of the wind-organ, as it then existed. " The organ is an instrument composed of divers pipes, formed into a kind of tower, which, by means of bellows, is made to produce a loud sound : and in order to express agreeable melodies, there are in the inside, movements made of wood, that are pressed down by the fingers of the player, which produce the most pleasing and brilliant tones." But, as Sir John Hawkins justly remarks, whoever is acquainted with the exquisite mechanism of this instrument, and considers the very low state of the manual arts at that time, will find it difficult to suppose that the organ of the eighth century bore any very great resemblance to that now in use.

time it began to yield to the superiority of the pneumatic organ, which at first, was blown by hand bellows. Still, it was not till the seventh century that its use was introduced at Rome. Vitalian was the first pope that embellished divine service with this noble instrument; and in France, it did not make its appearance till 757, when the emperor Constantine Copronymus the Sixth, as Sigebert relates, presented one to Pepin.

It is remarkable, that Bede, who lived till near the middle of the eighth century, makes no mention of the use of organs, (even when he is minutely describing the manner in which the psalms and hymns were sung) though it is well known, that a hundred years before that period, their introduction into the church had become pretty general. It is not easy to account for the appearance of the organ in England before it was employed in Italy and Germany. That this was the fact, we cannot doubt, since we find Mabillon and Muratori saying, that during the tenth century, organs became common in Italy and Germany, *as well as in England.* Julian's epigram gives the invention of the wind-organ to Greece: from Greece, therefore, to England it must have passed direct; but by virtue of whose zeal it is not possible to determine *. Though music, long before the tenth century, had been received into churches and religious houses, and sanctioned by all the dignitaries of the Christian church, the novelty of the organ, perhaps, forbad for a while its being *orthodox;* and

---

* Zarlino, in his *Sopplimenti Musicali,* intimates, that the prevailing opinion was, that the modern organ was first used in Greece, and that it thence found its way to Hungary and Bavaria; but this he refutes, as he does also the supposed antiquity of an organ in the cathedral church of Munich, pretended to be the most ancient in the world, with pipes of one entire piece of box, equal in magnitude to those of the modern church organ.

Italy and Germany were willing to witness its effects on the people of another country before they ventured on its adoption. Finding that it was not only well received by the religious in England, but calculated to heighten the general fervour of piety, they resolved to avail themselves of its influence; and the organ became the universal accompaniment to the voices of the choir. From a celebrated missal of the tenth century*, we obtain an idea of the manner in which the organ was made to relieve the monotony of the service. In the midst of the lesson from *The Song of the Three Children*, after the 27th verse, we read, " Here the priest begins to sing *with the organ.*" In the tenth century, then, the use of this noble instrument was, it is evident, established throughout Christendom. But still the organs of England retained their superior character. And if we admit the fact, that the organ was introduced into this island before it made its appearance in Italy, Germany, and France, we shall not be surprised that its progressive improvement here should have more than kept pace with its advances in those countries. The more natural will it appear, that this should have been the case, if we consider, that the fondness of the English for music, was always great; and that consequently, no encouragement would be wanting, to stimulate the ingenuity of the artist †.

Music, certainly, according to every information of history, when once planted among us, flourished rapidly; loved the soil, and grew abundantly. If for a long time, it here consisted merely of chants applied to psalms and hymns, it

---

* Among the Barberini manuscripts at Rome.

† Giraldus Cambrensis does not scruple to assert, that the natives of Wales and the northern parts of Great Britain were *born musicians.*

was, at least, as forward in its maturity as the music of other nations. Our *Canto Fermo*, if the monkish historians are to be credited, was cultivated and taught by almost all the ingenious among the clergy, who, they assure us, were well skilled in music. As early as the seventh century, Theodore, Archbishop of Canterbury, and the Abbot Andrian, introduced into all our places of worship the Roman manner of singing, which, till then, had been practised only in Kent; though soon afterwards, it spread over the whole kingdom *. Hollinshed, in his Chronicles, Vol. I. thus describes the progress of vocal music in our churches :—

" Also, whereas before-time, there was in a manner no singing in the Englishe churches, except it were in Kent; now they began in every church to use singing of divine service, after the ryte of the church of Rome. The Archbishop Theodore, finding the church of Rochester void by the death of the last bishop, named Damian, he ordeyned one Putta, a simple man in worldly matters, but well instructed in ecclesiastical discipline, and namely, well seene in song, and musicke to be used in the church, after the manner as he had learned of Pope Gregorie's disciples." And afterwards, when Ethelred, king of the Mercians, invaded the kingdom of Kent with a great army, destroying the country before him, and amongst other places, the city of Rochester; the cathedral church was also spoiled and defaced, and Putta driven from his residence; upon which, as the same historian relates, " he wente unto Scroulfe, the Bishop of Mercia, and there obteyning of him a small cure, and a portion of ground, remayned in that country; not once

---

* The first singing-master in Northumberland, except John, was Edde, surnamed Stephen, who was sent thither out of Kent by Wilfred, primate of all England.

labouring to restore his church of Rochester to the former state, but went about in Mercia to teach song, and instruct such as would learne musicke, wheresoever he was required, or could get entertainment."

This both proves, that the English clergy of the seventh century were good musicians, and that music itself was in such credit and esteem, as to render the art of teaching it worthy the occupation of the dignitaries of the church. Yet, what the music actually was, the mystery of which the clergy undertook to communicate, is not possible to ascertain. Perhaps, (to speak with Dr. Burney) had we examples of their labours, they would not much exalt our notions of their science and ingenuity : but to judge of their musical accomplishments as compared with the science of a thousand years later, would be unjust. Equally distant from equity were it, to estimate their mechanism by the present scale of merit in that province of human art. To judge of the talents of our Saxon ancestors as *organ-builders*, we must compare them with those of their own time in other countries; not with those of the present age, or even of the last two or three centuries. As a question of comparative genius, the subject includes the consideration of comparative opportunities. The present state of mechanical science sanctions the boldest hopes in every thing within its sphere of operation, and some of the most daring expectations have been realized ; but the paucity of experience and dearth of knowledge in the tenth century, far from entitling us to expect more than was then performed, leave us to be astonished, that so much was really achieved.

CHAP. XIII.

STATE OF MUSIC FROM THE TIME OF GUIDO TO THE FORMATION OF THE TIME TABLE.

W E are now in the middle ages, and among the Goths, Vandals, and Huns, Germans, Franks and Gauls, in whose music we cannot reasonably look for any thing like maturity or perfection. Where, and when, the ideas are crude, the language harsh, and the manners savage, the advancement of science and the arts, will be almost imperceivably slow, unless the task of their culture happily fall into the hands of some one gifted with genius, and endued with patience, to penetrate and pursue, to discover and enhance, to bring the diamond's light from the darkness of the mine, and by an improved disposition of things, make it the luminary of a new creation. Such a diamond, such a luminary, was *Guido Aretinus*, a monk of Arezzo in Tuscany, though, with respect to the more northern parts of Europe, a light shining at a distance. To Guido modern music was indebted for the invention of *counterpoint ;* or, at least, for the first suggestion of that great and important advancement in composition.

Of Guido's various tracts on the science, the principal is the *Micrologus*, written in the eleventh century ; it is not long, is written in monkish Latin, and contains an account

of the author's method of teaching boys to sing*, with
rules for the composition, and just performance, of the plain
chant. Of the several inventions attributed to this musician, so distinguished in his own time, we do not find him
expressly claiming any one in the work just mentioned;
though he clearly disowns all title to the honour of adding
the Greek *gamma*, (G on the first line in the bass) to the
bottom of the ancient scale. It has been doubted by some,
whether B flat (or B *rotundum*, because it was designated
by a round or Italian *b*) was first introduced by Guido; or
whether some prior musician had stationed it between A and
B natural, (or B quadrum, because its sign was a square or
Gothic B, thus: ♮.) But the second chapter of the work
to which we are now alluding, shows this semitonic interval
to be really his. He was the founder of the *hexachord*, or
diatonic ascent from the key note to its sixth; to which six
sounds he applied the syllables *ut, re, mi, fa, sol, la* †, taken
from Paulus Diaconus's hymn to St. John the Baptist, of
each hemistich of which, they respectively formed the first
syllable; as thus:

Ut *queant laxis* RE*sonare fibris*
MI*ra gestorum* FA*muli tuorum*
SOL*vi polluti* LA*bii reatum*
> *Sancti Johannes!*

Also he was the inventor of the use of *points ;* and the
author of an improved method of discanting, which, till he
suggested something better, consisted of an under part,

---

* Guido's method of teaching to sing, was that of guiding the
voice by the aid of the monochord.

† The modern Italians use the syllable *do*, instead of *ut*, as more
soft.

called the *organum,* sung to the *cantus,* or plain song, in fourths, or elevenths ; thus :—

It was permitted to double either the plain song, or the organum; in the latter case, an uninterrupted succession of fifths was produced between the duplicate of organum and the cantus ; as thus :—

---

* The under *part* of a *discant,* or harmony dupla, or tripla, was called the *organum.*

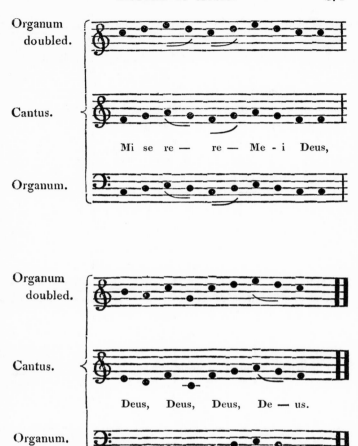

Till Guido's time, it seems, this barbarous dissonance was bearable. The change he made, it must be confessed, did not amount to its entire removal; but nevertheless he considerably diminished the jargon; and though he was cautious of making too free with the ditone, or major third, (a combination numbered with the discords, by the ancients)

the honour is to be allowed him, of having elevated it to the rank of a concord.

Dr. Burney is not satisfied that Guido was really the inventor of *counterpoint ;* and I agree with the Doctor, that, looking at the specimens of some of the combinations he has left, we are obliged to admit that he had large strides to make, before he could arrive at the formation of any thing like pure and regular harmony *. Among the various treatises of this ingenious churchman, some of which are in the royal library at Paris, some in the Vatican, and others in the British Museum, there is one containing a section under this title : *Quid est Armonia ?* What is Harmony ? In this part of the work we find him giving a fair definition of the word *harmony,* as harmony is now understood. He enumerates the ecclesiastical tones, and completes the scale, or septenary †. Fortunately, the study of music had an intimate connexion with Guido's holy profession, and he fully availed himself of the opportunity it afforded him of cultivating his favourite science ; a science, by his success in the practice, study, and improvement of which, he has established a reputation which has lasted eight hundred years. The Greek *gamma* added to the scale, the settling the *lines* and *cliffs* ‡, his adoption of the alphabetical names

---

* Dr. Brown, speaking in his Dissertation on Poetry and Music, of the time of Guido's first appearance, says, " After many centuries had passed in darkness, Guido arose ! and with a force of genius surpassing that of all his predecessors, invented the art of counterpoint, or composition in parts. " But Dr. Brown was not a musician.

† In doing this, he quotes Virgil: *Orpheus Obloquitur numeris septem discrimina vocum.*

‡ The use of parallel lines was introduced before the time of Guido ; but the regular stave of four lines was not generally adopted till the thirteenth century. Also the Greek *gamma* is said to have

of notes, still used, his introduction of the *harmonic hand*, his *hexachords* and *solmization, points, counterpoint,* new method of *discant,* and invention of the *Polyplectrum,* or spinnet, are testimonies of his talents and industry, and will support his name as long as the art whose powers he extended, shall continue to gratify the ears, and flatter the passions of mankind.

Some dispute has arisen respecting the credit given to Guido by many, for the introduction of the five lined stave, as now used. Kircher positively asserts, that it was not used till his time ; and as strenuously insists upon his being the inventor of counterpoint, and the polyplectrum, honors which have been denied him by others. With respect to the five-lined stave, if Guido was not the first who employed it, still he was the first who gave it the latitude of accommodation it now affords ; since, till his time, either the lines only were used, or the spaces only. Confident of the service he had rendered music by this improvement, in the prologue to his *Antiphonarium,* he speaks of its importance in the following terms :

" By divine assistance, I have pointed out such a method of notation, that by a little help from a master at first, an intelligent and studious person may easily acquire the rest

---

been suggested by the Abbot Odo, a century earlier than when the work of Arezzo flourished. But this assertion is founded on a passage in a work of Odo called the *Enchiridion,* where the *gamma* is mentioned ; and this very passage is confessed to have been interpolated by Guido. With respect to *cliffs,* they originally consisted of the letters of the alphabet, one of which was placed at the beginning of each line and space, to declare its name, and the sound of the notes placed upon or within it. These letters were called the *claves signatæ,* and were, after a time, reduced from seven to two. For a description of the *harmonic hand,* see note, page 274.

by himself. And if any one should suspect my veracity in this assertion, let him come to our convent, let him make the experiment, let him examine the children under my care, and he will find, that though they are still severely punished for their ignorance of the psalms, and blunders in the reading, they can now sing correctly without a master, the chants to those psalms of which they can scarcely pronounce the words." He then explains the use of the lines and spaces, and tells us, that " all the notes which are placed on the same line, or in the same space, denote the same sound: and that the name of the sound is determined, either by the colour of the line, or by a letter of the alphabet placed at the beginning of it: a rule of such consequence," he adds, " that if a melody be written without a letter, (that is, a cliff) or coloured line, it will be like a well without a rope; in which though there be plenty of water, it will be of no use."

Certain it seems, that Guido first taught the modern notation, and the method of discovering by the eye all the different intervals, and of singing melodies merely from the view of the signs of their sounds: and though the honour of the *solmization*, has been partially denied him, the invention is positively ascribed to him by writers who immediately followed the period in which he lived. One of these, Sigebert, a monk of Gemblours, who flourished as early as 1028, says, " he (Guido) excelled all his predecessors; as by his method, children were taught to sing new melodies, with more facility than by the *voice* of a master, or the use of an instrument: for by only affixing six letters, or syllables, to six sounds, (all that music admits of, *regularly*) and distinguishing these sounds by the fingers of the left hand *,

---

* This was effected by what was called the *harmonic hand*, consisting of a representation of the left hand, bearing on the joints of

their distances ascending and descending through the whole diapason, are clearly presented both to the eye and the ear." This evidence, by a writer who was his cotemporary, in fa-

---

the thumb and fingers the names of the several notes, according to the then newly-established solmization. Though this *manual diagram* is generally denominated the *Guidonian hand*, in honour of its reputed inventor, its use, like several other of Guido's improvements, has, by some writers, been attributed to the ingenuity of his predecessors. It is true, that no proof of the invention being his, appears in any of his works ; but since it was in common use during his time, and there is no certainty that it was known till then, it seems but just to conclude, that it owed its introduction to the author of the other musical inventions. The different *hexachords* will be best elucidated by the following samples of notation by *points*. But it is necessary to premise, that in the time of Guido, only three different keys were in use ; C, F, and G ; and to explain that F not being allowed to be made sharp in the key of G, the harshness of the interval between F natural and B natural, occasioned the *hexachord* of G to be called the *durum*, or *hard* bexachord ; while that of F, requiring, and obtaining, B flat, which removed the harshness of the tritone F, B natural, was denominated the *molle*, or *soft* hexachord ; and that of C, in which the B flat was unnecessary, the *natural* hexachord.

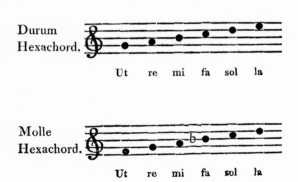

Durum Hexachord.

Ut   re   mi   fa   sol   la

Molle Hexachord.

Ut   re   mi   fa   sol   la

vour of Guido, as being the inventor of the improvements
generally attributed to him, is powerful, and, by every candid
reader, will be felt as decisive.   But should doubts still

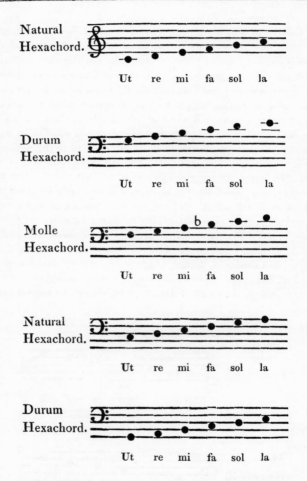

Natural
Hexachord.

Ut   re   mi   fa   sol   la

Durum
Hexachord.

Ut   re   mi   fa   sol   la

Molle
Hexachord.

Ut   re   mi   fa   sol   la

Natural
Hexachord.

Ut   re   mi   fa   sol   la

Durum
Hexachord.

Ut   re   mi   fa   sol   la

The reader will bear in mind, that though the hexachord, by its
very name, could include only six notes, the seventh had been intro-

remain, the testimony of Carpentier, in his Supplement to the Latin Glossary of Du Cange, (art. *Gamma*) will surely remove them. That learned writer gives a passage from the *Chronicle of Tours,* under the year 1033, which makes Guido the certain author of the scale, and the art of solmization. The words of this passage are, " Guido Aretine, a wonderful musician, flourished in Italy about this time. He constructed the gamut and rules for singing, by applying those names to the six sounds, which are now universally used in music. For, before, practitioners had no other guide than habit and ear." And certain it is, that though some writers have endeavoured to shear Guido of many of his honours, and in some few instances, perhaps, the integrity of history might require the spoliation, yet in the times they adorned, his merits were unequalled, and demand our veneration. An obscure monk, the rays of whose genius could penetrate the pontiff's palace, whose lucubrations were destined to form future authorities, and whose inventions were to be received in almost [every part of Europe, must be allowed to have conferred considerable benefits on society, and to have entitled himself to a place among those whose labours are rewarded with admiration and esteem. Of such a man, no apology need be offered for presenting the reader with an ample biography.

Guido, as already observed, was a native of Arezzo, a city

---

duced by Guido; but was generally omitted, even by himself, as extraneous and irregular. With respect to his object in bringing forward the above hexachords, he modestly declares, that he writes merely for the *church*, where the pure diatonic genus was first used. I ought not to conclude this note, without observing, that the sound added next above *la*, that is, the *seventh* of the key, is supposed to have received for its appellation the syllable *si*, from Le Maire, a French singing-master, in the beginning of the seventeenth century.

in Tuscany. From the station of a monk of the order of St. Benedict, he rose to that of abbot of the Holy Cross at Avellano, near Arezzo. Of the minor incidents attending his clerical and musical career, but little is known; and for that little we are chiefly indebted to himself. Fortunately, the preservation of an epistle from him to his friend Michael, a monk of Pomposo, which Cardinal Baronius has inserted in his Ecclesiastical Annals, affords us the opportunity of becoming acquainted with particulars not to be collected from his works, and which cannot but be acceptable to every musical connoisseur.

In his time, the beginning of the eleventh century, the state of learning being very low, and the subjects for study few, merely including theological controversy, church history, logic, and astrology, left to the musical taste and abilities of Guido, sufficient opportunities for their exertion, gratification, and improvement. All the time spared him by his monastic functions, (and even they, we must bear in mind, were partly musical) he devoted to the serious study of his favourite art; particularly attending to that province of it which embraced the system of the ancients, the method of whose notation he had, early in life, determined to reform. His ultimate object was, to facilitate the instruction of those who were employed in the choral service, and to render them capable of a more decent style of performance *. The legendary accounts in some old monkish manuscripts, would persuade us, that he was assisted in this pious intention by immediate communications from heaven. Some

---

* The difficulties arising from the notation then in use, to youth under tuition for the church offices, were so great, that, as we learn from himself, ten years were generally consumed, barely in acquiring the knowledge of the *plain-song.*

writers have not scrupled to impute his invention of the application of syllables to the gamut, to immediate inspiration; and Guido himself seems to have indulged the same opinion; for he expressly says, That it was revealed to him by the Lord in a dream. But graver historians are contented with stating, that being at vespers in the chapel of his monastery, it happened that one of the offices appointed for that day was the hymn to St. John the Baptist, (which the reader has seen) and that its performance suggested the important improvement of the hexachord, and a more perfect notation.

The conversion of the ancient tetrachords into hexachords was, indisputably, a bold as well as an ingenious idea; and he had to reckon upon the sturdy opposition of all the old musical scholiasts, to his *innovation* upon the *established scale*. But whatever were the difficulties to be apprehended, or from whatever source they might arise, he resolved to persevere; and at length his fertile mind suggested the one thing wanting, to complete his design: that of a method of effectually discriminating the tones and semitones. During the performance of the hymn, he remarked the iteration of the words, and the frequent recurrence of the syllables *ut, re, mi, fa, sol, la;* at the same time, he was struck with the closeness of the syllable *mi,* and the broad, open sound of *fa,* which he conceived could not fail to impress the mind with an idea of their congruity in respect of the sounds to which they might be applied; and immediately formed the conception of employing them as the distinguishing appellations of his new hexachord.

Delighted with this discovery, he retired to his study, and laboured incessantly till he had perfected his system, and prepared it for practice. When, however, he communicated his invention to the brethren of his own monastery, they received it with the coldness he might have expected. Their

envy, however, very luckily, was not a match for the interest
he had with the abbot; who allowed him to try the efficacy
of his new method on the boys then training under him
for the choral service ; and its success exceeded his most san-
guine expectation, fully justified the abbot's compliance with
his wishes, and quickly spread abroad *the fame of the Monk
of Arezzo*.   Kircher tells us, that his method was speedily
adopted by the clergy of other countries; and that Her-
mannus, bishop of Hamburg, and Elvericus, bishop of
Osnaburg, availed themselves of its advantages : and the
authors of the *Histoire Litteraire de la France*, assure us,
that it was readily received in that country, and taught in
all the monasteries in the kingdom.

Cardinal Baronius states, that the reputation of Guido's
great talents, and the singular service he had rendered the
church by his musical improvements, having reached the ears
of Pope Benedict VIII. that pontiff in the year 1022, invited him to Rome, where he received him with honour, and
treated him with the greatest kindness *.   The splendour of a
court, however, it seems, did not so dazzle the imagination,
or flatter the feelings of Guido, as to induce him to remain
long under the patronage of Benedict.   He soon returned
to Arezzo, and John XX. (or, as some compute, the 19th)
who in 1024, succeeded Benedict, sent three several mes-
sengers for him, before he was prevailed upon to revisit
Rome.   His second reception at that city, as his own letter
to the monk Michael informs us, was even more gracious

---

* When the invitation arrived from his Holiness, the very brethren
who had, before, so coldly viewed his new method, were the first to
advise him to accept the invitation : and it was agreeably to their
united resolution, that he was attended to Rome by Grimaldo the
abbot, and Peter, the chief of the canons of the church of Arezzo.

than his first. The new pontiff frequently conversed with him with the greatest freedom, on the subject of his musical discoveries; and when Guido first shewed him his *Antiphonarium*, or notation of the mass for the whole year, his Holiness regarded it as a prodigy, and would not quit his seat till he had learned to sing a chant in it under the author's personal direction : he then confessed himself convinced of that which he should have found it difficult to believe, without his own personal experience of its verity. The pope was desirous that he should remain at Rome; but Guido's indifferent state of health rendering him fearful of encountering the bad air of that city, (for the summer heats were approaching) he took his leave, promising to have the honour of revisiting his Holiness, and of explaining to him more fully the principles of his new system. On his passage back, he made a visit to the Abbot of Pomposa, a town in the duchy of Ferrara : With the Abbot's earnest solicitations to settle in his convent, he was, after some hesitation, induced to comply; in hopes, as he says, of rendering that great monastery still more famous, by his labours under its roof.

In this monastery it was, that he wrote several of his musical tracts; among which, some reckon his *Micrologos*, which he dedicated to Theobald, Bishop of Arezzo; and which, according to a memorandum found on the back of the original manuscript, he finished in the thirty-fourth year of his age*.

---

* Vossius speaks also of another musical work, which he wrote at the same place, and dedicated to the same person. Divers others, among whom was Mersennus, mention also his being engaged in the controversy with Berenger, concerning the Eucharist : and Du Pin, in his Ecclesiastical History, includes Guido, or Guimond, as one who in opposition to Berenger, maintained the real presence in the Eucharist. But it seems, that Mersennus and the other writers were

When, where, at what age, and under what circumstances,
Guido died, are facts not communicated to us. It is, however, sufficient for this part of our history, to have made
evident the force and extent of his genius, and to have shown
that by his sedulous application to the improvement of the
harmonic science, the perfection to which that science was
destined to be carried, was considerably accelerated. Guido,
indeed, effected so much, that we are left to wonder at its
tardy progress during the next three or four centuries immediately following his own. This appears the more extraordinary,
when we consider the estimation in which music continued
to be held. That enthusiasm which induced Alfred to en-
join and encourage the study of music among the liberal arts
in his new university, was not suffered to cool. The
church found its interest in the promotion of the science,
the monks cultivated it as necessary to their profession, and
every one, less or more, derived pleasure from its vocal and
instrumental appeals to the external sense: yet it does not
appear, that either in practice or theory, the art was much
advanced, till after the period when the *Time-table* was
settled.

One reason, perhaps, to be justly assigned for the slow
progress of music in the church, is, that besides being themselves backward to change and innovation, the monks were
often forbidden by their superiors to deviate in any thing
from their accustomed course *. But then, on the other

---

mistaken in their opinion of the identity of Guido and Guimond.
The indefatigable Boyle has detected the error, and set the matter
right, by showing that Guido and Guimond were two distinct persons:
and that it was not Guido the monk of Arezzo, or Abbot of the Holy
Cross, but Guimond the Bishop of Avers, that contended for the
presence of the body and blood of Christ, in the sacrament of the
Eucharist.

* *Thirds*, at their first introduction as concords, were censured as

haud, it is to be recollected, that, generally, besides the ca-
nonical hours of chanting in concert during the celebration
of their religious rites, they were allowed to sing in their
cells, when those who might possess any genius or imagination, would have an opportunity to give them exercise. Yet
so imperceptible were the gradations of improvement, that
Patience would not pardon my fatiguing the reader's attention with the dull detail of the advance of music during the
eleventh and twelfth centuries.

New powers of execution, however, even in spite of
monkish indolence and monkish prejudice, crept in upon the
vocal performers of the church; and at length, *discant* implied
not only *harmony in dupla*, or *concord in two parts*, according to the strict and original sense of the expression, but the
graces, broderies, and *flourishes* of florid song. That an
inclination to vary the plain song, or *canto fermo*, should
accompany the ability to execute embellishments, was perfectly natural; and, by degrees, this increased ability seduced
the chanters into what was thought licentious alterations, and

---

innovations; and while the new art of counterpoint was extending its
limits, and forming its code, great scandal was thought to be given to
piety, simplicity, and ancient usages: and complaints having been made
to Pope John XXII. that " the abuse of *discant,* the principles of
the antiphonary and gradual were so much contemned as to render it
impossible for the singers to know upon what foundation their melodies were constructed; and that they manifested such ignorance in
the tones or modes of the church, as to neglect all distinction, and
exceed the bounds that had been prescribed to each ;" a bull was
issued at Avignon, by the advice of the Conclave, about the year
1322, to suppress these licenses under very severe penalties. And
John of Salisbury had, indeed, long before this, severely censured
what he called " the wanton modulations, effeminate inflexions, and
frittered notes and periods, with which monks were in the habit of
profaning the *penetralia,* or awful sanctuary itself."

levities inconsistent with the solemnity and simplicity of church music.

Of all the numerous cultivators of the science between the age of Guido and the introduction of the *time-table*, only two seem to deserve a place in this chapter; Franco of Cologne, and Walter of Evesham; both men of talents and industry.

Franco was the next harmonist, in point of time, to Guido, and made deviations from the Micrologus which merit the name of discoveries. He was the inventor of new concords, and the author of new precepts for their use. His system divides the concords into three classes; *perfect, imperfect*, and *mean :* of this last kind are the fourth and the fifth, which, though less perfect than the unison and octave, are more pleasing to the ear than the *two thirds* which were first called *imperfect* by this author. Franco divides discords into *perfect* and *imperfect*. Of the first class, are the flat second, sharp fourth, sharp fifth, and sharp seventh, which, says he, the ear is unable to tolerate. Of the second class, are the major sixth, and the minor sixth; which, he tells his readers, may be borne in discant, though not very pleasing. Besides his novelties in counterpoint, Franco produced a tablature, or scheme of notation, so improved in method and clearness, that it continued in use for some centuries.

Dr. Burney, judging of Franco's progress in practical harmony, by the precepts he found in an Oxford manuscript, feels himself sanctioned in asserting his great superiority over Guido, in intermixing *imperfect* concords with the *perfect*, and thereby producing a better evolution of harmony. The Doctor determining, if possible, to decypher one of his specimens of counterpoint (all which he found miserably dislocated and erroneous, in the copy he examined) after considerable labour, was able to make out the following sample, which he presents to us as tolerably, if not entirely faithful.

If the modern contrapuntist smiles at this specimen of *harmony in dupla,* he will do so, because he does not make due allowance for the general state of musical consonance at the period almost immediately preceding that in which it was produced; or because he does not consider the infancy of the science of *combination* in Franco's time, and the natural slow-

---

* Thus far melody and harmony had proceeded, since the establishment of the Christian religion. Franco has, it is true, left a Treatise on *Music, Measure,* and *Florid Counterpoint;* but his examples of discant are all in diatonic intervals ; and the words which he has placed under his melodies, are wholly fragments of psalms or ecclesiastical hymns. It should be noticed, that he speaks of his *Discantum cantilenes Rondellis,* or discant to airs called roundelays; which continued long in favour, and gave birth to the present *rondeau.*

ness of every art in the earlier stages of its cultivation. This
is the progress melody and harmony had made in the service of
the church, since the establishment of the Christian religion ;
and it must be allowed, that however much Franco left to
be achieved by the genius and labour of his successors, he
effected much himself; and opened the door to a rational
union of *part* with *part*.

To Franco succeeded Walter Odington, a monk of
Evesham in Worcestershire, author of a treatise, now in
Bennet College, Cambridge; it has been said, that it is so
copious and complete with respect to every part of music
which was known when it was written, that if all other
musical tracts from the time of Boethius to Franco and
John Cotton, were lost, our knowledge would not be much
diminished, provided Walter's manuscript remained.

Walter of Evesham (for so he is commonly called) figured
in the early part of the thirteenth century, during the reign of
Henry III.; and was distinguished, not only by his profound
knowledge in music, but his proficiency in astronomy, and mathematics in general. The translator of Dugdale's Monasti-
con, speaking of him among the learned Englishmen of the
order of St. Benedict, says, " Walter, a monk of Evesham,
was a man of a facetious wit, who applying himself to literature,
lest he should sink under the labour of the day, the watch-
ing at night, and continual observance of regular discipline,
used, at spare hours, to divert himself with the decent and
commendable diversion of music, to render himself the
more vigilant during the performance of his other duties."
This mode of accounting for a Roman priest's addiction to
music is curious, as entirely overlooking the fact, that the
study and practice of music were among a churchman's
principal obligations. A monk without some knowledge of
its theory, and skill in its performance, would have been an
anomaly in the clerical profession ; and hence, it is with still

greater surprise, that we afterwards find the same writer, almost in the language of lamentation, saying, That his extreme partiality to music diverted him from other studies *.

Of the musical work of this author at Cambridge, it will be sufficient to take a broad and general view. It is divided into six parts, or books. The *first* of these contains ten chapters on the division of the scale, and the harmonical proportions. The *second*, comprizes eighteen chapters; and merits a more particular notice. The author, after an eulogium upon music, in which he pays due honour to the nine Muses, gives the invention of instruments to Tubal, relates the manner in which Pythagoras discovered the harmonical proportions; and speaks of David's power over the evil spirit of Saul. The relative properties of the major and minor third, and major and minor semitones, are there considered; after which, the different kinds of human voices, from the shrill cries of the infant to the deep tones of an aged man, are fully described. We are next informed why the ancients regarded thirds as discords, then presented with a list of concordant *discords*, (concordes discordiæ) which he makes to consist of the minor and major third, the major sixth, the tenth (or octave of the third) and the eleventh, formed of the diapason (the eighth) and the diatesseron (the fourth of the eighth.) In the *third* part, the author proceeds to treat of harmonies; explains the formation of the scale, divides the monochord, by numbers, and lays down rules for the proportions of organ pipes; and the casting of bells. He next speaks of the three kinds of melody; *De tribus generibus cantilenæ,* and describes the *diatonic, chro-*

---

* Nevertheless, we are told by Pits, Bayle, Tanner, Moreri, and other of his biographers, that he wrote *De mortibus Planetarum,* et de Mutatione Aëris, and on other learned subjects.

matic, and *enharmonic* genera of the ancient Greeks; and
from these, we are led to an illustration of the ecclesiastical
modes. The *fourth* part contains a digest of the laws of
rhythm. The *fifth*, consisting of eighteen chapters, is, for
the most part, curious and uncommon. From the chapter
entitled *De Signis Vocum*, we learn, that in *his days*, musical tones were expressed by the first seven letters of the
alphabet; great, small, and double : and that *longs* and
breves were in common use, in the chanting, or plain song,
which were then uniformly written on a stave of five lines *.
The *sixth* chapter of this work, so luminous in regard of the
information it conveys upon the subject of the state of music
in the time of the author, treats of the art of *organizing of
chants*, that is, the composition of *organic* or second parts to
chants, in the course of which we meet with many of the
technica of later times, as *tenor, motetus, coloratus, cantilena*,
and *rondellus*.

From the writings of Marchetto da Padova, which are
preserved in the Vatican Library, we collect, that in the
thirteenth century, Italy began to cultivate *secular music*.
This author presents us with many attempts at new combinations, some of which have been retained to this day,
though others have necessarily been rejected. In some instances, as where he treats of *harmonics* and *temperament*,
the chromatic semitone and enharmonic diesis, or quarter
tone, his ideas neither correspond with those of the ancients
nor the moderns. Of his counterpoint, Dr. Burney pre-

---

* The remainder of this part of the work is chiefly employed in
describing different kinds of ecclesiastical chants, and in giving rules
for their composition. Some pages of it are devoted to the separation
of the modes into *authentic* and *plagal*, and to examples of *Canto
Fermo*, which appear more florid than appear in missals of the same
period.

sents us with some examples, which, brief as they are, will be viewed with satisfaction, as throwing some *direct* light upon the state of counterpoint in this writer's time. The *first* of the single staves of the following examples, represents the bass cliff on the *second* line *, and the notation as it stands in the manuscript; except that, in the manuscript, the characters are square: The *second* single stave exhibits the two parts according to the power, or meaning, of the F or bass cliff, when placed on the *fourth* line of the stave ; where, in modern music, it constantly stands. The *first two* staves represent the two parts of the discant *separately*, and according to the powers of the F or bass cliff, on its usual line, and the C or tenor cliff on the fourth line ; and the *second two* staves represent the two parts according to the bass and treble cliffs, which adjustment raises the upper part an octave higher than it stands in the manuscript, but accommodates those who are not familiar with the tenor cliff.

DIATONIC COUNTERPOINT.

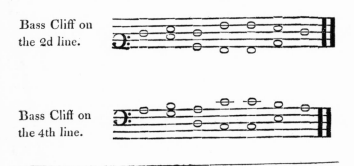

Bass Cliff on the 2d line.

Bass Cliff on the 4th line.

* It may be necessary to remind the reader, that the F or bass cliff being here placed on the *second* line of the stave, a note on that line indicates the very same pitch or sound, as a note on the *fourth* line of the stave, when the F or bass cliff is placed on the fourth line.

Tenor

and

Bass.

Treble

and

Bass.

The following examples present us with the most ancient adoption of sharps and flats.

Tenor Cliff on the 4th line.

Tenor

and

Bass.

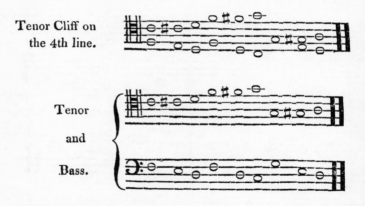

* Of the *elegance* of this specimen of the *style* of Marchetto's discant, we will, in charity, say nothing. However, there is not any thing in the *combination* that strikingly militates against the laws of modern counterpoint.

Treble

and

Bass.

Tenor

and

Bass.

Treble

and

Bass.

Tenor Cliff on the
3d line, changed
to the Tenor Cliff
on the 4th line.

Counter Tenor

and

Tenor.

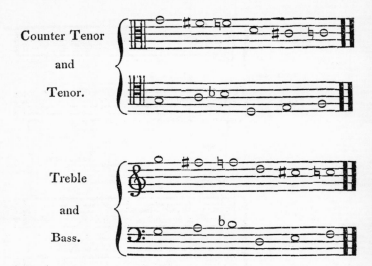

Treble

and

Bass.

The above passage requires no great alteration, to form a modern refinement.

To Marchetto the credit is due, of having been the first musician who suggested the resolution of discords; and who laid down the rule that disallows two consecutive sevenths, or fourths, discordantly used.

As music advanced, the difference between the compositions of the church and the secular melodies, became greater and greater. The former, cultivated exclusively by the choir, notwithstanding their uninterrupted, though slowly-increasing refinement, and all the innovations against which, from time to time, so much was urged by some of the more austere of the superior clergy, retained, in a great measure, their primeval simplicity; while the strains of pleasure and amusement, frequently alike estranged from science and decency, deviated into wildness, as if emulative of the licentiousness of the poetry they often accompanied; and were as ungoverned and capricious as the passions they excited. The bards and minstrels, who haunted every country of Europe, and not only visited the castles of the nobility, and attended weddings and banquets, but wandered through the several kingdoms, mixing with the common people, were, in general, without any knowledge of the theory of music; and uttered with the voice, and performed with the hand, what they

---

the honour of having first dared to use the *Settima Diminuita*, or diminished seventh, is due to Jomelli or Galluppi; as both these eminent masters hazarded this piquant transition so near the same time at different places, the one in a song composed at Venice, and the other in a song composed at Turin, that it is easier to imagine the invention due to both, than that either should arrogate to himself the merit of another. Jomelli, however, first carried it into Germany, where the elder Stamitz and the symphonists of the Manheim school, and after them, the contrapuntists of every other school, introduced it in almost every movement, without *always* waiting for a favourable opportunity."

learnt by their ear: and as the object of their vocation was, for the most part, to excite mirth and pleasantry, and that very often of the coarsest kind, their music was as loose as their manners, and pleased most when it was least chaste and orderly.   But more of the minstrels in a future chapter.

The reader having been conducted to a period when the laws of harmony had made some advance towards a settled code, at least, as far as concerned *simple counterpoint*, or note against note; and when it seemed only to want a TIME-TABLE, to perfect written *discant*, or *Musica Mensurabilis*, which constituted florid counterpoint, the origin and progress of that great *desideratum* will form the next object of our inquiry.

CHAP. XIV.

INVENTION OF THE TIME-TABLE, AND THE FURTHER PROGRESS OF HARMONICAL COMPOSITION.

SO necessary is a systematic division of *Time* to the due performance of music in which two or more parts move in consonance, that it is difficult to conceive how harmonized melodies could be sung or played, without such a regulation. Whether the notes were similar, or dissimilar in form, if no relative lengths or durations were assigned to them, and if no measure commenced and terminated the corresponding phrases of the parts, the unions would be in continual danger of becoming false, and of misrepresenting the design of the composer : however simple the counterpoint, the particular sounds in either part might or might not, be given simultaneously with the sounds in the other part, or parts, in conjunction with which they were meant to be heard. The principal provision against the dissonance that would almost continually result from this deficiency, would be *a previous agreement to give equal lengths to the harmonizing notes ;* that is, to begin and end the corresponding sounds at the same time, in the manner of a modern congregation, singing in unison the equallized sounds of the common parochial psalmody *. Another partial resource would be in the

---

* The ancients have left us no rules for *rhythm, time,* or *accent* in Music, but what concerned the verses that were to be sung ; and we

observance of the long and short syllables of the verse; but still, the relative durations not being precisely ascertained, but left to the loose determination of feeling, and the general rules of prosody, it would often happen that the harmonizing sounds would not meet, and that a discordancy would ensue as great as if the parts of which the composition consists had been constructed, without any view to a harmonized conjunction. Hence there is no reason whatever to doubt that the necessity of *time* in *florid counterpoint* first suggested its adoption.

If, then, the want of a *Time-table* would be so sensibly felt while music had not yet advanced beyond *simple consonance*, much more necessary was it when composition had arrived at figurative and florid counterpoint. Time, indeed, is so important to music, that without it, the greatest variety of sounds will have no spirit or meaning, while even the repetition of the same sound may derive energy and sentiment from a diversity of durations *.

Before the invention of *counterpoint*, music, as it seems, consisted merely in *Canto Fermo*, or melodies equally simple; and on this the first *harmony* was founded. But the most important improvement that music has ever received, was derived from the invention of characters for *time*, which enabled it to disengage itself from syllabic restraint, to assume a kind of independence, and in a degree, rely upon its own strength. It is to *time* that music is indebted for the

---

are not certain, that in high antiquity, they possessed any melody purely instrumental, unless we yield our credence to the stories of the contention of Marsyas and Apollo, and of Minerva throwing away her flute.

* Upon this principle it is, that the monotonous drum seems to express different tunes, when their times are beaten upon it agreeably to their various accents and measures.

force of its *instrumental* appeals ; of its power, *without the aid of poetry,* " To move, to stir, to shake the soul." It is by virtue of *time,* that it has those proportions, contrasts, punctuations, members, phrases, and periods, which render it a rich, expressive, and picturesque language. Music, without this liberating adjunct, was the slave of her sister art, to a degree, that in *her* she may be said to have had her life and being. But made the mistress of her own motions, she immediately began to display her innate powers ; and lent to poetry the grace and strength she had used to borrow. It was then, that quitting the dull practice of *a unity of sound and syllable,* she launched out into *a plurality of notes to the same syllable,* gave, by her *divisions,* new beauty to verbal expression, and to poetical sentiment more brilliant ornaments.

From the few memorials that have been recorded concerning the invention of the *time-table,* (respecting its inventor, we have no certain account) it is natural to suppose, that the benefit of its introduction was not at first very obvious to the generality of musicians. As the originator of characters of *time,* John de Muris, who flourished early in the fourteenth century, has been mentioned by many writers, but erroneously ; as appears by a manuscript work of his own in the Vatican library. It is a tract written under the title of a *Compendium of Practical Music ;* in which, treating of musical characters for *time,* he introduces the subject, with a short chronological list of anterior musicians who had merited the title of their *inventors ;* beginning with Tubal, and proceeding to Guido ; who, says he, " constructed the gamut, or scale for the monochord, and placed notes upon lines and spaces ; after whom came Magister Franco * ; the inventor of the figures, or notes, of the *cantus*

---

* The Benedictine monks made it a great blemish in the religious and moral character of Franco, that he studied profane science, and

mensurabilis. With respect to Franco, Marchetto cites him
in his *Pomœrium, de Musica Mensura,* as the inventor of
the four first musical characters; and Franchinus Gaforius,
in his *Practica Musicæ,* quotes him as the author of the
time-table : and ascribes to him the completion of counterpoint, by his contrivance of moving in different melodies at
the same time ; meaning his invention of musical characters
for measure. In the Bodleian Library at Oxford, there is
a tract by Franco, entitled *Ars Cantus Mensurabilis,* containing six chapters under the following heads :

1. Prologue, and Definitions of the Terms used in this
Treatise.

2. Of the Figures, or Representations of single sounds.

3. Of Ligatures, or compound Notes.

4. Of Rests, or Pauses.

5. Of the different Concords used in Discant.

6. Of the Organum, and of other Combinations of
sounds.

Speaking of " the theory and practice of *plain Music,* or
chanting," he says, " that both had been sufficiently explained by several philosophers ; particularly the theory, by
Boethius, and the practice, by Guido." He subsequently
adds, " that the ecclesiastical tropes or modes, had been
settled by St. Gregory." And then he says, " Nor let any one
suppose, that I have undertaken this work through arrogance,
or for my own convenience, but merely for the sake of its
evident truth, the ease with which it may be comprehended by
the student, and because it contains the most perfect method
of teaching all the modes of *Measure, Music,* and their

---

presumed to attempt the squaring of the circle. Yet they allowed
that he exercised his faculties not wholly without discretion ; that is,
that he did not neglect his ecclesiastical studies and spiritual interests.

notation. For, as there are several authors, as well modern as ancient, who in their treatises give many good rules concerning *Measured Music,* and on the contrary, are deficient and erroneous in other particulars, especially in the appendages of the science, we think their doctrines require some correction from their errors and defects. We therefore propose giving a compendious explanation of *Measured Music,* in which we shall not scruple to insert *what others have said on the subject,* to correct their errors, and to support by good reasons, *whatever we ourselves may have newly invented."* This is evidence sufficient, in proof that Franco was not the original inventor of *musical notes* for *time;* though he might have had the merit of improving their forms, or increasing their number*: and it well corresponds with what we find in a Latin treatise among the Cotton musical manuscripts : Speaking of the *Canto Fermo* of a certain period, the author says, " Though music was at that time not measured, it was approaching *towards* measure, when Franco appeared, who was the first *approved author,* or writer, on *measured music.*

The *Definitions* and other didactic passages in Franco's *Ars Cantus Mensurabilis,* threw so much light on the state of musical knowledge in his time, especially as regarding

---

* This tract likewise chiefly informs us, that there were in his time treatises *de Mensurabili Musica,* or, at least, that doctrines had been proposed and laid down concerning musical notes, and the different duration of sounds, by writers who had flourished before his time ; and the work proves itself to be only a collection of old rules, intermixed with his own. Did a single doubt remain, it would be removed by certain passages in the fourth chapter, in which he speaks of the great error which *some* have committed, by tying together three *longs* in tenor parts ; and of the still greater mistake which *others* have made in tying a *long* between two *breves.*

time and its representative characters, that we cannot apply to better resources for authentic information. I shall therefore detain the reader's attention while I make a few elucidative quotations. After his introduction, the author proceeds to his definitions. In the first of these he says,

" *Measured Music* is regulated by long and short *times*, or portions of measure.

" *Measure* is the regulated motion of any series of sounds, whether quick or slow, different from plain-song, in which no such regularity of music is observed.

" A *time* is the stated proportion of a lengthened tone, or of a *rest* of equal duration.

" *Measured Music* is of two kinds; *wholly*, and *partly* measured.

" Music *wholly measured*, is discant, which is measured throughout; and that which is *partly* measured, is the simple chant, or plain-song, which, though measured by time in some degree, is neither *organum* nor discant, as it is commonly called by those who sing the ecclesiastical chants.

" *Discant* is that *consonance of different melodies*, in which those different melodies move in sounds of various lengths, as *longs, breves,* and *semibreves,* proportioned to each other, and expressed in writing by adequate notes or characters.

" A *mood* is the representative of the time of measured sounds, expressed by *longs* or *breves*, or long and short notes. As moods are of different kinds, their number and arrangement are differently made by different musicians. Some multiply them to six, and some to seven; but *we* allow only five, because to this number all others may be referred."

He then explains the five moods, saying, that the first consists wholly of *longs ;* the second of a *breve* and a *long ;* the third of a *long* and two *breves ;* the fourth of two *breves* and a *long ;* and the fifth of *breves* and *semi-*

breves ; which moods, by modern notation, would be represented thus * :

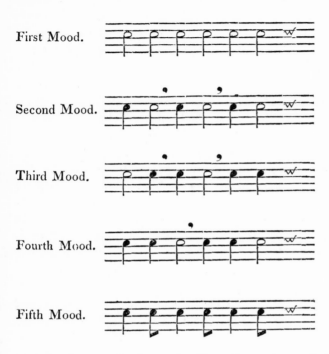

First Mood.

Second Mood.

Third Mood.

Fourth Mood.

Fifth Mood.

From the second chapter in this work, we learn, that the
notes, or characters, were of three kinds; and consisted of
the *long,* the *breve,* and the *semibreve* †. These are *per-*

---

* These five moods afford no great variety of measures. The ancients had been in possession of a far greater number of combinations
in their poetical feet.

† No mention is made of the *large* or the *minim*. The *long, breve,*
and *semibreve,* bore the same relative proportion as they do at present:
the breve was double of the semibreve, and the long was double of the

fect, or *imperfect,* as they are dotted or not dotted. The *perfect long* is the first and principal of all, because in that all the other notes are included. The *perfect* note is that which is *measured by three times,* or portions ; the *ternary* division being the most perfect of all, *as it had its name from the Holy Trinity, which is true and pure perfection.*

Franco's definition of *Plica* is not very clear. He calls it " a note of division of the same sound, ascending or descending." (*Plica est nota divisionis ejusdem soni in grave et acutum.*) Dr. Burney thinks, that the *Plica* was a note of *prolation ;* that, like the point or dot, it augmented the length of the note to which it was applied. Rousseau describes, but does not define it. " The *Plica,*" says he, " is a kind of ligature in our ancient music. It was a sign of augmentation or increase of a note's length ; a *signum morositatis,* as Muris says. Like the ligature, it was used in any group of notes, from the semitone to the fifth, ascending or descending.

In his third chapter, Franco treats of ligatures, or compound notes. He describes the *ligature* agreeably to what the word implies ; and says, that it is used to *link* or *bind* notes together ; and that some are ascending, and some contrarywise *.

The fourth chapter treats of *rests* and *pauses,* or discontinuity of sound. Of these, there were six kinds, all consisting of thick, single, double, and triple vertical lines of various lengths, placed within the stave. But the most cu-

---

breve ; and the dot, as now, added to the note after which it was placed, one half of its duration ; consequently, the *dotted long* was equal in length to *three breves,* and the *dotted breve* to *three minims.*

* Though, at present we tie only the stems of quavers and notes of shorter duration, the old masters linked together the heads of square notes. The ascending *ligature* is when the end of the note is higher than the beginning or first part of the character.

rious part of this chapter is that which seems to point out the
origin of *bars*, which are placed, in the musical examples,
as pauses for the singers to take breath at the end of a sentence, verse, or melody. And this was the only use then
made of bars in *Canto Fermo*. The following fragments,
the first of which consists of *trochees*, and the second
of *iambics*, are given (with a subjoined bass) in modern
characters, from the samples presented to us by Franco in
longs and *breves*. They are regularly phrased, and by no
means so quaint or barbarous as from the age in which they
were produced, many would expect.

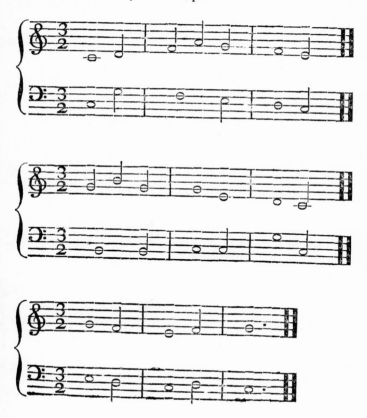

If the reader imagines the double bars in these fragments to be single, and the single bars removed, he will have in his mind the real representation of the manner in which music was originally divided.

When we consider the simplicity and clearness of Franco's notation, as compared with that of Guido, the properties of prolation and diminution in his characters, his suggestion of the *bar* and the *dot*, or *point of augmentation*, we are obliged to allow him considerable praise, and rank him among the benefactors of the harmonic science.

Between the time of Franco, and that of the invention of printing, many strange and fantastical forms of notes were proposed; but to the *long* and the *breve*, only the *minim* and *crotchet* were added; and it was not till the fifteenth century, that full or black characters were used. With respect to the diversified forms of the notes that were first employed to mark the *time*, while the *situations* of the characters in the stave signified their particular pitch, or degree of elevation, they are all to be deduced from the old black square note called a *breve*, the first and almost only note used in *Canto Fermo ;* which, with a stem or tail added to it, is a *long*, and if doubled in breadth, a *large *.

By this time, the reader has become convinced, that Franco was the worthy successor of Guido, and that it has not been without reason, that more pains have been taken to point out and explain the musical doctrines of these theoretical and practical musicians, than of any others of the middle ages. In fact, their treatises have been received, and respected, as original institutes which succeeding writers have done little more than transcribe and illustrate †.

---

* The present Chinese, we are told, know nothing of the use of notes. Indeed, both their music and poetry, are, to this day, very crude and irregular. The former, as they pretend, was formerly brought to the highest perfection among them, and greatly esteemed. Confucius is said to have been an admirer and master of the science. For its present rude state they account, by saying, that the books which treated of the art, have long since been lost. However this may be, their system, if we can allow that they possess any, consists now of little more than an uncouth jingle of sounds. Of harmony, contrast, or variety of *parts*, they are perfectly ignorant ; and their music, in its best specimens, scarcely equals the most vulgar of our common airs. Their instruments are limited to bells, drums, trumpets, flutes, and a few of the stringed kind. To these they add their principal favourite, the gong. But adapted as Music may seem to the gay, airy genius of the Chinese nation, it is cultivated among them with indifference, and seldom used, either vocally or instrumentally, except in plays, festivals, funerals, or other solemnities.

Martini, Hist. Sinic. imp. 3. Du Halde, Le Compte, &c.

† John Cotton is the principal commentator of Guido, as Robert de Handlo is of Franco.

John de Muris, by some styled a doctor and canon of the
Sorbonne, by some a mathematician and philosopher, and
by others a chanter of the church of Notre Dame at Paris,
though not the inventor of the time-table, was by his numerous
writings a great improver and benefactor of music *. Since
both the country and profession of this distinguished man
have been disputed, and little or nothing of his personal
career is known, a complete list of his musical works, with
a few remarks on their contents, will be as much as the
reader's curiosity can expect †. Scattered through the se-

* The country of John de Muris is disputed. Some say he was
born at Meurs in Normandy, whence he had his name ; others, that
he was an Englishman.

† Concerning the various writings of John de Muris that are still
preserved among the manuscripts of the Bodleian and Museum
Libraries, Dr. Burney has transcribed the account given in Tanner's
Bibliotheca Britannica ; in which it will be seen, that Tanner, copying Pits and Bayle, makes him a native of England.

" John de Muris, or Murus, an Englishman, and an eminent philosopher, mathematician and musician, wrote *Ex Stellarum position-
ibus prophetiam.* Lib. 1. ' Infra Annum certe Mundi.' *Arithmeticam
Speculativam.* Lib. 1. MS. Oxon. in Bibl. publ. Impress. Mogunt—
Tractatum Musicum. Lib. 1. ' Quoniam Musica est de sono relato ad
numeros.' MS. Bodl. N. E. F. 10. 11. *Artem componendi* (metiendi)
fistulas Organorum Secundum Guidonem. Lib. 1. ' *Cognita conso-
nantia in Chordis.*' Ibid. *Sufficientiam Musicæ Organicæ editam*
(ita habet MS.) *a Mag. Joanni de Muris, Musico sapientissimo, et
totius orbis subtilissimo experto.* Pr. Princeps Philosophorum Aristo-
teles. Ib. *Compositionem Consonantiarum in Symbolis Secundum Boë-
tium.* Pr. ' Omne Instrumentum Musicæ.' Ib. Canones super Ta-
bulas Alphonsinas. Pr. ' Quia secundum Philosophum. 4to. Phisi-
corum.' MS. Bodl. Digby 168. f. 132. *Collectionem Prophetiarum
de Rebus Anglicis,* per Joh. de Muris. MS. Cotton. Vespas. EVII. 8.
In MS, Bodl. Digby 190. fol. 72. extat *Prologus in opus* cui Titulus:
"Tractatus Canonum minutiarum Philosophicarum et Vulgarium, quem
composuit Mag. Johannes de Muris, *Normannus* A. MCCCXXI. a

veral public libraries of Europe, they, by their preservation, afford grounds for rational conjectures concerning
some circumstances of his life. In the Vatican there is a
" Treatise on Time, or Measured Music ;" a " Compendium of Counterpoint;" and " Musical Theorems explained
in Verse." In the library at Paris, we find his " Mirror of
Music *." In the Bodleian Library his " *Quoniam Mu-*

---

quo eodem anno (verba sunt autoris) *Notitia Artis Musicæ* proferendæ
et figurandæ tam mensurabilis quam planæ, quantum ad omnem mo-
dum possibilem discantandi, non solum per integra, sed usque ad mi-
nutissimas fractiones: *Cognitioque circuli quadraturæ* perfectissime
demonstratæ: expositioque tabularum Alphonsi regis Castelliæ: et
Genealogiæ Astronomiæ nobis claruit," &c. *Canones de Eclipsibus.*
Pr. ' In oppositione habenda aliud.' MS. Bodl. Digby 97. ubi ha-
betur hæc nota: ' Hos Canones disposuit Johannes de Muris *Parisiis*
in A. MCCCXLV. Pr. ' Tres Principes ex Militia.' MS. Bodl.
Digby 176. Bal. XI. 74. Pits *app.* p. 872. seq."

    * This (divided into seven books) is the chief and most diffuse of
his works. It is mentioned by Mersennus, Du Cange, and Rousseau,
who tried, but without success, to deduce from it proofs of his having
been the inventor of the time-table. Indeed, the latter of these
writers has, in his Musical Dictionary, made two quotations from the
" Mirror of Music." (See Art. *Discant*) " According to John de
Muris," says Rousseau, " *Discant* is"—and then speaking in the
words of his author, he adds—" *The singing extempore with one or
more persons in different concords, in such a manner as to produce
one harmony.*" Rousseau then tells us, That having explained what
he (Muris) means by consonances, and the choice which it is necessary to make between them, sharply censures the singers of his time
for using them indiscriminately : and proceeds to quote again from
his great authority.—" *How great is the audacity, if our institutes are
good, of those who, without the least comprehension of the rules necessary for the proper choice of concords, presume to compose the discant !
Of those who know not which to avoid, nor which to select ! Of those
who are ignorant of the places eligible for their introduction, and, indeed, of every thing in the knowledge of which real science consists!*

sica est de sono relato ad Numeros." In Bennet College, Cambridge, is deposited his tract beginning *" Quilibet in Arte:"* and in the Bodleian Library a tract commencing with *" Omne Instrumentum Musice:"* in the same volume with which is a " Treatise on the Art of Music, teaching and describing in figures, or notes, both measured and plain-song, with every possible kind of discant, not only by integers, or long notes, but by the shortest and most fractious."

With respect to the place of Muris's birth, we have three different suggestions. By some writers, he is supposed to

---

When they concord, it is merely by chance. Their voices wander about the tenor or plain song, without any law, or rational guide; and harmonize with it just as often as they are befriended by fortune, or Providence. Their sounds are thrown out at random, like stones awkwardly aimed at a mark, which, perhaps, they hit once in a hundred times." " Then the good Master Muris," says Rousseau, "gives the corruptors of the pure and simple harmony of his time (corruptors as numerous as those of our own age) a severe flagellation." " *Alas! in these our days, some, by empty verbiage, endeavour to gloss over their want of skill. This, they say, is the new method of discanting, and these the new concords. But how grievously do they offend both the ears and the understandings of those who are qualified to judge of their defects! For, surely, where they ought to awaken delight, they induce sadness. O incongruous language! O, miserable gloss;—irrational excuse! O monstrous abuse of things,—most rude and brute-like ignorance,—to mistake an ass for a man, a goat for a lion, a sheep for a fish, a snake for a salmon! For no less is their error, when they so confound concords with discords. O if the learned and skilful masters of former times heard such discanters, what would they say? What would they do? Doubtless, they would chide them, saying, This discant, which you have introduced, you never received from us. Your songs are not framed to be concordant with ours. Why, then, do you thus thrust yourselves forward,—you that do not agree with us,— you who are our adversaries and our scandal? This is not* concording, *but most doating and delirious* discording. *O that you were dumb!"*

have been a Norman, by some a Parisian, and by others an Englishman. Pits, in his account of him, says, that he was living in 1352. From his description of his mental characteristics, we learn, " that he was a man of genius, but possessed of too daring a curiosity ; for, while he was studying philosophy, he addicted himself to mathematics, and to that more sublime part of astronomy which contemplates celestial predictions; and in the exercise of his talents for calculation, had the presumption to anticipate future events ; thus persuading the ignorant, that by the aspect of the stars, he could penetrate the decrees of Providence." He even published celestial secrets under the title of *Prophetiarum*, or *Of the Prophecies*. Bayle calls Muris a *mathematician* and a *conjuror ;* and Fabricius joins him, as well in that assertion, as in saying that he was an Englishman. In regard of his heinous offence in studying the stars, it is not *mal-a-propos* to observe, that most of the musical writers of those times studied the stars, and professed to understand astrology *.

The *Cantus Mensurabilis*, though not invented by John de Muris, was certainly indebted to him for some improvement. It is impossible to read the following passage, quoted by Dr. Burney, from the *Art of Counterpoint*, (*Ars Contrapuncti*) without feeling assured, that its author could not be an idle spectator of any musical defects, for the amelioration of which he was so amply qualified.

" Beyond the octave, all is repetition ; but within it there are six species of concord ; three perfect, and three im-

---

* Walter of Evesham is said to have been " an able astrologer and musician:" and the same is reported of Simon Tunsted, and Theinred of Dover. Astrology was the *fashionable folly*. Not only musicians, and priests, but kings and princes, pretended to *predict;* and one instance of correctness among twenty examples of error, explains the quality of their prophetic wisdom.

perfect: of the first kind are the unison, eighth, and fifth ;
and of the second, the two thirds and major sixth. The
first of the perfect kind is the *unison*, which, though by
some not allowed to be a concord, yet, according to Boethius, is the source and origin of all consonance. The unison naturally requires after it a minor third ; which minor
third, for variety, is best succeeded by a perfect concord.
The fifth, being of the perfect kind, is well followed by a
major third, and *è contra*. The octave, another perfect
concord, may be succeeded by the major sixth ; after which,
either a perfect or imperfect concord may be taken. It is
the same with the minor third, which, being of the imperfect kind, may be succeeded either by a perfect or imperfect
concord. The major third, though best followed by a fifth,
may yet be succeeded by another third, but then it must be
minor. The major sixth, too, though best followed by an
eighth, may yet, for the sake of diversity, be succeeded, either
by a perfect or imperfect concord of another species ; it
can be followed by a fifth only, when the under part rises a
major or minor third ; but by thirds and sixths at pleasure.
Every composition should begin and end in a perfect concord ; and it must be remembered, that no two parts should
ascend or descend in perfect concords, though imperfect
may be used without limitation : and lastly, care must be
taken, that when the under part ascends, the upper shall
descend ; and the contrary."

These precepts, most of which had been given before by
Franco, though not with equal clearness and precision, shew,
as in a glass, the state of harmonical knowledge in the middle
of the fourteenth century ; and if tried by the following
examples, given in modern notation, will not be found to impose any construction capable of shocking our more cultivated ears.

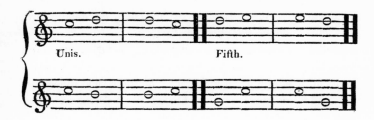

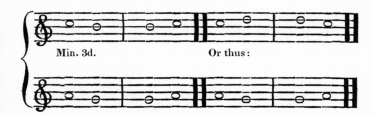

It was a curious circumstance, that the minor sixth should be esteemed a discord, while its inversion, the major third, was ranked among the concords *.

Philippus de Vitriaco, the first distinguished writer after De Muris, not only merits our particular notice as a luminous musical author, an ingenious composer, and the soundest contrapuntist of his day, but as the inventor of a new character of time,—the *minim*. The name of this musician so frequently occurs in ancient authors, that it is a circumstance of wonder, it should not have become more generally known. An anonymous Latin author in the Cotton musical manuscript, not only speaks of him as the first who suggested the use of the *minim*, but that he was the author of some excellent motets, and universally admired in his time †.

When Vitriaco flourished, *motets* were very prevalent in the church, as *rondelli*, *motelli*, and *conducti*, were among the secular compositions. In Gerbert's History of Church Music, there are *motets* in *two parts*, between four and five hundred years old; and Franco speaks of *motets* in *three parts*. It appears that *motets* were in their nature a lighter species of composition than that of the old ecclesiastical chant; and that in their less formal cast and texture, they were

* Prosdocimus de Beldemandis, in a tract upon counterpoint, written 1412, set the first example of admitting the minor sixth among the concords.

† Thomas Tewkesbury calls him "the flower of musicians in the whole world." Morley, Ravenscroft, and Butler, express the most exalted opinion of him: and the former says, that for some time his motets were esteemed *the best of all others, and most used in the church.* With respect to the minim, it is worth observation, that the unknown author of a tract in the Cotton MS. expressly says, that Vitriaco was the inventor of that note, and that its introduction led to that of the semi-minim, or crotchet, though Vitriaco would never countenance the *licentious innovation*.

liable to assume more levity than was thought becoming the solemnity of the church; and a passage given by Carpentier, from the manuscript constitution of the Carmelite Friars, censures it as indecorous and profane *.

Of all the numerous writers who mention and eulogize Vitriaco, only one names his country. Tunsted says he was of Auvergne, and if he be correct, the talents, learning, and period in which Vitriaco flourished, will countenance the supposition entertained by some, that he and Philippes de Vitry, Bishop of Meaux, were the same person; especially since Vitry, according to John de Vinette, a writer in the fourteenth century, says, " that he applied himself to music and poetry with so much success, that for the time in which he lived, he may be ranked among the most excellent of their votaries."

Of the general state of musical composition, as used in religious houses, between four and five hundred years ago, we might form a tolerably correct idea from the following specimen, could it possibly be relied upon as correct. It is from a manuscript of St. Blaise, of which the learned Gerbert was abbot, and is inserted by him in the first volume of his History of Sacred Music. The two words, *Benedicamus Domino,* of which alone the verbal part of this piece consists, were appointed to be sung by the religious of some orders at the end of every hour, as a grace. The characters in which the original is written, are *longs, breves,* and *semibreves;* and these are all full and black; for *white, open* notes were not yet in use.

---

* Musicians of the thirteenth and fourteenth centuries gave the name of *motetus* to the part which is now called counter-tenor. The name *motetus* was afterwards used in common with *motellus,* a kind of tune or melody; and consequently the *motet* had then become more gay and airy. At present, the appellation *motet* is applied to all compositions set to Latin words for the use of the Romish church.

PER BISCANTUM *

* This composition not only explains to us the state of *counter-point* in the middle of the fourteenth century, but exhibits the *Neumæ* or divisions, in which the monks were permitted to indulge on festivals; and the use of which, was not neglected in their cells, and on other days, when their superiors were not near enough to be disturbed by their *harmonious relaxations.*

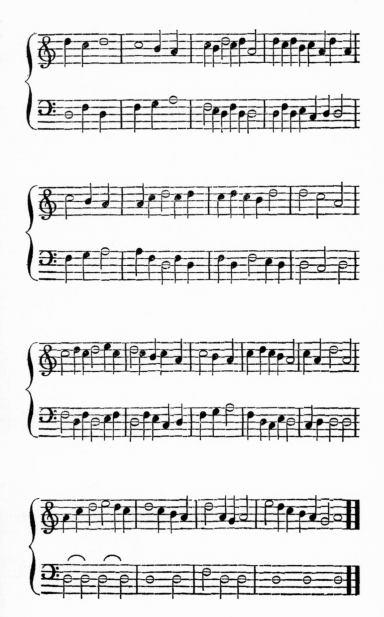

This composition is so anomalous,—so void of melody, destitute of measure, and hostile to harmony, that judgment cannot stoop to its criticism.   If I did not possess a positive knowledge of the profound science of my late learned friend Dr. Burney, and the most unlimited confidence in his integrity and his care, I should have taken it for granted, that the above copy (transcribed from one of his own) of the samples of the compositions used at the church of the abbot of St. Blaise, is not a true representation of the fac simile transmitted by Gerbert.   Extremely probable, however, is it, that Gerbert may not have been faithful to the original manuscript ; I shall therefore make no further remark upon it than to say, that besides its being out of the pale of regularly-measured time, almost the only concords to be found in it, are consecutive fifths and eighths.

From Franco's discant, it is obvious, that the harmony practised in the church under the title of *organizing*, was not equal to that of the period immediately following the time of Guido.   A jealous adherence to the old *diaphonics*, long subsisted in the church ; and kept its compositions stationary ; while secular music, on the contrary, unrestrained, and ever open to improvement, made daily advances towards that ease and freedom of melody, and force and variety of expression, which it has long since attained.   It appears obvious that the excellent rules (excellent for the time) given by De Muris, Vitriaco, and others of the fourteenth century, were at least disregarded, if not rejected, by ecclesiastical contrapuntists ; and hence the admission of many wretched compositions into the pale of the church ; compositions, that for her own credit and honour, religion should never have permitted to disgrace her temples.   The church, at that time, as if determined that superstition and bad counterpoint should not be divided, seems to have been as fond of darkness in *music* as in *divinity*.   The light of superior doc-

trines, and the beauty of better compositions, were obtain-
able ; but monkish indolence preferred brutal ignorance ;
and the dormant powers of the mind, and finer susceptibilities of the external sense, were alike refused cultivation.

To the church, however, one great merit must always be
allowed ; that of having gradually established a *time-table ;* a
system of notation by which we are benefited at this very day.
By what marks or characters the ancient Greeks designated
the different quantities of sound, or whether they possessed
any means whatever of measuring them with precision, is not,
nor ever can be known.   Their rhythmopœia is irrecover-
ably lost; and the *numbers* of modern poetry are, in their construction, as different from theirs, as they are inferior in force
and energy *.   St. Augustine and Bede seem to have written
upon some metrical principle, and the general structure of
the Runic poetry, or the songs of the bards, would sanction
the opinion, that these compositions were framed to regular
measures.   Consequently, the want of metrical harmony
would not be discernible in vocal music, however its absence might be felt in melody, distinctly considered.   The
musical sounds, in respect of their duration, were subservient
to the poetical metre, and received from its laws the regulations
of their own movements.   Of music merely instrumental,
the time, of course, was unguided by any system; or at most,

---

* The signatures contained in the introduction of Alypius, are
evidently of a kind very different from those used by the Greeks, to
imply their several *quantities* of musical sound ; and were confined to
the marking the different degrees of acuteness and gravity.   Neither
Aristides Quintilianus, Porphyry, Bryennius, or even Ptolemy,
affords us any real intelligence upon the subject of the ancient division
or measurement of *time ;* and of course, the learned modern, Dr. Wallis,
(as indeed he himself confesses) is still farther from being qualified to
furnish information upon this point.

it could only proceed by slow and equal divisions, better calculated to fatigue attention, than to animate the passions. Nothing, therefore, could be more obvious, than the want of a metrical regulator ; a notation that should give a continual but
governed variety to the motion of mere melody, render music
independent of poetical rhythm, and add to the fascination of
sonorous sweetness, the charm of diversified movement.

By the successive labours of Franco, De Muris, and Vitriaco, this *desideratum* was gradually supplied ; and music,
while it daily improved in the formation of its *consonant
parts*, began to assume that systematic order in its *time*,
which laid the foundation for a richer and more elaborate
construction of harmony, and could not but lead to that
artful and complicated disposition of transient and protracted sounds, which, in the hands of genius, have since
given so much beauty, energy, and grandeur, to the higher
species of composition.

Could a single doubt remain, that the superior enjoyment
of one description of music over another, depends in a great
measure upon the education, or *artificial* capacity of the ear,
(as I have asserted in page 76 of this volume) it would be
removed by the facts explained in this and the preceding
chapter ; in which, at one time, we have seen no combinations admitted, except regular *successions of naked fourths :*
at another, none enjoyed but those of *consecutive fifths ;* and
at another, all sanction refused to *thirds* and *sixths !* So
different, indeed, was what the primitive Christians called
harmony, from the simple *unisons* and *octaves* of the ancient Greeks, or any other consonances producible from
their enharmonic and chromatic genera ; and again, so far
removed is the present system of harmonization from that of
the earlier ages of church composition, that had nature, in
those different periods, formed the human ear upon dissimilar and distinct principles, it would not, in regard of mu-

sical concordance, have indicated feelings more diverse, more opposite. Some writers have observed, that there is a *mode,* or *fashion* in music : but, since Nature is uniform in her construction of the exterior senses, the remark ill explains Why those combinations, which, by their proportions, were always harmonious, should have been considered as dissonances, while others, in themselves naturally discordant and forbidding, were listened to with approbation and pleasure.

CHAP. XV.

MINSTRELS, TROUBADOURS, &c. &c.—GENERAL STATE OF MUSIC FROM THE INTRODUCTION OF THE TIME TABLE TO THE FOURTEENTH CENTURY.

FROM the contents of the foregoing chapter, the reader will form a tolerably accurate idea of the state of musical science in or about the fifteenth century. It now remains to take a nearer view of its general application in Europe at that period; to examine it in the various provinces of its *practice.*

It appears that long before the fifteenth century, the lyrical productions of the Provençal and other itinerant poets, had begun the great work of raising Europe from the barbarous ignorance into which she had been plunged. This race of rhyming songsters had now become very numerous in the different countries, but no where more abounded than in *Provence,* which country Nostrodamus, brother of the astrologer of that name, calls *The Mother of Troubadours and Minstrels.* The points of history on which they dwelt, and which their labours served to record, and the enthusiasm and courage excited by their allusions to the glory of warfare, added to the fascination of the two arts they so well combined, rendered their presence at the courts of princes

and barons highly acceptable; and by these munificent patrons they were treated with the greatest consideration and
respect.   Patriots heard the interesting events of their
country's career in power and civilization; warriors listened
with zeal and with pride, to the eulogies of valour and conquest; and the ears of beauty drank them with a delight that
was not always concealed, and a gratitude that was sometimes tenderly demonstrated.   The success with which a
happy few of these poet-musicians sung their tales of love,
encouraged the hopes of others, excited their exertions in
the exercise of their art, and accelerated their progress towards perfection.

But though, as will ever be the case, where excellence of
execution so greatly depends upon native genius, some very
far exceeded others, we do not learn, that during the cultivation of Provençal literature and music, any one Troubadour
transcended another to a degree to be considered as the supreme pattern for his cotemporaries, or a standing model for
his successors.   Insensible to classical authority, these modern versifiers followed no other rules than those suggested
by their own imagination; consequently their strains were
marked by a kind of independent variety, the elements of
which were sometimes tolerably consistent, but generally
wild and unconnected, and always quaint and capricious.   It
is a curious fact, that two years elapsed after the introduction
of the time-table, without affording any records of secular
music, except those of the Troubadours or Provençal poets.
Yet, though this province of the harmonic art appears to
have been wholly in their hands, they were so neglectful in
its cultivation, as to continue to dispense with the regulations
of *time;* and leave us to wonder how, with so important a
deficiency, they could make those impressions, of which
we are assured by the most respectable writers, and lay

a foundation for the future compositions of Italy, and of France *.

If the period of Provençal poetry is interesting to literature, equally so to the musical world are the melodies to which it was sung. But the knowledge of what these melodies were, possesses an interest beyond itself; since, as inseparably connected with a new species of verse, these melodies contributed to produce, not only a revolution in literature, but improved manners, and purer principles of thinking.

Provençal poetry arrived at a very high degree of perfection as early as the twelfth century ; and it was about that time, that it began to be sung to the sound of instruments ; a time when *violars,* or performers on the vielle and viol; *juglars,* or flute-players ; *musars,* or performers on other instruments ; and *comics,* or comedians, abounded universally. Those musical poets, formerly known in France under the title of *jongleurs,* travelled from province to province, and received as the reward of the pleasure their performances afforded, presents of clothes, horses, arms, and money. When it happened that a troubadour was unwilling, or not able, to rehearse his own verses, he applied to a jongleur to perform that task. The troubadours, it seems, held a higher rank than those strolling musicians, the jongleurs, and were considered as following a more regular and

---

* *Air,* like the several species of Italian poetry, seems to have originated in the genius of the troubadours. The most ancient strains that have been spared by time, are such as accompanied their songs. To modern ears, they are crabbed and grotesque: but it is easy to perceive, that to an age whose taste was a stranger to the refinements with which we are become so familiar, they might seem excellent, and worthy of enthusiastic admiration.

respectable profession than men whose qualifications were confined to vocal and instrumental execution *.

The *bard,* properly so called, was no less a literary than a musical character. His qualifications gave him rank, and his rank recommended his qualifications ; so that persons of the very highest orders in society were ambitious to cultivate arts that delighted universally, and threw splendour round their possessors. Some of the most ancient poems in the Provençal language, were written by William IX. Count of Poitou, born 1071 ; and in the twelfth century, Richard I. King of England, exercised his talents in lyric composition, and produced *one* song, in conjunction with Blondel, a bard who enjoyed that monarch's friendship ; a fact to which it is impossible to allude, and not feel impelled to relate the interesting event to which it afterwards gave birth, and from which it will never be separated.

" Blondiaux," says a faithful translation of the old *Chronique,* " was a poet, of whom it is not told exactly when he was born, or when he died ; but he is found to have been known to Richard I. of England, who died in the year 1200.

" Richard having had, in the Holy Wars, a quarrel with the Duke of Austria, was unwilling, at his return home, to pass in his public character through the Austrian dominions, on account of the Duke ; or through those of France, for fear of Philip Augustus ; and therefore travelled in disguise. But the Duke being informed of his arrival, seized him and con-

---

* The fragments of these bards form the principal materials for the history of this dark period. Without their aid, the annals of Europe would have been very defective ; and the light they served to throw upon some important events, greatly sanction Bayle in saying that a collection of old ballads is not an unprofitable companion to an historian.

fined him in a castle, where he remained prisoner, none knowing for a long time where he was.

" Richard had retained in his service and friendship a
minstrel or bard, whose name was Blondel. The bard
losing his patron, felt his subsistence cut short, and the happiness of his life very much impaired. He found the account well verified, of the king's departure from the Holy
Land, but met with none that could tell with certainty whither he was gone ; and therefore wandered over many countries to try whether he could find him by any intelligence.

" It happened, after a considerable time thus spent, that
Blondel came to a city near the castle in which Richard was
confined, and asking his host to whom it belonged, was told
that it was one of the fortresses of the Duke of Austria.
Blondel then inquired whether there were any prisoners in
it, which was a question that he always took some indirect
method of introducing ; and was answered by his host, that
there was one prisoner, who had been there more than a
year, and that he was not able to tell who he was.

" Blondel having received this information, made use of
the general reception which minstrels find, to make acquaintance in the castle ; but though he was admitted, could
never obtain a sight of the prisoner, to know whether he was
the king ; till one day, he placed himself over against a
window of the tower in which Richard was kept, and began
to sing the French song which they had formerly composed
together. When the king heard the song, he knew that the
singer was Blondel ; and when half of it was sung, he began
the other half, and completed it. Blondel then knowing the
residence and condition of Richard, went back to England,
and related his adventure to the English barons."

The song here alluded to is preserved in an old French
romance, entitled *La Tour Tenebreuse,* or the " Black

'Tower." The original is in the ancient language of Provence. The following translation will enable the reader to
judge of the ideas and sentiments :—

> Your beauty, lady fair,
>   None views without delight;
> But still so cold an air
>   No passion can excite;
> Yet this I patient see,
> While all are shunn'd like me.
>
> No nymph my heart can wound,
>   If favour she divide,
> And smile on all around,
>   Unwilling to decide:
> I'd rather hatred bear,
> Than love with others share *.

A troubadour of the name of Gaucelm, another favourite
of Richard, and who accompanied him to what has been
called the *Holy War*, has left a poem on the death of his
benefactor (now in the Vatican, among the MSS. bequeathed to that library by the Queen of Sweden) with the
original music, by the *bard himself*, who was no less applauded for the music than for the words of his compositions.
Gaucelm, it appears, had tasted of misfortune before he lost
his royal patron, which event completed his misery, and ex-
torted from him the poetical expression of his grief. The
melody, Dr. Burney tells us, is the most ancient which he
had seen to Provençal words. The following is reduced
from the original, to modern notation, by the Doctor himself, who has added to it a bass of his own, from which I
have but little deviated.

---

* Walpole's *Catalogue of Royal and Noble Authors*, includes the
Lay, or Song of Complaint, written by Richard during his impri-
sonment.

SONG.

Words and Melody by Gaucelm, Friend and Troubadour of Richard I. King of England.

Now Fate has fill'd the mea - sure of my woes, And rent my heart with grief unfelt be - fore; No fu - ture blessings wounds like these can close, Or mi - ti - gate the loss I now de - plore, The

valiant Richard, England's mighty king, The

first and chief of all that's good and brave,

Of tyrant Death has felt the fa - tal

sting: A thousand years his equal may not

bring,   The world from mean-ness and con-

tempt   to   save.   The world from

mean - ness   and   contempt   to   save.

Among the church melodies of this time, many were very
florid and embellished, compared with the plain-chant: and
it has been reasonably supposed, that such indulgences of
the fancy were appropriated, and confined, to festivals and
holy times; at which seasons, certain portions of the service
were allowed to be performed with additional ornaments and

graces, and in *faux-bourdon*, or counterpoint *. It seems, indeed, extravagant to suppose, that in those times of religious fanaticism, these lighter melodies and portions of the church service were used in common, and made the topics of public festivity; for certain it is, that a *holy day* was a day of rejoicing and merriment, and that our word *holiday* is not more directly a compound of *holy* and *day*, than our seasons of mirth are the relics of religious banquets. On these occasions the *florid* chant of the church was the vocal music employed; and in France, SONGS did not become common till the reign of Philip Augustus †. The most ancient of these are called *lays*. M. L'Eveque de la Ravaliere says, in his *Ancienté des Chansons*, that " these compositions were amorous elegies, or tender laments." The origin of this species of song, he then proceeds to inform us, " is such as render it necessarily plaintive; as the word *lai* is imagined to have been derived from the Latin word *lessus*, signifying complaints and lamentations." " However," adds he, " there are some lays which describe moments of joy and pleasure, rather than sorrow and pain; and others upon sacred subjects ‡."

---

* The French have always been passionately fond of music. Pepin made the chants of the church (which were indeed Roman) his particular study; and his son Charlemagne had Roman masters to teach it, and establish schools for it in all parts of his empire.

† Gautier de Coincy, an ecclesiastic of St. Medard de Soissons, composed a considerable number, which are still extant in MSS.

‡ Chaucer never uses the word *lay* in any other than a plaintive sense.

> And in a lettre wrote he all his sorowe,
> In manere of a complaint or a *lay*,
> Unto his fair freshe lady May. CANT. TALES, v. 9754.

In Spenser, however, we find its signification extended to the more cheerful sentiments.

The editor of ancient *Fabliaux et Contes François* says, with every appearance in his favour, that tales and songs were the most ancient species of Gallic poetry. The French, naturally gay, mirthful, volatile, and more attached to this kind of composition than other nations, communicated their predilections to their neighbours. Of these songs or tales, they must have produced a great number; since in social meetings, the unvaried custom was, for each of the company either to sing a song, or relate a story; as appears by the conclusion of the fable of the priest, *qui ot Mere à force:*

> *A cest mots fenist cis Fabliaux*
> *Que nous avons en rime mis,*
> *Pour conter devant nos amis.*

And from the ditty of the Sacristan of Clugny, by John Chapelain, we collect, that it was customary for a bard to pay his reckoning with a story, or a song:

> *Usage est en Normandie,*
> *Que qui habergiez est, qu'il die*
> *Fable ou Chanson a son oste*
> *Ceste costume pas n'en oste*
> *Sire Jehans li Chapelains.*
>
> In Normandy a song or tale
> Is current coin for wine or ale;
> Nor does the friendly host require
> For bed and board a better hire.

The songs of the thirteenth century were of various kinds: some moral, some mirthful, and others amatory. But secu-

---

To the maiden's sounding timbrels sung
In well attuned notes a *joyous lay.*   FAIRY QUEEN.
Shakspeare and Milton use it as a general appellation for *song.*

lar melody had yet deviated but little from the florid chant of the church; and like that, was written in square notes upon staves of four lines, in the C cliff, and without any signs for time *. Not only the embellishments depended upon the taste and abilities of the singer, but the movement itself was left to his choice and judgment: and when he accompanied himself, a practice almost universal, the notes of his instrument were in unison with those of his voice. The two prevailing instruments at this time were the harp and the viol. Of these the harp was considered as the most dignified; and hence the romancers place it in the hands of their princes and great men, as Homer and the other Greek bards give the *lyre* to their heroes and sages.

The *harp* was so highly esteemed, that its powers were made the subject of a poem. This poem was called *Le Dict de la Harpe*, or "the Ditty, or Poem, upon the Harp." In extolling the instrument, it speaks of it as "too good to be profaned in taverns, or places of common amusement;" and declares that it should be used "by knights, esquires, clerks, persons of rank, and ladies with plump and beautiful hands;" and that "its courteous and gentle sounds should be heard only by the elegant and good †."

The *viol* was frequently used as an accompaniment to the harp; and excepting that it had frets, and possessed more than four strings, was the same with the modern violin: at

---

* It was not till towards the end of St. Lewis's reign that the stave consisted of five lines.

† The harp of these times contained twenty-five strings. It is a fact too curious not to be noticed, that upon each of these the poets bestowed an allegorical name. One string was called *Liberality*, another *Wealth*, a third *Politeness*, a fourth *Youth*, a fifth *Beauty*, and so forth. Thus, in order to compliment his mistress in the highest possible strain of gallantry, the bard compared his mistress to a harp.

least, the violin had its foundation in this instrument. The viol, though *fretted*, was played with a *bow*, and was wholly distinct from the *vielle*, the tones of which were produced by the friction of a wheel. The former is thought by some to have been an early favourite in France : an idea sanctioned by the exterior of an antique bason, or ewer, dug up near Soissons, upon which is the representation of a musician performing on a viol with a long bow ; the engraving of which was thought by the late antiquary, L'Abbé Le Beuf, to be the workmanship of the seventh or eighth century. But, indeed, many ancient and respectable monuments in France, upon which the viol is seen, offer their proofs of the esteem in which it has so long been held in that country ; as well as that they seem to show, that those *minstrels* who performed upon it, must have been in the highest estimation with the public. The following verses of an old French poet, quoted by Duchesne in his edition of Alain Chartier, do not ill describe the office of those musicians who accompanied such bards as sung their own historical songs at the festivals held by the great.

> *Quand les tables otées furent,*
> *Cil jugleour in pies esturent,*
> *S'ont viols et harpes prises*
> *Chansons, sous, vers et reprises,*
> *Et de gestes chanté nos ont.*
>
> Roman du Tournoyement de l'Antechrist.

> When the cloth was ta'en away,
> Minstrels strait began to play ;
> And while harps and viols join
> Raptur'd bards in strains divine,
> Loud the trembling arches rung
> With the noble deeds we sung *.

---

* Dr. Burney justly observes that there were four different species of performers, all included under the old French term *jouglerie*. The

Though strolling musicians, who abounded in France, were, in the time of Charlemagne, so irregular in their conduct, that he forbade their admission into convents; and during the reign of Philip Augustus, the troubadours and minstrels were so far involved in the same disgrace, that, for some time, they were banished the kingdom; yet they were the only living depositaries of that knowledge and politeness, upon which the fate of letters and civilized manners then depended. L'Abbé de Longchamps, in his *Tableau Historique de Gens de Lettres*, does not hesitate to pronounce the jougleurs, or troubadours and minstrels, to have been the fathers of literature in France. " It was they," says he, " who banished scholastic quarrels and ill breeding, and who polished the demeanour, established the rules of gentility, enlivened the conversation, and purified the gallantry of its inhabitants. That urbanity which distinguishes the French from the people of other countries, was the fruit of their *songs;* and if it is not from them we derive our virtues, they at least taught us how to render them amiable."

From a metrical tale still subsisting in the libraries of France, and in the Bodleian Library, we collect some idea of the several talents that were necessary to qualify a minstrel of the twelfth and thirteenth centuries. The piece is entitled *Les Deux Menestriers*, the Two Minstrels. The subject matter consists of the representation of the meeting of two companies of minstrels at a castle, who endeavour to amuse its lord by counterfeiting quarrels. One of each party being selected for the wordy war, it commences by the first speaker's assertion of his superior professional skill. His

---

troubadours, who set and sung their own verses; the *singers*, who rehearsed the compositions of others; the *romancers*, who chanted their metrical histories; and the mere harpers, or violists, who accompanied those who sung, or performed without any singing at all.

boast is, that *he* can tell stories in verse, both in the Ro-
manse and Latin tongue; can sing forty *lays* and *heroic
songs,* as well as every other kind of songs which may be
called for; that also he knows tales of *adventures,* particularly those of the *Round Table;* and in short, that he can
sing innumerable romances, such as *Vivian, Reinbold the
Dane,* &c. and relate the stories of *Flora* and *White Flower.*
He finishes the enumeration of his talents, by facetiously
informing his opponent and the spectators, that " he did not
choose his present employment for want of knowing others;
for he was possessed of many secrets, by which he could
soon have made a fortune. He knew how to circle an egg,
bleed cats, blow beef, and cover houses with omelets. He
also knew the art of making goats' caps, cows' bridles, dogs'
gloves, hares' armour, joint-stool cases, scabbards for hedg-
ing-bills; and if he were furnished with a couple of harps,
he would make such music as they never heard before."
The other now, in turn, extols himself in much the same
strain, and concludes with the following song; which, while
it serves as a sample of the poetry of this strolling, lower
order of minstrels, informs us of some of the instruments
then in use *.

---

* In the thirteenth century, the French had more than thirty different musical instruments. Among them were flutes, harps with ten
strings, hautbois, bassoons, trumpets, small kettle drums carried by a
boy and beaten by a man, the cymbalum, tambour de basque, two
long speaking-trumpets, two large hand-bells, guitars, bagpipes of
various forms and size, a dulcimer in shape, but held against the
breast and thrummed with the fingers, a vielle, viols, or rebecs with
three string, and regals, or portable organs. Of the style and character of the music, which was then performed upon these instruments, the following piece, said to have been composed about that
time, will serve to give the reader some idea.

All the minstrel art I know,
  I the *viol* well can play ;
I the *pipe* and *syrinx* blow,
  Harp and *gigue* my hand obey.
Psaltery, symphony, and *rote,*
  Help to charm the list'ning throng,
And *Armonia* lends its note
  While I warble forth my song.
I have tales and fables plenty,
  Satires, past'rals, full of sport.
Songs to *vielle* I've more than twenty,
  Ditties too, of ev'ry sort.
I from lovers tokens bear,
  I can flow'ry chaplets weave,
Am'rous belts can well prepare,
  And with courteous speech deceive.

RHYDLAN MARSH, or THE TUNE OF MORVAH.

It is to be regretted, that with respect to the melodies to which the metrical romances were sung, we have no certain information. The most rational conjecture is, that they were nearly, if not quite, as simple as the ecclesiastical chants; and that, as these tales generally ran out to a great length, the air, or tune, was, by necessity, often repeated. The author of an old romance called *Gerard de Roussillon*, professes to have written it from the model of the *Song of Antioch*, which we may suppose to mean, that its measure is adapted to the same tune *.

Of the *military* and *love* songs of the French it behoves me to speak with some particularity. They are of remote antiquity; and exhibit a gallant and polite people equally

* To write new songs to old tunes, was as common at that time as ever it has been since: and the modern practice of making variations upon old melodies, is by no means a novel resource of dulness.

prompt to celebrate the courage of their heroes, and the charms of their mistresses.

The *military* songs were generally sung in chorus by the whole army, while advancing upon the enemy; and the privilege of leading off the strain appertained to the bard by whom it had been composed. Charlemagne, like our Alfred, was highly partial to these heroic songs; and like him, commanded that they should be collected; and even learnt many of them by heart. However, new achievements form new topics, and these, by degrees, take place of, and obliterate the subjects of prior compositions. The victories of Alfred eclipsed the glory of his predecessors, and were echoed through the land in strains that superseded the old popular songs, and gave a fresher and warmer ardour to their interested auditory. The same result occurred on other occasions. The ballad in praise of Roland silenced the songs it followed, was sung by a French knight, at the landing of William the Conqueror, and continued in favour among the soldiers of France, as late as the battle of Poictiers, in the time of their King John; who, upon reproaching one of his men for singing it at a time when there were no Rolands, was shrewdly answered, that *another Charlemagne* would soon produce a *new Roland*. The words of this ballad, popular as they were in the fourteenth century, have not come down to us entire. The Marquis de Paulmy has collected what he could of them; but even these would be too long for insertion in a history purely musical. The *melody* the reader is entitled to expect. It is simple, bold and varied; and is calculated to impress us with a high idea of the ballad music of near four hundred years back.

CHANSON DE ROLAND.

Gaiment.

Sol - dats Fran - çois, chantons Ro-
land, de son pa - is il fut la gloi - re, Le nom d'un
guerrier si vail - lant, est le sig - nal de la vic - toi-
re. Roland e - tant pe-tit gar - çon, faisoit sou-

vent pleu - rer sa mere, Il etoit vif et poliss-

on tant mieux dis - oit Monsieur son pe - re ; à la

force il joint la va - leur nous en fe - rons un mili - tai-

re. Mau - vaise tête avec bon cœur c'est pour réus-

sir à la guer - re. Soldats François chantons Ro-

land de son pa - is il fut la gloi - re Le nom d'un

guerrier si vaillant est le sig-nal de la vic - toi - re.

TRANSLATION.

Soldiers ! the valiant Roland sing ;
    Of France is he the proudest glory ;
From Roland Gaul's best honours spring ;
    Through him she shines in deathless story.
Brave Roland, e'en in earliest years,
    Display'd the future hero's merit ;
While flow'd his mother's timid tears,
    His sire approv'd his dawning spirit.

" His rising strength, what courage joins !"
The father cried, his joy declaring ;
" If wild his mind, his heart combines
A warrior's fire and warrior's daring."
Soldiers ! the valiant Roland sing ;
Of France is he the proudest glory ;
From Roland Gaul's best honours spring ;
Through him she shines in deathless story.   BUSBY.

On the subject of love, no songs in the French language
are more tender and pathetic than those of the unfortunate
Chatelain de Coucy *. Not less distinguished by his pas-

---

* The story of Chatelain de Coucy, given in a chronicle written
about the year 1380, is truly tragical. " In the time of Philip Augustus and Richard I. Coucy, a valorous and accomplished knight in
Vermandois, six leagues from Noyon, in Picardy, was extremely
enamoured with the wife of the lord of Fayel, his neighbour. After
many difficulties and sufferings incident to such an attachment, the
lover determined to take the cross, and accompany the kings of France
and England to the Holy Land. The lady of Fayel, when she discovered his intention, wrought for him a beautiful net, with a mixture of silk and her own hair, which he fastened to his helmet, and
ornamented the tassels with large pearls. The parting of these lovers
was of course extremely tender. On the arrival of Coucy in Palestine, he performed many gallant and heroic actions, in hopes that
their fame would reach the ears of the beloved object whom he had
left in Europe ; but unfortunately, at a siege, in which the Christians
were repulsed by the Saracens, he received a wound, which was soon
pronounced to be mortal ; upon which he entreated his esquire, the
instant he should be dead, to have his heart embalmed, and carry it
to the lady of Fayel, together with the ornament which she had
worked for him, in a little casket, and other tokens of her affection,
and a letter full of tenderness, written with his own hand, on his
death-bed.

In this request he was punctually obeyed by his friend and esquire ;
but unfortunately, on his arrival in France, when he was hovering
about the castle of the lady's residence, in order to seize the first

sion and his talents, than his untoward fate, he has left behind him many poetical specimens of amatory elegance, among which are some that may rank with the most affecting lyrics of any age or country. The following words, and sample of his taste for melody, will exhibit him in the character of a musician as well as a poet.

---

opportunity that offered of delivering the casket into her own hands, he was discovered by the lord of Fayel, her husband, who knowing him, and suspecting that he was charged with dispatches to his wife, from the *Chatelain*, whom he hated more than any other human creature, he fell upon the esquire, and would have instantly put him to death, had he not begged for mercy, and informed him of the business with which he was entrusted by his late master. The enraged husband therefore seizing the casket, dismissed the affrighted esquire, and went instantly to his cook, whom he ordered to dress the embalmed heart, with such sauce as would make it palatable, and serve it up for dinner. In this he was obeyed by the cook, who at the same time prepared a similar dish, in appearance, for his lord's use, of which he ate, while his lady dined upon the heart of her lover. After dinner, the Seigneur de Favel asked how she liked the dish of which she had been eating. On her answering, ' very well ;' ' I thought,' said he, ' you would be pleased with it ; supposing it to be a viand of which you were always very fond, and for that reason I had it dressed.' The lady suspecting nothing, made no reply ; but her lord continuing the subject, asked her if she knew what she had been eating. She replied in the negative. ' Why then,' said he, ' for your greater satisfaction, I must inform you, that you have eaten the heart of the *Chatelain de Coucy.*' To be thus reminded of her friend, made her very uneasy, although she could not believe that her husband was serious, till he shewed her the casket and letter ; which, when she had examined and perused, her countenance changed ; and after a short pause, she said to Fayel, ' It is true, indeed, that you have helped me to a viand which I very much loved ; but it is the last I shall ever eat ; as, after that, every food would be insipid.' She then retired to her chamber; and as she never more could be prevailed upon to take any kind of sustenance, fasting and affliction soon ended her existence.''

CHANSON

Du Châtelain de Coucy.

Quand li Ro - si - gnol jo - lis chante seur la flor d'Esté que naist la Rose et le lis et la rou - sé - e et vert pré plains de bou - ne vo - len-

té chauté - rai confins, a - mis mais d'itant

sui esba - - his que j'ai si

trés haut pen - - - sé qu'a paines iert a com-

plis · li, ser - virs dont ja - ie gré.

TRANSLATION.

When the nightingale shall sing
  Songs of love from night to morn ;
When the rose and lily spring,
  And the dew bespangles thorn:
Then should I my voice expand,
  Like a lover fond and true,
Could I but its tones command,
  And the tender strain pursue ;
But his love who fears to tell,
Notes of passion ne'er can swell.

In the Bodleian Library is a copy of an ancient metrical romance called the *Roman d'Alexandre,* begun as early as 1150, but continued by two other authors, and finished in the thirteenth century *. In the middle of the poem is the following song, set to music in Gregorian notes. The melody, though scanty and monotonous, is so regular, facile and smooth, that it might pass for a production of the present time. For its reduction into modern notation, the reader is obliged to the ingenious industry of the late Dr. Burney. For the purpose of relieving the sameliness of the air, I have given some diversity to the bass.

---

* The *Roman d'Alexandre* had great celebrity in its time, and long continued to delight the lovers of metrical narration. The account transmitted respecting it by a learned friend of Dr. Burney's at Paris, was, that it is " divided into three parts, and was written by three different authors." Each of these parts, it seems, has a different title : the first is called *Le Roman d'Alexandre ;* the second *La Vengeance d'Alexandre ;* and the third *La Mort d'Alexandre.* The whole poem comprises near twenty thousand lines.

SONG

In the Roman d'Alexandre.

Thus blindly   he proceeds, whom Love at

pleasure leads; As all who live must bear The ills which

mortals share. So all who love with zeal,

Must pain and anguish feel. Thus blind - ly

he   proceeds, Whom Love   at   pleasure leads.

At the head of the *French* songs that have been preserved, are those of Thibaut, king of Navarre, while the ballads best known in the Provençal language, were from the pen of Guillaume IX. Duke of Aquitain. Of Thibaut, it is related, that he was the admirer of Queen Blanche of Castile, mother of St. Lewis, in praise of whom many of his songs were written. *Les Grandes Chroniques de France* inform us, that to allay the violent and hopeless passion he had conceived for Blanche, he was advised to devote himself to the study of music and poetry, which he did so successfully, that he produced "the most beautiful so ngs and melodies that have ever been heard." At any rate, they are curious, not only as further samples of the state of music in France at that early period, but as specimens of royal talent in the compound exertion of a poet and musician*. Of these pieces, I shall present the reader with two: one serious, and one gay. Both are copies from the fac similes made by Dr. Burney, from the originals, found among the MSS. of the Queen of Sweden, in the Vatican: and are reduced by the Doctor into modern notation, with bars, and a base of his own subjoining.

---

* Bards in this king's time, whether professional or of any other rank, were expected to be able to set their own verses to music. Of William Count of Poitou it was said, that *il sut bien trouver et bien chanter:* that is, that he could write verses, and compose music for them.

SONG

Written and composed by Thibaut, King of Navarre.

I hop'd to van quish mighty love, But
find myself de - - ceiv'd; For ev'ry hour, a-
las! I prove the conquest un - a - chiev'd.
By day I seek for ease in vain, Or

call on sleep by   night,   Sighs, tears, com-

plaints, increase   my pain, Nor does a hope, ye

pow'rs! remain, That she will e'er my love re - quite.

SONG

Written and composed by Thibaut, King of Navarre.

Gaiment.

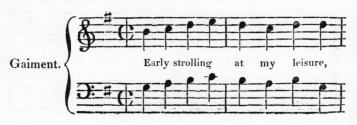

Early strolling   at   my   leisure,

'Twixt an orchard and a grove; While a damsel

for her pleasure, Sweetly sung the pains of love.

Thus began her am'rous strains: "Cupid holds me

fast in chains." Eager I approach the maid;

Hoping she who could so warble,   Had a heart not

made of marble,   When " Good day, Sweetheart," I said.

CHAP. XVI.

GENERAL STATE OF MUSIC, FROM THE BEGINNING
OF THE FOURTEENTH CENTURY TO THE TIME OF
HAMBOIS, THE FIRST DOCTOR IN MUSIC.

THE specimens already given of musical composition,
in France, have been purely melodial. It was not till the
early part of the fourteenth century, that written discant
was generally employed in that country; at least, no remains of *French* counterpoint of an earlier date have reached
us[*]. Indeed, the first samples of French music in parts,
properly so entitled, appeared in a volume of *Virelais, ballads,
rondeaux,* and other poems, by Guillaume de Machau, who
flourished about the middle of the fourteenth century, and
by the Count de Caylus, has been styled *poet and musician.*
Some of these pieces the author set to music for a single
voice, and others in four parts, *triplum, tenor, contratenor,*
and another part, which he has not named. By the appearance of the *scores,* the melody, in full compositions, was
always given to the *tenor.* At this period, notes of a lozenge form were very generally used; which, when their
heads were *full* or *open,* were called *minims;* but a still
quicker note being occasionally wanted, the white or open
note received that appellation, and the black were called

---

[*] It has been pretended, that compositions in counterpoint of a date
earlier than this have been preserved; but they must consist of wild
and irregular combinations not properly ranging under the head of
what we now mean by *music in parts.*

les noirs. The dissection of notes, for the purpose of expressing an accelerated motion, became now very common; and
was carried to an extent that gave great offence and scandal to pious and sober Christians! But so different was
even this advanced state of notation from that which has
been used within the last century and a half, that to the generality of modern musicians it would be utterly unintelligible *. In the British Museum, there is, among the fragments of three musical treatises, the music of a French song
composed as late as the end of the fourteenth century, which
is without bars, and possesses no other indication of its
measure than what is to be collected from the intermixture
of black, lozenge-formed, or square notes. According to
these, its proper division, in modern characters, would be as
follows :—

AIR OF A FRENCH SONG;

Composed at the latter end of the Fourteenth Century
(Words in the MS. illegible).

---

* In the Pepysian Collection, Magdalen College, Cambridge,
there are copies of music, of the fourteenth, fifteenth, and sixteenth
centuries, which only musical antiquaries can decipher.

The reader cannot have proceeded through this long
course of observations on the early French music, without
the desire of becoming acquainted with the state of composition in Italy, the land whose *language is music,* *—the
land destined to produce the finest vocal composers of which
the world can boast.

According to Conticelli, *(Eloquenza Toscana)* the first
Italian poetry was lyrical: but he thinks that the first songs

---

* Metastasio has pronounced the Italian language to be *Musica
Stessa :* and Gravina says, that the Tuscans brought the people over
to their democratic opinions by the sweetness of their tongue. Muratori asserts, that the French, Spanish, and Italian languages, were
little more than different modifications, not of the pure and elegant
Latin used by the higher and educated orders of the ancient Romans,
but of a rustic, plebeian dialect, spoken only by the lower and ignorant classes. He, however, justly insists, that there is more pure
Latin in the Italian, than in any other modern language.

of the moderns were written in Sicily, whence he says, the
art of composing them passed to the troubadours of Provence *, and thence to the Italians, among whom the art
arrived about the middle of the thirteenth century, the time
when, if we are to believe Crescimbeni, the Italian language
was almost completely formed.   Muratori says, (and his
assertion is probable), that music did not perish in the
middle ages.   In support of this opinion, he mentions from
the History of Malaspina, a procession of women singing
through the streets, accompanied with cymbals, drums,
flutes, and other musical instruments, in the year 1268, when
Prince Conrad was marching against Charles I. King of
Sicily.   Also he says, the Pagan custom was continued, of
hiring women (*præficæ*) to sing and weep at funerals, and
chant epithalamiums, at the weddings of the wealthy.   In
Tuscany, and other parts of Italy, actors, musicians and
singers, under the titles of *Giullari* and *Giocolari*, were
retained at the courts of princes, or in the habit of frequently appearing there, to amuse and exhilarate the company.   Their pay was munificent; but did not consist
wholly of money.   Costly and gorgeous robes were often a
part of their reward.   Benvenuto Aliprando, an old rustic
poet, describes a marriage at the *great court* of Mantua in
the year 1340; upon which occasion the musicians were
presented with a variety of rich and precious vestments: and
the same author tells us, that at the nuptials of Lionel, Duke
of Clarence, son of Edward III. of England, and Violante,
the daughter of Galeazo Visconti, Duke of Milan, the

---

* Petrarch doubted whether the Sicilians were indebted to the
Provençals, or the Provençals to the Sicilians, for the art of lyrical
poetry.

bridegroom presented five hundred superb dresses to the attendant minstrels and singers *. This custom, during the fourteenth century, travelled into England, where it continued till the establishment of the king's band.

The most ancient melodies to be found in Italy, originally set to Italian words, are in a collection of *Laudi Spirituali,* or sacred songs, preserved in a manuscript of the Magliabecchi Library at Florence †. These religious poems became very popular throughout Italy. At Florence, as early as 1310, a society was formed expressly for their practice and performance. In 1485, and soon afterwards, several collections of them were published; and in the following century, many more, among which were productions of Politian, Bembo, Lodovico Martelli, and other eminent poets. These spiritual canticles were, at first, little more than chants ; and were unaccompanied with a bass ; but they gradually assumed a *harmonized* form ; and were successively sung in two, three, and four parts. " There are at Florence," says Sansovino, in his Commentary on Boccaccio (published in 1546) " several schools of artizans and mechanics, among which are those of Orsanmichole, and Santa Maria Novella. Every Saturday, after nine o'clock, these assemble in the church, and there sing five or six *laudi,* in four parts; the words of which are by Lorenzo de Medici, Pulci, and Giambellari; and at every *laud,* they change the

---

* Musicians were always addicted to *dress.* Virgil speaks of the *flowing vest* of Orpheus. Arion leaped into the sea *richly attired;* and Antigenides wore a *saffron robe* and *Milesian slippers.* Even in the time of Petrarch, poets and musicians were distinguished by their habiliments ; and Dante, it is said, was buried in *the poetical stole.*

† Father Menestrier thought that hymns, canticles, and mysteries, in the vulgar tongues of Europe, had their origin from the pilgrims who went to the Holy Land.

singers, and to the sound of the organ, discover a *Madonna,* which finishes the festival. And these singers, who are called *laudesi,* have a precentor, whom they denominate their captain or leader."

The following is a specimen of the melodies sung by the *laudesi·*

TO THE BLESSED TRINITY.

Al - la   Tri - ni   ta   be-

a - ta   da noi   sem - pre   a - do-

ra · ta   Tri - ni · · tà   glo - ri-

a - ta   u - ni - ta   me - ra - vig-

lio - sa   Tu   sei   Man - na

sa - por - o - sa   E - tutt'-

o   de — si - de — ro - sa.

Of the state of secular music during this dark period, the memorials are but few, and those few but scanty in their intelligence. But the time was not very distant when the progress of the harmonic science in its provinces of passion and temporal amusement, would not only procure for it a larger portion of the historian's notice, but raise it to a dignity not dependent upon poetical support. In consequence of the multiplication of characters for the expression of different durations of sounds, a species of composition arose, which proved capable of affording exquisite pleasure to the ear, and a high gratification to the mind, without the aid of poetical numbers, and the melodious articulations of the human voice. Nevertheless, it continued to add its force to the charms of verse; and the sonnets of a Petrarch were indebted to its mellifluous aid for an influence over the heart, which, without the influence of sound, even their own intrinsic excellence had scarcely commanded. It is much to be lamented, that none of the original melodies exist, to which those exquisite effusions of Petrarch's muse were originally set; not because we can reasonably suppose that they competed in beauty with the poetry they accompanied *,

---

* The arts of Poetry and Music have never advanced in any country with equal steps. The principal reason of which may be, that music is a language constituting a science in itself; a science which the student may acquire, and yet remain ignorant of the higher rules of composition; as he may learn those rules, and yet find himself unqualified to compose. The elements of poetry are *words*, the sense of which every one comprehends, while those of music are *sounds*, with the relations and bearings of which only musicians are acquainted. Poetry cannot be enjoyed without being understood; but music can delight the uninitiated. Poetry exists by its own ideas, conveyed to us through a medium common to all minds; music speaks under a regulation of laws not necessary to be explained to the hearer. In a word, the import of the materials of poetry is forced upon us, from

(for probably, they were no more to be compared to the airs of modern times, than the music Henry Lawes set to Milton's Comus, to that applied to the same drama by the late Dr. Arne;) but they might have thrown a light upon the then state of secular composition of which history now would be happy to avail herself. By some writers it has been said, that in Italy, music was the last cultivated of any of the polite arts; and one author, even of the last century, has gone so far as to affirm, that in that country, it is not yet established upon true principles: and, with Muratori, he complains of the degeneracy and corruption of music in Italy, and of its having ceased to copy nature, and to appeal to the heart.

That *music* in *parts*, that is, figurative counterpoint, and performance in concert, had in the fourteenth century, arrived at some respectable degree of improvement, seems evident, from an account published in Padua, 1549, of the ceremonies of Petrarch's coronation. It informs us, that in the procession, there were " two choirs of music, one vocal, and the other instrumental, which were constantly singing and playing by turns in sweet harmony." And in the Chronicle of Frankfort, published in 1360, it is observed, " that music was amplified by new singers, and a figurative kind of composition unknown before." Also, from a writer, who survived Petrarch only two years, we collect some interesting particulars. The *Decamerone* of Boccaccio tells us, that during the plague at Florence, one of the methods resorted to, for alleviating the horrors of that dreadful calamity, was that of musical exercise, vocal and instrumental; a resource, of which the respectable inhabit-

hour to hour; while that of the elements of musical composition can only be attained by a long course of indefatigable exertion.

ants at least, could well avail themselves; for the author
adds, that all the ladies and gentlemen were not only skilled
in song, but *able instrumental performers*. But to what
latitude we may justly extend the sense of these expressions,
is doubtful. If we consider how simple and inartificial was
the music of the middle ages, speaking generally, we shall
find ourselves obliged to conclude, that no very extraordinary powers were necessary for its performance : and it is
worth observing, that the writers of those times are not
very lavish of their praises of musical execution. The first
instance of reported skill, accompanied with the author's
avowal of his admiration, is in the *Lives of Illustrious Florentines,* by Philip Villani, who flourished about the middle
of the fourteenth century. Speaking of Francesco Cieco,
that biographer says, " Many are the Florentines who have
rendered themselves memorable by the art of music ; but
all those of former times have been far surpassed by Francesco Cieco, who, during childhood, was deprived of sight
by the small-pox. He was the son of Jacopo, a Florentine painter, of great probity and simplicity of manners ;
and being arrived at adolescence, and beginning to be sensible of the misery of blindness, in order to diminish the
horror of perpetual night, he began in a childish manner to
sing ; but advancing towards maturity, and becoming more
and more captivated with music, he began seriously to study
it, as an art, first by learning to sing, and afterwards by applying himself to the practice of instruments, particularly
the organ; which, without ever having seen the keys, he soon
played in so masterly and sweet a manner, as astonished
every hearer. Indeed, his superiority was soon acknowledged
so unanimously, that, by the common consent of all the musicians of his time, he was publicly honoured at Venice, with
the laurel crown for his performance on the organ, before
the King of Cyprus and the Duke of Venice, in the manner

of a poet laureat. Cieco died in 1390, and is buried in the church of St. Laurence." The musical abilities of Cieco, distinguished as they were, appear to have at least been equalled, if not transcended, by the celebrated Antonio, surnamed *dagl' Organi*. Of this organ performer, Christopher Landino, in his commentary upon Dante, says, " We have seen and heard in our own times, the famous Antonio, of whom it might be observed, that, as many persons went from Cadiz, the remotest part of Spain, to Rome, in order to see the historian Livy ; so many most excellent musicians have come from England, and the most distant regions of the north ; crossing the sea, Alps, and Appenines, in order to hear the performances of Antonio." By these striking instances of excellence in organ performance, it would seem that at this time that noble instrument was much and very generally practised. The powers of Cieco and Antonio, regarded by themselves, would only prove that organ music was successfully cultivated in Italy ; but, if we take into view the circumstance of their talents attracting the atten- tion of the musicians of *England, and the most distant regions of the North*, we shall be obliged to conclude that the organ was also a favourite in England, and most of the countries of Europe ; and that, consequently, *good organists* formed a considerable portion of the professional musicians of the fourteenth century.

But of all the instruments in use at this time, no one appears to have been so highly and so generally esteemed as the *harp*. One of its great advantages over the organ, no doubt, was its portability. The bards and minstrels could bear it about with them in their peregrinations, when it would serve the purpose, either of entertaining the auditors with its tones, independently of those of the voice, or as an accompaniment to the melody of song. In Wales, the ballads of which country are of very high antiquity, the

harp was so great a favourite, and the ability to perform
upon it deemed so high an accomplishment, as to be necessary to the completion of a gentleman's education *·
With the Saxons and Danes the harp was an instrument of
equal estimation. The songs sung to it for the victory obtained by Athelstan, and those on the occasion of the death
of Edgar, as also the use to which Alfred was able to
turn his command of that instrument, are strong proofs of
its ancient and general practice. This predilection, as
already observed, it chiefly owed to the bards. Not only
was it easy of conveyance, but it possessed a most material
preference over the flute and hautbois, in that its performance was no impediment to the exercise of the voice, with
which its tones most attractively amalgamated.

With respect to *British harpers,* we have proofs abundant, that they were famous long before the Conquest. To
his *bard,* Doomsday Book records the bounty of our first
Norman sovereign; and Henry III. it will be remembered,
gave forty shillings and a pipe of wine to Richard his harper.
Whether under British, Saxon, Danish or Norman kings,
the inhabitants of this island appear to have been long partial to the music of the harp. The ancient poems were
sung to this instrument on Sundays and festivals; and the
minstrels themselves were as much esteemed, as their performances were admired. They were often the attendants
and the companions of princes; who prized their professional powers, and experienced their attachment and fidelity †.

---

* The northern annals abound with instances of princes and great
personages, who were proficients on the harp. Eustace, the author
of *Le Brut d'Angleterre,* or the Metrical History of Brutus, represents Gabbet, one of our ancient kings, as the most able musician of
his time.

† An incident connected with our Edward I. strongly proves the

Of the *privilege* formerly granted to itinerant minstrels at the Midsummer fair at Chester, few readers have not heard; but the *particular occasion* of the immunity is not so generally known. It happened that in 1212, during the observance of this fair, Randal, one of the Earls of Chester, was suddenly besieged by the Welsh in Rhydland, or Rothelan Castle, in Flintshire; when Robert de Lacy, Constable of Chester, heading the people assembled at the fair, marched them, *animated by the minstrels*, to Rhydland, and effected his relief. " In memory of this notable exploit," says Dugdale, " that famous meeting of minstrels has been duly continued to every Midsummer fair, at which time the heir of Hugh de Dutton, accompanied with diverse gentlemen, having a pennon of his arms borne before him by one of the principal minstrels, who also weareth his surtout, first rideth up to the east gate of the city, and there causeth proclamation to be made, that all the musicians and minstrels assembled within the County Palatine of Chester, shall, during the time of the fair, be safe in their persons, notwithstanding any misdemeanors, of which they may have been guilty, provided they commit no new offence."

Another privilege, equally curious, and not less barbarous, is related by Dr. Plot, in his History of Staffordshire. This was granted by John of Gaunt, Duke of Lancaster,

---

sentiment of good faith with which the minstrels were capable of being animated towards their patrons. Walter Heming, in his Chronicle, tells us, that this prince, a short time before he ascended the throne, took his harper with him to the Holy Land; and that when he was wounded at Ptolemais, his harper *(Citharœda Suus)* saved his life, by rushing upon, and killing the assassin: a service that aggravates, if any thing *can* aggravate, the murderous enormities afterwards committed by this monarch of infamous memory, whose name, with that of many another of our royal criminals, ought, for the honour of England, to be blotted from its history.

at the inauguration of the first king of the English minstrels, at his castle of Tutbury, in the year 1381. The
account is so long, that I need not apologize for substi-
tuting for the narration itself, its more acceptable abridgment.

Among the concourse of persons who partook of the
liberal hospitality of the ancient Earls and Dukes of Lancaster, were always a great number of musicians. Jealou-
sies and quarrels sometimes arising between them, for their
better regulation and government, a ruler was appointed by
the name of a KING. To this musical monarch the following charter was granted.

" John, by the grace of God, King of Castile and Leon,
Duke of Lancaster, to all them who shall see or hear these
our letters, greeting. Know ye, we have ordained, constituted, and assigned, to our well-beloved the King of the
Minstrels in our honour of Tutbury, who is, or for the
time shall be, to apprehend and arrest all the minstrels in
our said honour and franchise, that refuse to do the services
and minstrelsy as appertain to them to do from ancient
times at Tutbury aforesaid, yearly on the days of the Assumption of our Lady; giving and granting to the said
King of the Minstrels for the time being, full power and
commandment to make them reasonable to justify, and to
constrain them to do their services, and minstrelsies, in such
manner as belongeth to them ; and as it hath been there,
and of ancient times accustomed. In witness of which
thing we have caused these our letters to be made patent.
Given under our privy seal, at our castle of Tutbury, the
twenty-second day of August, iu the fourth year of the reign
of the most sweet King Richard the Second."

The defaulters generally numerous, and the amerce-
ments, perhaps, sometimes rather unreasonable, controversies
between the offenders and the officers, rose to such a
height, that it was found necessary to erect a court to hear

complaints. At this court, which was held " on the mor-
row after the Assumption, being the sixteenth day of August," the steward of the honour presided. On this occasion, the minstrels assembled at Tutbury in great form,
having previously met at the house of the bailiff of the
manor, whence, preceded by music (the King of the Minstrels for the year past being between the bailiff and the
steward, and followed by four officers immediately under the
king, bearing white wands) they walked in procession, two
and two together, to the church, where they heard a sermon
suitable to the occasion. From church they proceeded to
the castle hall, or court. Here the ceremonies commenced by an *O yes*, made by one of the minstrel-officers,
commanding the attendance and attention of all the minstrels dwelling within the precincts of Tutbury, and owing
suit and service to his Majesty's Court of Music. Then a
jury being chosen, the steward proceeded to give them his
charge ; in which he never failed to remind them of the real
origin of all music, both vocal and instrumental ; its antiquity, its excellence, and its power over the affections ; its
high office in sounding the praise and glory of God, and the
honour it shares, in ranking in the schools among the liberal
arts. He then exhorted them to be careful in preserving
their reputation ; and to elect for officers men skilled in their
profession, and of good life and conversation.

The charge being finished, the jurors retired, to make
choice of officers for the ensuing year ; one of which officers
was elected king. On their return into court, they presented to the steward their new monarch, who received from
the old king a little white wand, the token of royal authority.
They then proceeded to hear and determine upon the complaints brought before the court : levying upon the convicted offenders fines proportioned to their faults ; one half
of which fines went to the king, the other to the stew-

ards. To this ceremony succeeded a sumptuous dinner, which being finished, the minstrels went forth to receive a bull, (first the gift of the Prior of Tutbury, afterwards of the Earl of Devonshire) which, to the disgrace of the times, after having his ears cropt, his tail amputated close to his body, his hide smeared over with soap, and his nostrils blown full of pepper, was turned loose by the prior, or the Earl of Devonshire, to be pursued and hunted by the minstrels; and when taken, was staked and baited *.

The following movement, copied from Mr. J. S. Smith's *Musica Antiqua*, presents a favourable specimen of the instrumental tunes composed about this time.

DANCE TUNE.

In modern Notation, with a Bass, added by J. S. Smith.

---

* The author, of whose account the above is a faithful compression, observes, "that as much mischief often occurred from this bull-hunting, as from the *Jeu de Taureau*, or bull-fighting, practised at Valencia, Madrid, and many other places in Spain; whence, perhaps, this our custom of bull-running might be derived, and set up here by John of Gaunt, who was King of Castile and Leon, and lord of the honour of Tutbury; for why might not we receive this sport from the Spaniards, as well as they derive it from the Romans, and the Romans from the Greeks?

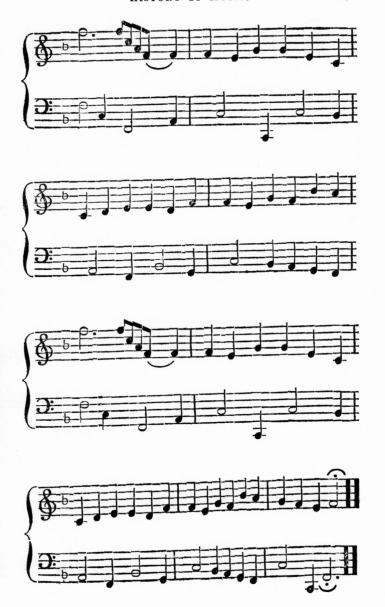

A more important period of English poetry and English melody, does not, perhaps, present itself to the investigator of our progress in the elegant arts, than that of the latter end of the fourteenth century, in which the genius of Chaucer displayed itself. Of this poet, his own works will ever remain the best eulogium, and place him immeasurably higher in the scale of excellence than his cotemporaries, Gower, Lydgate and Occleve, while his incessant allusions to the charms of vocal and instrumental music, demonstrate the power with which it then appealed to the ear and the passions. Speaking, in his tale of *The Cock and the Fox*, of his hero, Chaunticlere, he says,

> His voice was merrier than the merry *organ*,
> On massè days, that in the churches gon.

From which it is but reasonable to conclude, that in the poet's time, organs were very generally employed in the embellishment of divine service; an opinion further sanctioned by the history of Cecilia, in his *Nonne's Tale :* where he says,

> And while that *organs* maden melodie,
> To God alone thus, in her best sung she * :

---

* Respecting Cecilia's character as a *musician*, or *musical patroness*, Dr. Burney was at considerable pains to discover something more than is generally known, but could obtain nothing on that point, certain or satisfactory. " Neither in Chaucer, nor in any of the histories or legendary accounts of this saint," says he, " which I have been able to consult, does any thing appear, that can authorize the religious veneration which the votaries of music have so long paid to her; nor is it easy to discover whence it has arisen. Chaucer's account is almost literally translated from the Life of St. Cecilia, in the *Legenda Aurea* of Jacobus Jannensis. Bede in his Ecclesiastical History, mentions her church at Rome, as the place where Vilbrord was ordained pope in the year 696 ; and in his Martyrology, he tells us,

No English music in *parts,* of a date so distant as that of Chaucer, is now extant * : but certain passages in his poems seem to prove, that in his time, *full services* were not uncommon. In his *Dream,* describing a concert of birds, we find him saying—

> And everiche song in his wise
> The most sweete, and solemne *service,*
> By note, that evir man I trowe,
> Had herde, for some of 'hem *songe low.*
> Some *high,* and *all of one accorde.*

It is a curious fact, recorded by Thomæ de Elmham, that at the coronation of Henry V. the only instruments em-

---

that her intended spouse, Valerian, and his brother Tiburtius, suffered martyrdom in the time of the Emperor Alexander Severus. Mabillon has proved, that the festival of this saint was celebrated in France before the time of Charlemagne, by a *Gallican* missal, which he has published, and which must have been in use before the Gregorian chant was received in that country. Fortunatus of Poictiers, the most ancient author who speaks of her, says, that she died, or rather, suffered martyrdom, in Sicily.''

During the pontificate of Clement VIII. there was a solemn festival at Rome, for the discovery of the body of St. Cecilia, among the relics with which that land of Catholicism and superstition abounds. Of the ceremonies observed on that occasion, Cardinal Baronius, who was an eye-witness of them, has left a clear and full account.

* Indeed, all our secular music produced before the beginning of the fifteenth century, has perished. Stowe collected many ballads that bore Chaucer's name, and John Shirley made a voluminous collection of songs by Chaucer, Gower, Lydgate, and others, which are still subsisting; but not one of the tunes to which they were sung, are any where preserved. This is to be regretted; for though our early poets acknowledge the pleasure they received from the melodies of their time, and seldom lose an opportunity of describing their effects, a single *example* of their popular tunes, or their counterpoint, would afford us a clearer idea of their claims to admiration, than is to be derived from any verbal description.

ployed were harps; of which, however, the historian says
there were a prodigious number. It appears, that when
this prince entered the city of London, after the battle of
Agincourt, among other devices for celebrating his recent
victory, children were placed in temporary turrets to sing
his exploits; for which personal adulation, he, however, had
so little taste, that by a formal edict, he forbade its repetition. One of these songs, or one written soon after the
battle, is preserved in the Pepysian Collection at Magdalen
College, Cambridge *. The original is written upon vellum
in Gregorian notes. Dr. Burney made a journey to Cambridge for the purpose of seeing it; and tells us, he found
it so ill written, that it was with considerable difficulty he
reduced it to modern notation.

The two following airs, both composed in the fifteenth
century, will, as far as regards the object of conveying an
idea of the style of secular vocal composition in England
at that period, be found tolerably satisfactory.

SONG

Of the 15th Century.   Preserved in the British Museum.

The Melody transposed from the Tenor Cliff.—The Bass by Mr:
J. S. Smith.

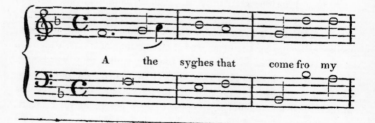

A   the   syghes that   come fro my

---

* This song has been inserted in the *Reliques of Ancient Poetry*.

hart — They grieve me passying

sore — — Syth I must

fro my love de - part, ffare-

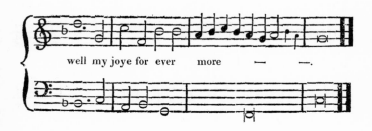

well my joye for ever more — —.

2

Oft to me wyth hir goodly face
   She was wont to cast her eye,
And now absence to me in place
   Alas! for woo I dye, I dye.

3

I was wont hir to beholde,
   And takyn in armys twayne,
And now with syghes many fold,
   Ffarewell my joye and welcome payne.

4

A methynke that I schud yete
   As wolde to Gode that I myght,
There myght no joyes compare with hyt
Unto my hart to make it lyght.

HUNTING AIR.

Composed about 1470, *by John Cole.*

Blow thy horne   hunter   cu   blow thy horne on

hye,   In   yonder wode ther   lyeth   a doo In

fayth she wolt not dye cu blow thy horne

hunter cu blow thy horne joly hun - ter.

So fast did the music of the minstrels continue to hold the love and partiality of the aggregate of the people, that even the turbulent and unhappy reign of Henry VI., was so far from being unpropitious to their importance, that they were often better paid than the clergy *. This, at least, has been confidently asserted; and the opinion derives some support from the fact, that in 1430, at the annual feast of the fraternity of the HOLIE CROSS, at Abingdon in Berkshire, twelve priests received only four-pence each for singing a dirge; while the same number of minstrels were severally remunerated with two shillings and four-pence, besides provision for themselves and their horses. And the *History of English*

---

* The clergy, however, it is to be observed, were at this time, all unmarried: besides which, they almost universally, as members of some fraternity, were not only furnished with a habitation, but provided with a regular table.

Poetry informs us, that " In the year 1441, eight priests were hired from Coventry, to assist in celebrating a yearly obit in the church of the neighbouring priory of Mastoke; as were six minstrels called *mimi*, appertaining to the establishment of Lord Clinton, who lived in the adjoining castle of Mastoke, to sing, harp, and play, in the hall of the monastery, during the extraordinary refection allowed to the monks on that anniversary. Two shillings were given to the priests, and four to the minstrels; and the latter are said to have supped in the *camera picta*, or painted chamber of the convent, with the sub-prior; on which occasion the master furnished eight massy tapers of wax. That the gratuities allowed to priests, even if learned, for their labours, in the same age of devotion, were extremely slender, may be collected from other expences of this priory. In the same year, the prior gives only sixpence for a sermon to a DOCTOR PRÆDICANS, or an itinerant doctor in theology of one of the mendicant orders, who went about preaching to the religious houses."

By this it would appear, that the music of the minstrels was not only highly estemed by the laity at large, but was considered as useful by churchmen; since, whenever the church has been lavish of its stores, some substantial reason has appeared in excuse for its liberality. The value of music to religion at this time, will be the more evident, if we consider the general ignorance that prevailed, and that the embellishments of divine worship would consequently be better understood, and, even, if for that reason alone, more enjoyed, than the verbal formulary, or the mystic comments of the school divines. About this time, the church service, in every country, began to assume much of that pomp which it afterwards exhibited. The choirs were better supplied with vocal priests, or as they are now popularly called, *singing-men ;* and not only was the organ very generally used, but the instrument was improved in its powers, and opened a new scope for the display of the performer's talents and science. In a word, music, rising above the character of an almost unimportant adjunct, to religious ceremony, which it had originally been, now became indispensable to the solemnity and the dignity of public worship; and was honoured and rewarded by the priesthood, because it rendered great and momentous services to the clerical profession.

CHAP. XVII.

HITHERTO, we have seen Music receiving encouragement from the church, and admiration and honourable notice
from the great and wealthy, as well as from the people at
large; now it is about to be exhibited, clothed in new
honours, and formally taking its rank among the liberal
sciences, by giving its professors a station among the higher
graduates of our great national seminaries. It is true, that
during the middle ages, as we have before remarked, Music
was considered as one of the seven scholastic arts, but it had
not attained the power of conferring degrees on its students; and as Dr. Burney pertinently observes, it is a curious fact, that of the seven sciences of which itself constituted one, (grammar, rhetoric, logic, arithmetic, music, geometry, and astronomy) music should, in England, be the only
faculty that bestows titular distinction.

According to the original spirit of the institution, the dis-
tribution of musical degrees, was confined to speculative
candidates; that is, to the learned in acoustics, as comprehending the doctrine of harmonics, and the ratio of grave
and acute: and to be able to read and expound certain books
in Boethius, was to be qualified to receive the degree, either
of Bachelor or Doctor of Music. But statutes upon more

liberal principles, have at Oxford, superseded requisitions profitless to composition and practical music; and now, proceeders to academical honours, become qualified by observing the following regulations. Before a student becomes a candidate for a bachelor's degree, it is necessary that he should have employed seven years in the study and practice of music; and that previous to his supplication for his grace towards this degree, he compose a song or anthem in *five parts*, and perform the same publicly in the music-school, with vocal and instrumental music. Of a bachelor proceeding to the degree of doctor, it is required that he shall have studied five years after he has taken his bachelor's degree; and that he compose a song, or anthem, in *six or eight parts*, and publicly perform the same " *tam vocibus quam instrumentis etiam musicis.*"

It is asserted, and with every appearance of correctness, that the degree of Doctor in Music was first conferred in the year 1463, when John Hambois, of whom we are about to speak, received the title. None who are concerned for the honour of the science, will regard with indifference an era that raised the musical composer to an elevation competing with that of learned men, and those whose genius confer honour upon literature and general science. The following short deduction of the progress of music between the year 1300 and the middle of the fifteenth century, explaining how music became entitled to this distinction, will not, perhaps, be uninteresting.

The discrimination between the liberal, and the manual or popular arts, is at least as ancient as the fourth century. But in how barbarous a manner the sciences were taught, the treatise on them by the famous Alcuin, the preceptor of Charlemagne, sufficiently demonstrates. In most of the schools, the public teachers ventured no further than grammar, rhetoric, and logic; though a few proceeded to arith-

metic, music, geometry, and astronomy; and thence to the
study of Cassiodorus and Boethius. This exhibits to us
the track prescribed to the musical student. Utterly ignorant of the language in which the rules of harmony were originally delivered, only qualified to view them through the
medium of a Latin version, he studied Marcianus Capella,
Macrobius, Cassiodorus, Boethius, Guido Aretinus, and
other writers on the tones, and on the *Cantus Mensurabilis;* and to this species of musical learning it was, that the
honour of degrees was granted; and even to this species,
only by the universities of Oxford and Cambridge. The
honour, however, was nominally awarded to *music;* it was
therefore, only necessary to give to the statutes the new form
which the reader has seen, in order to divert that honour
from the professors of dry speculation, to those who are
learned in harmonical combinations and evolutions, and
whose genius imparts life to embodied sounds, and teaches
them to raise the mind, and interest the heart.

Among the musicians of this description, was John Hambois. He is said by Bayle to have been " a man of great
erudition :" and several writers speak of him as learned in
all the arts, though they admit, that among his various studies,
music held the first place. His knowledge in harmony, and
skill in the construction of concords, and preparation and
resolution of discords, were superior to what any other musician of his time could boast. He wrote, in Latin, several
tracts, among which was one entitled *Summum Artis Mu-
sices;* and another called *Cantionum Artificialium diversi
generis.*

At what precise period Hambois received his diploma,
and whether he was a member of Oxford or Cambridge, has
never been ascertained. But since he was the first upon
whom the title of *Doctor in Music* was conferred, and academical degrees are traceable only up to the year 1463,

when Henry Habengton was admitted to the degree of Bachelor of Music at Cambridge, and Thomas Saintwix,
Doctor in Music, was made Master of King's College, in
the same university, it is probable that Hambois' admission
took place but a short time earlier.   Far, indeed, is it from
extravagant to suppose, that his extraordinary merits might
give birth to the institution of musical degrees, and that he
was not only the first musician upon whom *any* academical
distinction was conferred, but the individual in honour of
whose learning and abilities *musical* distinctions were instituted.

Hambois, we are told, flourished about the year 1470;
but Wood, in his Fasti, does not produce any names of
musicians whom the university of Oxford enrolled among its
graduates before the sixteenth century, though some time
previous to that date, Cambridge created several. About Hambois' time, musical composition assumed a regularity of disposition in its melody, a contrivance in its harmony, and an
ingenuity in the imitations and responses of its *parts*, that
demonstrate a very considerable advance in the art of counterpoint.   Dr. Burney has presented to the public a production of about this period, which he found in the British
Museum, whose merits attest the state of musical harmonization in the fifteenth century, and prove, that though the laws
of composition, as they are now understood, were then not
thoroughly known, or too frequently disregarded, light was
flowing upon the science ; a light that had begun to expose
the past chaos, and to induce a wish for that order and beauty
which was about to be called forth by cultivated genius.
The production to which I am alluding, is a descriptive
song; its subject, The approach of summer. The score
comprises six *real parts*. The upper four constitute a canon
for many voices, in the unison ; the two beneath them are
free, and introduced alternately, with the same notes in a
kind of drone, or burden, to each of which the author gives
the name of *Pes.*

CANON,

From an ancient MS. in the British Museum.

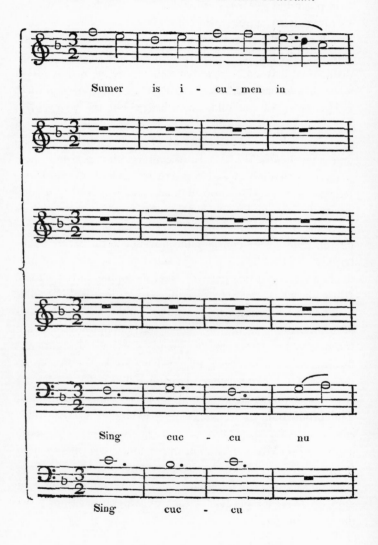

Sumer is i - cu - men in

Sing cuc - cu nu

Sing cuc - cu

groweth   sed   and   bloweth   med   and

lhude   sing   cuc - cu

Sumer   is   i - cumen   in

sing   cuc - cu   nu

sing   cuc - cu

springeth the wde nu.

groweth sed and bloweth med and

lhude sing cuc - cu

Sumer is i - cumen in

sing cuc - cu

sing cuc - cu nu

after   calve   cu

Awe   bleteth   after   lomb lhouth

Sing   cuc - cu

springeth   wde   nu

Sing   cuc - cu   nu

Sing   cuc - cu

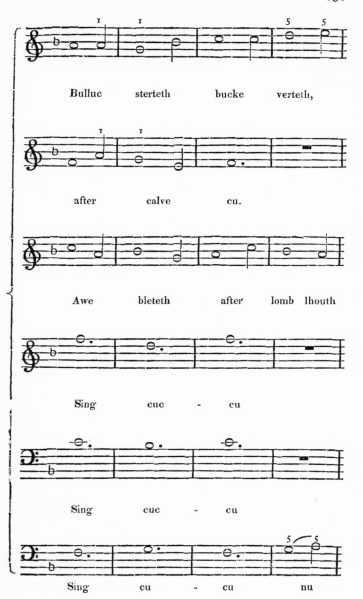

cuc - cu cuc - cu

murie sing cuc - cu

Bulluc sterteth bucke verteth

after calve cu

Sing cuc - cu.

Sing cuc - cu nu

Groweth   sed   and   bloweth   med   and

Lhude   sing   cuc   -   cu

Sumer   is   i   -   cumen   in

thu   naver   nu.

Sing   cuc   -   cu   nu

Sing   cuc   -   cu

spring'th   the   wood - è   nu.

Grow - eth   sed   and   blow - eth.

Lhu - de   sing   cuc - cu.

Sumer   is   i - cumen.

sing   cuc - cu.

sing   cuc - cu *.

* The true import of the words of this canon, seems to be as follows:

Summer is a-coming in,
    Loud sing cuckoo.
Groweth seed, and bloweth mead,
    And springeth the wood new.
Ewe bleateth after lamb;
    Loweth after calf, cow;
Bullock sterteth, buckè verteth,
    Merry sing cuckoo,
Well sing'st thou cuckoo,
    Nor cease thou ever, now.

With consecutive fifths and eighths this composition abounds. The figures of reference will point them out to the musical reader, and show him how little the law prohibiting successive perfect concords in the same direction, was regarded by the ablest composers of the fifteenth century : I say the *ablest* composers : because this specimen of harmonical structure (the first example of counterpoint in six parts) with all its defects, is very superior to any thing extant, of the same early period. It is airy, pastoral, and simple ; yet, exhibits a good deal of thinking; so much, indeed, that we cannot but feel surprized that the propriety of imitating the notes of the cuckoo, should have so entirely escaped the composer's attention ; an advantage so obvious as to have been attended to by all subsequent writers, whether for the voice or for instruments, whenever the subject of their compositions offered an occasion. Vide the Madrigals of Walker and Bennet ; the Concertos of Vivaldi, Handel, and Lampe, and Dr. Arne's " When daisies pied and violets blue," in " As you like it."

The above canon would sanction the supposition, that in the fifteenth century, vocal composition in parts was much studied ; and that much of it was consequently produced : but, either from a dearth of genius, or the neglect of subsequent times in preserving what was left, so little music of that period has reached us, that it is impossible to determine with what success the art of composition, whether vocal or instrumental, was cultivated. With respect to instrumental music, since the minstrels continued to be encouraged, it is natural to imagine that at least the species of it which came within the province of their practice was carried to some degree of excellence. It is scarcely in the nature of things, that instrumental melody should be in constant course of performance in the balls of princes and nobles, and in the principal monasteries where minstrels

were generally retained, and from which they received regular salaries *, and not occasionally give birth, in even ordinary imaginations, to many an agreeable novelty.

But though the minstrels enjoyed a considerable degree of
the esteem of all ranks of society, they did not till the reign
of Edward the Fourth, acquire the solid dignity and stability
of a corporate body. That prince, by his letters patent,
bearing date the twenty-fourth of April, 1469, did, ' for him
and his heirs, give and grant licence unto Walter Haliday,
Marshall, John Cuff, and Robert Marshall, Thomas Grove,
Thomas Calthorne, William Cliff, William Christian, and
William Eynesham, the MINSTRELS of the said king, that
they by themselves should be in deed and name, *one body
and cominality,* perpetual and capable in the law, and should
have perpetual succession ; and that as well the Minstrels of
the said king, which then were, and other Minstrels of the
said king and his heirs, which should be afterwards, might at
their pleasure name, chuse, ordaine, and successively constitute from among themselves, one marshall, able and fit to
remain in that office during his life, and also two wardens
every year, to govern the said fraternity and guild," &c.†

In a scarce book, called *Liber Niger Domus Regis,*
published by Bateman, another remarkable regulation of the

---

* It is recorded that Jeffery the harper, so early as the reign of
Henry II. received a corrody, or annuity, from the Benedictine
Abbey of Hide, near Winchester ; and several of the abbies in
Wales retained a bard.

† About a century before this, a charter was granted to the French
minstrels, by which they were incorporated, and had a *king* set over
them. The original charter of Edward IV. is preserved in Rymer's
Fœdera : and when Charles I. in the eleventh year of his reign, granted
a new patent to the professors of the art and science of music, its
form was grounded upon that of Edward.

minstrelsy is recorded, together with a general account of the household establishment of this monarch, including the musicians retained in his service, as well for his domestic entertainment as for the service of his chapel. The ordinance to which I allude was evidently the origin of the present musical establishments of the Chapel Royal and King's band. It includes the detail of the several employments and rewards of the musicians, which though rather long, is too curious to be omitted.

" Minstrelles thirteen, thereof one is Virger, which directeth them all festyvall dayes in their statyones of blowings and pypyngs to such offiyces as the offiyceres might be warned to prepare for the King's meats and soupers; to be more redyere in all services and due tyme; and all thes sytying in the hall together, whereof some be trompets, some with the shalmes and smalle pypes, and some are strange mene coming to this court at five feastes of the yeare, and then take their wages of houshold, after iiij *d.* ob. by daye, after as they have byne presente in courte, and then to avoyd aftere the next morrowe aftere the feaste, besydes theire other rewards yearly in the King's Exchequer, and clothinge with the houshold, wintere and somere for eiche of them xx *s.* And they take nightelye amongeste them all iiij. galones of ale; and for wintere seasone thre candles waxe, vj. candles pitch, iiij. tale sheids; (fire-wood cleft into billits) lodging suffytyente by the Herbengere for them and theire horses nighteley to the courte. Aulso having into courte ij. servants to bear theire trompets, pypes, and other instruments, and torche for winter nightes, whilst they blow to suppose of the chaundry; and alway two of thes persones to contynewe stylle in courte at wages by the cheque rolle whiles they be presente iiij. ob. dayly, to warne the King's ridynge houshold when he goeth to horsbacke as oft as it shall require, and that his houshold meny may followe the more redyere after by the blowinge of theire trompets. Yf any of thes two Minstrelles be lete blood in courte, he taketh two loves, ij. messe of greate meate, one galone ale. They part not at no tyme with the rewards given to the houshold. Also when it pleasethe the King to have ij. Minstrelles continuinge at court, they will not in no wise that thes Minstrelles be so famylliere to ask rewards.

" A wayte, that nightelye from Mychelmas to Shreve Thorsdaye pype the watche withen this courte fower tymes; in the somere nightes iij. tymes, and makethe bon gayte (good watch) at every chambere doare and offiyce, as well for fear of pyckeres and pillers. He eateth in the halle with mynstrielles, and takethe lyverey at nighte a loffe, a galone of ale, and for somere nightes ij. candles piche, a bushel of coles; and for wintere nights halfe a loafe of bread, a galone of ale, iiij. candles piche, a bushel of coles; daylye whilste he is presente in court for his wages in cheque roale allowed iiij d. ob. or else iij d. by the discresshon of the steuarde and tressorere, and that, aftere his cominge and diserninge: also cloathinge with the houshold yeomen or minstrelles lyke to the wages that he takethe; and he be syke he taketh twoe loves, ij. messe of great meate, one galone ale. Also he partethe withe the housholde of general gyfts, and hathe his beddinge carried by the comptrollers assygment; and under this yeoman to be a groome watere. Yf he can excuse the yeoman in his absence, then he takethe the rewarde, clothe-ing, meat, and all other things lyke to other grooms of houshold. Also this yeoman-waighte, at the making of Knightes of the Bathe, for his attendance upon them by nighte-tyme, in watchinge in the chappelle, hathe to his fee all the watchinge-clothing that the knight shall wear uppon him.

" CHILDREN OF THE CHAPELLE viij. founden by the King's privie cofferes for all that longeth to their apperelle

by the hands and oversyghte of the deane, or by the master
of song assigned to teache them, which mastere is appointed
by the deane, chosen one of the number of the fellowshippe
of chappelle after the form of sacotte, as well as in songe in
orgaines and other. Thes children eat in the hall dayly at
the chappell board, nexte the yeomane of uestery; taking
amongeste them for lyverye daylye for brekefaste and all
nighte, two loves, one messe of greate meate, ij. galones ale ;
and for winter seasone iiij. candles piche, iij. tale biads, and
lyttere for their pallets of the serjante usher, and carryadge of
the King's coste for the competente beddynge by the oversyghte of the comptrollere. And amongeste them all to
have one servante into the court to trusse and bear their
harnesse and lyverye in court. And that day the King's
chappelle reneweth every of thes children then present re-
ceaveth iiij*d*. at the grene clothe of the compting-house for
horshire dayly, as long as they be jurneinge. And when any
of these children comene to xviij. years of age, and their
voyces change, ne cannot be preferred in this chappelle, the
nombere being full, then yf they will assent the King assyne the
them to a college of Oxeford or Cambridge of his founda-
tione, there to be at fyndyng and studye bothe sufficiently,
tylle the King may otherwise advance them."

Between the time of Hambois and the invention of printing, many musical tracts were written, some of which deserve
particular notice.

One, called *Musica Guidonis Monachi*, was compiled by
John Wylde, the præcentor of Waltham Abbey. It is not a
Treatise by Guido, as the title would imply, but a general
explanation of the Guidonian and other principles. The
whole, however, seems to be chiefly founded on the Micrologus. The work is divided into two books. In the first,
consisting of twenty-two chapters, the subjects treated are,
the monochord, the scale, the hand, ecclesiastical tones,

solmization and clefs, which are succeeded by a battle between B flat and B natural. The second book, containing thirty-one chapters, speaks of a Guido minor, surnamed Augensis, as a writer on the ecclesiastical chant*. After *the battle between B flat and B natural,* (B molle and B durum) in the first book of this work, the reader will not be surprized to hear, that in the second, the author draws a parallel between *the tone and semitone,* and *Leah and Rachel,* Jacob's wives.

In another work, entitled, *De Origine et Effectu Musicæ,* the chief object is to inculcate, " that music is the science of number applied to sound, or an art dependent on calculation," we find the author making heavy complaints of the fashionable singers of his time; who " corrupt and deform the diatonic genus, by making the seventh of a key a semitone." It is principally on account of this curious passage that I have mentioned the work. We learn from it that counterpoint had made a considerable progress, and that harmony had invaded the simplicity of the ecclesiastical chants, which, never including any other sounds than those of the natural scale, formed in different keys, different species of octaves: for instance, the key of G major, by not including F sharp, would have a whole tone between its seventh and eighth; and the key of F major, being without B flat,

---

* Who this Guido Augensis was has never been known. Some, from having seen in the Vatican library a musical treatise, entitled, *Tractatus Guidonis Augiensis,* which corresponds in many particulars with the Micrologus, have imagined the author of that celebrated work to have been a native of Auge in Normandy, and not of Arezzo in Tuscany. But as no such Guido appears in the annals of literature to sanction such an idea, it would be as unreasonable as unjust to deprive Italy and the Monk of Arezzo of the honour they have so long enjoyed.

would have a whole tone between its third and fourth, and half a tone between its fourth and fifth. The author querulously says, " Many now, when they ascend to G from D, as D, E, F, G, make a semitone between F and G ; and when they have D, C, D, to sing, or G, F, G, make semitones of C and F." This proves what habit will effectuate with regard to the ear. Nothing could more shock a modern musician than a close prepared by the flat seventh. At the time when this tract was written, a sharp seventh (except in the key of C) was deemed so licentious, that even those who presumed to use it in performance, were not bold enough to commit the infringement to paper.

A work by Simon Tunsted, called *Metrologus Liber*, is only remarkable on account of the author's whimsical attempt to prove the analogy between Music and Heraldic Colours. This idea, however curious, was not new. The Greeks spoke of a *white* voice, and a *black* voice, and the Romans of a *brown* voice : but this was no more than a figurative appellation of the impressions made by light upon one sense, to those effected by sound upon another ; as when we talk of the *sweet* or *brilliant* tone of a piano-forte. The seven primary colours have been compared with the seven sounds of the octave. But it is now pretty generally known that each of the prismatic colours is simple and unmixed, while every single sound of the octave is a combination of sounds. Besides, in this comparison, what are we to do with the intermediary sounds of the octave ? What relation have they with the compound colours ? Purple is composed of blue and red ; and green of blue and yellow : but F sharp not a union of the sounds of F natural and G natural, nor B flat a commixture of B natural and A natural.*

---

* I am not unmindful of the blind-man, who on being asked, what sound he thought the colour of red most resembled, is reported to have

Were any music extant of the beginning of the fifteenth century, a treatise, called *Regulæ Magistri*, written by John Torkesey, would greatly assist us in reading it. In this work, we are told, that though there was only three specific square characters used in musical notation (the *large*, the *long*, and the *breve*), these are modified into six species of simple notes : and here we also learn, that about a century after the introduction of the *minim*, a still shorter note was invented, called by some *crochetum*, and by this author and a few others, the *simple*.

His accompanying diagram is as follows, except that the *rests* are added.

Simple.   Minim.   Semibreve.   Breve.   Long.   Large.

The *rests*, as the reader will not fail to notice, are in their *imperfect state*, as at that time they were called, when used in duple proportion, or even time. In their *perfect state*, or triple proportion, a square note was considered as equal in duration to three of the next shorter notes in degree, without a dot, or point of perfection †.

---

answered, " *the sound of a trumpet.*" Admitting the fact that a blind-man so answered such a question, (though it is much more probable that the story was invented by a man that could see), it tells for nothing : because the blind-man having no idea of what colour is, could have no reason for the comparison he was making. Of the sound of a trumpet he had a perfect conception ; but of the colour which he is said to have assimilated to that sound, he could have no idea but that with which he was impressed by the sound itself.

† It is a remark made by Dr. Burney, that all these notes being originally black, when a hook was applied to the *minim*, it would

After giving a table of concords and discords no way distinguished from those seen in other similar works, Torkesey presents us with a most curious notation of distances upon the interval of the *comma* to that of the *disdiapason*. In this system of signs the square B, 𝕋, or natural, is used to indicate all the accidental semitones, ascending; and the round B, ♭, to distinguish the same intervals, descending. The character called a sharp, ♯, though its invention is traceable up to the time of Marchetto da Padua, was not yet in general use*.

Another tract, written by Thomas Walsingham, on the simple and compound figures of notes, and their perfect and imperfect powers, the moods, and whatever concerned the time, or measure, is so clear and explanatory on all those points as to be very instructive and truly valuable.

---

have, to a modern eye, the appearance of a *quaver*, to which the name of crotchet is now improperly applied. After these notes were opened, adds the Doctor, it was no uncommon thing to see white crotchets, or as we now denominate them *quavers* ♪♪, which were then only one degree quicker than the minim. The signs of prolation were orignally limited to four; two for *perfect*, or triple time, and two for imperfect or common time. The circle with a point of perfection in the center, thus ⊙ was the sign for the *great mode perfect*, in which all long notes were equal in duration to *three* of the next shorter in degree. The simple, unaccompanied by the point, was used for notes of a shorter duration, but with the same triple power. These two moods may be compared with our present measures of $\frac{3}{2}$ and $\frac{3}{4}$, where each note is occasionally rendered perfect, or equal to three others by a point, instead of the general augmentation implied by the circle, which the old masters placed at the beginning of a movement.

* The *comma* he calls the difference between G sharp and A flat; the *diesis* that between C sharp and D; while the interval between F natural and F sharp is denominated a minor semitone, and that between E and F a major semitone.

These and many other treatises calculated to advance the theory and promote the practice of music, were written during the fifteenth and sixteenth centuries, and at once bear testimony to the ingenuity and industry of its professors, both ecclesiastical and secular, and manifest the encouragement the science received, and by consequence, the esteem in which it was held in our own country.

But Italy and Germany, shared the honour of fostering the principles of harmony and melody. In both those countries, treatises, masses, and motets, as well as amusive compositions of every description, were continually issuing from the laboratory of inventive genius, adding to theoretical knowledge, and promoting practical excellence. But as the musical talents of the natives of Germany and Italy in different provinces of the art, will be amply considered in the next chapter, I shall content myself at present with only noticing, that during the sixteenth century, the songs of the Germans were set to melodies formed upon the scale of Guido, and accompanied with the best harmony then known. According to Bede, the Saxons had poetry and songs as early as the eighth century. Yet the most ancient music applied to German words, that is now known, was set to the hymns of the first reformers. In fact, the relics of ancient German compositions are very few. But a nation whose theorists, during the last hundred and fifty years, have illumined the musical world upon every topic of combined and evolutionary sound, and whose composers have produced such striking, grand, and brilliant exemplifications of the profound rules those theorists devised and established, can afford to lose whatever honour might have attached to the preservation of its fugitive melodies of the sixteenth century.

CHAP. XVIII.

STATE OF MUSIC FROM THE INVENTION OF PRINT-
ING TO THE TIME OF JOSQUIN DEL PRATO.

HAVING passed those periods when melody was confined to the *plain chant*, and consonance limited to a few
meagre and false combinations, (the first unmarked by any assigned measure, and the second not dictated by nature or any
rational rule), we are now entering upon an æra replete with
materials for more regular composition. To the advantage
of a settled *notation*, and an established *time-table*, the art of
printing was added ; which as it were, opened a passage for
the mutual communication of light between one country and
another, and sensibly promoted the progress of science and
of taste. The laws of musical composition, even such as
till now they were, had, by the pride and artifice of the
monks, been secreted from the laity. But now, no longer
locked up in the obscurity of the Latin tongue, but presented
by the press to general use in the current language of each
country, many of the various tracts then existing, poured
forth their no longer hidden treasures, while enlarged systems
and improved theories made their appearance, and extended
the general stock of harmonical knowledge.

For the musical historian, it is fortunate that the productions of the theorist are not equally transient with those
of the composer, and the reputation of the mere practi-

tioner. Without knowing whether Boethius, Guido, or John de Muris were good, vocal or instrumental performers, by their theoretical remains, we are reminded of their genius and their science, while the name of many a once distinguished practical musician has long since sunk into total oblivion*. Theorists, in every science, are a species of legislators; and the dignity and authority they enjoy while living, continues to conciliate respect, and exact obedience, after their departure.

Of the theorists whose doctrines were disseminated by the press, Franchinus Gafurius was one of the first. His principal work, entitled *Theoricum opus Armonicæ disciplinæ*, was published at Naples in the year 1480. He speaks only of five different characters of time; the *maxima*, or large, the *long*, the *breve*, the *semibreve*, and the *minim;* though in the writers of the early part of the sixteenth century, we find the *crotchet*, *quaver*, and *semiquaver;* forming the following time-table:

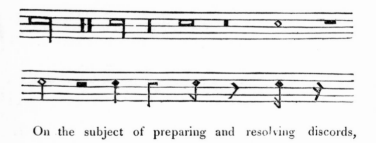

On the subject of preparing and resolving discords,

---

* It is remarkable, that in Dr. Priestley's chart not one musician appears from the commencement of Christianity till the eleventh century, where Guido is placed in a desert. In the sixteenth century we see Palestrina without a rival or neighbour; nor did the author find another musician whom he thought worthy a niche, till he arrived at the age of Lulli.

Franchinus is not very copious, or even intelligible. Indeed, the only discords used for nearly two hundred years after the publication of his book, were the seventh, the fourth and fifth, the fifth and second, the fifth and sixth, and the ninth*. In vocal music, for the occasional union of two, three, or more of these notes, to one and the same syllable, *ligatures* were used, similar to our present slurs, or *bindings* of notes. The classes of voice, as formed by the difference of sex, or of age, were four; these ranked in the great compass of sounds a third above each other; and their particular ranges or scales were expressed by the bass and tenor cliffs, placed on different lines. The lowest compass of voice was called the *tenor*, the next above it, the *contratenor*, the third, the *motetus*, and the fourth and highest the *triplum*. To this division, succeeded another, consisting of scales, or departments: Of these, the lowest was denominated the *bass*, the next above it the *baritono*, or tenor-base, the third the *tenor*, the fourth, the *contralto*, or counter-tenor, the fifth the *mezzo soprano*, or under treble, and the sixth and highest, the *soprano*, or upper treble. In the following diagram, the scale of each species of voice, according to this latter division, is first exhibited agreeably to the cliffs and their several stations, as formerly and scientifically used; and afterwards is designated according

---

* The semibreve, at all times, apparently, the unit or standard measure of time, (and now the largest note in common use) was formerly placed in the middle of the diagram: a *large* was said to be equal in duration to eight *semibreves*, a *long* to four, and a *breve* to two; that is, a *semibreve* was one half as long as a *breve*, and hence its appellation, which it bears to this day: hence too, of course, the figures $\frac{3}{2}$ imply three halves of a *semibreve*, that is, three *minims*, in a bar; the figures $\frac{3}{4}$ three fourths of a *semibreve*, or three crotchets in a bar; and the figures $\frac{2}{4}$ two fourths, or two crotchets in a bar.

to the modern popular mode of notation, by the bass and treble cliffs only *.

1. Bass.

2. Baritono, or Tenor-Bass.

3. Tenor.

4. Contralto, or Counter-Tenor.

* It is however, necessary to observe, that these are only the scales of the several classes of voice, as they are generally found to extend. In particular instances it will happen, that they considerably exceed the limits here allotted to their several ranges. Double F is often reached by a bass voice, and sometimes F in altissimo by soprano : two notes that include a diapason of four octaves.

5. Mezzo Soprano, or Under Treble.

6. Soprano, or Upper Treble.

1. Bass.

2. Baritono, or Tenor-Bass.

3. Tenor.

4. Contralto, or Counter-Tenor.

5. Mezzo Soprano, or Under Treble.

6. Soprano, or Upper Treble.

It is a curious fact, that all written counterpoint was at
this time composed for voices. But though *parts*, in Italy
and elsewhere, were multiplied greatly beyond the above six,
those used in the compositions of the Pope's chapel,
amounted to no more than four : *bass, tenor, altus,* and
cantus. The music of the church continuing to be set to
Latin words, and the technical terms were in the same language. Hence, if an additional *part* was by chance introduced, it was called *quinta pars;* and a second additional
part *sexta pars* *.

The boundaries of the different species of the voice
being thus determined, their assemblage in harmony became
greatly facilitated. To have a thorough knowledge of notation, that is, a precise and intimate acquaintance with the
different stations in the great scale, as expressed by the
notes according to the cliffs by which they were governed,
was to have before the mind's eye a picture, or map, of the
whole site upon which the harmonical combinations were
to be formed, and their evolutions executed. The ground
being thus prepared, the first endeavour with contrapuntists
appears to have been, to settle *the accompaniment of the
octave.* But the laws of harmony, though less mutable
than those of melody, were far from becoming fixed ; and
all that musicians could then effectuate, was but precursory
to a better state of things ; to a *formula* that, at a future
time, was to supersede most of their rules and regulations,
and give birth to an edifice as far transcending in order
and beauty, the monument of their industry and talents, as
their own structure surpassed that of the first architects of

---

* About the year 1474, the terms became so numerous, that John
Tinctor published a collection of them under the title of ' *Terminorum
Musicæ Diffinitorium.*' It was printed at Naples, and was the first
musical dictionary that ever issued from the press.

harmony. The accompaniment of the eight notes of the scale, ascending and descending, called by the French the *Regle de l'Octave,* consisted, at that time, almost wholly of common chords. The single instance in which they indulged themselves with a deviation from that harmony was at a *close.* It is particularly to be remarked, that the middle of the sixteenth century arrived before composers ventured to accompany the seventh of the key with a sixth. And major fourths and minor fifths were so abhorred, that rather than have their ears offended with their discordancy, harmonists would flatten the seventh of the key, even before a close *. To modern musicians, this prejudice will be inexplicable. But every new glance we take at the state of harmony previous to the middle of the fifteenth century, is an additional proof, that the musical susceptibilities of the ear are dependent upon its cultivation. If any construction of consonance would be more offensive to our auditory faculty than a continued series of fourths and fifths, (the *diatessaronare* and the *quintoier* of our ancestors) that construction would be found in a *close* prepared by the flat seventh of the key †.

In the ancient music, the bass notes C D, C E, and E G, accompanied with their common chords, perpetually occur; as thus:

---

* " Si *contra* Fa *est diabolus,*" said an eminent musical writer, so late as the beginning of the last century.

† The musicians of the times to which we are here alluding, seem to have retained of the ancient music, only the Pythagorean intervals. Of the elegance of what *we* call melody, they appear not to have had an idea; and what, in general, their harmony must have been, their rules enable us to conceive.

And the second bar of the following chant of Palestrina presents us with A, G, F, under similar circumstances.

During the sixteenth century, musicians arose with ears too perfectly constructed to be satisfied with uninterrupted successions of *perfect harmonies*, and whose minds were courageous enough to presume upon the introduction of *discords*. These combinations, however, for a considerable time, were very sparingly employed. The innovators seem to have proceeded with the caution of boys venturing upon new ice; and did not dare to take a fresh step, till authorized by the experienced safety of the past *. In a fragment of *Canto Figurato*, composed in 1473 by Bonadies, the master of Franchinus, we only find the discord of the *seventh*, thus prepared and resolved.

After this period, the relations and dependencies of con-cords and discords became, every day, better and better understood, and *harmony* assumed a state which indicated

---

* Dr. Burney, on *scoring* the first masses that were printed in Italy, and those composed before the Reformation in England, found few discords regularly prepared and dissolved. The fourth descended into the fifth, and the seventh into the sixth; but with the chords of the *second*, the *ninth*, and the *fifth* and *sixth*, he very seldom met. The order in which the discords were introduced, appears to be as fol-lows:—First, the *seventh* was used; secondly, the *fourth;* thirdly, the *fifth* and *second;* and fourthly, the *ninth.*

the perfection to which, under the guidance of genius and
industry, it might in future be carried. But *melody* was not
cultivated with the same zeal and success. Confined, in a
great measure, to psalmody, she, for a long while, lacked
the opportunity of evincing her susceptibility of grace, elegance, and every embellishment which taste can suggest.
Nevertheless, she at length burst from the confines of
the cloister; and, once admitted into the gay and scenic
world, proved her power to charm all who listened to her
flights; and derived from, and imparted to, the stage, an increased importance, and a higher admiration. As counterpoint commenced by adding *parts* to plain chant, and harmonizing old tunes, so florid melody had its birth in the
variations given to existing melodies, such as they were; for
at first, few composers had the presumption to attempt the
invention of new tunes.

But to whatever extent the fascinations of *melody* operated
upon the public ear, the cultivation of *harmony* was not neglected. Most of the ancient music that has come down to us,
proves, that not only plain counterpoint, but *fugue* and
canon, made considerable progress after the charms of *air*
were better felt and acknowledged *. According to Padre
Martini's opinion, this species of composition originated in
the endeavour of the first contrapuntists, so to order the
part they superadded to *canto fermo*, as to render it as
similar as possible, at least in its subject, to the *canto fermo*
itself. And certainly the skeleton of the ecclesiastical
modes, authentic and plagal, strongly sanction the idea, that

---

* The song or round, " *Sumer is i cumen in,*" is an early proof
of the cultivation of those branches of the harmonic art; and the
sacred music composed in the fifteenth century, is full of canons and
fugues very artificial in their construction.

this purpose of *imitating* in one part, the interval of another, in the unison, the octave, or one of what may be called the two first related keys (the 5th and the 4th) formed the foundation of the fugue, and all the various modes of musical response.

ANTHENTIC and PLAGAL MODES.

Anthentic.

Plagal.

The fifth above and fifth below, or in other words, the fifth and fourth of a key, are the only connected scales, or varied keys, in which the answer of a regular fugue or canon can be made. All other responses, however legitimate their appearance upon paper, are nothing more than *imitations ;* the very name, indeed, which is applied to such passages, to distinguish them from those which belong to, and characterize, the fugue and the canon. The following little movement will prove that a fugue in appearance is not necessarily a fugue in reality.

---

* Here we have all the keys ; and if these fixed and fundamental intervals were filled up with the intermediate notes, we should have all the scales whence the melody of fugues and canons was deduced, during almost three centuries.

But the underwritten is a *fugue* in reality, as well as in appearance.

Though in the fifteenth century, the science of harmony was earnestly and successfully cultivated in most of the countries of Europe, it flourished in a higher degree at Rome than elsewhere. While the priests, almost universally, visited that city to acquire the best style of performing *canto fermo,* composers studied the figurative music in four, five, and six parts, composed by the Italians for the use of the Pope's chapel. At Rome it was, that the musical author felt a two-fold excitement to exert his genius; the certainty of a liberal reward, and the equally certain pleasure of hearing his productions well executed. Rome had her college of musicians, possessed within herself the best models of composition and performance, and was resorted to for instruction, and examples of excellence, with as much confidence and devotion, as the ancient Romans travelled for improvement to Greece, or the Grecians to Egypt. But if Italy at this time drew to her capital musicians from every part of Europe, Flanders soon afterwards distributed

---

* Counterpoint and fugue, have generally been thought to have had their origin in the Netherlands ; but it is due to Guido, Marchetto da Padua, and Franchino Gafforio (all Italians) to observe, that the *first* furnished the scale and system still in use, the *second* introduced modern chromatic, or secular modulation, and the last presented the world with the first practical treatise upon composition.

over Europe many excellent composers. The knights-
errant, Charles V. and Francis I., both of them lovers and
encouragers of music, spent much time in the Netherlands;
and the fine arts, which followed wherever they led the way,
became familiar to the Flemings, in general, but especially
to the inhabitants of Brussels, Antwerp, Mentz, and Cam-
bray, where those munificent princes frequently resided.
But, nevertheless, England, in the early times of *part* composition, appears to have cultivated harmony with a degree
of success that might vie with the progress made by almost
any other country in Europe : and, indeed, it may be fairly
questioned, whether Flanders, or even Italy, can produce
a more ancient specimen of vocal harmony than that of the
song or round, " *Sumer is i cumen in.*" The Italians, undoubtedly, were the *best musicians ;* but it remains to be
determined whether they were the *first composers* of harmonical and complicated music *.

Among the contrapuntists who flourished in the fifteenth
century, no one, perhaps, is more deserving of notice than
John Okenheim; no one, certainly, on the continent, produced earlier specimens of harmony. This ingenious and
scientific Netherlander produced many learned and elaborate
compositions for the church : and had the honour of including Josquin among his numerous pupils †. It has been

---

* Bonadies, the master of Franchinus, lived as early as any other
good composer in *parts*, of whom any thing is preserved; but it must
be allowed, that we are still in possession of works by Okenheim,
Josquin, Isaac, and Brumal, who were neither Englishmen nor Italians, that surpass in excellence all that can be produced, of equal
antiquity, by the inhabitants of England, Italy, or any other part of
the world.

† His scholars, by whom he was much loved and respected, were
not only numerous, but highly successful in their studies. If they

asserted by Duchat, that Okenheim was a native of Hainault; but if it be considered that his cotemporaries, Tinctor and Franchinus, always spoke of him as a Netherlander, it will be difficult to doubt of his real country. To this we may add the evidence of the *Deploration*, or dirge, written upon his death, which his scholar Josquin set to music in five parts, as also that of the following elegy, set by Crespel:

> *Agricola, Verbonnet, Prioris,*
> *Josquin des Pres, Gaspard, Brunel, Compere,*
> *Ne parlez plus de joyeux chants, ne ris,*
> *Mais composez un* NE RECORDERIS
> *Pour lamenter nostre Maistre et bon Pere.*

From the writers of the sixteenth century we learn, that Okenheim composed a motet in *thirty-six parts*. But were we to waive the comparing this effort of patient genius with that still mightier exertion of our countryman, Bird, a song in *forty parts*, or even to withdraw from the scientific Netherlander's reputation all the increase it received from his polyphonic composition, the fragments of his labours preserved in the *Dodecachordon* of Glareanus, would be sufficient to challenge our respect, and excite our wonder.

It appears that Okenheim was partial to the species of cantus called the *Catholica;* a melody so constructed, that it may be sung in various modes, or keys, at the pleasure of the performer, observing only the ratio, or relation of consonant notes in the harmony; the performance of which,

---

were fortunate in the talents and science of their master, he, for the most part, was happy in the abilities and attention of his disciples; and produced many excellent musicians. By Padre Martini, Okenheim is styled, *Il famoso Maestro:* and by other writers, *Musicorum principem.*

in fact, amounts to this: that the cantus being led off, the other singers should give the answer, by discovering the accidental sharps or flats, as they proceed. From the following *single part*, presented to us by Dr. Burney, together with its *solution*, two other parts may be educed, each a fifth lower than that immediately above it, and succeeding it at the distance of a *perfect breve*, or whole measure*. The answers, it will of course be perceived, are not, strictly speaking, *in canon;* that is, the corresponding intervals in the several parts are not directly similar: and this is agreeable to a law which permitted the *canon* to deviate from a *perpetual fugue*, and made it sufficient that there should be in the plan some mystery for the performer to unravel: and Tinctor says accordingly, *Canon est regula voluntatem compositoris sub obscuritate quadam ostendens.*

CANON.

In epidiapente.

---

* The circular modal sign at the beginning of the stave, proves the *time* to be *perfect*, or triple: and the expression " *In epidiapente*," implies that the responses are to be given in fifths below.

† The cantus is here given in the key of G minor; but not only may it be led off in any key, but that key may be either minor or major.

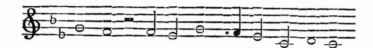

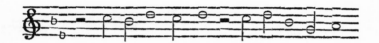

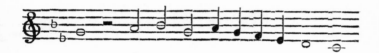

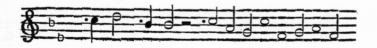

SOLUTION.

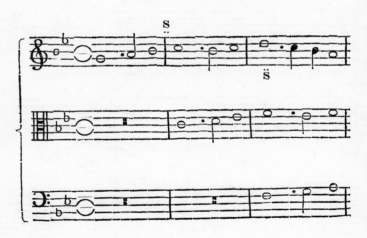

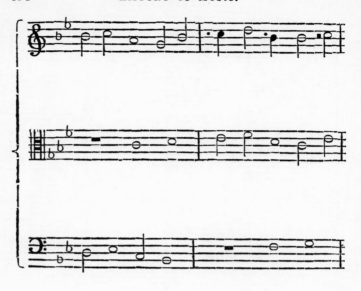

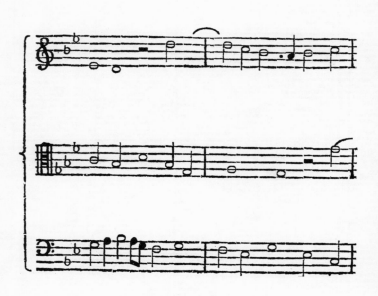

It is a striking fact, that in Music, a science the great and immediate object of which is to move and interest the mind by flattering the sense, labour and patience should have preceded taste and invention. But this, perhaps, chiefly, if not wholly, is to be attributed to the circumstance of the chants of the church being almost the prescribed ground-work of all composition at the period to which we are alluding. The monotonous gloom of the cloister, usurped the regions of fancy, and forbad even the appearance of the flowers of nature to relieve the complexity of art.

Composers, proceeding in this province of study, acquired great facility in every species of music imitative of itself; and fugues were contrived, some of which sung both backwards and forwards; or, to speak technically, *recte et retro;* while others sung *per arsin et thesin;* that is to say, their construction was such, that one part rose, while the other descended. These, and many other forms of composition, equally difficult, equally perplexed, and equally inefficient, in regard of gratifying the ear, or moving the heart, made their appearance during the fourteenth and fifteenth centuries; after which, the charms of a chaste and cheerful melody began to make their appearance, and to be generally felt.

The above observations are, however, to be understood with some limitation, as the two following compositions will evince.

PAVANE à QUATRE PARTIES.

Extracted from the Orchesographie de Thoinot Arbeau.

First published in the year 1558.

Bel - le qui tiens ma vi-
Bel - le qui tiens ma vi-
Bel - le qui tiens ma vi-
Bel - le qui tiens ma vi-

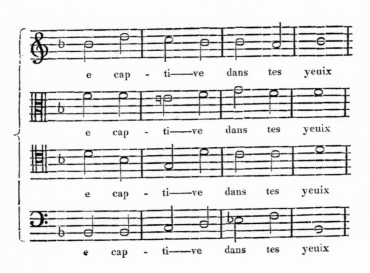

e cap - ti——ve dans tes yeuix
e cap - ti——ve dans tes yeuix
e cap - ti——ve dans tes yeuix
e cap - ti——ve dans tes yeuix

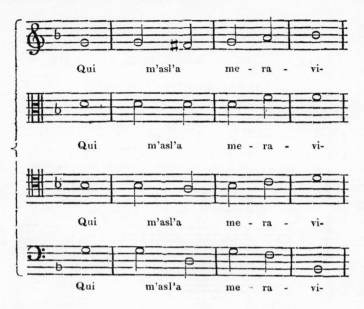

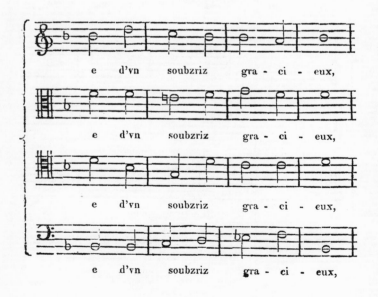

Viens tost me se - cou - rir

Viens tost me se - cou - rir

Viens tost me se - cou - rir

Viens tost me se - cou - rir

Ou me fauldra mou - rir.

Ou me fauldra mou - rir

Ou me fauldra mou - rir.

Ou me fauldra mou - rir.

SONG.

From a MS. of about the year 1580.

so in - tent to   move   her.   I

stept in her waie, she stept a - wrie, But

she I shall   ever   love   her.

CHAP. XIX.

JOSQUIN DEL PRATO; AND THE STATE OF MUSIC DURING THE EARLY PART OF THE SIXTEENTH CENTURY.

JOSQUIN DEL PRATO*, already spoken of as the pupil of Okenheim, was the next distinguished contrapuntist of the Flemish school. If the sacred compositions of this great musician have long since become obsolete, it is to be attributed to the mutability of notation, and the caprice of fashion, rather than to their deficiency of merit, even of the most exalted kind. If we admire Palestrina, Orlando di Lasso, Tallis, and Bird, whose labours adorned and enriched the musical libraries of the sixteenth century, how much more ought we to be struck with the powers of Josquin, who, a hundred years before, not only vanquished all the existing difficulties of Canon, Fugue, Imitation, and

---

* Josquin is enumerated by Guicciardini *(Descritt. di tutti i Paesi bassi)* among Flemish musicians. But the addition of *del Prato* to his name, or, as he was styled in Latin, *Pratensis*, indicates him to have been a Tuscan. Also, he is frequently mentioned by Italian writers under the name of Josquino, Jodoco del Prato. Franchinus, when speaking of his extraordinary ingenuity and learning, as a composer, gives him this denomination ; and in so naming him, is followed by almost every theoretical author.

every species of learned contrivance and ingenious contexture of consonant combination, but invented new structures of harmony, original adjustments of *part* with *part,* and was, in a great measure, the father of modern polyphonic composition.

A more striking proof of Josquin's high reputation as a composer cannot well be adduced than the following incident, taken from Castiglione's *Cortegiano.* Insisting upon the incredible extent to which, in common minds, prejudice is often carried, respecting the merit of literary productions, this author illustrates his position by describing the rapturous delight with which a polite company of his acquaintance had read a copy of verses, announced to them as the production of Sanazaro, and the exalted terms in which they continued to extol them, till they discovered that they were not of his composition, when their applause was instantly converted to as vehement a condemnation. And then he proceeds to corroborate his argument by adding, " So a Motet sung before the Duchess of Urbino, was totally disregarded till known to have come from the pen of Josquin, when it excited universal ecstacy." As a proper companion to this narrative, I give the following from Zarlino. The Motet, *verbum bonum et suave,* having been long performed in the Pontifical chapel at Rome, as the production of Josquin, was esteemed one of the finest compositions of the time; but the celebrated Willaert, having quitted Flanders, in order to visit Rome, and finding that this Motet was listened to as the composition of Josquin, declared it to be his own work. He was believed; the piece was immediately condemned, and never performed again. So high, indeed, stood Josquin's merit that his name would have been a passport for almost any production; and almost any production would fail to please that wanted that high recommendation. This prejudice in the ignorant, however, as far as it re-

spected the merit of Josquin, stood upon a basis sanctioned
and confirmed by the opinions of the best judges. Franchinus, speaking of the great masters of his own time,
makes the most honourable mention of this musician, and
ranks him with the most delightful of composers *. To this
evidence of Franchinus, Zarlino zealously subscribes; and
also places Josquin among the *pratici periti*, the most skilful performers: and Adami, in his " Laws for the Regulation of the Pope's Chapel," awards to Josquin the highest
honours after those due to Guido, as a cultivator and supporter of church music. He calls him *Uomo insigne per
l'inventione*, a man renowned for the stretch and splendour
of his imagination; and informs us, that during the time of
Sixtus the Fourth, he was a chorister in the Pontifical
chapel.

Quitting Italy, Josquin became Maestro di Capella to
Lewis XII. of France. His fame had flown to that country before him, and prepared for him the most favourable
reception. If he was happy in his new patron, the French
king was proud of having such acknowledged talents in his
service, and it would be difficult to say whether the musician
or the monarch had most reason to be satisfied with the connexion. Lewis, indeed, was so sensible of his good fortune in monopolizing such abilities as those of Josquin,
that, in the ebullition of his royal pleasure, he promised him
a benefice†. But the promises of princes are not quite so

---

* Franchinus, as appears from his own writings, was personally
acquainted with Josquin. Speaking *(Angel. ac. Div. opus Musicæ
Tract.)* of some inaccuracies in the sesquialteral proportion, he says:
Di questi inconvenienti ne advertite gia molti anni passati Jusquin des-
priet *et* Gaspar, dignissimi compositori.

† Lewis having a great *penchant* for music, and incapable of gra-

easily remembered as made, and the Maestro di Capella found it necessary to quicken his Majesty's recollection. This he took occasion to effect publicly, though inoffensively. Being required to compose a Motet for the Chapel Royal, he selected for the words, part of the hundred and nineteenth psalm : *Memor esto verbi tui servo tuo ;* " O think of thy word unto thy servant;" which he set in so appropriate and significant a manner, that the King felt and acknowledged its application to his neglect of his word, and soon afterwards realized the promised preferment; when Josquin, not less sensible of the royal kindness than he had been of his Majesty's previous inattention, and prompted by a gratitude quite as intense as had been his vexation, immediately composed another Motet, the words of which he chose from another part of the same psalm, *Bonitatem fecisti cum servo tuo Domine ;* " O Lord, thou hast dealt graciously with thy servant." This anecdote ought not to be dismissed without adding, that Josquin having, in consequence of Lewis's procrastination of his promise, repeatedly applied to a certain nobleman to refresh the King's memory, and continually

---

tifying his taste with his own performance, thought himself, perhaps, the more indebted to those who were peculiarly qualified for administering to him a pleasure he so highly valued. It is said that his voice was so weak, and inflexible, as to be incapable of the simplest execution ; and that he defied Josquin to compose a piece of music in which he would be able to perform a part. The musician did not shrink from the challenge, but produced a canon for two voices, to which he added two supplementary parts, one of which consisted of a single sound occasionally sustained, and the other of the key note and its fifth, taken in alternate succession. Of these two parts the king preferred the first, and after many strenuous and patient trials, found himself, in spite of nature, able to perform the drone to a canon!

received for answer, " Leave the business to me, I will take care of it—*Laisse faire moi*"—and finding that he obtained nothing from him but that fruitless assurance, he turned the phrase into *solmization,* and composed an entire mass on these syllables of the hexachords : *La sol fa re mi**.

According to all that can be collected from the best authorities, Josquin, in his day, was the prince of musicians. No one seems to have possessed an equal influence over the affections and passions of the lovers and patrons of music. Rabelais, in his prologue to the third book of Pantagruel, gives him the first place among the fifty-nine excellent masters whom he had formerly heard : and his compositions appear to have been as well known in his time, as now are those of the most favourite of the modern masters. Of these, our Henry VIII. when Prince Henry, and Anne Boleyn, during her residence in France, collected and learned a considerable number. His French songs, for three and four voices, are very numerous : and several of his masses, some of which consist wholly of canons, in the different intervals of diatessaron, (the 4th); diapente, (the 5th); and diapason, (the 8th), comprise upwards of twenty movements. Among this latter species of his compositions, that upon the old tune, called *l'Homme Armé,* is one of the most curious, as well as most ingenious. Dr. Burney found it at the British Museum, in a printed collection, the first that issued from the press after the invention of printing. The Doctor's intention was, to transcribe from it only two or three movements, but his mind was so drawn onward, and amused, by the well-studied contexture, and happy contrivance of the composition, that he scored the whole mass. In Josquin's fine *Sine nomine,* consisting of

---

* This mass is preserved in the British Museum, among the other productions of Josquin, and is an excellent composition.

a series of canons, we find two that are very curious; one of
them in the second above, and one in the second below. The
reader will think them well worthy of being transcribed. They
are printed in the tenor cliff on the third and fourth lines; but
for general convenience, they are here given in the treble.

CANON,

Un ton plus haut.

CANON,

Un ton plus bas.

The themes of these movements are supposed to be original; but in the time of Josquin, it was a common practice
to adopt, for the subjects of canons and fugues, some old
chant or tune. This custom prevailed as late as when Zarlino flourished, who tells us, that every mass then composed,
was founded upon a certain subject, borrowed from some
popular motet or song †. This habit in church composers,

---

* Though no rapidity of execution is required by these compositions, they could not be correctly performed without much previous
study and frequent rehearsals. In the originals there are no bars ;
and the value of the notes is often changing, as well by their position,
as by the operation of the modal signs.

† Glareanus also says, that in his time, scarcely a mass was composed, that had not some well known air, or passage, for its theme.
And Bayle (Art. Marot.) tells us, that Francis I. and all his court,
sung Clement Marot's translation of the Psalms, to the tunes of fa-
vorite songs.

of *adopting a theme,* had it been confined to the borrowing
from chants and the solemn *canto fermo,* would have been
subject to no other objection than that it checked imagination, and excluded originality ; but extended to the taking up
the light and licentious strains of the vulgar, it appears to have
been not only extremely unappropriate, but highly objection-
able, inasmuch as it must have tended to throw an air of levity
over the whole composition, and frequently, by an unavoidable association of ideas, have brought to the minds of the
performers the subject matter of the words originally attached to the melody, and have utterly annihilated the
sense and sentiment of the sacred text they were singing *.
In his motets, Josquin not only avoided this error, but to
the ambition of making them wholly his own, added that of
exhibiting in them, generally, an excellence surpassing that of
his other compositions. Their style is transparent and
graceful, their contexture more artful and elaborate, and if
he ever descends to forego the exercise of his own abundant invention, it is in favour of some beautiful and solemn
chant of the church, which he so variously and liberally
treats, as to render it his own property. The principal fea-
tures of this portion of Josquin's works, are the simplicity
and grandeur of their fugue subjects, the grave and reve-
rential style of their accompanying parts, the ingenuity of
their interwoven imitations, and the general purity of their

---

* It seems, by all that can be collected on the subject, that, like
the Turks, who, according to Gio. Battista Donato, have a limited
number of tunes, the Christians at this time circumscribed the variety
of their melodies. Certain it is, that in England, the secular and
popular airs were very few. Invention and novelty were so little
thought of, that even such composers as Bird, Morley, Bull, Farnaby,
and Gibbons, were content to make variations upon the tunes of old
and well-known ballads.

harmony. These excellencies, when music was so greatly confined to the church ; when there was such a paucity of melody, and so little of the grace of arrangement, were of high value, and sufficient to place the composer who could command them, in the first rank of his profession. They were aimed at by all, but attained by few ; and by none displayed in so eminent a degree as by Josquin, in his motets *.

If this *great man* (for he well merits the appellation) depreciated his compositions by any material defect, it was the excess in which he indulged himself in the fault of his time ; the courting difficulties for their own sake. *Augmentation, diminution,* and *inversion,* and every possible position, and even distortion of melody, formed the ruling passion of his contemporaries; with whom, to please the eye, was a compensation for every neglect of the ear. Regular canons were prized beyond fugues, rigid fugues preferred to free ones, and these again to accidental imitation, merely on the principle of giving the higher value to the greater degree of complexity. That such compositions, as exercises, are useful to the aspiring student, and form the best school for those who are ambitious of becoming sound and distinguished contrapuntists, cannot be denied : but it is only because, to execute difficult things with freedom and facility, it is necessary in our practice, to *heighten* their difficulty, as public dancers perform their private exercises, loaden with weights. It has been contended, and certainly with reason, that since the invention

---

* In the third and fourth collection of motets published at the beginning of the sixteenth century, under the title of *Motetti della Corona,* are some of the finest specimens of Josquin's talent in that province of composition ; among these a *Miserere* for five voices claims a distinct notice. In every view of it, it is admirable, and presents a model of choral composition.

of counterpoint, a great composer never existed who had not
submitted to the labour of studying and of producing these ab-
struser kinds of musical combination. If formerly, such productions were revered on their own account, they ought now
to be respected as magazines of theoretical materials, and models of ingenious disposition and contrivance : and it is not because good taste has banished them from the theatre, that
they are not proper in oratorial, and still more so in ecclesiastical music. The indefensible fault in Josquin was, that,
overflowing with science, he poured too much of it into his
secular compositions. Hence they are often grave when they
should be gay, and elaborate when they should be light. But
in this he was more than countenanced by the practice of his
contemporaries ; for if his compositions were sometimes too
serious, their's were still more sombre. But though others exceeded him in ponderosity and dryness, they never reached his
clearness, dignity, and majestic manner. Indeed, he is pretty
generally allowed to have been the type of all musical excellence at the time in which he flourished, and to have exhibited
in his person that *one original genius* with which in any art
or science, an age is sometimes, by the bounty of heaven,
indulged and adorned.

It is not more a subject of lamentation to every reflecting
reader, than of disgrace to Italy, that while he remained in
that country, neither his exalted merit, nor wide-spread fame,
were sufficient to shield him from the mortification of seeing
fashionable buffoonery basking in the sunshine of public mu-
nificence, frolicking in ill-earned splendor, while he was
left to endure comparative narrowness of income, and even
penury. In the *Sopplementi Musicali* of Zarlino, we find
the following sonnet, written on the regretted occasion, by
Serafino dall'Acquilla *.

***

* This author, Crescimbiri informs us, was much esteemed for his

SONNET

ON

JOSQUIN DEL PRATO, OR JOSQUIN DES PRES.

Giosquin non dir che'l ciel sia crudo e empio,
  Che t'adornò si soblime ingegno :
  Et s'alcun veste ben, lascia lo sdegno;
  Are di ciò gode alcun buffone ò sempio
Da quel ch'io ti dirò prendi l'essempio ;
L'argento e l'or che da se steli e degno,
  Si mostra nudo, e sol si veste il legno,
  Quando sòrdorna alcun Theatro ò Tempio :
Il favor di costor vien presto manco,
  E mille volte il dì, sìa pur giocondo,
  Sì muta il stato lor di nero in bianco.
Ma chì hà virtù gioca a suo modo il mondo ;
  Com 'huom che nuota e hà la Zucca al fianco,
  Metti 'l sott' acqua pur, non teme il fondo.

TRANSLATION.

Say not, O Josquin, Heav'n hath been unkind ;
Heav'n that endow'd thee with so bright a mind ;

---

excellence in the arts of poetry and music. He died in the year 1500;
and the following was his epitaph :—

  Qui giace Serafin : partiti hor puoi,
  Sol d'aver visto il sasso che lo serra,
  Assai sei debitore agli occhi tuoi.

TRANSLATION.

Here Serafino lies : thy way pursue ;
Soft sighing, to his ashes bid adieu.
The stone thou'st view'd, that o'er his body lies,—
Enough art thou indebted to thine eyes.

                                        BUSBY.

Nor to buffoons that borrow'd plumage grudge,
That decks as well the culprit as the judge.
Pure metals by intrinsic splendor glow,
Shine of themselves, and outward grace bestow
Glitt'ring with silver'd wood, or gilded stone,
Temples and theatres their value own.
On worthlessness bestow'd, soon favors fade ;
Soon the lost gloss betrays the native shade ;
While virtue braves misfortune's roughest tides,
Like him who, buoy'd by cork, the stream in safety rides.

                                          BUSBY.

Josquin died early in the sixteenth century. Walther, in his *Musical Lexicon,* says that he was buried in the church of St. Gudule, at Brussels. From the *Athenæ Belgicæ* of Swertius, the same author cites his epitaph *.

> *O Mors inevitabilis !*
> *Mors amara, Mors crudelis,*
> *Josquinum dum necasti*
> *Illum nobis abstulit ;*
> *Qui suam per harmoniam*
> *Illustravit ecclesiam,*
> *Propterea die tu musicæ :*
> *Requiescat in pace.   Amen.*

TRANSLATION.

O bitter, ruthless death !
Whose pow'r all beings dread,
With Josquin's tuneful breath,
Devotion's rapture fled.
Religion mourn'd thy sway,
Felt Harmony's decease ;
To Harmony then say—
" Repose in endless peace."

                                          BUSBY.

---

* Several Latin poems were written on the occasion of his death, the music to two of which is preserved in the seventh collection of

The account of this celebrated musician cannot be better concluded than with the insertion of the following additional specimen of his science and talents, as a composer in the style, or manner, which prevailed in his time.

French Songs, in five and six parts, printed at Antwerp, in 1545, and preserved in the British Museum.

One of these poems has been set twice: by Benedictus, and by Nicholas Gombert, one of Josquin's disciples. This circumstance was thought the more worthy of notice, as offering an opportunity of instancing the power and promptitude of unfounded conceit: because both compositions are in the key of E minor, with a minor second as well as minor third, M. de Blainville, a scholar and musician of the last century, produced them as evidences of the existence of a *third mode*, different from our major and minor. (See *Musica de France*, 1751.) And since this mode partakes, as he asserts, of the modulation of both our major and our minor mode, he calls it the *mixed mode*. Rousseau, remarking in his dictionary upon this novel conception, expresses himself as follows :

" This new mode not being given by the analysis of three concords, like the modes major and minor, is not, like them, determined by harmonies essential to the mode, but by an entire gamut suitable to it, as well in ascending as descending ; so that while in our two modes, the gamut is given by the concords, in the minor mode, the concords are given by the gamut."

The musical lexicographer then proceeds to demonstrate, that the essential difference between the *mixed-mode* and ours, in regard to the melody, is in the position of the two semi-tones ; the first of which, in the *mixed-mode*, is invariably between the tonic and the second, and the other between the fifth and sixth. And in respect to its harmony, that, he tells us, in the opening of a piece, bears on the minor third, but in the process, on the minor or the major third. All this, however, Rousseau states, only in explanation, not in support, of what the utmost of his own extraordinary ingenuity would have found it impossible to defend. With that view, and that view only, he adduces the following example of the gamut and accompaniment (in harmony) of M. Blainville's *mixed-mode*. —

CANON,
Duo in Uno.

O Je - su Fi - li Da-

Should it be urged in favour of M. Blainville's notion, that the old music of the church was often composed upon this plan; the answer will be, that it was barbarous, and not to be tolerated upon any principle of harmony and the allowed relation of chords. The keys of such compositions were, at most, but equivocal; and the compositions themselves anomalous.

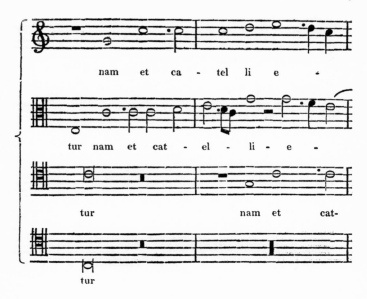

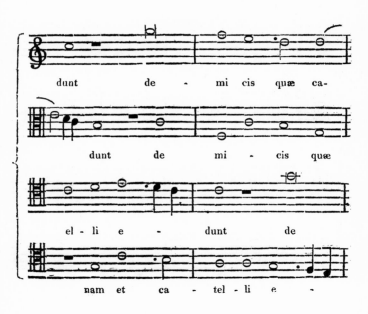

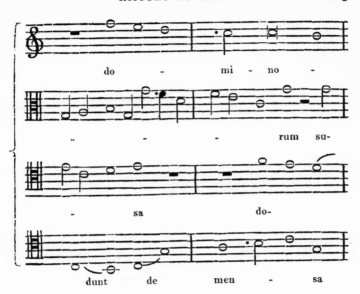

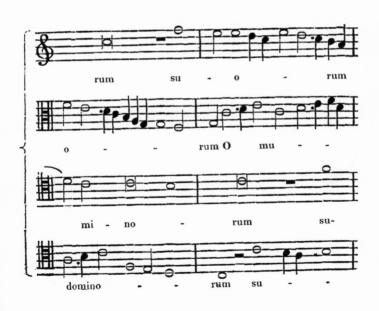

- O mulier mag - na est Fi -

lier mag - na est Fi - -

o - - rum O muli er mag-

- - rum O mulier mag - na est

- - - des tu - a

- - des tu - a.

na est Fi - des tu - a.

Fides tu - - - a.

The next musician of eminence after Josquin, was Henry Isaac, by some named Arrigo Tedesco. Of this contrapuntist Politian, and other Florentine authors, speak in very exalted terms. While Tinctor was at the head of the Neapolitan school, and Josquin at that of the Roman, Isaac was Maestro di Capella of the church of St. John, at Florence. During Carnival, certain songs called *Canti Carnascialeschi*, used to be sung through the streets of that city by persons in masks. Antonio Francesco Grazzini, who published a collection of these songs, says in his preface, that the first of them which was performed in this manner in the time of Lorenzo il Magnifico, was set in *three parts* by Isaac *.

Glareanus agrees with Politian in extolling the merits of this composer; speaks of his great genius and erudition, and says, that he " embellished those ecclesiastical chaunts in which he found any majesty or force, with such harmony as rendered them superior to any new subjects of modern times. He was particularly fond of making *one* of the parts sustain a note, while the others were in motion, like the waves of the sea eddying about a rock, during a storm." How Isaac obtained the second name of Arrigo Tedesco does not appear. Glareanus, glancing at the circumstance, observes, that " Politian celebrates Henry Isaac by a corrupt name, foolishly calling him Arrigo. Several of his compositions are preserved; and considering the state of *Music in consonance* at the time he wrote, great praise is due to his science, and the ingenious disposition of his score. If in his melodies, he does not discover any remarkable facility of fancy, his power of *imitation* is conspicuous, and his harmony sound. At the

---

* Soon afterwards, many songs of this kind were composed in four, eight, twelve, and even fifteen parts; a proof that the employment of counterpoint was not confined to sacred music.

same time, however, candour must admit, that by adhering too rigidly to the mode which he denominates *Mixolydian*, he sometimes renders his combinations somewhat crude and uncouth. For a composer of the latter end of the fifteenth century, he made remarkably free with discords ; and in one of his compositions still extant, he introduces a naked ninth.

Jacob Hobrecht, a Fleming, was of high standing in his time ; and much celebrated both for his celerity of invention, and solidity of judgment. Among his scholars was the renowned Erasmus : and Glareanus, who was a disciple of that great man, tells us, that he has frequently heard his preceptor speak of Hobrecht as a musician who was without a rival. In evidence of his wonderful facility in writing, it is mentioned that he composed an entire mass, a very excellent one, in a single night.

The time of Hobrecht's birth is not known : but as his mass *Si Dedero* was printed at Venice in 1508, he was probably born about 1480*. The *melody* of the period in which this eminent contrapuntist lived, was, as compared with that of aftertimes, so dry, and little varied ; and what is now meant by *air*, was so far from the composer's aim or pursuit, that it would scarcely be reasonable to look for it in the productions of Hobrecht, high as was his rank among the masters of his day. His harmony and modulation are of the first order of excellence ; and are so formed and conducted, as to make upon the mind and ear a most majestic impression. He was remarked for equally avoiding quaint and pedantic passages, and those which were unusual and affected : a merit which could not, in every instance, be

---

* Dr. Burney scored this composition, and says of it, that " though the movements are somewhat too similar in subject, that the counterpoint is neat, clear, and masterly."

claimed by his predecessors, Okenheim, Josquin, and Isaac.

Of this high period there were several composers whose works were of sufficient merit to attract the public attention; but none, except John Mouton, Pierre de la Rue (by Walther called a Netherlander) Anthony Brumel, cotemporary with Josquin, and Gaspar and Feum, or Fevin, whose productions have come down to us, or at least, that are worthy of being mentioned. Of these, Mouton, whom Glareanus calls a Frenchman, though Guicciardini pronounces him to have been a Netherlander, is the only master deserving our particular notice. As the place where, so the exact time when, this composer was born, is not positively known: but it is beyond dispute, that the chief part of his life was devoted to the services of Lewis XII. and Francis I*. He was a pupil of Josquin's, and approached the nearest to the excellencies of his master, in his *motets*, the polish and smoothness of

---

* In the Memoirs of M. De la Foret, ambassador from Francis I. to Solyman II. emperor of the Turks, for the conclusion of a treaty between them, in the year 1543, we read, that the king, a warm amateur of music, and willing to please his new ally, sent him a band of accomplished musicians, making the Turk, as he conceived, a present worthy of his magnificence. Solyman received them with much civility, and listened attentively to three different concerts performed by them at his palace, and in the presence of all his court. He expressed the pleasure and satisfaction he received from the music; but having observed that it tended to enervate his mind, he apprehended that it might still more decidedly affect his courtiers. He much applauded the skill and exertion of the musicians: but fearing the established introduction of music among his people might occasion as much disorder as a permitted use of wine, he dismissed the musicians with a handsome reward, after having ordered all their instruments to be broken, with a prohibition against their ever returning to that country, upon pain of death.

which are attributed to his having lived in a *court*. Among this species of his productions, one of the most pleasing and masterly is his *Non nobis Domine*, composed for the birth of Renée, the second daughter of Lewis XII. by Anne of Bretagne, in the year 1509. The only rival he produced to this composition, is the motet *Quam pulchra es Amica mea*, from the Song of Solomon. Besides these pieces, he wrote many masses, which were highly admired by Leo X. A *Miserere* for four voices, of his composition, has been preserved by Glareanus, in his Dodecachordon, as also the following hymn, the merit of which demands, while its brevity permits, my presenting it to the reader.

HYMN.

For Four Voices.

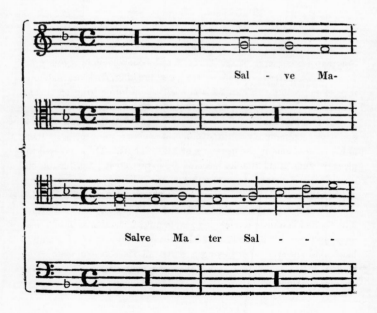

ter   sal   -   -   -   va-

-   -   va - to   -   -

to   -   -   ris

ris   Sal   -   -

Sal   -   ve - Ma-

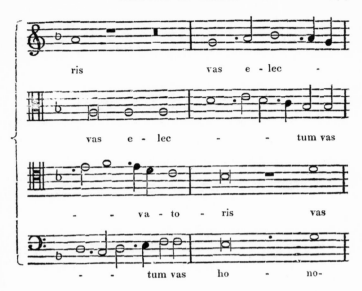

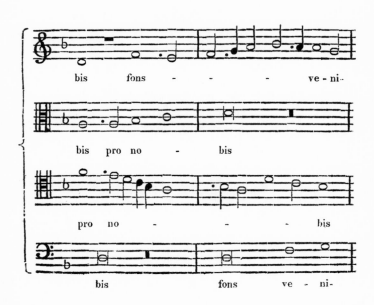

CHAP. XX.

STATE OF MUSIC FROM THE EARLY PART OF THE
SIXTEENTH CENTURY, TO THE REIGN OF ELIZABETH.

ACCORDING to the existing testimonies of merit left
us by the musicians of the various countries of Europe, it
appears that none laboured more sedulously, and with more
success, to bring the science of harmony to a state of consistency, purity, and elegance, than those of Flanders.
During the latter half of the sixteenth century, the Low
Countries abounded with masters whose productions proclaimed the talents and the science of their authors, and
seem to have challenged the acknowledgments, and rivalled
the abilities, of the Italians themselves. This temporary
advantage of the Flemings, over the composers of a country
uniformly renowned for the musical genius of its natives,
may fairly be attributed to a kind of voluntary *halt* made by
the latter in the march of their counterpoint, and harmonical
knowledge, for the purpose of changing their track, or establishing a new style of composition, founded upon the precepts of Franchinus. Weary of the *Cantus Gregorianus*,
both the Italian clergy and laity were desirous of seeing introduced into the church service, a greater freedom and variety of melody *. The masters of Italy, of intellects too

---

* Leo X. who is said to have *loved music to a fault*, was the first
Pope that suggested this improvement in choir composition, which,

ductile to be long posed, or detained by the proposed
change, soon became familiar with a more easy and flowing
manner, and shewed themselves capable of rivalling the
Flemings in the composition of madrigals, and other forms
of secular harmony, in which their superior powers of invention and contrivance, as well as their natural freedom and
floridity of fancy, soon became conspicuous.

While the Flemings and Italians were thus polishing melody, and giving to harmony a new and improved cast, the
English, as if emulous of their rival advances, were earnestly regarding, and ambitiously imitating, their progress, in
both provinces of the science. Indeed, as early as the
fifteenth century, not only *masses* in four, five, and six parts,
were produced in our country, but *secular songs*, in two
or three parts, the counterpoint of which, at the time of its
production, was equal to that of any other country.

Among the English musicians of the sixteenth century,
we find the eminent Dr. ROBERT FAYRFAX, a graduate
both of Cambridge and of Oxford, who flourished during the
reigns of Henry VII. and Henry VIII. By a curious manuscript collection of ancient English songs, still preserved,
it appears that Dr. Fayrfax was a composer of secular as
well as sacred music; and that he and Syr Thomas Phelyppes were distinguished above the other musical professors

---

indeed, was carried so far, that the Council of Trent, taking the state
of church music into consideration, felt alarmed at what it was
pleased to call its *abuse*, and issued a decree against *curious singing*.
Among other things, this decree, quite as *curious*, as could be the
singing it reprobates, forbids " *l'uso delle musiche nelle chiese con
mistura di canto, v' suono lascivo, tutte le attioni secolari, colloquii
profani, strepiti, gridori.*" That is, the use in churches of music
mixed with lascivious songs, all secular action, profane dialogue,
noises and screeches.

of their time. Bishop Tanner informs us, that Fayrfax was a native of Rayford, in the county of Hertford, and that he died at St. Albans, of the abbey church of which place he was organist, and in which cathedral he was buried. Among his remaining compositions, we find the following; which appears worthy of being presented to the reader. In the original the two upper parts are written in the counter-tenor, and tenor cliffs; but for the purpose of general accommodation, they are given in the treble cliff.

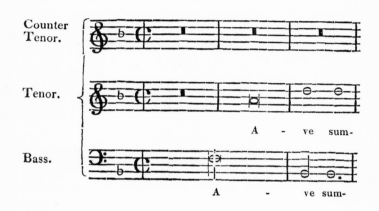

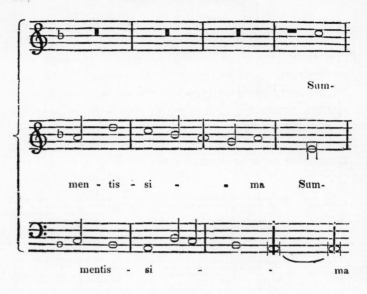

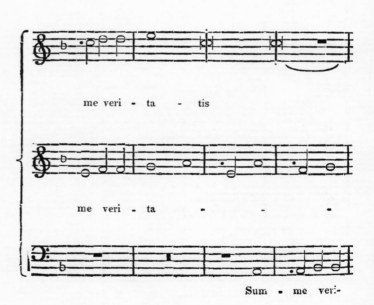

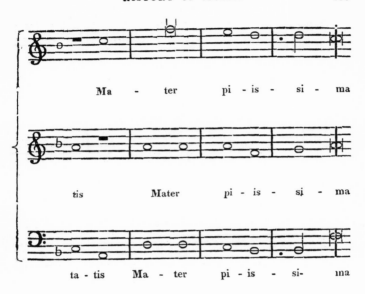

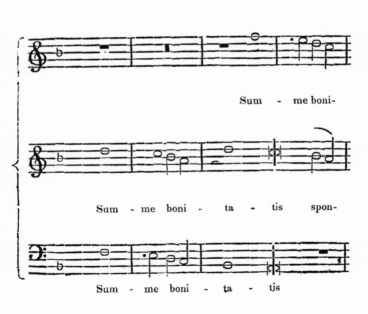

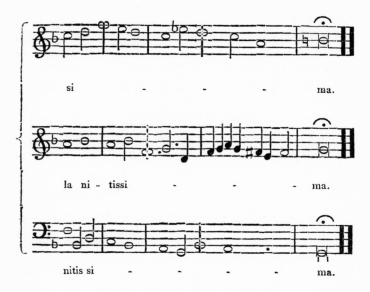

In the manuscript volume containing the songs of Dr. Fayrfax, are many others, by various masters, among whom we find John Taverner, Dr. Tye, John Shephard, John Marbec, and Robert Parsons, as well as several others, who appear to have been more of secular than ecclesiastical composers.

JOHN TAVERNER was organist of Boston, in Lincolnshire, and of *Cardinal,* now *Christ Church* College, Oxford *. The view of preferment in this, Wolsey's new-

---

* It is necessary to distinguish between the present John Taverner, and another musician of the same name, who, in the year 1610, was chosen Gresham professor. The truth is, that the organist of Cardinal College is the musician always meant when men speak of John Taverner. The *professor* of whose merit little or nothing is known, was the son of the well-known Richard Taverner, who in the year 1539, published a new edition of Matthew's Bible, with corrections and alterations of his own. It is a fact Sir John Hawkins has thought

founded college, drew Taverner, together with John Frith the martyr, from Cambridge. It seems that these, and a number of other persons, the eyes of whose understanding had been opened by the doctrines of Luther, to the existing abuses of the church, held private conversations upon the subject of religion. Those meetings, and their purpose, being discovered, the communicants were accused of heresy, and immured in a deep cave under the college : an enclosure, the air of which was rendered so impure by the salt fish, of which it was the constant repository, that several of them were killed by the stench *. The evidence against Taverner

---

worth relating, that in 1552, this Richard Taverner, though a layman, (there being then a scarcity of preachers) obtained of Edward VI. licence to preach in any part of his dominions, and preached before the king at court, wearing a velvet bonnet, a damask gown, and a gold chain ; and in the reign of Queen Elizabeth, being then high sheriff of the county of Oxford, he appeared in the pulpit at St. Mary's, then of stone, with a sword, and a gold chain about his neck, and made a sermon to the scholars, which had this hopeful beginning :—" Arriving at the mount of St. Mary's, in the stoney stage, where I now stand, I have brought you some biscuits baked in the oven of charity, carefully conserved for the chickens of the church, the sparrows of the Spirit, and the sweet swallows of salvation." Taverner, as already observed, was a layman ; but such was the general style of pulpit eloquence in the sixteenth century, that the flowers of Mr. Sheriff Taverner's eloquence would not have disgraced a cardinal.

    * One of these unfortunate persons, John Fryer, was removed to the prison of the Savoy, where, according to the information of Wood, " he did much solace himself with playing on the lute, having good skill in music, for which reason, a friend of his would needs commend him to the master ; but the master answered, " Take heed, for he that playeth is a devil, because he is departed from the Catholic faith." This devil, however, the Catholics, for some reason now unknown, did afterwards set at liberty ; and he whose soul was lost

only proved his having hid some *heretical* books under
the flooring of a school; on account of this, and the respect procured him by his eminence in his science, the cardinal extended to him his mercy, and he escaped. Frith,
however, his friend and companion, was not equally fortunate. He was tried, convicted of heresy, and burnt in
Smithfield, together with Andrew Hewet, another of the
same Lutheran society.

The first reformers, trusting more to reason and principle,
than to show and ceremony, were so far from being anxious
to preserve the ancient embellishments of the church service, that their first care was, to gradually reduce, if not
abolish, all its exterior dependencies. With its visible splendor and formalities, the grandeur and the portion of its music were curtailed; and the adoption of hymns and psalmo-
dic versification, sung to plain and simple tunes, superseded
in parish churches, figurative harmony and florid counterpoint. In the cathedrals, however, the choirs of colleges,
and private chapels *, the former style of composition and
performance, in a great measure still continued to prevail.
It was, in fact, a luxury with which even the reformed religion could not altogether dispense. It imparted a flattering
magnificence to what may be called the *spectacle* of worship, heightened its solemnity, and contributed to the dis-

---

beyond all redemption, became a physician, and restored the ailing
bodies of many.

* The magnificence of some of the private chapels equalled that
of a cathedral. The *Gentillmen* of the Earl of Northumberland's
clerical establishment consisted of " x parsons—as to say—two at x
marc a pece—three at iiijl a pece—two at v marc a pece—oone at xl *s.*
and oone at xx *s.* viz. ij basses, ij tenors, and vj counter-tenors.—
Childeryn of the chapell vj. after xxv *s.* the pece."

tinction which it was thought proper to preserve between
the service of the cathedrals and the royal and private chapels, and the parish or plebeian worship.   The study of
counterpoint, as exercised in sacred music, was therefore
still encouraged to a certain degree; and hence the preservation of many of our *early church compositions*, and that
addition of *modern harmony*, which reflects so much honour
on the talents of our country.   The question, *What were
the genius, taste, and science of Taverner?* will be best
answered by the following composition, written originally in
the key of **F**, and for a treble, soprano, and counter-tenor;
but here transposed one note lower, for the double purpose
of better accommodating the generality of voices (for the
composer carries his treble up to B ♭ in alt) and avoiding
the use of the soprano and counter-tenor cliffs.

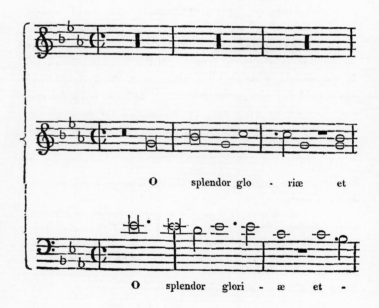

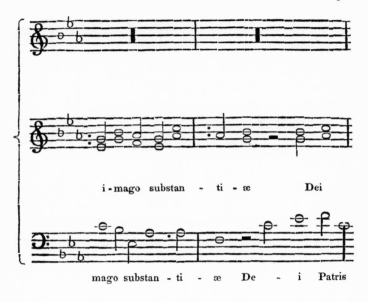

i - mago substan - ti - æ Dei

mago substan - ti - æ De - i Patris

Je - su Chris -

Patris omnipoten - tis Je - sus Chris-

omni po ten tis Je - su Chris - te

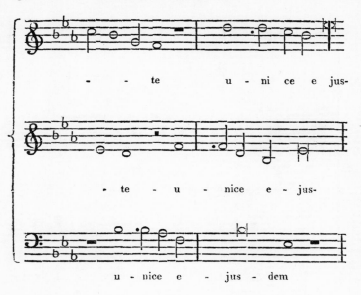

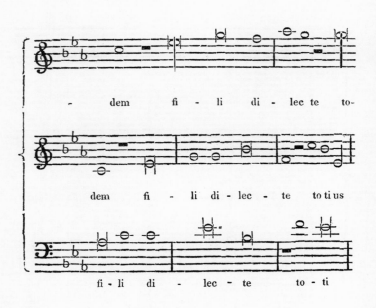

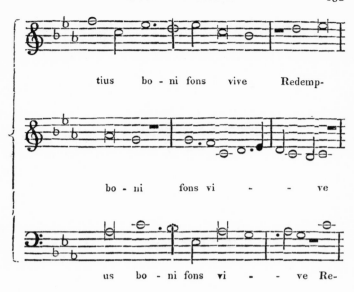

tius   bo - ni fons   vive   Redemp-

bo - ni   fons vi –   –   ve

us   bo - ni fons vi   –   –   ve Re-

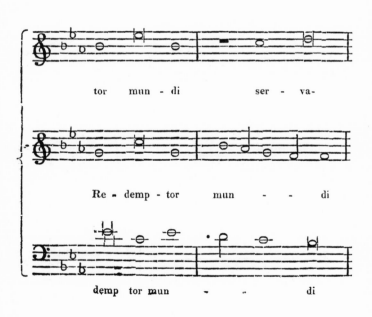

tor   mun - di   ser - va-

Re ▪ demp - tor   mun –   –   di

demp tor mun   –   ▪▪   di

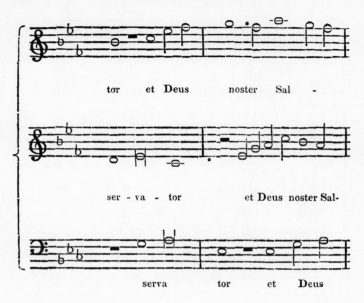

tor   et Deus   noster   Sal -

ser - va - tor   et Deus noster Sal-

serva   tor   et   Deus

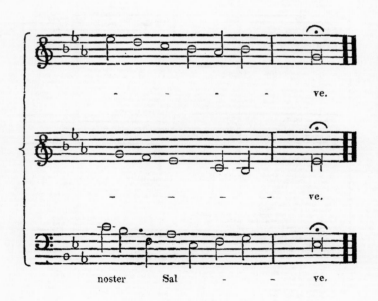

-               -   -   ve.

-              -   -   ve.

noster   Sal   -   -   ve.

To no musician of the sixteenth century is the English cathedral-service more indebted than to JOHN MARBECK, organist of Windsor. His industry undertook, and his genius executed, the formidable task of resetting all the preces, prayers, responses, &c. &c., and in a word, furnishing the church with much of the very music that is used at this day *. In 1549, he was admitted to the degree of Bachelor in Music, at Oxford. By Bale, he is honourably mentioned, because he was persecuted by the Catholics; but Pitts, for the same reason, omits his name. Both from Fox's *Acts and Monuments*, and Burnet's *History of the Reformation*, we learn that Marbeck, more honest than prudent, and less patient than zealous, outstript in his activity, the spirit of the time in which he lived, and was near becoming a martyr to his new sentiments. Condemned to the stake with three other persons, who were burnt for heresy, he escaped only by the earnest intercession of Sir Humphrey Foster †.

---

* Marbeck's notation of the English cathedral service, was published under the following title :

The Book of Common Praier,

Noted,

1550.

Imprinted by Richard Grafton, Printer to the King's Majestie, *cum privilegio ad imprimendum solum.*

It appears, by this publication, that the assertion of Marbeck's having re-set the whole church service, is to be understood with allowance ; since it contains the music of the *Te Deum laudamus*, and some other portions of the formulary, in nearly the same state as it had been long before the Reformation.

† Marbeck was more immediately connected and involved with Robert Testwood, who suffered for his principles. By this it would

The chief of the portions of Scripture, or hymns of the church that have been set by English musicians to Latin words, were produced during the reign of Mary. And by the time Elizabeth ascended the throne, a school of counterpoint was formed in England, that did not yield to that of any other country of Europe. It must not, however, be forgotten, that if Music, like *commerce*, flourished in this island, like commerce, it first reared its head in Italy, whence it spread to the Hanseatic towns, the Netherlands, and every part of Europe; that the choir of the papal chapel was its first and great generator, and that it was only left to other countries to receive the model, and by its excellence, to be instigated to its imitation.

The general practice of the composers of the sixteenth century, was that of constructing harmony upon an ancient ecclesiastical chant; a species of musical fabrication, in which few were more distinguished than ROBERT PARSONS of Exeter, first of the Chapel Royal, and afterwards organist of Westminster Abbey. Of this kind of composition by Parsons, there are remaining many excellent specimens, in the manuscripts of Christ Church College, Oxford; among which is an *In Nomine*, founded on an ancient chant to that part of the mass beginning *Benedictus qui venit in nomine Domini*, which at that time, was a favourite theme with the English masters.

As a loss to our curiosity, rather than our taste, we have

---

appear, that Marbeck, like many others of his professional brethren, compromised his conscience. That such accommodations of opinion were not uncommon among the musicians of that age, is evident from the chapel establishments of Edward, Mary, and Elizabeth, which shew their choristers constantly tuning their consciences to the court pitch: that is, becoming in perfect unison with the *Supreme Head of the Church.*

to regret, that the remains of our *secular* music are very limited. Of songs, ballads, and other compositions dedicated to public and private amusement, there must have been an abundance: but their subjects were too temporary, and their texture too slight, to survive the age in which they were produced. Though printing gave them circulation, they had no permanent registers, like those provided for the compositions of the church; and the lays of each year giving place to those of the next, were successively produced, and successively laid aside and forgotten. The nobility continued to retain in their service a number of musical performers, most of whom occasionally visited the neighbouring monasteries, where they regaled the monks with music, both vocal and instrumental: and as, in general, without variety, pleasure ceases, and nothing more urgently requires relief than an *old song*, new compositions appeared with every rising sun, and were as constantly swept away by the very force and fulness of their own tide.

The *state* of keeping a *master of the revels*, was not, at this time, confined to royalty. Almost every nobleman had such a domestic officer, whose especial province was the *overseyinge and orderinge of plays and interludes plaid in the* xii *dayes of Crestenmas* *. But all the establishments of this kind among the nobility, yielded in pomp, grandeur, and extent, to the chapel of Cardinal Wolsey. Indeed, according to the account published after the death of this ambi-

---

* In these dramatic pieces, the gentlemen and the children of the chapel were the principal performers; for which service, as well as for their acting upon other great festivals, they received certain distinct and stipulated rewards. The dramas, the subjects of which were sacred, were called *Mysteries*. At Christmas was represented " the play of the Nativity;" at Easter, " the play of the Resurrection."

tious priest, by Cavendish, his gentleman-usher, it seems, in the splendor of its decorations, and number of its officiates, to have even surpassed that of the Roman Pontiff. By Cavendish it is thus described :—

" First he had there a deane, a great divine, and a man of excellent learning ; a sub-dean, a repeatour of the quire, a gospeller and epistellor ; of singing-priests ten, a master of the children. The seculars of the chapell, being singing-men, twelve ; singing children, ten, with one servant to wait upon them. In the vestry, a yeoman and two grooms ; over and besides other retainers that came thither at principal feasts. And for the furniture of his chapell, it passeth my weak capacity to declare the number of the costly ornaments and rich jewels, that were occupied in the same. For I have seen in procession about the hall, 4 rich copes, besides the rich candlesticks, and other necessary ornaments to the furniture of the same."

It was to sustain the *pomp and vanity* of this establishment, that Wolsey exercised his tyrannical power upon the sixth Earl of Northumberland, by demanding of that nobleman all his choral books. Letters still preserved in the family, represent the Earl saying, " I do perceayff my Lord Cardinal's pleasour ys to have such boks as was in the chapell of my lat Lorde and ffayther (wos sol Jhu pardon). To the accomplychment of which, at your desyer, I am confformable, notwithstandinge I trust to be able ons to set up a chapell off mine owne. I shall with all sped send up the boks unto my Lord's Grace, as to say iiij *Antiffonars,* (Antiphoners) such as I think wher not seen a gret wyll— v *Gralls* (Graduals) —an *Ordeorly* (Ordinal)—a *Manuall*— viij *Prossessioners* (Processionals)."

Among the musicians of the time of Henry VIII. we have to include that monarch himself. He was both a performer and a composer. From Erasmus, and also Burnet, we learn, that he set to music offices for the church; and in the books of the Chapel Royal, there is an anthem of Henry's, for four voices *.

The fact is, that this Henry, whose history disgraces our country, studied music so early in life, and became so well acquainted with its laws and properties, that its influence ought to have softened his savage nature. Lord Herbert of Cherbury, in his life of this royal sacrificer of wives, and enemy of every just and humane feeling, says, that " his education was accurate, he being destined to the Archbishoprick of Canterbury, during the life of his elder brother, Prince Arthur. By these means, not only the more necessary parts of learning were infused into him, but. even those of ornament; so that, besides being an able Latinist, philosopher, and divine, he was (which one might wonder at in a king) a curious musician; as two entire masses composed by him, and often sung in his chapel, did abundantly witness †." We also collect from Hollinshed, that during his progress from one place to another, singing, playing on the recorders, flute, virginals, and setting songs to music, were his principal amusements: indeed, it is universally allowed, that he was highly skilled in manual execution; and a suffi-

---

* In a collection of church music published by John Barnard, in the year 1641, this anthem is given to William Mundy; but the late ingenious Dr. Aldrich, after taking great pains to ascertain the real composer, pronounced it to be a genuine production of Henry; of whose composition there is also a motet still extant, a genuine copy of which was in the possession of the late Dr. William Hayes, *Musical Professor* of the University of Oxford.

† His musical taste, however, far from being confined to church compositions, was so strongly turned to songs and ballads, that the light and "*jocular*" melodies produced by the secular clergy, since the time of Edward III. received, from the high favour he shewed them, the collective appellation of *King Henry's Mirth.*

cient adept in counterpoint, to be qualified to compose the pieces' that bear his name *. In a collection of anthems, motets and other church offices, in the hand-writing of one John Baldwin, of the choir of Windsor, which collection appears to have been completed in the year 1591, is the following composition for three voices, with these words, " *Henricus Octavus*," at the beginning; and these, " *Quod*

---

* At this time, the accomplishment of music was deemed necessary to the completion, not only of a gentleman's but a prince's education. We read in Sandoval's Life of the Emperor Charles V., that " he was a great friend to the science of music, and after his abdication, would have the church offices only accompanied by the organ, and sung by fourteen or fifteen friars, who were good musicians, and had been selected from the most expert performers of the order." " He was himself so skilful, that he knew if any additional singer intruded ; and if any one made a mistake, he would cry out, *Such a one is wrong;* and immediately mark the man. He was earnest too, that no *seculars* should come in ; and one evening, when a contralto, from Placentia, stood near the desk with the singers, and sung one verse with them eminently well, before he could sing another, some of the barbarians ran, and told the prior to turn him out of the choir, or, at least, bid him hold his tongue."

" The emperor understood music, and felt and tasted its charms : the friars often discovered him behind the door, as he sate in his own apartment, near the high altar, beating time and singing in parts with the performers ; and if any one was out, they could overhear him call the offender names ; as *redheaded blockhead*," &c. " A composer from Seville, of my own acquaintance," continues his biographer, " whose name was Guerrero, presented him with a book of motets and masses ; and when one of these compositions had been sung, as a specimen, the Emperor called his confessor, and said—'See what a thief, what a plagiarist, is this son of a —— ! why here,' says he, ' this passage is taken from one composer, and this from another,' naming them as he went on. All this while, the singers stood astonished, as none of them had discovered these thefts, till they were pointed out by the Emperor."

Rex Henricus Octavus," at the end of the cantus, or upper
part. The science it displays, will, to many, appear more
than can well be imagined, to be possessed by a king, unless
they keep in mind, that Henry was intended by his father
for the church, and that a competent acquaintance with the
principles of music was then necessary to the clerical profession. The words are taken from the *Canticum Can-
ticorum*, and are supposed to have been addressed by him to
one of his favourite females, whom, in his early years, he had
under his protection at Greenwich *.

In the transcript from which the composition is copied, the
parts are written for two counter-tenors, and a tenor. For
the same reasons that the cliffs are changed in the piece by
Taverner, that liberty is taken here ; but without varying the
key.

* Her lodging (Puttenham, in his *Arte of English Poesie*, tells
us) was a tower in the park of the Old Palace. When he visited

et   quam   de - co - ra   et   quam

co   -   ra   quam pulchra   es et quam

de co   -   ra   quam   de - co-

Quam   pul - chra

de - co - ra

her, he generally went by water in his barge, attended by Sir Andrew Flamock, his standard-bearer, a man of humour, who entertained him with jests and merry stories. The king, as the signal of
his approach, used to blow his horn at his entrance into the park.

ra   Quam   pulchra es   et   quam

es   Quam   pulchra es et quam de - co-

de co •   -   ra   Charis-

ra et quam   de - co - ra

Cha - ris - si-

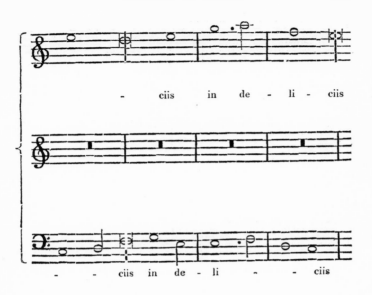

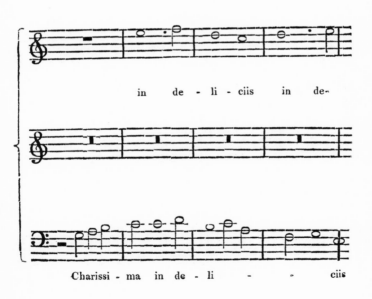

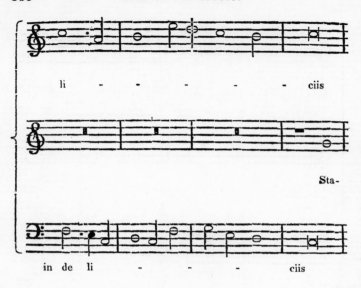

li - - - - - ciis

Sta-

in de li - - - ciis

tu ra - tu - a as si mi - la ta est   Pal -

Sta - tu ra tu - a as si - mi - la ta

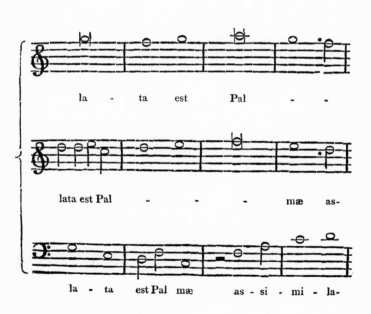

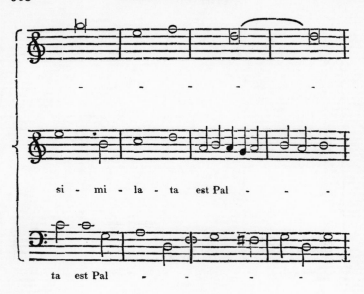

si - mi - la - ta est Pal - - -

ta est Pal - - - -

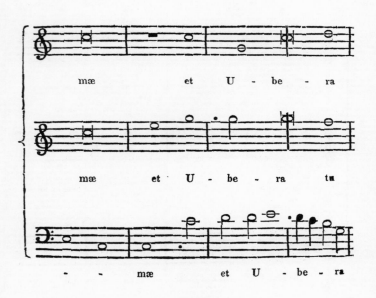

mæ   et   U - be - ra

mæ   et U - be - ra   tu

- - mæ   et U - be - ra

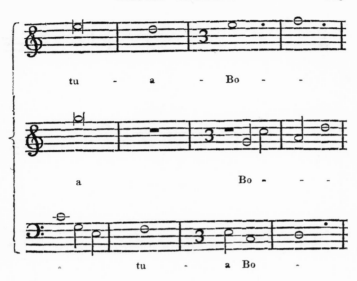

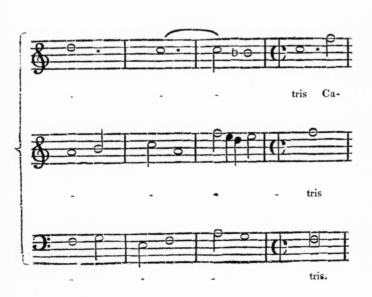

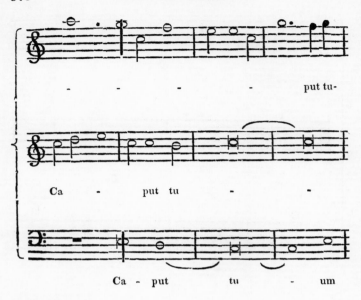

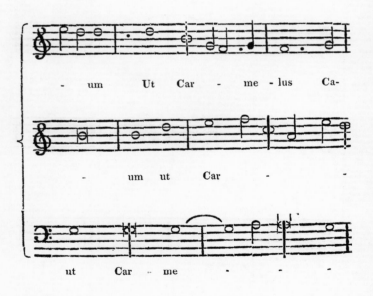

put tu - um   Ut   Car -

- me - lus   Ut

lus   Ut Car-

Car

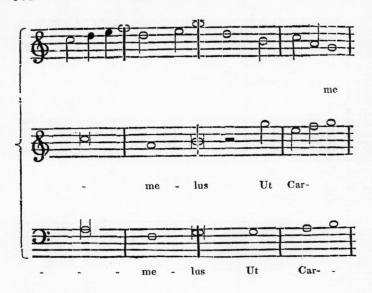

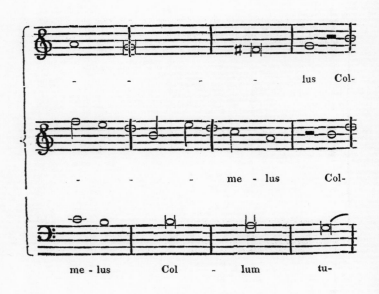

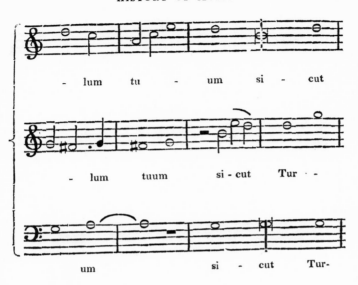

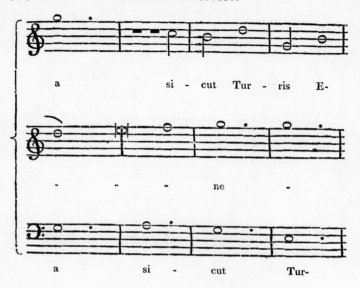

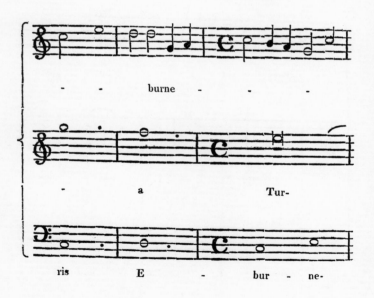

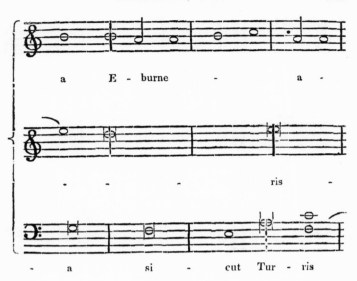

a   Ve - ni di-

Ve - ni di - lec -

a   Ve - - -

lec te mi di - lec te - mi   Ve - ni di-

- - te - mi   Ve - ni di - lec -

- - - ni - di-

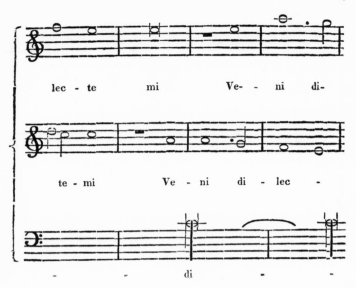

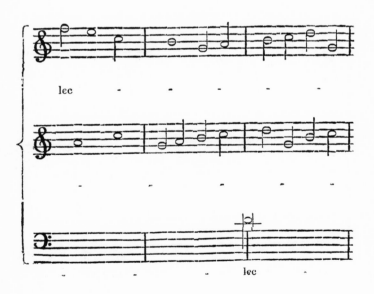

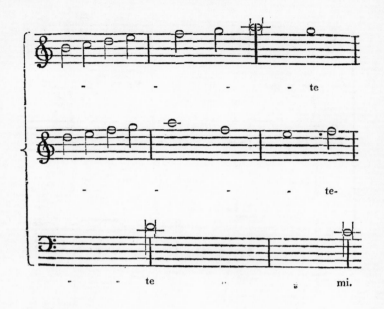

-     -   -   - te

-     -   -   - te-

-     - te   mi.

mi.   E - grediamur   E gre di-

mi.   E - gre   -   -

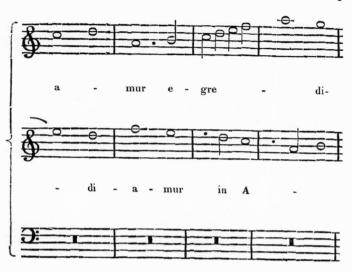

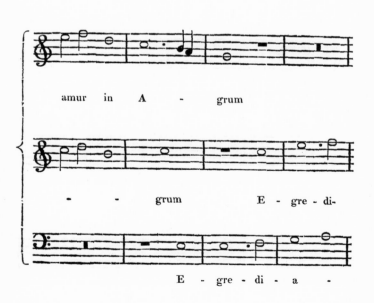

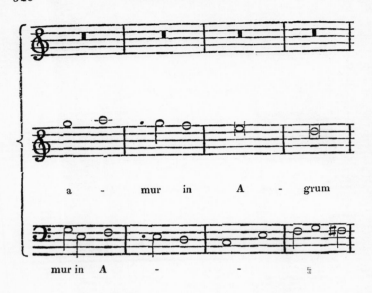

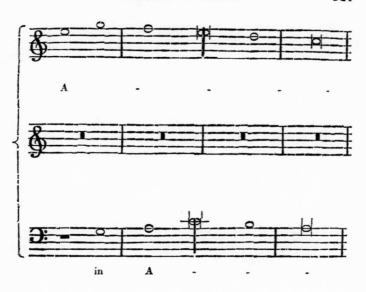

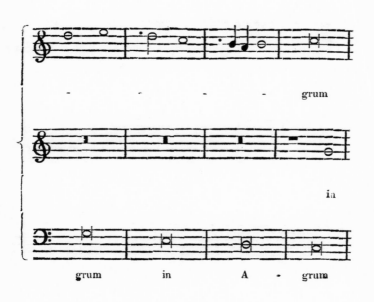

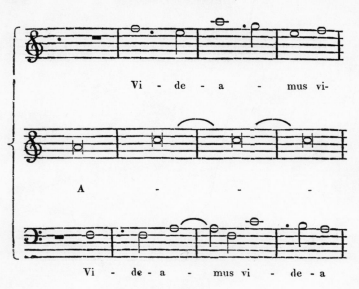

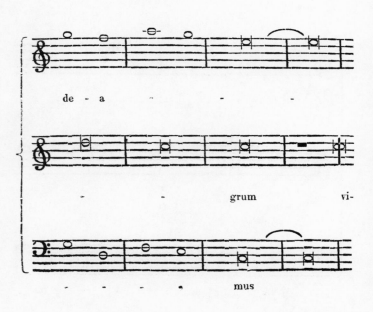

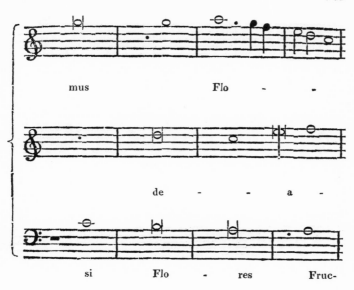

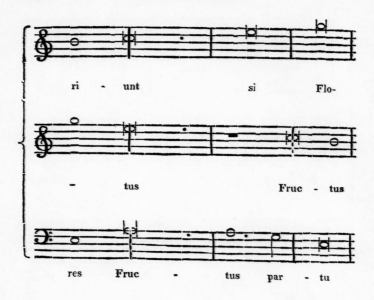

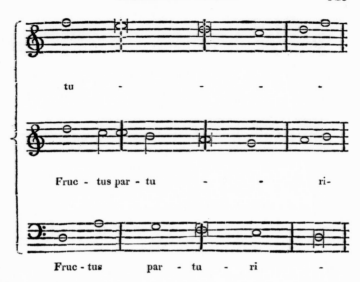

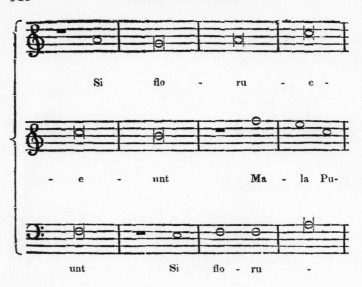

Si   flo -   ru - e -

- e - unt   Ma - la Pu-

unt   Si   flo - ru   -

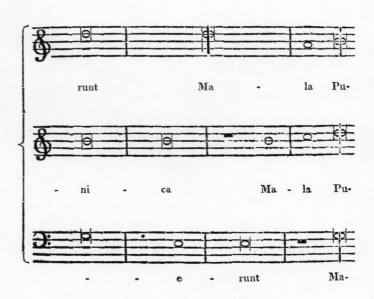

runt   Ma   -   la Pu-

- ni - ca   Ma - la Pu-

-    -   e - runt   Ma-

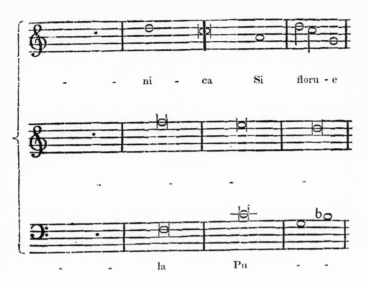

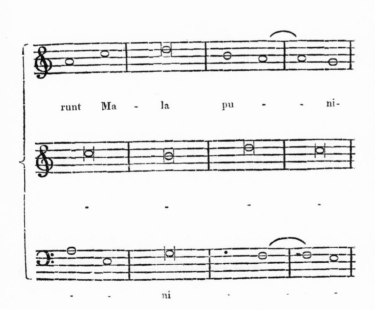

da - bo ti - bi U - be - ra
bo - ti - bi U - be - ra me -
- a U - be - ra me-

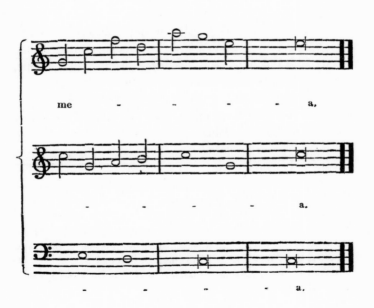

me - - - a,
- - - - a.
- - - - a.

Notwithstanding the progress of the spirit of reformation, a considerable number of English musicians adorned with their genius and science, the church music of this century; among these are to be reckoned William Cornish, some of whose compositions are respectfully mentioned in Thoresby's " History of Leeds *." Bishop Tanner speaks of the excellence of his productions, and considers him as one of the ornaments of his age.

About the same time with Cornish, flourished John Dygon, who, as appears by a composition of his, was Prior of St. Austin's in Canterbury, and a very skilful musician. He afterwards became an abbot of the monastery of St. Augustine, to which dignity, it is supposed, he was raised, on account of his great musical proficiency. According to the Fasti Oxon, Dygon was admitted in that university to the degree of Bachelor in Music.

George Etheridge (in Latin, Edricus,) was a native of Thame in Oxfordshire, and became a member of Corpus Christi College. Besides being deeply skilled in music, he was so excellent a scholar as to be thought worthy of the chair of Regius professor. Being a determined Catholic, Elizabeth removed him from that station; after which he acquired considerable wealth by instructing the sons of gentlemen in his own communion, in the rudiments of grammar, logic, and music †. Etheridge was an excellent poet, and

---

* Either this William Cornish, or his father, wrote a curious poetical dialogue, comprising many stanzas of seven lines each; which he entitles " A Treatise between Trowthe and Enformation." It contains a parable, almost wholly consisting of allusions to music and musical instruments; and which, in many respects, is so great a curiosity, that I regret its being too long for insertion.

† Among the pupils of Etheridge, was William Gifford, afterwards Archbishop of Rheims.

possessed a profound knowledge of the mathematics; and according to Anthony Wood, his musical compositions, like his manual performance, were of a very superior order. Leland, who was one of his intimate friends, says of him—

> Scripsisti juvenis multâ cum laude libellos,
> Qui Regi eximie perplacuere meo.

And his portrait, as drawn by Pits, is " Erat peritus mathematicus, musicus tum vocalis, tum instrumentalis cum primis in Anglia conferendus, testudine tamen et lyra præ cæteris delectabatur. Poëta elegantissimus. Versus enim Anglicos, Latinos, Græcos, Hæbreos, accuratissime componere, et ad tactus lyricos concinnare peritissime solebat."

While these, and many other men of learning and science, of whom no memorials are now remaining, were enriching the harmony of England, some distinguished composers and theorists flourished on the continent, whose names have not yet been mentioned ; but without a knowledge of whose merits, the reader would be very imperfectly acquainted with the music and musicians of this century.

Before giving the biography of Henricus Loritus Glareanus, styled by Gerard Vossius, " *a man of great and universal learning*," it is necessary to observe, that the translation of the Greek harmonicians had excited a general wish to revive the ancient modes ; an inclination not a little promoted by that celebrated work of Glareanus, to which the public disposition had itself given birth *.

This theorist, a native of Switzerland, flourished about the

---

* The design of Glareanus, in writing this book, was to establish the doctrine of twelve modes, in opposition to the opinion of Ptolemy, who allows of no more than there are species of the diapason, and those are seven.

year 1540. His principal preceptor was Johannes Coch-
læus; but he derived much instruction from his friend and
tutor, Erasmus. Speaking of Erasmus, and alluding to a
proverbial expression in the *Adagia* of that great man, in
which any sudden, abrupt, and unnatural transition of whatever kind, is compared to " *the passing from the Dorian to
the Phrygian mode*," his words are—" I am not ignorant of what many eminent men have written in this our
age concerning this *Adagium*, two of whom, however, are
chiefly esteemed by me, and shall never be named without
some title of honour, Franchinus and Erasmus Roterdamus;
the one was a mute master to me, but the other taught me
by word of mouth; to both of them I thought myself indebted in the greatest degree. Franchinus, indeed, I never
saw; although I have heard that he was at Milan when I
was there, which is about twenty years ago; but I was not
then engaged in this work (the *Dodecachordon*): However,
in the succeeding years, that I may ingenuously confess the
truth, the writings of that scholar were of great use to me,
and gave me so much advantage, that I would read, and
read over again, and even devour the music of Boetius,
which had not for a long time been touched; nay, it was
thought not to be understood by any one. As to Erasmus,
I lived many years in familiarity with him; not indeed in the
same house, but so near, that each might be with the other
as often as we pleased, and converse on literary subjects, and
those immense labours which we sustained together, for the
common advantage and use of students; in which conversations it was our practice to dispute and correct each other:
I, as the junior, gave place to his age; and he, as the senior,
bore with my humours: sometimes chastising, but always
encouraging me in my studies; and at last I ventured to appear before the public, and transmit my thoughts in writing;
and whatsoever he had written in the course of twenty years,

he would always have me see beforehand; and really, if my own affairs would have permitted it, I would always have been near him. I have corrected several of his works: he did not take it amiss to be found fault with, as some would do now, provided it were done handsomely; nay, he greatly desired to be admonished, and immediately returned thanks, and would even confer presents on the persons that suggested any correction in his writings. So great was the modesty of the man."

The *Dodecachordon*, which was published during the last year of Henry VIII. though highly esteemed, both by scholars and musicians, did not carry to the minds of its readers entire conviction of the truth of Glareanus's doctrine of the twelve modes. Nevertheless, his work was greatly admired and praised for its erudition, and the classical purity of its style; and it would be illiberal not to say that it is entitled to the attention of the learned *. To prove that the author was distinguished in more than one province of literature, it will be sufficient to observe, that the emperor Maximilian I. presented him with the poetic laurel and ring.

Erasmus having received invitations from France, to teach the sons of some exalted personages, (a task which did not accord with his disposition and views) warmly recommended Glareanus; and in a letter addressed to the Bishop of Paris,

---

* Glareanus, throughout his book, discovers great partiality for the music of the Greeks. Struck with the wonderful relations of Plutarch, Boetius, and many other writers respecting the ancient music, he entertained the hope of restoring that very practice to which such astonishing effects had been imputed. And the fond expectation was cherished, not only by himself, but many other musicians of his time.

and still extant, speaks of him in the highest possible terms.
He died in the year 1563, in the seventy-sixth year of his
age. The following is the sepulchral inscription to his memory :—

" Henricus Glareanus, poeta laureatus, gymnasii hujus
ornamentum eximium, expleto feliciter supremo die, com-
poni hic ad spem futuræ resurrectionis providit, cujus ma-
nibus propter raram eruditionem, candoremque in profi-
tendo, senatus reipublicæ literariæ, gratitudinis et pietatis
ergo, monumentum hoc eternæ memoriæ consecratum, pos-
teritati ut extaret, erigi curavit*."

Damianus A'Goës, a Portuguese knight, and intimate
friend of Glareanus, was distinguished for his learning and
accomplishments. He loved poetry and music, composed
verses, and sung with great taste. His great musical merit
procured him the countenance of Emanuel, King of Por-
tugal, whose chamberlain he became, as well as that of his
successor, and was employed in several foreign negotiations
of great moment. In these engagements, he did not testify
more fidelity and address, nor in the exercise of his poetical and musical talents, a greater degree of imagination and
science, than he evinced of skill and courage in his defence
of the city of Louvain, in 1542, when it was besieged by
the French. During the latter period of his life, he was
engaged in writing the history of his country, and had made

---

* His life happily closed, here reposes, in hope of a future resurrection, Henry Glareanus, poet laureat, and the distinguished
ornament of this school. To the honour of his rare learning, and
urbanity in its communication, the Senate of this republic of letters,
in token of its gratitude and affection, and to transmit to posterity
the knowledge of his great merit, caused to be erected this monument, consecrated to his eternal memory.

a considerable progress in the task, when a fit, which seized him in his study, in the year 1596, terminated his existence.

In music, A'Goës was ranked with the most eminent masters of his time. The following hymn of his composition, is published in the *Dodecachordon* *.

HYMN.

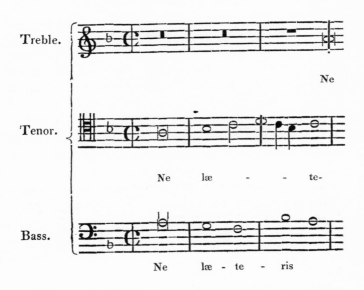

* Could this work boast of no other merit than that of assembling a great number of the best compositions of the sixteenth century, it would be valuable. Many of them are of such intrinsic excellence in regard of their harmony and the curious contexture of their *parts*, as not only to form eligible studies for the young contrapuntist, but to be qualified to highly gratify the lovers of ecclesiastical music. They have also considerable claims to our esteem, on the score of their antiquity; being, with the exception of a few examples in the writings of Franchinus, the oldest symphoniac productions now extant in print.

in i - mi ca   in - i - mi ca me-

ca mea in - i - mi - ca me   -   -

- a   in - i - mi ca me-

- - a   su - per me su-

- a su - per me su - - per

- a   su-

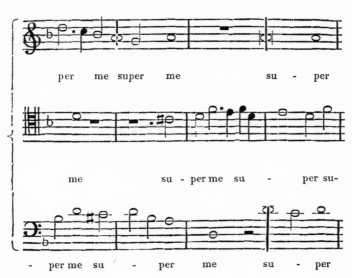

ce - ci - di   qui - a ce - ci-

di   quia ce - ci - - -

a   ce - ci   -   -   - di

di   quia   ceci   -   - di quia

-    - di   quia   ceci   -

qui - a   ceci   -   -   -

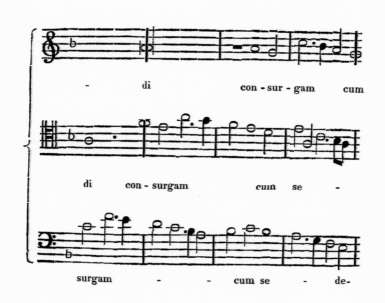

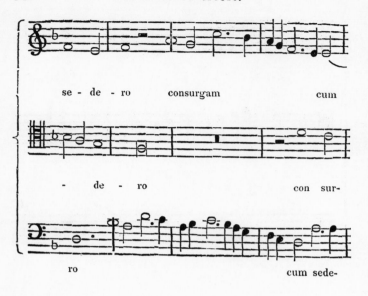

se - de - ro   consurgam   cum

- de - ro   con sur-

ro   cum sede-

se de - ro   in te - ne-

gam   con - surgam   cum se   -

ro   consur - gam   cum se - de - ro

mea est Do - - - mi-

nus lux me - a est Do - -

lux me - a est Do-

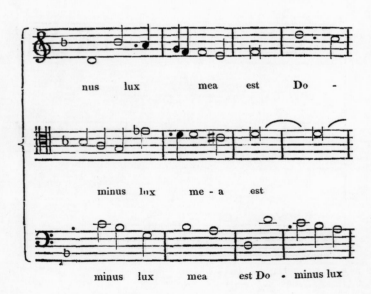

nus lux mea est Do -

minus lux me - a est

minus lux mea est Do - minus lux

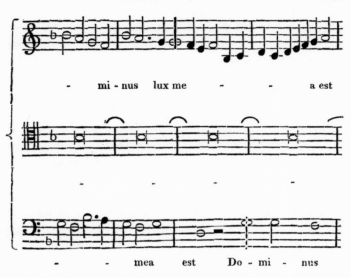

In an account of the distinguished composers of this period, to omit the notice of ORLANDUS LASSUS, or, as he
is more generally denominated, Orlando de Lasso, would be
to leave a blank in the list of the musical geniuses of the
sixteenth century.

It appears that, like many others whose talents have
adorned the harmonic profession, Orlando de Lasso was
led to it by the extraordinary excellence of his voice, when
a child. Thuanus, in his history, speaks of him in the following words:—

" Orlando de Lasso was a native of Mons in Hainault;
for this is the chief praise of Belgium, that it abounds in
excellent teachers of the musical art. And he, while a boy,
as is the fate of excellent singers, was, on account of the
sweetness of his voice, forced away, and for some time retained by Ferdinand Gonzaga, in Sicily, in Milan, and at
Naples. Afterwards, being grown up, he taught for the
space of two years at Rome. After this, he travelled to
France and Italy, with Julius Cæsar Brancatius, and at
length returned into Flanders, and lived many years at Antwerp; from whence he was called away by Albert, Duke of
Bavaria, where he settled and married. He was afterwards
invited, with offers of great rewards, by that generous
prince, Charles IX. of France, to take upon him the office
of his chapel master *. In order to reap the benefit of this
promotion, he set out with his family for France ; but before
he could arrive there, received the news of the sudden
death of his expected patron. Thus disappointed, he was

---

* That prince, tasteful as generous, constantly retained, and well
rewarded, some chosen and distinguished musician, as his Maestro di
Capella.

recalled to Bavaria, by William, the son and successor of Albert, and reinstated in his former office. At Bavaria he continued to live till his death, which occurred in 1595, in his seventy-third year, and after he had rendered himself highly celebrated through Europe, by the great excellence of his compositions, both sacred and secular *.

For the very liberal treatment which Orlando de Lasso experienced at the hands of that " *generous prince*," Charles IX. it is but just to remark, that he was principally indebted to the troubled conscience of his royal patron. The king, after having not only consented to the massacre of the Hugonots in Paris, but so far forgotten his regal dignity, as well

---

* This account, by Thuanus, does not, however, entirely concord in its dates, with the inscription on his tomb.

ORLANDUS LASSUS, Bergæ, Hannoniæ urbe
natus, Anno MDXXX.
Musicus et Symphoniacus sui seculi facile princeps :
Primâ ætate admodum puer, ob miram vocis suavitatem
in canendo, aliquoties plagio sublatus :
Sub Ferdinando Gonzaga prorege Siciliæ, annis fermè sex
partim Mediolani, partim in Sicilia, inter symphoniacos educatus.
Neapoli dein per triennium, ac demùm Romæ amplius biennium
Musico præfectus Sacello longè celeberrimo.
Post peregrinationes Anglicanus et Gallicanus cum
Julio Cæsare Brancacio susceptas, Antverpiæ
totidem annis versatur.
Tandem Alberti et Gulielmi Ducis Bojorum, musicæ Magister
supremus per integrum vicennium.
A Maximiliano II. Cæs. nobilitatus : à summis imperii Principibus
ac Proceribus summe honoratus.
Cantionibus Harmonicis tam sacris quam profanis omnium
linguarum in orbe universo celebratissi
Obiit Monaci anno Sal. MDXXCV. Æt. LV.

as the claims of humanity, as to be personally concerned in its execution, found his nightly repose disturbed by the reflections of self-reproach, he was glad to avail himself of the sweet melodies of Orlando performed in his chamber by the children of his chapel, whose mellifluous strains might soothe the storm that raged in his tormented bosom. But the summary vengeance of Heaven did not permit him to make the experiment *.

This great musician had two sons (able musicians) both of whom were too sensible of their father's merit, not to be induced to follow his profession. The elder, Ferdinand, became chapel-master to Maximilian, Duke of Bavaria, and the younger, Rudulph, was preferred to the situation of organist to the same prince. Besides several collections of madrigals presented to the public by Orlando himself, there is still extant a large folio volume of his motets, published by his sons after his death, under the title of " Magnum Opus musicum Orlandi de Lasso, Capellæ Bavaricæ quondam Magistri, complectens omnes Cantiones, quas Motetas vulgo vocant, tam antea editas, quàm hactenas nondum publicatas à 2 ad 12 voc. à Fernando Serenissimi Bavariæ Ducis Maximiliani Musicorum præfecto, & Rudulpho, eidem, Principi ab Organis ; authoris Filiis summo studio collectum, & impensis eodem Typus mandatum. Monachii, 1604."

It is worthy of remark, that Orlando de Lasso and Zarlino, are the only persons of the musical profession whose merits Thuanus has condescended to record. Orlando was so

---

* By Mezeray, and other historians of those times, we are assured, that in the scene of undistinguishing butchery here alluded to, this royal assassin, with the utmost coolness and composure of mind, issued from his palace with a loaded fowling-piece, and deliberately fired at those who fled from their pursuers.

distinguished an ornament of the age in which he lived, that it would, certainly, have been as unjust as extraordinary, had that historian overlooked his claims to honourable notice. This composer, the most excellent of the sixteenth century, was the first great improver of figurative counterpoint ; and equalled only by the scientific and elegant Palestrina.

On his monument is the following humorous epitaph, supposed to have been written by himself.

> Etant enfant, j'ai chanté le dessus,
> Adolescent, j'ai fait le contre-taille,
> Homme parfait, j'ai raisonné la taille ;
> Mais maintenant je suis mis au bassus.
> Prie, Passant, que l'esprit sort là sus.

TRANSLATION.

> A *child*, I sang the *treble part*,
> A *youth*, the *counter* claim'd my art ;
> A *man*, the *tenor* was my place,
> But *now* I'm station'd in the *bass*.
> Kind passenger, if Christ you love,
> Pray that my soul may chant above.

Though the composers above enumerated, include the principal English, as well as foreign musicians of the early part of the sixteenth century, there were others of eminence sufficient to render it a subject of regret, that no memorials of them, of any consequence, are now remaining ; the preservation of a few of their compositions being the only honour that their country has awarded to their merits. These are, indeed, very few ; and though the general destruction of pious books and manuscripts which attended the suppression of religious houses, will account for the loss of many sacred compositions, we cannot so easily perceive why almost the whole of the *secular* music of those times should have disappeared. Among those professors whose science and abilities served to entertain and ornament the age in which they lived, were, Sir Thomas Phelyppes, John Charde, Richard Ede, Henry Parker, John Norman, Edmund Sheffield, William Newark, Richard Davy, Edmund Turges, Gilbert Banister, and others, of whom, at present, little more remains than their names.

About the period adorned by the talents of these masters, the clamour raised against cathedral music, on account of the indifferent and negligent manner in which it was performed, became so great, and its enemies, especially the reformers, took so much advantage of the resolutions passed by the Council of Trent, for the correction of its abuses, that it is, perhaps, a matter of just astonishment, that figurative church music survived the century of which we are speaking. Had not Henry's partiality for the compositions of the choir descended to his offspring, they would in all probability, have been wholly rejected from the public service*. At the Reformation, agreeably to a propensity in human nature to pass from one extremity to another, a plan of church discipline so purely spiritual, was adopted, that the idea of moving the mind through the medium of the external senses, seems, as far as possible, to have been shunned. The former antiphonal singing became not less obnoxious to the ears, than the ancient clerical habits to the eyes, of the Protestants: and choral service was in danger of being banished. We owe its preservation, and the consequent production of some of the finest compositions that do honour to musical science and musical talent, to the injunctions is-

---

* Edward VI. practised the lute; and both Mary and Elizabeth were proficients on the virginals.

sued by Edward VI. requiring the Litany to be said or *sung;* and to the permission expressed in his rubric to melodize the " *Venite exultemus;*" and other hymns, both at *mattins* and *even-song;* as well as to the proviso in his second liturgy, for using the *anthem,* a species of composition so peculiar, as well as essential, to cathedral service *. The music of the choir, however, was not entirely freed from danger, till the moderation and sound sense of Elizabeth prevailing in the disciplinarian controversy which arose at the beginning of her reign, determined the differences of those reformists, who, having withdrawn themselves to Geneva and Frankfort, from the persecutions of Mary, now returned to indulge their liberty of conscience †. The queen having the satisfaction to find, that her opinion in favour of the use of the higher and more refined species of church composition accorded with the general sense of the nation, did not hesitate to authorize and sanction its conti-

---

* The known partiality of Luther to the use of music in the church, added its influence, no doubt, to whatever other favourable circumstances might occur. That the reformist really was so, is manifested by many passages in his writings. In the third volume of his works, page 464, (Altenburg Edition) we find him saying, " It is by no means my intention to insinuate, that I expect the Latin language to be used in our religious worship ; the whole of my design is the improvement of our youth. And were it in my power, and the Greek and Hebrew were as common with us as the Latin, and contained such excellent church music and psalmody, as doth the Latin, it would be my wish to use all the four languages alternately, Sunday after Sunday, so as to sing and read in German, Latin, Greek, and Hebrew."

† Elizabeth, in the *Statute of Uniformity,* made in the first year of her reign, established the second liturgy of Edward; and with it, the continued use of cathedral music.

nuance in the reformed religion : and since that time, it has never ceased to aggrandize and embellish the service of our cathedrals *.

---

* It is to be regretted, that a style of musical performance less refined than that of the choir, and less coarse and vulgar than the psalmody of our parish churches, has not been adopted for parochial service.

END OF VOL. I.